KARGI

From Surprise to Victory

General V.P. Malik was the Chief of the Army Staff (India) from
1 October 1997 to 30 September 2000. Concurrently, he was
chairman, Chiefs of Staff Committee, from 1 January 1999 to
30 September 2000. In both these posts, he played a vital role
in planning, coordinating and overseeing the military operations
that enabled India to evict the Pakistani intruders in Kargil and
thus turn the tables on Pakistan.

A graduate from the Defence Services Staff College and
Madras University, General Malik is an alumnus of the National
Defence College, New Delhi. He has been a member of India's
National Security Advisory Board and has delivered lectures in
many prestigious civil and military institutions in India and abroad.
Currently, he heads the Institute of Security Studies in the
Observer Research Foundation, New Delhi.

General Malik's book...stands out as perhaps the most valuable contribution to our military literature since Independence.

The Tribune

Malik deserves credit for a frank and refreshing analysis of the first limited war fought by two nuclear powered states. His theory about the possibilities of further conflict would go a long way in shaping India's military strategy.

The Telegraph

General Malik's account...is comprehensive, straight from the shoulder and interesting to a range of readers.... This...volume will certainly be a reference point, not just in discussions on the Kargil conflict, but also in the way the Indian army perceives vital issues like nuclear deterrence.

Business Standard

...Malik's account is praiseworthy for its sobriety and objectivity, as well as generosity to comrades and colleagues...

Hindustan Times

[General Malik] has done a commendable job by providing a definitive glimpse into the politico-military-bureaucratic equations prevalent in India during the Kargil war.

Force

Malik gives us a fine and easily accessible narrative on the surprise that confronted India when it discovered that territory had been seized by Pakistan in May 1999 and on the victorious response to it.... All the phases of the conflict...are covered in impressive detail.

The Indian Express

As the first book of its kind, General Malik's book is a must read for everyone – military as well as civilian.

SP's Land Forces

A collector's item for students of military campaigns and military buffs!

Financial Express

It is a welcome contribution to the small body of literature in the realm of national security decision making in India.

Indian Foreign Affairs Journal

KARGIL

From Surprise to Victory

General V.P. Malik

HarperCollins *Publishers* India

First published in hardback in India in 2006 by
HarperCollins *Publishers* India

First published in paperback in 2010

Copyright © General V.P. Malik 2006, 2010

P-ISBN:978-81-7223-967-1
E-ISBN:978-93-5029-313-3

8 10 9 7

General V.P. Malik asserts the moral
right to be identified as the author of this work.

The views and opinions expressed in this book are the author's own and the facts
are as reported by him, and the publishers are not in any way liable for the same.

The author and the publisher thank Army Headquarters, New Delhi, for permission
to use some photographs and maps from the book *Heroes of Kargil* (2002) and also
Captain Amarinder Singh for permission to use some sketches and maps from
his book *A Ridge Too Far* (DK Publishers, New Delhi, 2001).

HarperCollins *Publishers*
A-75, Sector 57, Noida, Uttar Pradesh 201301, India
1 London Bridge Street, London, SE1 9GF, United Kingdom
Hazelton Lanes, 55 Avenue Road, Suite 2900, Toronto, Ontario M5R 3L2
and 1995 Markham Road, Scarborough, Ontario M1B 5M8, Canada
25 Ryde Road, Pymble, Sydney, NSW 2073, Australia
195 Broadway, New York, NY 10007, USA

Typeset in 11.5/13.5 Meridien
Nikita Overseas Pvt. Ltd

Printed and bound in India by
Thomson Press (India) Ltd

*For every single brave deed noticed and recognized,
there are many that go unnoticed in the fog of war.*

*To those unnoticed deeds and the gallant individuals
who performed them...*

Contents

Preface to the New Edition

KARGIL WAS A LIMITED WAR – THE FIRST OF ITS KIND AFTER India and Pakistan tested their nuclear weapons. The war took place despite the fact that, only a couple of months before, both nations had signed the Lahore Declaration, an agreement recognizing the principle of building an environment of peace and security and resolving all bilateral conflicts. This type of conflict has now become a more likely operational norm in a strategic environment where large-scale capture of territories, forced change of regimes and extensive military damage to the adversary is ruled out politically.

The war will always be remembered for its strategic and tactical surprise, the self-imposed national strategy of restraint in keeping the war limited to the Kargil–Siachen sector, military strategy and planning, and the dedication, determination and daring junior leadership at the tactical level. In fiercely fought combat actions, on the most difficult terrain that gave immense advantage to the enemy, we were able to evict Pakistani troops from most of their surreptitiously occupied positions. The Pakistani leadership was forced to sue for ceasefire and seek withdrawal of its troops from the remaining areas. Operation Vijay – the Indian codename for the war – was a blend of strong and determined political, military and diplomatic actions, which enabled us to transform an adverse situation into a military and diplomatic victory. As two prime ministers of Pakistan later acknowledged, 'Kargil war was Pakistan's biggest blunder and disaster.'

Many lessons emerged from the Kargil war, necessitating a holistic national security review as well as rethinking of the nature of conflict and conduct in the new strategic environment. Some important lessons were:

- There may be remote chances of a full-scale conventional war between two nuclear weapon states but as long as there are territory-related disputes, the adversary can indulge in a proxy war or a limited border or conventional war.
- A major military challenge in India remains political reluctance to commit a *proactive* engagement. This invariably leads us to a *reactive* military situation. Also, no loss of territory is acceptable to the Indian public and political authority. To deal with such situations, it is essential to have credible strategic and tactical intelligence and assessments, effective surveillance and close defence of the lines of control.
- Successful outcome of a border war depends on our ability to react rapidly in order to localize/freeze/reverse the military situation. The new strategic environment calls for speedier mobilization, versatile and flexible combat organizations and synergy amongst three services and other civil departments.
- A conflict may remain limited because of credible deterrence and *escalation dominance*. The adversary will then be deterred from escalating it into an all-out conventional or nuclear war due to our ability to respond with greater chances of success. This also gives more room for manoeuvre in diplomacy and conflict.
- A limited conventional war will require close political oversight and politico-civil-military interaction. It is essential to keep the military leadership within the security and strategic decision-making loop.
- Information operations are important due to the growing transparency of the battlefield – a comprehensive media and information campaign is essential.

The armed forces appear to have followed up on most of these lessons. Action has been taken to improve all-weather surveillance and defence of the border and lines of control. Individual service and joint services doctrines have been revised. Some Special Forces units have been added to the strength of each service, though the Army is yet to review the size of its large combat formations to make them more versatile and flexible. The Kargil war had highlighted gross inadequacies in our surveillance capability. This has now been made up for with indigenous satellites and aerial imagery with synthetic aperture radar. We have also acquired effective unmanned aerial vehicles and, most important, acquired and deployed hand-held thermal imagers, surveillance radars and ground sensors along the Line of Control.

At the politico-military strategic level, however, there has been little progress. The government had carried out a National Security Review in 2001–02. Many reforms were recommended in this Review to improve the higher defence control organization, its systems and processes. In terms of numbers, most of these reforms are stated to have been implemented. Many changes, however, have only been cosmetic. For example, there is hardly any integration in the Ministry of Defence. I feel that we need strong, competent and committed political leadership to bring that about.

The National Security Review had recommended the appointment of a Chief of Defence Staff (CDS) to provide single-point military advice to the government and to resolve substantive inter-service doctrinal, planning, policy and operational issues. This is necessary because turf wars, inter-service rivalries, bureaucratic delays and political vacillation in decision-making become major hurdles in defence planning and its implementation. Planning in defence tends to be tardy, competitive and thus uneconomical. In the new strategic environment of unpredictability and enhanced interactivity, it is essential to create synergy and optimize defence and operational planning. A face-to-face dialogue and military advice is critical for success in politico-military-strategic and operational issues. The creation of the post of CDS is still pending and interaction between the political authority and service chiefs continues to suffer due to inter-service rivalries and the dominant position retained by the civil bureaucracy.

Modernization of the armed forces continues to lag behind due to inadequate self-reliance, fear of scams and reluctance to procure essential equipment from abroad. Despite a large network of Defence Research and Development Organization laboratories, ordnance factories and defence public sector undertakings, we continue to import 70 per cent of our weapons and equipment. The newly established Defence Procurement Board has failed to speed up the process. Instead, it seems to have added one more tier in the clearance of proposals, causing further delays. There have been no major modernization procurements for several years. Despite that, in the financial year 2008–09, the Ministry of Defence returned to the central exchequer Rs 7,000 crores out of the Rs 48,000 crores that had been earmarked for modernization. There is no point talking about revolution in military affairs, information systems and net-centric warfare if we cannot induct relevant weapons and equipment in time. Efforts towards modernization of the armed forces have not borne fruit adequately primarily due to the absence of holistic and long-term defence planning. It is my belief that ten years after the Kargil war, India's deterrence capability stands further eroded.

A reflection on the Kargil war can never be complete without a mention of the brilliant junior leadership that we witnessed during battles. There were countless acts of the most extraordinary valour, courage and grit to achieve what would have appeared impossible under normal circumstances. Such acts by young officers and men can never be forgotten. They make us proud. Commanding officers of many infantry battalions displayed steely resilience and single-minded devotion to duty. There were actions by young artillery forward observation officers and battery commanders who took over infantry companies when their company commander colleagues were killed. And for every single brave deed noticed and recognized, there were many that went unnoticed in the fog of war. These legendary tales deserve mention not only in our military history books but also in school textbooks to serve as inspiration for young people. We must remember that those who fight for the nation and sacrifice their lives deserve memory and recognition. It sustains their families much more than any monetary compensation. It also sustains patriotism and contributes to nation building.

October 2009   **General V.P. Malik**

Preface

THE WAR IN KARGIL WILL GO DOWN IN THE HISTORY OF INDIA as a saga of unmatched bravery, grit and determination displayed on the battlefield by the Indian Army; a symbol of great pride and inspiration.

The main credit for achieving success in Kargil undoubtedly goes to the units that fought on the front. Behind the blaze of their glory, not much seen but of cardinal importance, were the yeoman contributions of the multitude of agencies providing vital inputs such as combat support, communications and logistics. And finally, due recognition also needs to be given to those behind-the-scenes individuals whose responsibility was to draw up strategies, formulate battle plans and facilitate decisions.

When a soldier goes out to perform his duty, he sublimates his individuality into that of his organization. He works in unison with his fellow-soldiers, trusting them completely. He strives to accomplish his mission whatever be the consequences – even if it means sacrificing his life. A single-minded focus on fulfilling his duty is all that matters to him. 'Pursuit of excellence' is, therefore, a goal for him not merely as an individual but as part of a team. Camaraderie and esprit de corps form a way of life and a collective trait for the whole Army. It was a privilege for me to lead such officers and men of the Army during the war.

Soon after my retirement on 30 September 2000, several friends advised me to write an autobiography or a book on the Kargil war. The idea of an autobiography never appealed to me. In India, except for his colleagues and a few others, no one is really interested in a soldier's autobiography or biography. Soldiers are quickly forgotten after a war or crisis is over. That is part of our post-independence strategic culture! After going through the quickies and other literature that had come out on the Kargil war, I sincerely felt the need to set the record straight. Consequently, I made up my mind to write this book. But after a great deal of self-introspection, I decided to wait for some time. There were two main reasons for doing so.

First, after leading a very long, sheltered life in Army units and cantonments, my top priority was to settle down in a place of our (my family members) choosing: it had to be outside New Delhi, far away from the hustle and bustle of a megapolis, but close enough to keep me busy vis-à-vis my routine activities and my commitments. Eventually, we opted for the picturesque Panchkula, very close to Chandigarh.

The second reason was more important. Writing about a war very soon after the event is not only difficult but also undesirable because raw emotions tend to block out objectivity. A war impacts a nation and a society much more than any other event. Lives are lost; significant geographical and political changes may take place; and, at times, a country's existence could be at stake. The charged feelings that suffuse the duration of a war are too intense to allow for instant verification, introspection or the application of academic rigour. No wonder, Ernest Hemingway stated: 'When war breaks out, truth is the first casualty.'

Although limited in scope, politically and militarily, the Kargil war, like all other wars, was marked by failures and successes, setbacks and achievements. And as the Kargil crisis occurred amidst a politically acrimonious atmosphere following the fall of a government and only a few days before the next general elections, it raised many questions and controversies that tended to blot out the achievements of both the nation and its soldiers that were responsible for the ensuing victory. The Army was at the receiving end of more than the usual quota of journalistic scepticism.

Under those highly charged circumstances, it would have been extremely difficult for any war chronicler to be objective about it or be perceived to be so. I, therefore, decided to wait for at least five years before attempting a book on the subject. This wait has been useful, not only because many more facts have now come to light but also because I could ascertain the views and perceptions of many more knowledgeable people from India, Pakistan and the USA.

My endeavour in this book has been to present the facts and to analyse and comment on related events before, during and after the Kargil war. The objective primarily is to highlight those lessons that would benefit the nation in general and its armed forces in particular.

Another crucial aspect that I have focused on relates to happenings within our neighbouring country and how they affected (and continue to affect) us. What made Pakistan, more specifically the Pakistan Army, take the initiative to wage war in Kargil? How did the military top brass plan the operations in Kargil and how did they set the ball rolling even as the Pakistani political leadership was engaged in a serious dialogue (resulting in the February 1999 Lahore Declaration) to improve relations with India? What role did Pakistan's leaders Nawaz Sharif and Pervez Musharraf play in carrying out both these activities simultaneously? What was India's political and military reading of the situation, and why? These are historically important questions. I have tried to answer these questions right at the start, which covers the geostrategic environment in the subcontinent a few years before the conflict.

The next section takes a close look at the Line of Control and developments related to it and also deals with India's intelligence and surveillance failures that led to the 'militants' bogey' in Kargil and a prompt but weak and uncertain response till the last week of May 1999. After that, the politico-military challenges, the political mandate and its rationale, the formulation of military strategy and its implementation are described.

No soldier knows about all these factors better than I do, and very little of that knowledge is in the public domain yet. It is necessary to make people aware of our systems and decision-making processes at the grand strategic level and at the military strategic level. Only such awareness can bring about further improvements in our security-related problems.

A victory in war is achieved because battles are won. I have described these battles and related activities towards the middle of the book. It is a macro-view from the level of the chief. But it is the most significant description of the war that reflects the spirit of the Indian armed forces.

Some readers may feel that the roles of the Indian Air Force, Navy and Headquarters Northern Command and 15 Corps of the Army have not been adequately covered in the book. This perception is correct. The reason: it was neither possible nor desirable for me to go into micro-details of their operational deliberations and planning. As the focus was on geopolitical and strategic levels, the tactical and some operational aspects had to be abridged. However, all military strategic aspects have been adequately covered. Simultaneously, I have also recounted the patrolling and other activities of the Chinese People's Liberation Army (PLA) on our northern border during the Kargil war period along with some observations on the Sino–Indian security relations.

The next section describes in detail how the war came to an end; it did not end as abruptly as many people believe, and there was no US pressure on the Government of India.

As the shrill rhetoric from Pakistan enabled the Western media, academics and even political leaders and officials to make much of the nuclear factor, I considered it appropriate to add a separate chapter on this subject.

At the level of service chiefs, and at the national level, factors such as the modernization of the armed forces, the politico-military relations and the role of the media during a conflict are extremely important. The media highlighted these factors during and immediately after the war. I have dwelt at some length upon these factors as well.

Towards the end, I have delineated the impact of the Kargil war on both Pakistan and India. There is a noticeable difference between the two: an almost total lack of debate and analysis in one country and sufficient, though politicized, debate in the other. For obvious reasons, post-war issues and developments in India have been covered in more detail.

I have rounded off the book with a survey of Indo–Pak security relations in the post-Kargil era. What major changes have taken place in these relations? How fragile is the current climate of peace? Is the 'peace dialogue' sustainable, given that the military rulers in Pakistan have yet to shun terrorism as an instrument of state policy? While one hopes for the best, political realism – keeping in view the tumultuous Indo–Pak relations since 1947 – warns all of us to remain prepared for the worst.

February 2006   **General V.P. Malik**

Prologue

The enemy has started the fight, but it is we who will fire the last shot and war will end only on our terms.

THE DATE: 30 SEPTEMBER 1997. THE PLACE: NEW DELHI. I HAD seen off my predecessor General Shankar Roychowdhury at the airport in the afternoon. In the evening friends and well-wishers were coming to felicitate us (my wife and myself) and convey their good wishes on our twenty-ninth wedding anniversary and on my taking over as the Chief of Army Staff (COAS).

At about 1700 hours, the Director General Military Operations (DGMO) rang up to inform me that heavy shelling had taken place in the Kargil sector. The town had been hit deliberately, which had resulted in several civilian casualties and damage to property. In panic, some people were leaving town. The civil administration was trying to control the situation and restore their confidence. Headquarters Northern Command would keep us informed and let us know its response, if any.

Later that night, I was informed that Prime Minister I.K. Gujral would hold a meeting the next day, my first day in office as COAS, at 1000 hours at his residence at 7 Race Course Road, New Delhi, to review the situation.

Kargil and the Srinagar–Kargil–Leh road have been vulnerable to the Pakistani Army's interdiction ever since the ceasefire after the 1947–48 Indo–Pak war. Many posts in this sector have changed hands between India and Pakistan for this reason. After the 1972 Shimla Agreement reached between Indira Gandhi and Zulfiqar Ali Bhutto, the Pakistan Army had, at times, indulged in firing and shelling on this road, which had become more frequent after 1996.[1] As offensive action would have involved crossing the Line of Control (LoC) for which political clearance was unlikely to come, on several occasions we had considered bypasses for vehicular traffic to avoid vulnerable sections of the road.

On 30 September 1997, the unusual bit, however, was the intensity of shelling and targeting of the civil population of the town. Around 2200 hours, GOC-in-C, Northern Command, Lieutenant General S. Padmanabhan (later, my successor as COAS) rang up. He gave me the details of the shelling, his assessment of the situation and his plan to hit Pakistani artillery guns the next morning, which I approved.

On 1 October 1997, I started official work in my new rank by laying a wreath at the Amar Jawan Jyoti at India Gate. After that, I reviewed a ceremonial guard of honour near my office in South Block. As expected, there were a lot of journalists. They followed me to the office, took photographs and asked me questions mainly about the shelling in Kargil the previous day. While climbing the steps to reach my office, I looked at my watch and wondered if we had retaliated as planned by Northern Command. In the office, my staff confirmed that we had, but I could not convey this news to the journalists till the meeting at 7 Race Course Road was over.

The prime minister held the meeting at the given time. The defence minister and some other ministers and secretaries

---

[1]According to General Jehangir Karamat, who was the COAS in Pakistan then and whom I met in January 2001, this firing was in retaliation for our attempts to interdict the Neelam Valley road in Pakistan-Occupied Kashmir opposite the Kupwara sector, from where maximum infiltration of militants takes place. After 1996, Pakistan started interdicting the Srinagar–Kargil highway regularly.

including the heads of the Research and Analysis Wing (R&AW) and the Intelligence Bureau were present. The situation was discussed in detail with inputs from all of us and from the Jammu and Kashmir State Government. The prime minister and his cabinet colleagues endorsed the retaliatory action of the Army in response to Pakistani shelling in Kargil on 30 September 1997.

I did not know then that one day a war in Kargil would become the most important event of my professional career.

Twenty months later, in the months preceding the summer of 1999, Pakistani Army personnel dressed as jehadi militants (Mujahideen) infiltrated through gaps between Indian defences in one of the world's most rugged terrain, to occupy several dominating heights between the LoC and the Srinagar–Kargil–Leh road (National Highway 1-A). The Pakistani Army's intrusion, taking advantage of the terrain and other factors, achieved a tactical surprise. But the ensuing Kargil war ended in a politico-military victory for India.

1

The Gathering Storm

You can do a lot with diplomacy but of course you can do a lot more with diplomacy backed up with firmness and force...sound defence is sound foreign policy.

The Nuclear Tests

THE EVENTS THAT TOOK PLACE AT THE TURN OF THE TWENTIETH century left an indelible mark on the relations between India and Pakistan and to some extent affected even the rest of the world. The newly formed National Democratic Alliance (NDA) Government in India stunned the world by carrying out nuclear weapons tests on 11 and 13 May 1998 and thus terminating its nuclear ambiguity. This step marked the implementation of a decision taken after decades of discussions within several Indian governments and after a series of public debates. The justification was not only the possession of nuclear capability in the immediate neighbourhood and the discriminate nature of the Non-Proliferation Treaty (NPT), but also the ever-increasing international pressure on account of the Comprehensive Test Ban Treaty (CTBT) and the Fissile Material Control Treaty (FMCT).

Pakistan followed the Indian example fifteen days later. That was not a surprise as its security policy has always been Indo-centric and its nuclear technical capability was known. The governments of both countries received massive domestic support after the events. But they faced sharp criticism and all types of sanctions from foreign countries.

In October 1998, while assessing the strategic scenario in a Combined Commanders' Conference, I stated:

> The strategic scenario in the last six months has quite matched the explosion and heat of the nuclear tests done on the subcontinent.... [The] Taliban's emergence, spread and now near-total control of Afghanistan is a serious, long-term

security threat in the region. If this experiment – conceived and supported by Pakistan – is allowed to succeed, the spread of Islamic fundamentalism may soon reverberate across South, West and Central Asia.... For us in India, [the] Taliban's consolidation has serious consequences. Intelligence reports have indicated the likelihood of Pakistan pushing 2000 Taliban into Jammu and Kashmir in the next one year.... Pakistan has made Jammu and Kashmir the centrepiece of Indo–Pak dialogue. The development of its nuclear capability is now being openly linked to its Jammu and Kashmir political and military strategy. This year, it has managed to upgrade proxy war. There is evidence of *(a)* more foreign militants and weapons that are more sophisticated, explosive devices and radio equipment, *(b)* extension of infiltration and militancy to Poonch, Rajouri, Jammu, Doda and Chamba and *(c)* higher intensity of firing along the LoC and [the] Jammu–Sialkot border. Some radio intercepts have indicated that Pakistan is prepared to continue proxy war for another ten–twelve years. In recent months, it has made three deliberate attempts to capture posts in Siachen: the last one on [the] night [of] 17–18 October (1998).

I have stated earlier and wish to emphasize again that we do not need to be defensive on Jammu and Kashmir. We need to step up exposure of Pakistan's terrorist activities and build [up] an international consensus on terrorism. We must progress [with] our diplomacy with Pakistan as per Kofi Annan's [the UN secretary-general] advice, "You can do a lot with diplomacy but of course you can do a lot more with diplomacy backed up with firmness and force.... Prime minister, ladies and gentlemen, sound defence is sound foreign policy".

Pakistan's nuclear tests unleashed two simultaneous and parallel developments within that country's two well-known power centres: one was positive and the other negative for the subcontinent. The positive development was at the political level. Pakistan decided to join India in developing confidence-building measures (CBMs) and to attempt resolving disputes through peaceful dialogues. The negative development was within its Army, to make use of the nuclear threshold for initiating a limited war against India. This aspect was not properly shared with the political bosses.

The Lahore Declaration

The international flak faced by both India and Pakistan and the imposition of sanctions on both countries engendered a new sense of responsibility in New Delhi as well as in Islamabad. The powers that be realized the non-viability of an all-out war in future. All these factors had a positive impact on the political leadership of both nations. In the next few months, direct and back-door diplomacy between India and Pakistan became hyperactive, which resulted in the Indian Prime Minister Atal Behari Vajpayee's historic bus journey to Lahore and the signing of the Lahore Declaration with Pakistan's Prime Minister Nawaz Sharif on 20–21 February 1999. In the declaration, both prime ministers recognized that the nuclear dimension had added 'to their responsibility for avoiding a conflict between the two countries'. They also reiterated their determination 'to implementing [sic] of [the] Shimla Agreement in letter and spirit' and agreed 'to intensify their efforts to resolve all issues, including the issue of Jammu and Kashmir'.

A significant part of the Lahore Declaration was made up of a memorandum of understanding (MoU) signed by the foreign secretaries of India and Pakistan for the two nations 'to engage in bilateral consultations on security concepts and nuclear doctrines with a view to developing measures for confidence building in the nuclear and conventional fields aimed at avoidance of conflict'. The MoU listed seven significant clauses on nuclear and conventional CBMs, mutual consultations and communication between the two sides (see Appendix 1).

My colleagues in the Chiefs of Staff Committee (COSC) and I had been consulted towards the end of the negotiations on the drafts of the Lahore Declaration and the MoU. After carefully examining the drafts, we recommended the inclusion of a separate paragraph on crossborder terrorism in the text of the main declaration and some minor changes in the MoU. I briefed Vivek Katju and Rakesh Sood, joint secretaries in the Ministry of External Affairs involved in the negotiations, about our recommendations and also spoke to the minister for external affairs, Jaswant Singh, and the national security advisor, Brajesh Mishra, before their departure for Lahore.

After returning, Rakesh Sood informed me that they were unable to get the suggested explicit mention of crossborder terrorism included in the Lahore Declaration. It was substituted with general statements that 'the respective governments agree to refrain from intervention and interference in each other's internal affairs' and they 'reaffirm their condemnation of terrorism in all its forms and manifestations and determination to combat this menace'. The amendments suggested by us in the MoU had been incorporated.

The Proxy War and the Lahore Declaration

Documents and diaries captured during the war have revealed that the Pakistan military had already put into motion the battle procedure for the Kargil war (Operation Badr, the Pakistani codename for the Kargil operation), as an extension of the proxy war, *before* the Lahore Declaration was signed by the two prime ministers.[1]

The proxy war in Jammu and Kashmir had been initiated by Pakistan soon after the Soviet withdrawal from Afghanistan in the late 1980s. By working in collusion with the Central Intelligence Agency (CIA) of the United States of America, Pakistan's Inter-Services Intelligence (ISI) and the Army had gained valuable experience in waging guerilla warfare. The ISI stepped up its efforts to subvert Kashmiri youth towards the end of the 1980s. Many young men were covertly exfiltrated to Pakistan-Occupied Kashmir through a porous LoC for religious indoctrination and arms training as was done in Afghanistan. These trained militants started pouring back into the Kashmir

---

[1]As per the captured diary of a Pakistani Army captain, Hussain Ahmad, of 12 Northern Light Infantry, his reconnaissance and firm base patrol entered the Kargil sector in February 1999. Pervez Musharraf visited this officer's patrol base on 28 March 1999, five weeks after the signing of the Lahore Declaration, and gave Rs 8000 'for sweets' to be distributed amongst 12 Northern Light Infantry personnel.

Valley in 1988. The period from 1987 to 1989 saw a spurt in violence, prolonged strikes in the Kashmir Valley and attacks on political leaders, the police and paramilitary forces. The kidnapping and subsequent release of Dr Rubaiya Sayeed, daughter of the then Union home minister, Mufti Mohammad Sayeed (who became the chief minister of Jammu and Kashmir in November 2002) in December 1989 in exchange for five top militants of the Jammu Kashmir Liberation Front (JKLF) proved to be the last straw. This event showed that the state administration had lost control and the militants had become more popular than the elected representatives in the state.

The elected chief minister, Dr Farooq Abdullah, resigned in January 1990. Governor's rule was imposed, which, as per the constitutional requirement, became president's rule in June 1990. The Army deployment started in April 1990, initially as an aid to civil authorities for maintenance of law and order. In July 1990, the complete valley and a 20-km belt along the LoC in Poonch and Rajouri districts were declared 'disturbed areas' and the Armed Forces Special Power Act (J&K), 1990, was promulgated. More Army units were inducted for counterinfiltration and counterinsurgency operations and also to restore normalcy. The ISI, however, continued to provide the militants with an assortment of sophisticated weapons, in addition to training and financial support. Over the years, many militant groups mushroomed. Of these, a majority were pro-Pakistan, with the JKLF and the Peoples' League being pro-independence. The ISI also encouraged the creation of the All-Party Hurriyat Conference in October 1993 to project a united political approach against the Government of India.

The important milestones in terrorism thereafter were: the siege of the Hazratbal mosque (in Srinagar) twice: first in October 1993 and then in March 1996; the spread of terrorist activities to Doda since 1994; the Charar-e-Sharif (a Sufi shrine) burning incident in May 1995; and the kidnapping and killing of five foreign tourists in 1995. The Army and paramilitary forces carried out protracted operations during this period to effectively contain terrorism and to create a safe atmosphere for the initiation of the political process.

Despite a desperate bid by the ISI-backed jehadi terrorists to stall the political process and subvert the elections, parliamentary elections were held in May 1996, and for the State Assembly in September–October 1996, paving the way for the installation of an elected government after seven years. Dr Farooq Abdullah's party, the National Conference, which had boycotted the parliamentary elections, joined the fray for the State Assembly elections. It won a comfortable majority. A voter turnout of 40 to 50 per cent re-established Kashmiri faith in the Indian Union and in democracy.

Parliamentary elections and State Assembly elections in Jammu and Kashmir ushered a fresh atmosphere of hope and enthusiasm among the people of the state. This turn of events dealt a severe blow to the Pakistan-sponsored proxy war. With a newly elected government in place and the people in the valley showing signs of disenchantment with militancy, the Army was withdrawn from Baramulla, Sopore, Srinagar, Badgam and Anantnag. Paramilitary troops were deployed to assist the civil authorities and civil police in maintaining law and order.

After 1997, Pakistan started focusing on the Muslim population in the interior areas of Poonch, Rajouri, Naushera and Doda districts. The proxy war was probably spread to these areas in a bid to make up for the lack of success in the valley and to trigger off a Hindu exodus from all Muslim-dominated areas. This situation resulted in an increased commitment of 16 Corps located south of the Pir Panjal range. Additional troops had to be inducted. Firing across the international border/LoC escalated. But both India and Pakistan continued to exercise restraint on using artillery in this zone. That was not the case in the area north of the Pir Panjal range, which was the responsibility of 15 Corps.

The infiltration attempts and violent incidents in the Kashmir Valley declined comparatively, but the frequency and intensity of high-calibre weapons and artillery firing across the LoC started showing an upswing. There were a few improvised explosive device (IED) incidents in Dras, east of the Zoji La pass, which had been free of militants' activities till then. Exchange of small arms fire, heavier direct firing weapons and artillery duels along the LoC became more frequent and intense. As the number of local terrorists waned, the ISI passed terrorism in Jammu and Kashmir onto the hands of foreign jehadi mercenaries.

Meanwhile, to conduct counterterrorist operations, two unified commands were established under the chief minister, Dr Farooq Abdullah: one each for the north and the south of the Pir Panjal range. Northern Command, with the largest number of troops, remained fully engaged in guarding the border, the LoC, the Actual Ground Position Line (AGPL) in the Siachen Glacier area and the Line of Actual Control with China, all of which fell within its sphere of responsibility. Northern Command also carried out counterinfiltration and counterterrorist operations.

There was some improvement in the overall situation immediately after the nuclear tests conducted by India and Pakistan in May 1998. Although some rumours spread that the ISI was infiltrating the Taliban into Jammu and Kashmir, they were effectively scotched.

From 17 to 29 August 1998, I undertook an extensive tour of Northern Command. General Officer Commanding (GOC) 16 Corps, Lieutenant General D. S. Chauhan, and GOC 15 Corps, Lieutenant General Krishan Pal, briefed me in the presence of their Army commander, Lieutenant General S. Padmanabhan. Thereafter, I visited forward deployments in Jammu, Naushera, Jhangar and Surankot (all covered by 16 Corps) and Srinagar, Kargil, Dras, Wujur, Khanabal, Phurkian Gali and Balbir Post (all covered by 15 Corps) to get firsthand briefings from local formation commanders.

By the time the Lahore Declaration was signed in February 1999, terrorism appeared to have been contained in Jammu and Kashmir. Common people had become disillusioned with this scourge and were keen to see the return of normalcy. The civil administration had started functioning better. Civil courts, schools and dispensaries started working more regularly and there was a noticeable increase in the commercial activity in the urban areas. Also, the number of tourists visiting the valley went up.

The Situation after the Lahore Declaration

A lot has been written about Pakistan Army chief General Pervez Musharraf's hesitation to greet Atal Behari Vajpayee during the latter's bus journey to Lahore. With 'Operation Badr' underway, it must have been difficult for him to indulge in doublespeak. As mentioned earlier, soon after the signing of the Lahore Declaration, he flew across the LoC in a helicopter to meet the 'advance elements' participating in 'Operation Badr'. This was a significant act of personal 'daring', which would have ensured that the Pakistan Army personnel understood his mind correctly and would not get carried away by the Lahore Declaration.

On the day the Lahore Declaration was signed, violence erupted in that city. The jehadi elements (Jamaat-e-Islami), which have had a long-standing alliance with the Pakistan military, started riots in many parts of the city to protest against the Vajpayee visit.[2] Indian military intelligence also intercepted several radio messages from across the border exhorting all jehadi elements inside Jammu and Kashmir to increase the level of violence.

There was a sudden spurt in the jehadi elements' activities in Jammu and Kashmir. On 20 February 1999, jehadi terrorists killed seven Hindu civilians at a wedding party at Bela Tilala in the Rajouri district. Four more were shot dead at Mora Putta in the same district. Home Minister L.K. Advani and Defence Minister George Fernandes, almost desperate, spoke to me several times on 21 and 22 February 1999. They wanted me to put Army units in the area on the alert and to take security measures to prevent further violence. We spread out the Army and paramilitary patrols over all potentially troublesome regions. For the first time, a few Indian Air Force attack helicopters

---

[2]In 2004, Nawaz Sharif claimed that intelligence agencies under the Pakistani military had orchestrated the agitation. 'It was later revealed to me that the stone pelting on the cars of diplomats and processions against Vajpayee's visit to Lahore in February 1999 were stage-managed and orchestrated by the agencies through a politico-religious party (Jamaat-e-Islami)', he said, in an interview to a weekend magazine of the *Dawn* Group (Pakistan). (See *The Times of India*, 11 October 2004. See also, 'Over 4000 Soldiers Killed in Kargil: Sharif', *The Hindu*, 17 August 2004.)

The Jamaat-e-Islami has been referred to as the 'Army's B team in matters ideological' by Ayaz Amir in his article 'Retrieving the Lost Years', *Dawn* (Pakistan), 5 December 2003.

were flown over sensitive areas in Jammu and Kashmir to play a deterrent role.

Between February and April 1999, there were 618 incidents of violence in Jammu and Kashmir in which 487 civilians, security forces' personnel and terrorists were killed. This figure marked a significant increase vis-à-vis the same period the previous year. Major terrorist incidents that took place during this period are as follows:

27 February: Five police personnel were abducted from their post in Kupwara district and later shot dead. In the Kokernag area of Anantnag district, terrorists blew up a bus carrying soldiers in a land-mine blast, killing five of them.

16 March: In Ganderbal, a group of six armed terrorists attacked police barracks and fired indiscriminately, killing at least three policemen and injuring many more.

28 March: A group of foreign mercenaries entered a house in the Poonch district and killed three young boys in front of their father, after chopping off his nose and one ear. In Anantnag town, terrorists lobbed a grenade into a crowded area, injuring twenty-eight people, including nine women.

20 April: Five persons were killed and twenty-nine others sustained injuries in an IED explosion at a shopping complex in Rajouri. In the Baramulla district, heavily armed terrorists intruded into a house and shot dead four members of a family.

29/30 April: Nine civilians were killed in indiscriminate firing by terrorists in the Kreshipora Nagri village of Kupwara district.

I visited Northern Command again on 10–11 April 1999 to take stock of the situation in consultation with the local commanders. On 12 April and again on 21 April, Prime Minister Vajpayee conveyed (through R.K. Mishra, a respected political leader and journalist who became his Track-2 interlocutor with Pakistan during this period) to his counterpart Nawaz Sharif that there was no let-up in the infiltration of militants from Pakistan. Nawaz Sharif replied that he *'would use his influence to correct the situation'*.[3]

---

[3]Robert G.Wirsing, *Kashmir in the Shadow of War: Regional Rivalries in a Nuclear Age* (M.E. Sharpe, New York, 2003, p. 29).

After the Lahore Declaration had been signed, our political leaders expected that crossborder infiltration and militants' activities in Jammu and Kashmir would gradually taper off. Both Defence Minister George Fernandes and Prime Minister Vajpayee enquired from me about the ground situation frequently. I asked the Directorate General of Military Operations to analyse the impact of the Lahore Declaration on the ground and make an assessment. Their assessment was: 'No change in the ground situation. There could, in fact, be some escalation in the proxy war in the immediate future due to Pakistan's internal compulsions and its politico-military situation.' This assessment was conveyed in review meetings in the Ministry of Defence and the Cabinet Committee on Security (CCS).

In my review and assessment of the strategic situation to the Army commanders in April 1999, I stated:

> The strategic environment, as expected, is changing fast and remains fluid. I would like to draw your attention to major factors evident in the last one year. These are *(a)* assertion and unilateralism of the post-Cold War era and *(b)* aftermath of nuclear and missile testing by India and Pakistan. The post-Cold War trend in coercive diplomacy, and even use of force, to assert and take unilateral action without UN approval and thus impinge on the sovereignty of weaker nations is on the increase. We have many examples of such happenings in the past one year. Other military and non-military pressures that have been displayed are *(a)* encouragement of secessionist elements, or proxy war, as [a] political instrument, *(b)* ready sale or transfer of arms and military equipment to secessionist elements, or [to] neighbours fighting with each other, or [to] a generally strife-prone area, *(c)* technological and financial sanctions, *(d)* attempts to politically isolate nations which do not...[subscribe to] unequal treaties like NPT, or even CTBT and FMCT and *(e)* trade embargoes.

> Two points should be noted in this scenario. First: These threats do not necessarily emerge from neighbours. Two: Developing countries, where ethnic and religious societies have not adequately gelled to safeguard sovereignty and nationalism, are more vulnerable than others.

There is no doubt that the nuclear haves of the world, and others who enjoy their protective umbrella, have put considerable political and economic pressure on both India and Pakistan after Pokhran II and Chagai Hills tests [both in May 1998]. [Pokhran I was in 1974.] Even the USA and China, which do not see eye to eye on many strategic issues, found this to be a challenge common to both. But what has been noticed, less than adequately, is the increased strategic and military cooperation between China and Pakistan: in terms of high-level visits; sale of arms and equipment; and on developments in Afghanistan.

The other positive impact of nuclear tests, i.e., the Lahore Declaration, has been lauded not only in India and Pakistan but also all over the world.

This diplomatic initiative has definitely opened the door for improving relations. But unless Pakistan translates it into ground realities, and stops sponsoring the proxy war, these CBMs cannot be expected to fructify. Pakistan's military has been and in the foreseeable future is likely to remain negatively Indo-centric. Despite [a] poor national economy, it has continued to receive support to upgrade its military potential. The military, including...ISI, is trying to force the issue of Jammu and Kashmir being central to the Indo–Pak dialogue. So our task and objectives have not changed. Pakistan's military strategy against India is based on low-intensity conflict or nuclear conflict: an all-or-nothing approach. We cannot accept this. We must be prepared to make use of the space between low-intensity conflict and nuclear war for conventional retaliation if Pakistan ups the ante in Jammu and Kashmir. This space would be limited in time, geography and scope and the threshold would need to be very carefully assessed.

So what are our deductions from these strategic environmental changes? These are: (a) defence capabilities and deterrence are necessary to be able to pursue our national interests including development; (b) strategic weapons do reduce chances of an all-out high-intensity war; (c) although conventional wars cannot be ruled out, these are likely to be limited in time, space and weaponry; and (d) lower threshold increases chances of low-intensity conflicts, which include low-level conventional war...

With conventional military capability in our favour, and nuclear capability lowering the threshold, Pakistan is likely to continue to resort to ISI-inspired insurgencies, where its instrumentality and expertise are in place and our vulnerabilities well known. It believes that a festering insurgency is a means of neutralizing our conventional edge and is keeping us engaged. Fuelling of insurgency and terrorism in India, a low-cost option, is likely to persist and should be seen as an adjunct to Pakistan's conventional war doctrine. The proxy war waged in Kashmir and other parts of the country needs to be handled with firmness, backed with effective deterrence.[4]

In conclusion of this chapter, it can be stated that, at the political level, the Lahore Declaration and the CBMs constituted a justified long-term approach and an attempt to bring about reconciliation. After the 1972 Shimla Agreement, the Lahore Declaration proved to be the next turning point in Indo–Pak relations, made possible by the two nations going nuclear. How much of the proxy war was discussed by political leaders, External Affairs Ministry officials and Track-2 diplomats with their Pakistan counterparts prior to signing of the declaration, other than what has been described earlier, was not known to the Army. But there were high expectations of reduction, if not termination of, crossborder terrorism and the proxy war itself. There was a kind of political anticipation in the air that one feared could lead to all-round complacency.

On 2 May 1999, I gave a planned interview to a journalist, in which I stated: 'The recent Lahore Declaration has not in any way changed the ground situation in Kashmir. If anything, the Pakistan Army and ISI are still active in aiding and abetting terrorism in the state.'[5]

---

[4] Author's address at the Army Commanders' Conference, New Delhi, April 1999.
[5] 'Malik Sees Trouble on J&K Front', *The Times of India*, 3 May 1999.

For military commanders in Jammu and Kashmir, countering the proxy war was part of their daily routine. They had to check infiltration, dominate and eliminate terrorists and minimize casualties of innocent civilians and of their own. In Army Headquarters, we were engaged with political and diplomatic efforts as well as military operational realities on the ground, in order to create a conducive operational environment for these commanders. We were also working on the futuristic strategic environment so that defence planning could be maintained on the right track and it did not suffer the vicissitudes to which political leaders and bureaucrats subject it to. While all formations in Northern Command were committed to counterinfiltration and counterterrorist activities, there was no intelligence about, or any indication of, a Pakistani attack by infiltration into the Kargil sector coinciding with the melting of snow in the higher reaches of the Himalayas.

On 10 May 1999, I left for an official visit to Poland and the Czech Republic.

2

War Planning or Conspiracy?

Five years after the Kargil war, Nawaz Sharif admitted: 'I blundered in making him [Pervez Musharraf] Army Chief.'

When Did Pakistan Decide to Attack Kargil?

IN AUGUST–SEPTEMBER 1998, PAKISTAN'S CHIEF OF ARMY STAFF, General Jehangir Karamat, had developed serious differences with Prime Minister Nawaz Sharif over the requirement for a National Security Council in Pakistan as well as its composition, apart from issues related to governance and ethnic violence. He also differed with his prime minister over the appointment of his successor. Jehangir Karamat was due to retire within a few months. On being criticized by Prime Minister Nawaz Sharif publicly, he decided to resign before his term ended.[1] Nawaz Sharif nominated General Pervez Musharraf as the Chief of Army Staff, thereby superseding two of his senior colleagues.[2]

---

[1]Some writers have suggested that Jehangir Karamat resigned as he refused to undertake the Kargil operation. This is not correct.

[2]According to a reliable intelligence source, Pervez Musharraf was not the first political or military choice as the Pakistan Army chief. Nawaz Sharif wanted to appoint Lieutenant General Khwaja Ziauddin who was way down in the Army hierarchy. Jehangir Karamat told him that this would not work and would create problems within the Army. The person more acceptable would be Lieutenant General Ali Kuli Khan, second in the hierarchy. When differences between the prime minister and the Army chief widened and Jehangir Karamat resigned on 6 October 1998, Nawaz Sharif appointed Pervez Musharraf, number three in the hierarchy, as Army chief. About a year later, on 12 October 1999, Nawaz Sharif tried to bring in Lieutenant General Ziauddin again by dismissing Pervez Musharraf. The Army carried out a coup and removed Nawaz Sharif.

Five years after the Kargil war, Nawaz Sharif admitted: 'I blundered in making him Army Chief.' ('Nawaz Sharif Speaks Out', *India Today*, 26 July 2004.)

(cont.)

After taking over, Pervez Musharraf made some quick changes in the top echelons of the Army. He brought in Lieutenant General Mehmood Ahmad as GOC, 10 Corps, in charge of all Pakistani Army deployments in Pakistan-Occupied Kashmir. Lieutenant General Mohammad Aziz Khan from the Inter-Services Intelligence (ISI), without commanding a corps as per the usual practice, was appointed Chief of General Staff, Pakistan Army. Probably an old contingency plan was updated.[3] Just when preparations for the Lahore meeting were going on, the Pakistan Army was busy planning and carrying out reconnaissance and logistic preparations from November 1998 onwards for 'Operation Badr' (the Pakistan Army's codename) with a view to:

- Altering the alignment of the LoC east of the Zoji La (pass) and denying the use of the Srinagar–Kargil–Leh highway in this area to India.
- Reviving jehadi terrorism in Jammu and Kashmir.
- Highlighting the Indo–Pak dispute over Jammu and Kashmir to the international community.
- Capturing Turtuk, a strategically important village located on the southern bank of the Shyok River in Ladakh through which an ancient trade route cuts through the Ladakh Range into the Northern Areas of Pakistan.

The planning and preparations were carried out only at the military level. This process included building up the strength of

---

When General Pervez Musharraf took over as the Pakistani Army chief, as normal courtesy, I wrote a letter of congratulations and good wishes to him, wherein I stated that I looked forward to improved Indo–Pak relations. I received a reply in February 1999 thanking me for the felicitations and good wishes. He also stated that he looked forward to our working together to improve relations. By this time, the Kargil war plan was already on the drawing board of the Pakistani Army and the process had been put into motion.

[3]All armies do prepare and keep ready such contingency plans against a likely adversary. According to Altaf Gauhar, a former Pakistan minister for information and broadcasting, this plan was prepared at the instance of (president) General Zia-ul Haq in 1987. It was dropped on account of military and diplomatic inappropriateness. Altaf Gauhar, 'Four Wars One Assumption', *The Nation* (Pakistan), 5 September 1999.

the Northern Light Infantry battalions that were required for infiltration, apart from stocking of artillery ammunition, limited development of tracks and helipads and the establishment of forward logistic bases. Here, soldiers were required to masquerade as jehadi militants. After carrying out further reconnaissance and establishing patrol bases from February to April 1999, the operation was to be launched in April–May 1999, under the direct command of Major General Javed Hassan, Force Commander Northern Areas (FCNA), to coincide with the melting of snow and the summer opening of India's National Highway 1-A linking Srinagar to Leh via Kargil.

General Pervez Musharraf and his team gambled on pulling off a 'Siachen type operation', i.e., pre-emption or occupation of tactically important heights before the adversary got to know what's happening.

Did the Pakistani Prime Minister Have Prior Knowledge of the Operation?

Did Nawaz Sharif have prior knowledge of this operation? If so, did he give his approval to it? These are frequently debated questions.

Nawaz Sharif has stated that Pervez Musharraf 'hid all Kargil details from me'. According to him: 'Initially, when this scuffle started, Musharraf said it was the Mujahideen that was fighting in Kashmir.' He also affirmed that the Pakistan Army chief did not brief him about the operation, or its intent, and added that he (Musharraf) 'didn't allow many of these inside developments' to reach him. He learnt about the Pakistan Army's involvement in Kargil from the Indian prime minister, Atal Behari Vajpayee. Nawaz Sharif has repeatedly put the entire blame of initiating the war on Pervez Musharraf. He also confessed: 'I suppose I should have known about all this. But, frankly, I had not been briefed.'[4]

A right-hand man of Nawaz Sharif, Chaudhary Nisar Ali Khan, has also stated that the prime minister '...did not get to know about the Kargil exercise at the *right* [italics added] time.... They [Pakistan Army] very consciously only provided him an

---

[4]'Nawaz Sharif Speaks Out', *India Today*, 26 July 2004.

outline of the exercise in which the focus was totally different. It did not involve the armed forces or crossing the LoC'.[5]

However, according to Pervez Musharraf, Nawaz Sharif had been on board all along.

Some post-war intelligence reports indicate that Nawaz Sharif was briefed about the Kargil plan first in December 1998/January 1999 and again in March 1999. Many Indian and Pakistani political leaders, with whom I have discussed this issue, believe that either Nawaz Sharif was not fully briefed about the plan and its political and military implications or he did not comprehend the implications. Nawaz Sharif, in 1998–99, was not known for showing much patience with military leaders, or for going into details of what was conveyed to him. My impression, which is confirmed by intercepted telephone conversations between Pervez Musharraf and his Chief of General Staff, Mohammad Aziz Khan,[6] is that during briefings of political leaders, there was considerable obfuscation. The Pakistan Army generals deliberately chose not to brief their political leaders about the detailed plan of 'Operation Badr' and its political and military implications. The chiefs of the Pakistan Navy and Air Force and some corps commanders too were not briefed. There can be three reasons for this. One: The Pakistan Army planners did not war-game this plan thoroughly and thus did not comprehend its strategic implications. Two: The concern for secrecy was so much that the plan was processed on a strict need-to-know basis. The Pakistan Army chief and his close planning staff did not consider it necessary to brief anyone outside their group. Three: The military planners feared that, as in the past, the political leaders might veto the plan.

What about Nawaz Sharif's role?

Nawaz Sharif's Government, notwithstanding the Lahore Declaration, had stepped up anti-India rhetoric in April 1999, especially after the test firing of Agni-2 by India. His foreign minister, Sartaj Aziz, and Senator Akram Zaki, chairman of the Senate Foreign Relations Committee, accused India of grave

---

[5] Interview with Rana Qaisar of *Daily Times* (Islamabad). 'Why Can't Generals Be Tried for Treason?' *The Indian Express,* 24 November 2003.
[6] For details of this telephone conversation, see Appendix 2.

violations of human rights in Jammu and Kashmir and called for self-determination in that area. Nawaz Sharif had appointed Lieutenant General (retd) Javed Nasir, former director general of the ISI, as the chief of the Pakistani Gurdwara Prabandhak Committee. A noticeable reception was given to a few Sikh secessionists such as Ganga Singh Dhillon during Baisakhi celebrations (13 April 1999), giving an impression to the Indian intelligence agencies that Pakistan planned to revive militancy in Punjab. Nawaz Sharif gave additional charge of acting chairmanship of the Joint Chiefs of Staff Committee to Pervez Musharraf and directed him to select and appoint a strategic force commander.

There is evidence to support the claim that Nawaz Sharif was using the Kargil intrusion to set up a fixed timetable for a solution of the Kashmir dispute in exchange for using his influence on the 'Mujahideen' to disengage.[7] He visited China and the United States of America. He pleaded with leaders there to exert pressure on India to make it agree to a ceasefire on terms favourable to Pakistan. He even told President Bill Clinton that if he did not agree to his pleas, on his return to Pakistan, his life would be in danger.[8] (These aspects will come up subsequently in greater detail.)

---

[7]Nasim Zehra, *The News* (Pakistan), 27 July 1999, and Amit Baruah, 'The Plan that Failed', *The Hindu*, 28 July 1999.

[8]Nawaz Sharif's meetings with President Clinton in Blair House (near Washington D.C.) on 4 July 1999 have been described vividly by Bruce Riedel in his paper 'American Diplomacy and the 1999 Kargil Summit at Blair House', Center for Advanced Study of India, University of Pennsylvania, May 2002, and by the deputy secretary of state, Strobe Talbott, in his book *Engaging India: Diplomacy, Democracy and the Bomb* (Brookings Institution Press, Washington D.C., 2004). Both of them have conveyed the impression that Nawaz Sharif had known about the operation but probably did not understand its strategic implications. During my visit to the USA in November 1999, I enquired from Matt Daley of the US Embassy in India if President Clinton had asked Nawaz Sharif as to why he permitted Pervez Musharraf to launch the operation in Kargil. Matt Daley, who was present in Washington D.C. during Nawaz Sharif's visit in July 1999, confirmed that the US president had asked this question and added that the Pakistan prime minister's reply was: 'Please don't ask me that question.' Strobe Talbott gave me the same impression when I spoke to him about this issue during his visit to India in September 2004.

Soon after the war, Nawaz Sharif accompanied Pervez Musharraf to the Northern Areas in Pakistan to pacify the highly agitated families of Northern Light Infantry soldiers who had participated in the war but got no credit, or had died inside Indian territory. The Pakistani Army had declined to accept their bodies after the war.

It is difficult to believe that a prime minister, who only a few months earlier had forced one Army chief to resign and had superseded two generals to appoint the next chief, would be doing all this under threats or pressure.

It is true that senior Pakistani Army officers did not fully explain the details of the Kargil operation to their prime minister. But there is also strong evidence to suggest that Nawaz Sharif had known *before* the Lahore Declaration could be signed that a Pakistan Army-controlled offensive action across the LoC was being undertaken in Kargil.

From the foregoing discussion, it appears that neither Nawaz Sharif nor Pervez Musharraf has stated the whole truth on this issue so far. Nawaz Sharif's conduct before and after the Kargil war is as suspect as that of the Pakistani Army leadership.

As this episode reflects on civil–military relations in Pakistan, which is an important factor in Indo–Pak security relations, it deserves further analysis and some comparison with India.

Civil–Military Relations in India and Pakistan

It is a well-known fact that most political leaders of the subcontinent have limited knowledge of their armed forces and little ability to understand their strategic and operational planning. In India, besides official military advice, the political leadership often obtained views from some cabinet colleagues like Jaswant Singh (a former Army man), bureaucrats and even heads of intelligence services. Also, personal equations of the kind that we saw between the prime ministers and Army chiefs in the 1965 and 1971 Indo–Pak wars (Lal Bahadur Shastri was the prime minister in 1965 and Indira Gandhi in 1971) and between Arun Singh (the minister of state for defence in Rajiv Gandhi's Government) and General K. Sundarji in 1986–87 have worked well for the system.

In Pakistan, on account of competing power centres, the civil–military relations are much worse. The political leaders have hardly any means to obtain information or inputs on security and related aspects other than what the military chooses to convey. They are seldom in a position to question the military, or get to know what the military may have deliberately left out in its briefing.

In the case of Nawaz Sharif, many people who have known him well have pointed out that his span of attention and comprehension of matters military did him no credit. He tended to speak dismissively, and even disparagingly, of his Army generals to outsiders, but was seldom in a position to contradict them.[9] At one stage, he had managed to vest in himself the power to appoint and dismiss chiefs of the three services through appropriate legislation. But he never acquired the political credibility to be able to exercise such authority.

Why did the Pakistani political and military leadership take this initiative without fully comprehending its strategic implications and international repercussions? One can only make an educated guess! My analysis is as follows.

Military Arrogance in Pakistan

Civil–military relations in a country are generally guided by its political structure, socio-economic conditions and its security environment. The armed forces tend to draw inspiration and motivation from the scriptures and military history of their countries. India and Pakistan are no exception. In India, we do so from multireligious scriptures. The military history in any case covers periods under Hindu kingdoms, Mughals and even British rule.

In the Pakistan Army, the soldiers' inspiration and motivation stem primarily from the Muslim cult of the warrior, a cult that puts warriors on a pedestal in that society. The general acceptance of wars, terrorism and violence in the Muslim world comes not from Islam but from the cult of the warrior that dominates the politics of most Islamic countries these days. The focus on external

---

[9]Personal conversation with a prime minister of India.

enemies causes them to admire power rather than ideas. Since independence, most public leaders in Pakistan have derived national pride less from economic productivity or intellectual output, but more from the rhetoric of 'destroying the enemy' and 'making the nation invulnerable'. The military in Pakistan has consistently taken advantage of this popular fascination. Over the years, the Pakistan Army as an institution has started viewing itself as the saviour of Pakistan above everyone and everything else. The Army tends to regard the civilians as incapable of understanding the dynamics of power and strategy.[10]

The other reason could be the equation among the power centres that has developed in the Pakistan polity over the last half a century. In Pakistan, issues such as Afghanistan, Kashmir and the nation's nuclear capability are specially important to the military.[11] The political leadership – whenever there is a civilian government – is neither briefed adequately nor is it in a position to assert itself on such crucial matters. This trend is almost traditional.[12]

The diametrically opposite paths followed by the Pakistani political leadership and the Pakistani Army hierarchy is also a reflection on the civil–military relationship of the recent period. That this could happen, despite the fact that the new Army chief had been hand-picked by the Pakistani prime minister, endorses the commonly held Indian view that the institution of the Pakistan Army, which is more powerful than the political authority, has a vested interest in maintaining tension with India. Such a vested interest and an Indo-centric view have compelled the Pakistan Army to enter into an alliance with, and use, jehadi elements

---

[10]Husain Haqqani, 'The Muslims' Cult of the Warrior', *The Nation* (Pakistan), 15 September 2004.

[11]Para II.6, '1947–1997 The Kashmir Dispute at Fifty: Chartering Paths to Peace,' report on the visit of an independent study team to India and Pakistan sponsored by the Kashmir Study Group (USA) in 1997.

[12]Even the Pakistan Air Force and Navy are often kept out of the loop. According to Air Marshal Nur Khan, former air chief of Pakistan: 'Top brass of Pakistan's Army did not take into confidence the country's Air Force and Navy when it started secret infiltration operation into Kashmir in 1965 that led to the Indo–Pak war.... I don't think they considered PAF and Navy important enough....' 'Pakistan Army to Blame for '65 War', *The Tribune*, 4 August 2005.

and terrorists not only in proxy wars but also in conventional wars. Both these factors put together have been responsible for most of the violence, including wars, in Afghanistan, Pakistan, India, Bangladesh and many other parts of the world.

Misperceptions and Self-Deception

While discussing Indo–Pak conflicts, one cannot but conclude that Pakistan has often made wrong assumptions and has developed misperceptions about India. Sometimes, Pakistan has indulged in self-deception vis-à-vis its bigger neighbour. These impressions have often been gained due to near opaqueness of military matters in Pakistan and the increasing transparency (as a result of debates and discussions in various fora) and parliamentary accountability on security issues in India. Any criticism of military-related issues in the Indian media tends to be highlighted, even exaggerated, in Pakistan. The Pakistan Army thus does not get a balanced picture about the Indian military capabilities.

Before Kargil, Pakistan had assumed that due to prolonged and excessive involvement in anti-terrorist and anti-insurgency operations in Punjab, Jammu and Kashmir and northeast India, the Indian Army was tired and not in a shape fit to fight; that its weapons and equipment were getting obsolete as no modernization had taken place for more than a decade; and that there was an acute shortage of officers especially at the junior levels. While addressing troops of Pakistan Army 1 Corps on 29 October 1998, General Pervez Musharraf declared: 'Don't be carried away by the rhetoric of the Indians whose armed forces are totally exhausted and whose morale is at its lowest.'

On 9 February 1999, while explaining the new Indo–Pak strategic environment, engendered as a result of the ongoing proxy war (and given the nuclear capabilities of both countries) to an academic institution[13] audience, I had observed:

If militancy grows too big, both the initiator, i.e., Pakistan and the affected nation, i.e., India, are tempted to use conventional weapons and forces. By now, Pakistan should realize that

[13]Maharishi Dayanand University, Rohtak (Haryana), India.

state-sponsored militancy is a double-edged weapon. It is like a wicked dog that bites the hand that feeds it. It can also lead to a conventional war. Having crossed the nuclear threshold does not mean that a conventional war is out. Space exists between the proxy war and the Indo–Pak nuclear umbrella wherein a limited conventional war is a distinct possibility. Nuclear deterrence only restricts an all-out war employing weapons of mass destruction.

This observation generated a strong reaction in Pakistan. A part of the vernacular media in that country misinterpreted my words, as if I was throwing a military challenge to Pakistan. Former director general of the ISI and intelligence advisor to Prime Minister Nawaz Sharif, Lieutenant General Javed Nasir, wrote a highly publicized article entitled 'Calling the Indian Army Chief's Bluff'.[14] The essential point made was that the Indian Army was incapable of undertaking any conventional operation. Javed Nasir's was not only a poor assessment of the adversary but also an indulgence in self-deception.

Brigadier Shauqat Qadir (one of the very few writers on the Kargil war from Pakistan), explaining the mindset inside the Pakistan Army before initiating the conflict in Kargil, has stated:

> Given the total ratio of forces for India and Pakistan, which was about 2.25:1, the (Pakistan) Military Operations concluded that the initial Indian reactions would be to rush more troops to Indian-Held Kashmir, further eroding their offensive capabilities against Pakistan. As a consequence, they concluded that it would not undertake an all-out offensive against Pakistan, since by doing so it would run the risk of ending in a stalemate, which would be viewed as a victory for Pakistan.[15]

---

[14]Lieutenant General Javed Nasir, 'Calling the Indian Army Chief's Bluff', *The Defence Journal*, Rawalpindi (Pakistan), February–March 1999.

[15]Shauqat Qadir, 'An Analysis of the Kargil Conflict 1999', *RUSI Journal*, Royal United Services Institute for Defence and Security Studies, Whitehall, London, April 2002.

There was a strong belief in the Pakistan Army top brass that the coalition government in India was weak and indecisive. It would either overreact or underreact on the 'Operation Badr' initiative. Whatever the Indian response, Pakistan would be able to lay the blame on India.

The Stability–Instability Paradox

Most analysts believe that the Pakistan Army started the war apparently believing 'that a stable nuclear balance between India and Pakistan permitted offensive actions to take place with impunity in Kashmir'.[16] Such a belief was held by senior military officers more strongly than by civilian leaders.

Stephen P. Cohen, the famous South Asia analyst in the USA, wrote in March 1984: 'A nuclear capability would paralyse not only the Indian nuclear decision, but also Indian conventional forces, and a bold Pakistani strike to liberate Kashmir might go unchallenged if Indian leadership was indecisive.' Further, he stated, '...a Pakistani bomb might enable Pakistan to reopen the Kashmir issue by threat of force: if nuclear weapons deter each other they may also inhibit direct military conflict between states that possess them; a Pakistani leadership that was bold enough could attack and seize Kashmir at a time when India was in disarray.'[17]

The stability–instability paradox is not new. This paradox has been articulated from the early Cold War days. In 1954, B. H. Liddel Hart stated: '...to the extent that the H (hydrogen)-bomb reduces the likelihood of a full-scale war, it increases the possibility of limited war pursued by widespread local aggression'.[18] Robert Jervis summarized this dilemma: 'To the

---

[16]Scott Sagan, 'The Perils of Proliferation in South Asia', *Asian Survey*, University of California, **41:6**, pp. 1064–86, ISNN: 0004-4687. He has supported the nuclear pessimists' views with organizational arguments.

[17]Stephen P. Cohen, *The Pakistan Army* (Himalayan Books, New Delhi, 1984, in arrangement with the University of California Press, Berkeley, California, pp. 153–54).

[18]B.H. Liddel Hart, *Deterrent or Defence: A Fresh Look at the West's Military Position* (Stevens and Sons, London, 1960 edition, p. 23).

extent that the military balance is stable at the level of all-out nuclear war, it will become less stable at lower levels of violence.'[19]

This implication of nuclearization had not been given adequate attention by most strategists in India. They generally held the deterrence optimists' view and predicted that such a situation would contribute to stability and peace in the subcontinent. However, it must also be emphasized that most strategists did not consider proxy war and terrorism as 'instruments of policy', which could be used by the states or non-state organizations such as the Taliban and the Al Qaeda. Proxy war and terrorism were not viewed as part of the 'spectrum of conflict', which could lead to limited or full-scale conventional wars. Since then, the Kargil war, post-9/11 wars waged in Afghanistan and Iraq and even the Indo–Pak military standoff in 2001–02 have now shown that proxy war and terrorism must be included in the 'spectrum of conflict'.[20]

The Revenge for Siachen

One of the motivating factors for, and one of the military objectives of, the Pakistani Army intrusion in the Kargil sector was to 'recapture' a part of the Siachen Glacier, to cut off vital Indian communication links to this area and thus disrupt its control. It is, therefore, necessary to understand the significance of the Siachen Glacier dispute for Pakistan.

The Siachen Glacier lies in the Karakoram Range, beyond the Ladakh Range. It is 75 kilometres long and between 2 and 8 kilometres wide. It covers a totally barren, uninhabited area of about 10,000 square kilometres. The glacier height rises from 12,000 feet to nearly 23,000 feet. The area is claimed by India on the basis of the Karachi Agreement of 1949, which described the ceasefire line beyond NJ 9842 (Saltoro Ridge and beyond)

[19]Robert Jervis, *The Illogic of American Nuclear Strategy* (Cornell University Press, Ithaca, 1984, p. 31).
[20]See V.P. Malik, 'Limited War and Escalation Control', Article Nos. 1570–1571, Institute of Peace and Conflict Studies, New Delhi, November 2004.

to be *'running Northwards to the glaciers'*. This line goes up to the southern Chinese boundary of Shaksgam Valley, an area that had been unilaterally handed over by Pakistan to China in 1964.

Unfortunately, the glacier area beyond Point NJ 9842 was not delineated in the post-1971 war exercise as no military forces had ever been deployed beyond this point. Later, Pakistan attempted cartographic aggression and started sending mountaineering expeditions to the Siachen Glacier and the mountain peaks around it. This resulted in some American civil and military maps showing a totally wrong alignment in the area: a straight line on the maps running northeast from Point NJ 9842 to the Karakoram Pass on the Sino–Indian boundary. Ever since, Pakistan has started laying claims to this area. India protested against these maps as well as the Pakistani cartographic aggression.

Meanwhile, intelligence reports disclosed that Pakistan was planning to occupy the Siachen Glacier by deploying troops there. This attempt was pre-empted by the Indian Army, which, in April 1984, launched 'Operation Meghdoot' (literally 'cloud messenger') and occupied the heights along the Saltoro Ridge. Pakistan launched its own military offensive called 'Operation Abadeel'. Thereafter, the line dividing the military forces of India and Pakistan in the area north of Point NJ 9842 came to be known as the Actual Ground Position Line (AGPL).

Whenever serving or retired Army officers from India and Pakistan have discussed violations of the LoC by either side, the Siachen Glacier area has figured prominently. After April 1984, when the Indian Army pre-empted Pakistan plans and occupied the Saltoro Ridge covering the Siachen Glacier, the Pakistani leader Benazir Bhutto had publicly taunted the Pakistani Army as 'fit only to fight its own citizens'. She did that again when, in 1987, Indian troops captured the 21,000-feet Quaid-e-Azam (the title given to Mohammad Ali Jinnah, the founder of Pakistan) Post in the area and renamed it Bana Post, after Naib Subedar Bana Singh who led the assault to capture it.

In Pakistan military circles, it is often mentioned that the former Pakistani Army chief, General Mirza Aslam Beg, suggested an operation in Kargil way back in 1987 to counter India's occupation of Siachen.

Siachen is considered a military setback by the Pakistan Army. That the Indians dominate the area from the Saltoro Ridge and Pakistani troops are nowhere near the Siachen Glacier is a fact never mentioned in public. The perceived humiliation at Siachen manifests itself in many ways. It is synonymous with Indian perfidy and a violation of the Shimla Agreement.

The occupation of the Siachen Glacier area has undoubtedly led to some financial drain on the Indian resources apart from a military effort of Herculean proportions. In Pakistan, Siachen is a subject that hurts, just like a thorn in its flesh; it is also a psychological drain on the Pakistani Army. Pervez Musharraf had himself once commanded the Special Services Group (SSG) troops in this area and made several futile attempts to capture Indian posts.

Kargil, therefore, was looked upon as a justifiable response by the Pakistan Army. General Pervez Musharraf, himself, has justified the intrusions in Kargil by pointing to Siachen.[21]

The Kashmir Obsession

The causes and the history of the Indo–Pak dispute over Jammu and Kashmir are well known. I shall not go into details here, except to mention that the Pakistani Army, ever since independence, has initiated two full-scale wars (in 1947–48 and in 1965) and made several smaller attempts to capture or nibble at part of the territory held by India. As stated earlier, it continues to support proxy war in this area ever since the late 1980s. The Pakistan military's obsession with Jammu and Kashmir is also well known.

Before the 1999 Kargil war, factors such as the successful conduct of elections in Jammu and Kashmir, a fair amount of normalcy returning to the area and considerable pressure on the jehadi militants exerted by the Indian Army had started causing concern amongst those in Pakistan who supported and

---

[21]During the Kargil conflict, particularly at the time of withdrawal of the Pakistani troops, the Pakistan Director General of Military Operations (DGMO) kept linking Kargil to Siachen. But we did not accept that linkage.

controlled the proxy war. The proxy war was to be continued, and calibrated, so that diplomatic and military pressure could be exerted on India, whenever desired. On this aspect, there was not much disagreement between Pakistani political authorities and the military. To that extent, the signing of the Lahore Declaration and Pakistan's proxy war policy in Jammu and Kashmir and other parts of India were not divergent strategies. The pressure generated by the proxy war and terrorism had greater utility during peacetime and peace talks. Nawaz Sharif had accepted that fact. He, therefore, tried his best to exert this pressure internationally and also during Track-1- and Track-2-level political dialogues during the Kargil war.

According to Brigadier Shauqat Qadir, 'in 1998–99, there was a growing concern in the Pakistani establishment that the Kashmiri cause was losing its international salience and the waning militancy in Jammu and Kashmir needed to be rejuvenated. The military operation, under the garb of a Mujahideen operation, would create a military threat that could be viewed as capable of leading to a military solution, so as to force India to the negotiating table from a position of weakness'.[22]

'Operation Badr' was a part of the Pakistan politico-military strategy, which among other objectives, was set in motion to highlight the Jammu and Kashmir dispute internationally, to exert diplomatic and military pressure on India, and thus to seek an early solution *favourable* to Pakistan. The entire planning for this operation was typical of the commando spirit of the new Pakistan Army chief. It was also an opportunity to prove his military leadership as well as tactical and strategic competence to Prime Minister Nawaz Sharif and to the people of his country.[23]

---

[22]Shauqat Qadir, 'An Analysis of the Kargil Conflict 1999', *RUSI Journal*, April 2002.

[23]K.Subrahmanyam, the doyen of strategic thinkers in India, has ascribed yet another reason. In a recent article, he has stated: 'Anti-India pronouncements of President Clinton during his trip to China in the immediate wake of Indian nuclear tests [in May 1998] and the publicly displayed Chinese anger and an increasing reliance of the US on Pakistan to deal with Osama bin Laden encouraged General Musharraf to try out [the] Kargil adventure, only to be rebuffed strongly both by President Clinton and the Chinese.' *The Tribune*, 30 May 2005.

3

A Line Uncontrolled

All defences in the mountains inevitably have gaps in between. It is neither physically possible nor tactically desirable to cover the entire length of any border with manpower.

THE STATE OF JAMMU AND KASHMIR IS DIVIDED BETWEEN INDIA and Pakistan along a 1049-km-long international border, the LoC and the AGPL. The AGPL terminates at the Indira Col near the Shaksgam Valley, 4853 square kilometres in area, which was unilaterally and illegally ceded to China by Pakistan in 1964, thus affecting the territorial integrity of the state.

To the southwest of Jammu and Kashmir is a continuation of the Indo–Pak international border through Punjab. The initial 199-km part of this boundary, up to Akhnoor (near Jammu town), runs as per the old alignment between the erstwhile state boundary of Jammu and Kashmir with West Punjab (now part of Pakistan). This part of the boundary is marked clearly on the maps as well as on the ground and is manned on the Indian side by the Border Security Force (BSF). To highlight the Jammu and Kashmir dispute, Pakistan, since the 1980s, has started referring to it as a 'working boundary'. This terrain is flat and consists of alluvial land with several stone-filled rivers and streams running north-south through it. Despite a series of infantry and tank battles that were fought in the 1965 and 1971 Indo–Pak wars, the international boundary in this area has not been altered. Any large-scale infiltration from Pakistan into India is not possible through this stretch due to lack of local support (the population is mostly Hindu and Sikh), easy mobility between border outposts and an obstacle system that runs parallel to the international border. However, small groups of terrorists have been able to cross over, mostly along the wide riverbeds.

The LoC is about 740 km long between the international border and Point NJ 9842 near Turtuk in Ladakh. This line is an outcome of the 1972 Shimla Agreement, wherein it was decided that the ceasefire line of 17 December 1971 would be

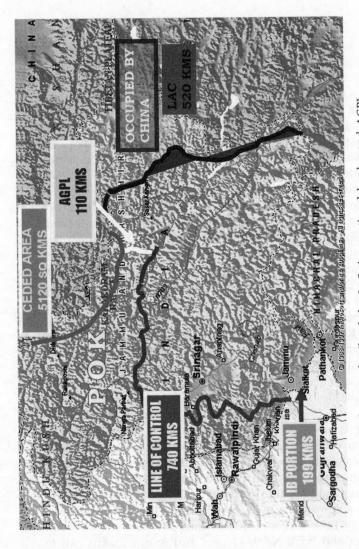

Map showing details of the LoC, international border and AGPL.

(*Note:* The map is neither accurate nor drawn to scale; it merely depicts the geographical area.)

clearly delineated. The delineation was done through a series of meetings between senior military commanders of both countries. The LoC is reproduced on two sets of maps prepared by each side, each set consisting of twenty-seven map sheets formed into nineteen mosaics. The two senior military commanders tasked for this mission have signed individual mosaics of all four sets of maps with the LoC marked on them. Representatives of the Governments of India and Pakistan, in a ceremony held in New Delhi on 29 August 1972, formally exchanged these sets of signed mosaics.

The first part of the LoC from Akhnoor to the Pir Panjal Range runs along riverine as well as forested hilly stretches, barring a small portion of mountainous region close to this range, where the heights go up to 9000 feet and there is snowfall during winter. The terrain in the hinterland is difficult to negotiate and underdeveloped with limited communication networks. A major road artery runs parallel to the LoC, linking Jammu with Rajouri and Poonch from which forward troop deployment areas are linked by feeder roads. Despite eyeball-to-eyeball deployment of troops on both sides and several stretches of minefields, this is a highly infiltration-prone area due to undulating terrain, forest cover and common ethnicity. Maximum infiltration during the 1965 Indo–Pak war took place in this sector. Many villages are located on the LoC or in very close proximity to it.[1] In the late 1990s, the Indian Army wanted the state government to shift sixteen such villages to the hinterland, but the latter declined to do so for political reasons. The state government also wanted the Army to give heavy compensation. The Army could not afford to do so.

Between Pir Panjal and Kaobal Gali on the Great Himalayan Range, the terrain along the LoC becomes more mountainous, with most of the Army posts located between 9000 feet and 13,000 feet. Some posts situated nearer the Great Himalayan Range are at 17,000 feet. While there exists a good communication network within the Kashmir Valley, the road

---

[1] I recall an old incident in which a villager on our side had drawn electricity connection from the village across the LoC to light up his house.

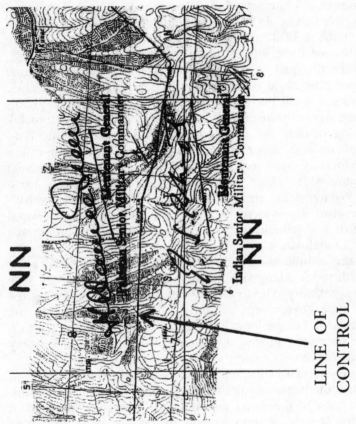

Clear-cut delineation of part of the LoC.

network in the forward areas is very limited. One major road each joins Srinagar with the Uri, Kupwara and Kanzalwan sectors. Thereafter, feeder roads and mule or foot tracks reach up to the forward posts. The tree line is approximately 10,000 feet and the Kashmir Valley bases lie between 5000 feet and 8000 feet. In this segment, the Shamshabari Range on the Indian side runs parallel to the LoC, separating the forward defences from the hinterland. There is a near-continuous deployment of troops in this segment also, except near the high ridgeline emanating from the Great Himalayan Range. In this Northern Gallies area, the deployment is comparatively thin on both sides due to the inhospitable nature of the terrain and the inability to support any large bodies of troops logistically.

For counterinfiltration purposes, this stretch presents even more difficulties due to steep slopes, deep valleys and heavy snowfall during winter. Here too, there are numerous villages at a stone's throw on either side of the LoC, particularly along Kishanganga (called Neelam in Pakistan) River. Some roads in the Pakistan territory are under our observation and thus vulnerable, but they are useful to the ISI for running terrorist training camps close to the LoC and for launching terrorist groups into our territory.

A distinct difference is noticeable in the terrain and the topography between the Great Himalayan Range and the Ladakh Range. The mountain sides are barren, steep and rugged. The terrain gets even more rugged from Chorbat La to Turtuk, an ancient trade-route village located on the southern bank of Shyok River that cuts through the Ladakh Range into the Northern Areas of Pakistan. The LoC runs along high mountain ridges/peaks with heights ranging from 16,000 feet to 21,000 feet. Many of these areas are glaciated. The winters are extremely severe. Dras is known to be the second coldest inhabited place on the earth outside the polar regions. The Shyok, Shingo and Indus Rivers, with the Zanskar Mountains in between them, divide this area into different parts. The only parts that are comparatively lower and inhabitable are on either side of these rivers and along a few traditional passes that go through these high mountains. Roads on either side of the LoC run parallel to it. These roads remain cut off from the mainland during winters as passes are blocked by heavy snow. On the Indian side, the Srinagar–Kargil–Leh road is the only surface communication link between Ladakh and the Kashmir Valley. This road remains closed from mid-November to early June due to the Zoji La pass being blocked. An alternative access to Ladakh exists from Himachal Pradesh along the Pathankot–Manali road to Upshi in Ladakh, which bypasses Jammu and the Kashmir Valley regions. This more difficult-to-traverse road also remains closed for nearly five months during winter.

On the Pakistan side, the road coming from Burzil towards Boyil and beyond passes over the Great Himalayan Range through the Burzil Bai pass. Another road comes from Skardu, as a feeder for the Northern Areas, opposite the Batalik and Kargil sectors.

This area is thinly populated but marked by considerable demographic variation. Of the approximately 10,000 Dras inhabitants, 95 per cent are Sunni and 5 per cent Shia Muslims. The total population of Kargil, Batalik and Turtuk is about 100,000, which is 80 per cent Shia, and the rest are mostly Buddhists. The majority population in the rest of Ladakh is Buddhist.

During my posting to Ladakh during 1962–64, Muslim (Shia)–Buddhist marriages were not uncommon. However, with the passage of time, the three ethnic groups have become considerably polarized, except in the Ladakh Scouts of the Indian Army, where all of them have a good representation and maintain complete harmony.[2]

Most Shia Muslims and all Buddhists oppose jehadi militancy. That is why, except for isolated incidents of infiltration and militants' activities, this area has remained largely unaffected even during the height of the proxy war. But, as mentioned earlier, the Pakistani Army artillery has often targeted vehicular movement near Kargil, and sometimes the town itself.

Ever since the map delineation was done as per the Shimla Agreement, the Indian and Pakistani Armies have, by and large, maintained the sanctity of the LoC. But there have been some

---

[2]During my tenure as Army chief, many local leaders approached me to raise separate Dras and Kargil Scouts, on the lines of the Ladakh Scouts. I dismissed such a proposal as it could further divide the society in this very sensitive border area.

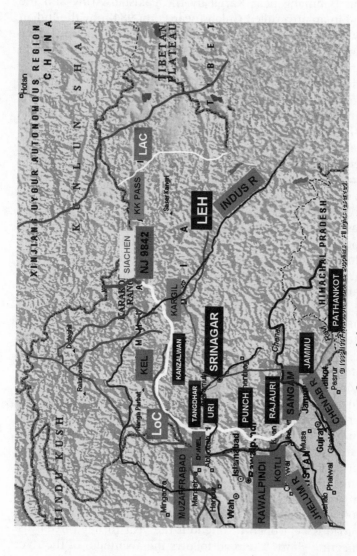

Status of the LoC Post-Shimla Agreement.

(*Note:* The map is neither accurate nor drawn to scale; it merely depicts the geographical area.)

violations too, most of them of a minor tactical nature. Two violations, which are significant, took place in the 1980s: the first in Dalunang near Kargil by the Pakistan Army and the second in an area called Gulab (near Point 9842) by the Indian Army. The latter was done to forestall repeated Pakistan Army attempts to outflank our defences in the Turtuk and Siachen sectors. Since then, the Indian Army has reacted violently to any attempt by the Pakistan Army at intrusion in these sectors and ensured vacation by launching low-level attacks, if necessary.

During the Kargil war, one of the 'disinformation campaigns' that the Pakistan Army tried to put across was that the LoC was vague; its exact location was not known at several places and, therefore, its patrols 'may' have crossed into Indian territory. This was untenable. Given the availability of precisely marked maps in both countries and of the global positioning system (GPS) capable of giving the exact location of any spot within 10 metres, it was not difficult to demolish the Pakistan disinformation campaign. We showed marked delineated maps signed by commanders from both sides to the media. And when a Survey of Pakistan map was captured at Tololing in June 1999, we were able to show the LoC markings on the Pakistan map also. At one stage, I told our DGMO to fax a copy of this map to his counterpart so that he did not talk about a 'vague' LoC in future.

Beyond Point NJ 9842 on the Ladakh Range is the 110-km long AGPL along the Saltoro Range going up to the Indira Col. This terrain, where the Siachen Glacier lies, is one of the bleakest and one of the most hostile terrains found anywhere in the world except the LoC portion short of it, which is only marginally better due to the absence of glaciers. The Nubra River coming down from the Siachen Glacier joins the Shyok River and then flows into Pakistan across the LoC near Turtuk. This area was taken back from Pakistan during the 1971 war. There is only one major communication link in the form of a vehicular road from Leh to Turtuk passing over Khardung La at a height over 18,000 feet, making it the highest motorable road in the world. This road is kept open throughout the year through extensive engineering effort. The road follows the alignment of the river in the Shyok Valley. A feeder road branches off from this road to the base of the Siachen Glacier along the Nubra River. On

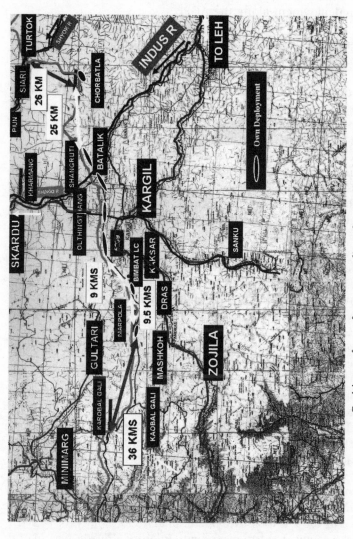

Positions of our forces guarding the LoC and AGPL.

(*Note:* The map is neither accurate nor drawn to scale; it merely depicts the geographical area.)

the Pakistan side, a road comes along the Shyok River upstream to act as a feeder from Skardu to Piun-Siari, just short of the LoC. From this main road emanates a feeder road to support troop deployment along the AGPL.

Operational Responsibility for Guarding Jammu and Kashmir

The operational responsibility for guarding Jammu and Kashmir along the international border, the LoC and the AGPL with Pakistan and Line of Actual Control (LoAC) with China, rests with Headquarters Northern Command, located at Udhampur, which lies in between Jammu and Srinagar. In 1999, at the time of the Kargil war, this responsibility was divided between 15 and 16 Corps. Here, 16 Corps was responsible for the southern portion: from the Ravi River up to the Pir Panjal Range. North of this range, the responsibility lay with 15 Corps. Both the corps were actively engaged in guarding the LoC, besides being involved in counterinfiltration and counterterrorist operations. The deployment along the LoC of 16 Corps and in the valley sector of 15 Corps was nearly continuous. Between them, the two corps had approximately fifty-eight Army and BSF battalions (all under the operational control of the Army) deployed along the LoC. Areas lying to the east of the Great Himalayan Range (Kaobal Gali and Zoji La), being more difficult for carrying out large-scale operations and given the threat perception, were held at selective places based on passes and other known tracks through high mountains. The operational responsibility for this stretch, along with the AGPL and the LoAC with China, lay with 3 Infantry Division (under 15 Corps), located at Leh.

During the 1971 Indo–Pak war, 3 Infantry Division had three brigades under its wing: 121 (Independent) Infantry Brigade with four battalions deployed in the Kargil sector, and 70 and 114 Infantry Brigades in eastern Ladakh. Later, after the deployment of troops in the Siachen Glacier area, 28 Infantry Division was raised in 1985. It took over operational responsibility for western Ladakh. Now, 121 (Independent) Infantry Brigade was placed under the new division. A new formation, 102 Infantry Brigade, took over operational responsibility of the Siachen Glacier sector, north of Chorbat La. The area between Chorbat La and Turtuk came to be known as Subsector West (SSW). The third brigade of the division, 53 Infantry Brigade, was nominated as a reserve for the whole of Ladakh.

After the Kashmir Valley got engulfed in militancy, Army Headquarters in consultation with Headquarters Northern Command carried out a strategic review in May 1991. As the militancy situation was expected to persist and develop further, it was decided to induct Headquarters 28 Infantry Division and 53 Infantry Brigade from western Ladakh to the Kashmir Valley. Since then, this division has been deployed in the area west of Kaobal Gali–Zoji La pass for guarding the LoC and also to carry out counterinfiltration and countermilitancy/terrorism operations. Next, 3 Infantry Division reverted to its pre-1985 responsibility of looking after western as well as eastern Ladakh. Also, 121 (I) Infantry Brigade remained deployed in the Kargil sector. An additional BSF battalion was allotted to this brigade for improving its defensive posture. The main disadvantage of this redeployment was that the reserves for offensive or defensive operations in Kargil and Ladakh were reduced.

As part of the same Army Headquarters review, 8 Mountain Division – which I was commanding and had moved it from Nagaland, Manipur and Arunachal Pradesh to Jammu and Kashmir in March 1990 – was concentrated in the Kashmir Valley (with headquarters at Sharifabad) to carry out countermilitancy/terrorism operations and to serve as the Northern Command Reserve.

The signing of the Peace and Tranquillity Accord with China in 1993 resulted in further reduction of forces in Ladakh. Headquarters 70 Infantry Brigade handed over its operational responsibility to 114 Infantry Brigade and was placed at Khalsi (Ladakh) as a reserve. In 1994, one infantry battalion and one mechanized battalion were moved out of Ladakh to the Kashmir Valley. Apparently, all this redeployment was accepted on account of the comparatively stable LoC with Pakistan (except for the Siachen Glacier) east of the Zoji La pass and the LoAC with China, and the difficulties that this high-altitude terrain posed for the conduct of any major operations.

In March 1997, prior to the Jammu and Kashmir State Assembly elections, Headquarters 70 Infantry Brigade was also moved to the Kashmir Valley and got sucked into countermilitancy/terrorism operations.

I have provided all these details because the gradual thinning out of troops from eastern and western Ladakh sectors between 1991 and 1997 would have definitely been noticed by Pakistan. This factor may have contributed to their decision to intrude into the Kargil sector in 1999.

In September 1998, after the improvement of the operational situation in the Kashmir Valley, Headquarters 70 Infantry Brigade with one battalion was moved back to Ladakh. The brigade had to leave behind two battalions as the reorganization of sectors in the Kashmir Valley could not be completed before the winter closure of the Zoji La pass.

On the eve of the Kargil war, operational deployment under 3 Infantry Division was as follows:

- 121 (I) Infantry Brigade with three infantry battalions and one BSF battalion, responsible for the area along the LoC between Kaobal Gali (Great Himalayan Range) to Chorbat La (Ladakh Range).
- 102 Infantry Brigade with three infantry battalions, responsible for the area along the LoC and the AGPL from the south of Turtuk (Ladakh Range) to Sia La (Karakoram Range).
- 70 Infantry Brigade with only one battalion located near Leh as a reserve in Ladakh.

Gaps in Defences

There has been considerable misunderstanding in the public mind about the gaps in the defences of 121 (I) Infantry Brigade.

All defences in the mountains inevitably have gaps in between. It is neither physically possible nor tactically desirable to cover the entire length of any border with manpower. In order to induct reasonable combat strength across the border/LoC and sustain that logistically, an aggressor (attacker) has to follow a reasonable axis, i.e., roads or tracks. The deployment by the defender is, therefore, based on the heights that dominate these roads or tracks, or where these may be constructed as part of the attacker's plan. The strength of troops in such deployments depends upon the terrain conditions and relative strength of the enemy in the sector. The aggressor is thus forced to attack and clear these (defender's) deployments and, in the process, the defender also gets a chance to move his reserves.

Gaps between such deployments are either held thinly, or only patrolled, but must be kept under constant surveillance. Our (and Pakistani) deployment all along the LoC and the AGPL was (and is) based on such a threat perception. This pattern of deployment with long gaps between defences was followed on either side of the LoC.

The deployment had acquired a traditional pattern over the last fifty-two years. Neither side had tried to occupy these gaps in strength owing to the difficult nature of the terrain and the limited threat perception. Such gaps in the 121 (I) Infantry Brigade sector were as follows:

- Chorbat La–Shangruti   25   km.
- Point 5299–Bimbat LoC   9   km.
- Bimbat LoC–Marpo La   9.5 km.
- Marpo La–Kaobal Gali   36   km.

In this sector, gaps in defences existed (and continue to exist, though smaller now) on both sides of the LoC. Such gaps were unavoidable due to the following reasons: (a) the terrain was (and is) barren and glaciated with high mountain ridges and limited roads and tracks; (b) due to the unsustainability of major offensive operations, the areas were accorded the lowest priority in the 'threat analysis' of the Corps Zone; (c) the conventional threat was limited to a force level of approximately one to two brigades along the available axes of maintenance, which were adequately defended; (d) the area was more suited for 'infiltration' by small groups rather than a conventional operation by the opponent; (e) the vastness of the area (stretching to almost 170 kilometres) coupled with the above, precluded continuous deployment due to constraints of manpower and maintenance requirements; and (f) balance had to be retained through the timely induction of reserves.

The responsibility for the defence of this sector, therefore, continued to be restricted to one infantry brigade with three infantry battalions and one BSF battalion to maintain a degree of surveillance over this tract.

During my tenure as Army chief, till the outbreak of the Kargil war, no recommendation was ever made to Army Headquarters for the deployment of additional formations in this sector.[3]

---

[3]During a brief visit to Kargil and Dras on 29 August 1998, I had conveyed to GOsC of 15 Corps and 3 Infantry Division and to the commander of 121 (I) Infantry Brigade that the infantry battalion in Dras required to 'be reorganized (redeployed) and made more effective on the LoC and along the 'route of maintenance' from Dras to its forward posts. This was one of the observations conveyed to Headquarters Northern Command in the tour notes of 15 September 1998, issued after my visit to 15 and 16 Corps in that command. After the Kargil war, I learnt that in response to this observation, Headquarters 121 (I) Infantry Brigade had informed Headquarters 3 Infantry Division on 26 October 1998 that 'the siting of defences in the brigade sector has been done tactically, after numerous war games and as a result of years of experience. Admittedly, some posts are non-tactically sited to meet the specifics of no-war-no-peace scenario'.

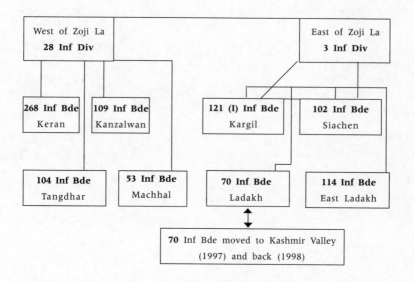

**Deployment – West and East of Zoji La:
1993–98**

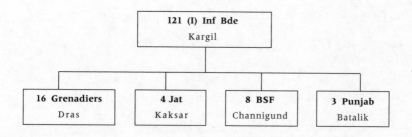

Deployment of 121 (I) Infantry Brigade: January–May 1999

4

The Dark Winter

The primary responsibility for providing intelligence about a likely military attack...rests with R&AW [Research and Analysis Wing] and the JIC [Joint Intelligence Committee].

A LOT HAS ALREADY BEEN WRITTEN ABOUT INDIA BEING TOTALLY surprised, about intelligence failure and about poor surveillance during the initial stages of the Kargil war. The Kargil Review Committee Report (see Appendix 3 for a summary) has stated that our intelligence agencies were weak in both gathering intelligence and assessing the inputs. Overall, the report came to the conclusion that the Pakistani intrusion was a complete and total surprise to the Government of India and its intelligence agencies. Some analysts have highlighted the general lack of awareness among political leaders about the critical need for assessed intelligence. Others have alleged overall complacency following the Lahore Declaration, even going to the extent of claiming that intelligence was skewed to suit the compulsions of the top-level decision makers. There are no two opinions as far as poor surveillance is concerned. To get a clearer picture, let us examine the facts closely and analyse the causes for the failures.

The Intelligence Factor

At the outset, it must be admitted that the task of the intelligence services is never easy. This fact became evident not only during the Kargil war but also on several occasions in military and non-military history. The failure of the intelligence agencies with the most sophisticated gadgets and highly trained personnel to anticipate the terrorists' strikes in the United States of America on 9/11 and other parts of the world after that and the failure to find weapons of mass destruction in Iraq are grim reminders of that reality. Both as a record for posterity and for learning objective lessons, it needs to be pointed out that our intelligence during the Kargil episode both at the strategic and tactical levels was deficient. There were no intelligence reports of a planned armed intrusion by the Pakistan Army before or even during the early stages of the war. There were some reports of jehadi militants' camps in Skardu and other areas, located approximately 50–150 km away from the LoC. Our civil and military intelligence agencies kept harping on the presence of jehadi militants in the conflict area almost till the end of the war without substantive evidence other than radio intercepts that were part of the Pakistani Army deception plan; in other words, a plant.

The failure to anticipate or identify military action of this nature on the border by the Pakistan Army reflected a major deficiency in our system of collecting, reporting, collating and assessing intelligence. This failure can be primarily attributed to the fact that, over the years, the Joint Intelligence Committee (JIC) had not been accorded due importance by the government. For many years, this committee was headed by a 'double-hatter', who, besides being responsible for running his own intelligence agency, was officiating as chairman, JIC. The importance of the JIC and its assessed intelligence thus got eroded. In the absence of an effective chairman, the JIC was hardly working to a plan and very little lateral coordination existed. The heads of the Research and Analysis Wing (R&AW) and the Intelligence Bureau fell into a pattern of reporting directly to the prime minister and the home minister and assiduously looking after their respective turfs. They developed a tendency to work more vertically and less laterally. Even the Military Intelligence Directorate became complacent when it came to providing feedbacks and attending the JIC meetings regularly at the appropriate level.[1]

In 1998, the JIC was absorbed into the newly formed National Security Council Secretariat (NSCS), headed by a secretary

---

[1]According to Kargil Review Committee Report, the level of participation by the Military Intelligence Directorate in the assessment process was low and often its representatives did not come fully briefed. That may be correct. However, it needs to be stated that the JIC/National Security Council Secretariat never reported this matter, or gave such a feedback, to Army Headquarters or to the Chiefs of Staff Committee (COSC).

working under the national security advisor.[2] The JIC intelligence assessments thereafter were prepared and issued from the NSCS.

At the national level, intelligence assessments play an extremely important role in formulating national responses including military action. These assessments are the total fusion of the capabilities, vulnerabilities, intentions and likely courses of action of the target nations, based on a wide range of factors: geopolitics, the ongoing national political developments, the health of the economy, the state of the armed forces and the sociological factors. The inputs can be strategic and tactical in nature; they can be either external or internal. The JIC (merged with the NSCS in 1998) received relevant inputs from all intelligence agencies: R&AW, the Intelligence Bureau, the Intelligence Directorates of the Army, the Navy, the Air Force, the Border Security Force and the Indo–Tibetan Border Police. The committee assessed these inputs at the strategic level, and then shared them with the key decision makers. The charter of the JIC, as laid down in 1985, was to assemble, evaluate and present intelligence from different sources pertaining to all developments that have a bearing on national security and prepare reports that help in policy formulations.

Strategic intelligence is concerned with broad issues such as evaluating the military capabilities and intentions of foreign countries, apart from assessing the political and economic scenario there. Relevant changes that affect the national power, including military capabilities of these countries, may be social, technical, tactical or diplomatic. These changes are analysed in combination with already known facts about the area in question with relation to factors such as geography, demography and industrial capacities.

Military intelligence is an essential discipline for the armed forces. This branch of intelligence focuses on gathering,

---

[2]Many of us in the strategic community believe that by merging the JIC with the NSCS, the independence and objectivity of the intelligence assessment process at the national level have been adversely affected. We now have a single organization – the NSCS, which is responsible for making intelligence assessments, appraisals, as well as coordinating and monitoring follow-up actions.

analysing and disseminating relevant information of a military nature about the adversary, the terrain and the weather in the area of operations or the area of interest, and ensuring security of our own military information. Military intelligence activities are conducted at all levels – from strategic, operational to tactical – during peacetime and during war.

In India, R&AW is responsible for gathering and analysing *all* external intelligence, including what relates to a potential adversary's military deployments and intentions. To assist it in collating and assessing military intelligence of a strategic nature, a military wing has been included in the organization of R&AW. The primary responsibility for providing intelligence about a likely military attack, therefore, rests with R&AW and the JIC.

In 1999, the role and the capability of directors-general of the Army, Air Force and Navy intelligence were limited. Their functions were restricted *mostly* to the collection of tactical military intelligence and signal intelligence. After receiving inputs from outside agencies, and from their own operational and tactical sources, they prepared assessment reports for dissemination within their respective services.

The foregoing discussion now leads us to a couple of crucial questions: What were the intelligence assessments of the designs of the Pakistanis on Kargil before the local agents discovered their presence there in the first week of May 1999? What kind of reports and assessments were they providing? We shall first examine the strategic intelligence reports and assessments.

Strategic Intelligence

In 1998–99, the service chiefs were briefed by the intelligence chiefs of the three services and by senior representatives of R&AW and the Intelligence Bureau during weekly meetings of the Chiefs of Staff Committee (COSC).

The JIC analysed inputs from various intelligence agencies and provided a monthly intelligence review to various places such as the Prime Minister's Office, the concerned ministries and the service headquarters. In the Army Headquarters, this review was studied by Military Intelligence and the Operations Directorates and then sent to the vice chief and the chief, with their comments. In addition, R&AW carried out a regular analysis and sent six monthly assessments to the armed forces, focusing on the war-waging potential/threat assessment from a potential hostile neighbour.

It needs to be emphasized that the armed forces did not have any agency of their own for providing strategic intelligence from outside the country for assessing enemy potential/intentions.

In April 1998, R&AW, India's primary external intelligence agency, had assessed that, for Pakistan, 'waging war against India in the immediate future will not be a rational decision'. Its subsequent assessment in September 1998 was that there was a serious financial resource crunch within Pakistan in general and its Army in particular. But elsewhere, the same September 1998 report suggested that a *limited swift offensive threat with possible support of alliance partners cannot be ruled out. Meanwhile, Pakistan will continue to indulge in proxy war in Kashmir and will keep the LoC volatile'* (italics added).

On receipt of this report, Army Headquarters immediately enquired about the likely areas for such a *limited swift offensive.* As per the laid-down procedure, Army Headquarters asked for monthly assessments/follow-up reports. There was no response from either the JIC or R&AW.

The assessment made by R&AW in March 1999, soon after. the Lahore Declaration, indicated a sobering effect on Pakistan's anti-India tirade and that the new Pakistan Army chief (General Pervez Musharraf) appeared to have dedicated himself to utilizing his forces for the improvement of national departments such as the Water and Power Development Authority (WAPDA), railways, prisons, customs, anti-narcotics, health and education. This assessment also reported heavy deployment of troops and artillery in 10 Corps in Pakistan-Occupied Kashmir and mentioned that (*a*) no major escalation had taken place since October 1998, (*b*) Pakistani troops had been consistently firing on the Dras–Kargil highway at night to offset disadvantage elsewhere and (*c*) diminution in the intensity of firing could be attributed to cold weather. Further, the report stated that there were indications that the troops 'were prepared for the contingency of *heavy exchange of artillery fire in April/May 1999'* (italics added), for which measures such as dumping of ammunition, the construction of emplacements and the activation of alternative gun positions had been put in place. This report assessed that the scenario of 'no threat of war with India' had emboldened the Pakistani Army to concentrate on reinforcing its deployment along the LoC from elsewhere. Pakistan was keeping its guns ready for the possible resumption of heavy exchange of artillery fire, which could erupt because it would begin abetting the infiltration of militants into the Kashmir Valley during the thaw in the coming months of April and May. After referring to the financial crunch being faced by Pakistan, the report concluded that *'waging a war against India in the immediate future would not seem to be a rational decision from the financial point of view...[the] Nawaz Sharif government would be left with little option but to pursue belligerence, abet infiltration, and indulge in proxy war in Jammu and Kashmir as part of an attempt to keep the hardliners subdued'* (italics added). This particular assessment made no reference at all to the 'limited offensive' of the previous report.

The R&AW, which was responsible for keeping track of the movements of Pakistan military units and for the order of battle of the Pakistan Army formations, showed no accretion in the force level of the Force Commander Northern Areas (FCNA) in Pakistan-Occupied Kashmir during a period of one year preceding the intrusion. The agency had not been able to detect and indicate accretion of two additional infantry battalions and artillery in this formation. Prior to the intrusion, the FCNA had realigned the areas of responsibility of its brigades and moved the reserve battalion, usually based in Gilgit, to the LoC. R&AW and military intelligence units in 3 Infantry Division did not notice these developments.

The Intelligence Bureau remained focused on jehadi activities. In June 1998, it had reported that some jehadi camps were located in Pakistan-Occupied Kashmir and the Northern Areas, about 50 to 150 kilometres north of the LoC, opposite Dras and Kargil. This report implied that jehadi infiltrations could take place in the Kashmir Valley or the Dras–Kargil sector. In none of these reports was there any hint of the impending military operation of infiltration with a view to occupying important mountain heights within Indian territory.

This report was addressed to the national security advisor with copies to the DGMO and other officials in the Home and Defence Ministries. An important aspect to be noted is that the jehadi militant groups do not infiltrate across the LoC with a view to occupying territory and holding ground defences. They normally follow 'hit-and-run' tactics.

The JIC monthly review of July 1998 stated that the Pakistani Army had been resorting to small arms and artillery firing presumably to facilitate the infiltration of trained jehadi militants into Jammu and Kashmir. In Kargil, such firing had been aimed at creating panic by threatening to cut off the Srinagar–Kargil–Leh highway. Along the international border in the Jammu region, the Pakistani firing had been aimed at stopping our work on fencing. The review also mentioned that during the US–Pakistan talks held in July 1998, the Pakistani representative had pushed the line that since Kashmir was the 'root cause of tension' and the 'core issue', the antagonism could lead to a conventional war and escalate to a nuclear war. There was no indication in this report or in any of the JIC reports received thereafter to support a possible Indo–Pak conflict.

The JIC April 1999 review underlined the possibility of increased anti-India rhetoric despite the Lahore Declaration, especially after test firing of India's medium-range, nuclear-capable ballistic missile, Agni-2. Pakistan, in a show of military superiority, had test-fired two missiles: Ghauri on 14 April and Shaheen the next day. The review predicted that the long-standing cooperation among China, North Korea and Pakistan was likely to continue. The report went on to mention that a nuclear command authority was likely to be set up in Pakistan soon, under the newly appointed chairman, Joint Chiefs of Staff Committee (Pervez Musharraf).

Nawaz Sharif's visit to Russia (which took place towards the end of April 1999) and the likely enhancement of economic cooperation between Pakistan and Russia were perceived by the foregoing review. The review also covered the strategic significance of Sino–Pakistan relations after the Chinese premier Li Peng's visit to Pakistan from 8 to 12 April and the likelihood of further cooperation with regard to projects in the field of defence. During Li Peng's visit, the Pakistanis used every opportunity to rake up the Kashmir issue.

To sum up, the focus of all these intelligence reports and assessments was on militancy. Some Intelligence Bureau reports indicated that additional groups of terrorists were being trained with a view to infiltrating them across the LoC. But these reports were not area specific. The report conveyed the impression that Dras and Kargil, which had experienced relatively less militancy till then, could become the jehadis' focus of attention.

The intelligence reports also indicated an enhanced level of artillery fire exchanges in Kargil during the forthcoming summer. But the possibility of a conventional conflict with Pakistani regular forces was consistently negated. On the other hand, the inputs and assessments reflected a lack of preparedness on Pakistan's part for a direct military conflict.

The scale and extent of the Kargil intrusion involved elaborate planning and preparation. The operation required well-trained, duly acclimatized troops familiar with the ground that would have to be carefully selected for the operation. Large quantities of snow clothing and other winter warfare equipment would need to be acquired. Some new roads and tracks would be required to be built. There would be a lot of movement besides dumping of artillery and ammunition and construction/ renovation of bunkers. A large number of porters would be needed for logistical back-up support. Additional infantry battalions and artillery units would have to be deployed along the LoC.[3]

No such information except dumping of artillery ammunition was picked up by any agency or included in the assessments. The first indication of Pakistan getting ready for a conventional war was received through a report from the NSCS dated 14 June 1999. This report stated that the operational situation in the Kargil sector and Pakistan's preparedness showed that that country was fully ready and economically capable of sustaining

---

[3]Two additional battalions were deployed by the Pakistani Army in the sector. These battalions could not be identified by R&AW in the order of battle of the FCNA.

the present conflict for a long duration and it was also capable of waging a short-term war.

But by then the war was already underway for over a month!

Operational and Tactical Intelligence

At the tactical level, apart from R&AW, the Intelligence Bureau and the intelligence agencies of the states, the Army has its own intelligence network for collecting tactical intelligence and making assessments.

At this level, there were few reports from the Intelligence Bureau (and other sources) regarding the initiation of militancy in Kargil by Pakistan and its plans to infiltrate militants during summer months of 1999. The activities of certain elements suspected to be harbouring a sympathetic attitude towards militants were being kept under surveillance. This fact had been brought to the notice of the Jammu and Kashmir State Government in 1998. There were also some indications that ammunition was being dumped and odd roads and tracks opposite the Kargil sector were being improved. These activities were attributed to the increased frequency – almost daily – and the heightened intensity of firing in the region. There was no indication that Pakistan planned to intrude with its regular troops and occupy the heights across the LoC.

In 1997–98, the Northern Army commander, Lieutenant General S. Padmanabhan, who had served as GOC 15 Corps and DGMI before taking over his present post, had restructured the intelligence set-up in Northern Command. This was done to meet intelligence challenges in the wake of the overall internal and external security situation in Jammu and Kashmir. Dedicated tactical intelligence resources were provided to formation commanders down to the brigade level. In the process, Headquarters Northern Command also absorbed some personnel from the Army Headquarters liaison units located in Jammu and Kashmir.

What came out after the war was that the intelligence agencies the at the tactical level, i.e., the brigade intelligence teams and the Intelligence and Field Security Unit, spent considerable time and resources to accomplish militancy-oriented intelligence missions. The ability of their officers in charge to gather worthwhile intelligence from across the LoC was limited due to the non-availability of volunteers, sparse population and inadequate incentives. Terrain conditions, limited operational seasons and demographic imbalance degraded intelligence-related activities. As a result, the intelligence teams were unable to find out that two additional battalions had been deployed and that field defences were being reinforced in the area opposite Dras, Kargil and Turtuk. The efforts of the corps intelligence groups remained mostly proxy war centric.

In 3 Infantry Division, incidents reported in different brigade sectors were neither linked together nor properly assessed. It appeared that most of the newly created intelligence teams remained obsessed with staff work and tended to neglect the fieldwork.

Post-operations, it also came to light that, in Kargil, liaison between Army units and the locals was, by and large, inadequate. Formation and unit commanders did not maintain close contacts with the civil population to obtain the ground-level feel in their areas of responsibility. In some cases, in fact, there was a 'strained relationship' between the locals and the men in uniform.[4]

Operational Surveillance

Operational surveillance demanded that the tactical area of responsibility be kept under vigil. Post-operations, it was revealed that no additional Pakistani infantry units from outside had been inducted into the FCNA in early 1999. Only troops from within the FCNA were employed and four Northern Light Infantry battalions with additional troops attached to them were infiltrated across the LoC. Tactical intelligence by way of operational surveillance should have picked up some telltale signs.

Poor surveillance at the brigade and division levels proved to be a major disappointment. These formations knew that the

---

[4]P. Stobdan, who comes from Ladakh and was then working in the Institute for Defence Study and Analyses (IDSA), New Delhi, after his tour of the area from 2 to 9 June 1999, reported these facts to me.

mountainous terrain in the Kargil sector, given their deployment pattern (which meant big gaps between defences), lent itself to infiltration. They were expected to carry out vigorous patrolling and surveillance of the gaps along the LoC to detect and check any intrusion as per the policy and instructions laid down by Headquarters 15 Corps and their own headquarters. The patrols were expected to submit reports along with comments on any unusual activity noticed. Investigations later revealed that patrolling was neither planned methodically nor executed resolutely. Gaps between defended locations were not fully covered. The patrols visited only the *nalas* (valleys and ravines) and that too halfway to the LoC. There was no patrolling along the ridgelines. In many cases, patrol reports were not sent to the Brigade Headquarters and, whenever sent, they were not given due importance by the formation commander and his staff. Briefing and debriefing of patrols were also not given due importance.

Since patrolling involves the physical movement of troops on the ground, it is greatly affected by the terrain and weather considerations. The patrols, which are usually led by young officers and junior commissioned officers, are however, not expected to give up easily. They never return halfway without the permission of the authority detailing the patrol. The local formations are expected to take all factors into account while laying out their policy and giving instructions; they are also expected to monitor these patrols. Regular patrolling in the sector, which would have ensured that troops were trained to operate in inclement weather and would have inculcated the determination and the will to accomplish missions despite harsh and difficult battle conditions, was conspicuously absent in this formation. It is evident that patrolling had been relegated to the level of routine activity. One can conclude that our most important and dependable means of surveillance was not conducted and supervised properly.

Even after the intrusion had been detected, the brigade commander did not realize the seriousness of the situation. He dismissed the intruders as a handful of militants and tasked the units accordingly.

Other methods of surveillance would include the deployment of radars and sensors apart from aerial surveys. Here, we needed unattended ground sensors and local surveillance radars, which were, unfortunately, not available with the Army. Apart from patrolling, the only other viable means was visual aerial surveillance or winter aerial surveillance operation (WASO). Aerial reconnaissance and WASO sorties were vulnerable to inclement weather. Besides, there were not enough helicopters, which could all the time be employed for aerial surveillance operations at the level of a brigade. Aerial reconnaissance without effective onboard surveillance equipment is not very effective. Again, this equipment was not available.[5] Between December 1998 and early May 1999, fifteen aerial reconnaissance and six WASO sorties were undertaken. But the observers did not notice any unusual activity. In 1999, the Indian Army and Air Force did not have any Unmanned Aerial Vehicles (UAVs) that could fly at these altitudes to carry out aerial surveillance.

Those responsible for safeguarding this sector considered 'that the threat was limited to infiltration of jehadi militants along with heavy firing to interdict the road'. They also felt that 'the intrusion of the type that ultimately occurred was considered unlikely'.[6] There is no military justification for such conclusions. If the militants could infiltrate, so could the regular Army personnel. 'Attack by infiltration' is a tactical technique in mountain warfare usually taught in the Army training establishments. The element of surprise comes from actions that are not anticipated. It appears that the local commanders' obsession with jehadi militants made them neglect this aspect.

No Intrusion Certificate

To ensure that all units and formations deployed on the LoC remained alert and vigilant and noticed any intrusion immediately, Headquarters 15 Corps had instituted a certificate to be submitted by the formation commanders every month to confirm that there was no fresh intrusion in their areas of responsibility. This

---

[5]This equipment was procured on a priority basis after the war.
[6]Statement of Brigadier Surinder Singh, commander 121 (I) Infantry Brigade, to the Kargil Review Committee. Para 8.14 of the Kargil Review Committee Report, Government of India, New Delhi, 2000.

practice was instituted some years before the Kargil intrusion. Every unit deployed on the LoC was required to give this certificate to its immediate higher headquarters in the chain of command. Units and formation commander of 121 (I) Infantry Brigade continued to give this certificate to Headquarters 3 Infantry Division till April 1999 despite the fact that infiltration – and intrusion – had been going on undetected in the sector since February 1999.

Wintry Perception on the Ground

The Kargil Review Committee has noted:

> Strategic surprise was achieved by Pakistan because this area had been free of LoC violations over a long period of time and was considered unsuitable for military operations, especially during winter. One significant infiltration operation undertaken by Pakistan in 1993 ended in their total rout. There was perhaps an unarticulated assumption in the military mind that a rational commander would not risk his troops at such avalanche-prone altitudes during winter. Captured diaries indicate that the Pakistani intruders suffered heavy avalanche casualties in Mashkoh in March 1999. Surprise was achieved by Pakistan by carrying out an operation considered unviable and irrational by Indian Army commanders. A determined foe can always achieve surprise provided he has clear objectives, is prepared to take risks and has the advantage of timing and operational flexibility.[7]

On the ground, there was an impression that the Kargil terrain during winter did not allow cross-country movement of large-scale forces and that even foot patrols could not stay away from their bases for any length of time.[8] Despite all these odds,

---

[7]Para 8.20 of the Kargil Review Committee Report.

[8]According to the Kargil Review Committee Report (Para 13.2): 'A number of former Army Chiefs of Staff and DsGMO were near unanimous in their opinion that a military intrusion on the scale attempted by Pakistan was totally unsustainable because of lack of supportive infrastructure and was militarily irrational.'

Pakistani forces were deployed in such wintry conditions and did suffer heavy casualties during their induction. As per one Pakistani officer's diary,[9] many soldiers perished in snowstorms and avalanches. But as disciplined, determined and acclimatized small bodies of troops, they overcame these obstacles. As a force, they suffered heavily due to poor logistics and inadequate combat support and could not sustain themselves for long. Nonetheless, they managed to achieve 'surprise' during the initial stages of the war.

Posts Vacated in Winter

There has been a lot of misinformation about the practice of the Indian Army vacating posts along the LoC during winter. That indeed was the practice in the past. There were many such 'winter-vacated posts' along the LoC (on both sides), due to heavy snow and blizzards, not to mention inaccessibility on foot. These posts were reoccupied during summer. Since Pakistan had attempted to capture some of our posts in the Siachen Glacier thrice in 1997 and eleven times in 1998, all field formations along the LoC had been directed to be extra vigilant and carry out a reassessment of the vacation of such posts during winter. Eight such posts existed in the defences of the Kargil sector, which used to be vacated during winters.

In the light of the threat mentioned above, 15 Corps Headquarters had ordered that no posts were to be vacated during the winter of 1998–99. An exception had been made by the 121 (I) Infantry Brigade/3 Infantry Division, which was not reported to higher headquarters and came to light only later. A post named 'Bajrang', to be occupied by eight to nine men, was located on the southwestern flank of defences in the Kaksar sector to keep a watch on the open glaciated flank. This post continued to be occupied during the winter of 1998–99, as were the other posts. But sometime in March 1999, when the snow level rose high, the post was ordered to fall back to the main defences at Point 5299 at the request of the battalion commander.

---

[9]Captain Hussain Ahmad's personal diary recovered after the war.

It was at this location that Lieutenant Saurabh Kalia and five jawans, while leading a surveillance patrol to locate and check the intrusion, were captured by Pakistani troops on 14 May 1999. Apparently, the intruders had come and occupied this post sometime between March and mid-May 1999. Apart from this post, no other existing post was vacated or occupied by Pakistani troops anywhere in the entire sector.

After the war, there was confusion as to who gave the orders to vacate the Bajrang post. Other related questions were: Who approved these orders? Why was this information not reflected in the daily situation reports? A court of inquiry instituted to investigate the matter opined that there had been an attempt at a cover-up at the brigade and division levels. After ascertaining facts, 'administrative action' as per Defence Services Regulations (Army) was taken by Headquarters Northern Command against all those held responsible for the lapses/wrongdoings.

Surprise and Deception

The Review Committee had before it overwhelming evidence that the Pakistani armed intrusion in the Kargil sector came as a complete and total surprise to the Indian Government, Army and intelligence agencies as well to Jammu and Kashmir State Government and its agencies. The committee did not come across any agency or individual [which or] who was able to clearly assess before the event the possibility of a large-scale Pakistani military intrusion across the Kargil heights. What was conceived of was the limited possibility of infiltrations and enhanced artillery exchanges in this sector.
The Kargil Review Committee Report, Para 13.1

Surprise is a principle of war. Both the attacker and the defender try to achieve surprise at every stage. In the beginning, the attacker always has the advantage because he initiates the war. He decides on the attack location, force level and methodology on the basis of the defender's vulnerabilities. The attacker very often adopts deception measures to achieve surprise. The art of military deception is as old as the art of warfare itself. To mislead the enemy as to one's intentions has always been the aim of commanders at all levels. Deception helps achieve this aim.

The defender, who has to react to the situation, thus starts on the back foot. This is because it is not possible for the defender to avoid some degree of vulnerability, as he cannot defend the entire border in strength. It is for these reasons that military experts prefer a proactive strategy to a reactive strategy. That factor, however, is more in the political domain. Due to political reasons, except in the 1971 conflict, the Indian military always entered a war *after* the adversary had taken the initiative.

Some of the measures taken by the Pakistan Army to achieve surprise and deception for the Kargil war were as follows:

- The plan was based on stealth and deception. It was kept a closely guarded secret among select commanders and military planners. As the intercepted telephone conversation between the Pakistani Army chief and the Chief of General Staff later showed (Appendix 2), even the prime minister and his cabinet colleagues were not given full details or the whole truth. Other service chiefs and corps commanders were briefed on a need-to-know basis, *after* Pakistani troops had been infiltrated across the LoC.
- Regular Army troops were employed in the garb of the jehadis. As a deception measure, deliberate radio transmissions in Balti and Pashto languages were made to convey an impression that it was the jehadis who had intruded and were occupying areas across the LoC.
- The deception that the jehadis were capturing Indian areas and that the Pakistan Army was not involved became the official line for political leaders and civil and military spokespersons of the Pakistan Government.
- Troops employed for the intrusion were mostly made up of locals and, as such, not much movement was involved. Battalions of the Northern Light Infantry, which were involved upfront and provided the combat base, and the Chitral and Bajaur Scouts, who assisted them in the logistics, were already located in the Northern Areas. They were fully acclimatized and had good knowledge of the terrain.

- The Pakistan Army chose the winter season to carry out initial reconnaissance of the area of operations and to establish firm bases. This is the period when there is minimum movement of troops and civilians on either side of the LoC. This operation involved considerable physical and logistic risks. The bulk of the troops infiltrated across the LoC in small groups in April 1999, with the thawing in the upper reaches of the mountains. (When combat was joined in the summer of 1999, poor logistics made a serious negative impact on their operation.)
- Ammunition and stores for the operation were put in place gradually over a period of months.
- According to an intelligence report received later, Northern Areas were placed under the Pakistani Army to deny access to the media and to facilitate optimal exploitation of local resources.

During the early stages of the Kargil war, the Pakistani Army was successful in maintaining its deception and disinformation campaign vis-à-vis the jehadi militants' façade. How was that possible?

Deception in war is the process of influencing the adversary by supplying incorrect information or withholding vital information so that he makes incorrect decisions. It is a purposeful attempt to manipulate the perceptions of the adversary decision makers in order to gain a competitive advantage. Deception has never been a principle of war; it is only a means to achieve surprise (which *is* a principle of war) and not an end in itself. Lately, deception has changed in magnitude and scope. It has evolved into a complex activity occurring at all levels of war.

Disinformation in the military context is the spreading of deliberately false information to mislead an enemy as to one's position or course of action. It also includes the distortion of true information in such a way as to render it useless. Disinformation is designed to manipulate the audience at the rational level by either discrediting information or supporting false conclusions.

The Jehadi Façade

Pakistan, since its very inception in August 1947, has built up considerable expertise in militancy and in the use of irregulars for war, on their own or as an extension of its Army. It made its first attempt to force the accession of Jammu and Kashmir way back in 1947–48 by sending in irregular forces (tribal hordes), fully supported by the Pakistan Army. The same strategy was followed in 1965. On both occasions, not withstanding this façade, the infiltration soon led to a regular conventional war.

In a recent interview, Gauhar Ayub Khan (Pakistan's foreign minister in 1998, former speaker of the Parliament and son of the late president, Field Marshal Muhammad Ayub Khan) admitted that, in August 1965, Pakistan had sent 5000 'Pakistani Commandos' in the guise of jehadis into Jammu and Kashmir to occupy some territory and help the so-called 'armed struggle of the local masses'. Every commando sent into Indian territory was given two rifles and additional ammunition. Each commando was supposed to keep one rifle with him and hand over the other to a member of the local population. The objective was to wage a massive indigenous war against 'Indian occupation'. Gauhar Ayub Khan later admitted that the intelligence reports received by Pakistan were 'doctored'. These reports painted a rosy picture to the effect that the entire Kashmiri population was eagerly waiting to receive the Pakistanis and help them in their mission. When these 'Pakistani Commandos' were trapped by the Indian armed forces and 'Operation Gibraltar' (the codename for this operation) turned into a disaster, Pakistan had to launch its conventional forces into the Akhnoor sector. The Chhamb–Jaurian front was opened by the Pakistan Army to force India to ease pressure on the besieged commandos.[10] Here, I shall not go into the details of the 1965 Indo–Pak war except to state that Pakistan's 'infiltration plans' went haywire due to faulty intelligence.

Since then, the Pakistan Army, with the help of the Inter-Services Intelligence (ISI), has been able to gain further expertise

---

[10]'Kashmiris "Misled" Ayub in 1965 War: Gohar [Gauhar] Ayub Khan'. Report by Rauf Klasra, *The News* (Pakistan), 1 June 2005.

in Afghanistan (in the 1980s) in planning and conducting integrated operations with jehadi militants. Pakistan's regular troops and ex-servicemen were trained and made to fight alongside the jehadis under a command and control organization, which was headed by serving officers of the Army.[11] This aspect was confirmed when Pakistani helicopter missions were launched to rescue their soldiers trapped along with the Taliban in Kundus (located in northern Afghanistan).

Even now, serving Pakistani Army officers go on deputation to the ISI for a fixed tenure and then return to their command. The ISI, at the strategic policy and planning level, is officered by regular Pakistan Army brass. Thus, there is near total integration between the Pakistan Army and the ISI with regard to strategy and operational planning.

In the Kargil war, the Pakistan Army once again resorted to this unusual step to achieve surprise and deception. Regular Army personnel shed their uniform and disguised themselves as irregulars to intrude and fight within Indian territory, contrary to Articles 43 and 44 of the Geneva Convention protocol. These articles require 'combatants' to distinguish themselves from civilians (which would include terrorists!). The Pakistan Army was thus able to make use of the ongoing irregular jehadi militants-instigated armed conflict, or the proxy war in Jammu and Kashmir, as a deception to launch and conduct a war with regular forces.[12] Some Chitral and Bajaur Scouts personnel, who were a routine part of FCNA formations, provided guidance and logistical support to Pakistani troops within the Indian territory.

During the course of the Kargil war, this deception succeeded till early June 1999 because (a) there were no intelligence reports on the Pakistani Army's involvement before the war,

---

[11]The Taliban phenomenon has further exposed the regular Pakistan Army soldiers involved in non-military irregular or guerilla war.

[12]Even the Pakistan Army has confirmed this now. Major General Nadeem Ahmed, GOC, FCNA, in one of his briefings on the Kargil operation in January 2003, is reported to have said that 'there were no Jehadis or Mujahideen that were operating in concert with the [Pakistan] Army'.

(*b*) all intelligence agencies continued to back their earlier reports focusing essentially on jehadi terrorist camps and concentrations in Pakistan-Occupied Kashmir and (*c*) the Pakistani electronic deception plan for conveying this disinformation was effective.

Many Pakistani writers and analysts have attempted to label the Northern Light Infantry battalions as irregulars and thus differentiate them from regular troops. This ruse is only to create confusion. The status of the Northern Light Infantry is, and has been, similar to our Ladakh Scouts. In any case, such a cover cannot be used to decide the status of these units. One has to take into account factors such as their organization, weapons and equipment profile, the officers' leadership pattern and the command and control hierarchy during both peacetime and wartime. The Northern Light Infantry battalions, composed of local men, specially organized and trained for high-altitude warfare, are fully integrated with, and form part of, the Pakistan Army brigades deployed in the Northern Areas. The units and their personnel are routinely trained at Pakistan Army schools, including a world-class mountaineering school in the same region. Their officers are assigned from the regular Army, who come on postings, similar to our practice in the Ladakh Scouts. Documents captured later showed that the strength of the officers had been built up well before the war. A large number of artillery officers were posted for observation and directing artillery fire in support of these battalions. Similarly, officers from the Special Services Group, Corps of Engineers and Signals were also attached. These officers infiltrated with Northern Light Infantry units into Indian territory and conducted the operations.

The jehadi façade was simply not workable for long. The Pakistan Army was able to achieve surprise because very few officers in their Army knew about the planning, preparation and launch of the operation. As mentioned earlier, information was disclosed on the need-to-know basis. But after the launching of full-scale operations and with casualties being reported on our side, the rest of the Pakistan Army and the country too would have learnt their real identity. For example, after the Kargil war, ninety-three Pakistani Army personnel (thirty-nine officers, eleven junior commissioned officers and forty-three non-commissioned officers) were decorated with gallantry awards, including two with Nishan-e-Haidar, the highest gallantry award of the country.[13]

Surprisingly, many people from the intelligence agencies and the media in India, Pakistan and elsewhere continue to persist with the jehadi façade even now. The relevant questions that need to be asked are: Had any jehadis been present in our area, would they have withdrawn in the organized manner in which the Pakistani troops did after 12 July 1999? If the Pakistan Army chief did not take the Air and Naval chiefs and even some corps commanders into confidence over the detailed operational plan, would he trust jehadi leaders and their outfits?

Post-Kargil, some more questions have been raised on this kind of façade: Had the people of Pakistan known that the Pakistan Army regulars and not the jehadis were to infiltrate across the LoC and thus would be involved in the Kargil conflict, how would they have reacted? How much domestic support would the Pakistan Army have received? Besides the past experience and ongoing proxy war in Jammu and Kashmir, did the nuclear factor and India's conventional superiority also influence the Pakistani Army's decision to use this façade? We shall reflect on these aspects later.

Political Circumstances

On our side too, a series of events and circumstances at political, strategic and tactical levels played a role in helping the Pakistanis to spring their surprise and obfuscate matters in the fog of war that followed the Lahore Declaration of February 1999.

Politically, considerable euphoria was generated, perhaps justified, after the Lahore Declaration. It was widely believed in political circles that Indo–Pak relations would improve and crossborder infiltration, which had become more intense immediately after the declaration, would taper off and eventually cease. Prime Minister Atal Behari Vajpayee asked me a couple

---

[13]Captain Karnal Sher Khan of the Pakistan Army, who was killed in Indian territory (near Tiger Hill) and whose body was returned by India to Pakistan, was awarded the Nishan-e-Haidar (posthumous).

of times about the ground reality, to which my answer was that there was no change in the pattern of infiltration. No one in the Indian political establishment expected that the Pakistan Army would undertake territorial aggression across the LoC. (This viewpoint, however, does not condone any complacency or lack of surveillance.)

Since early March 1999, not known to the Army (including me), the prime ministers of India and Pakistan were holding secret parleys through the Indian political journalist, R.K. Mishra, and a Pakistani diplomat, Niaz Naik, in New Delhi and Islamabad. Mishra kept complaining about the continuation of infiltration from the Pakistani side.[14] Nawaz Sharif promised that he would use his influence to correct the situation. He either did not want, or had no influence over the Army, to do that.

When the initial reports of armed intrusion into the Kargil sector started trickling in around mid-May 1999, there was a flurry of Track-2-level exchanges. The objective was to ascertain from the Pakistani prime minister as to what exactly was going on. On 17 May, Mishra complained to Nawaz Sharif in very strong terms about the infiltration in Kargil. He accused the Pakistani prime minister of knowing about the Kargil plan when he had signed the Lahore Declaration. Nawaz Sharif had no answer.[15] By now, Nawaz Sharif was riding a military tiger that he himself had unleashed, and as the unleashed tiger was achieving some tactical successes, he could not, or did not want to, question the Pakistani military.[16]

Was there any politics of intelligence failure? According to P.R. Chari, an experienced strategic affairs analyst, often there is an 'alacrity of the intelligence agencies in providing their

---

[14]According to an account given by Niaz Naik to Robert G. Wirsing on 1 April 1999, Vajpayee personally conveyed to Nawaz Sharif through Naik that the old pattern of infiltration in summer and artillery shelling across the LoC must not be repeated in the summer of 1999. This message was again conveyed through R.K. Mishra on 12 and 21 April 1999. Robert G. Wirsing, *Kashmir in the Shadow of War: Regional Rivalries in a Nuclear Age* (M.E. Sharpe, New York, 2003, pp. 29–30).

[15]Ibid., p 30.

[16]Also see, 'Nawaz Sharif Speaks Out', *India Today*, 26 July 2004.

clients with the conclusions they [political leaders] wanted'. He also observes: 'The lapse (in Kargil) occurred largely due to the complacency that followed the Lahore Declaration.... Moreover, there was a failure to anticipate that intrusions could take place during the harsh Himalayan winter.' Chari further feels that the '...Indian system is structurally designed to ensure that its leadership gets the intelligence it wants'.[17] There may be some truth in that statement. But it is difficult for a military person in India to pass judgement because he is not as close to the political leadership as the heads of intelligence agencies are. Also, because governments in India, unlike in the United States, seldom allow discussions on intelligence failures in public or in the Parliament.

Intercepted Telephone Conversations

It is not as if our intelligence agencies failed everywhere; they notched up some significant successes too. One such success was on 26 May 1999.

By that time, we in the Army were fairly certain that the intrusion in Kargil was not a jehadi operation but had been planned and executed by the Pakistan Army. We had now planned our military strategy and operations accordingly. Most of the intelligence reports, however, continued to point to the jehadi militants. It appeared that the intelligence sources were trying to defend themselves and protect their credibility by referring to memos sent by them about the location of jehadi camps in Pakistan-Occupied Kashmir. Meanwhile, things started hotting up. The Indian Air Force unleashed its fighter-bombers for the first time and struck known enemy-held positions on our side of the LoC. Headquarters 8 Mountain Division had arrived at Matiyan in the Dras sector. We (at Army Headquarters, New Delhi) wanted them to settle down and consolidate their position before launching further attacks. The Northern Army commander was visiting Dras, Kargil and Leh to ensure that that

---

[17]P.R. Chari, 'For Your Eyes Only: Politics of Intelligence Failure', *The Times of India*, 30 August 2004.

happened. We had ordered movement of 6 Mountain Division from Bareilly (in Uttar Pradesh) to 15 Corps. The tactical headquarters of the division moved by air to the Kashmir Valley that very day (26 May).

Around 9:30 p.m., I received a call from Arvind Dave, secretary, R&AW, on the secure internal exchange telephone. In a light-hearted bantering tone, he told me that his people had intercepted a tele-conversation, probably between two Pakistani Army officers, with one of them speaking from Beijing. He read out parts of that transcript and pointed out that the information could be important to us. He said that he would send the transcripts the next day. I realized that the secretary, R&AW, had by mistake rung me up instead of the DGMI. He was very apologetic when I identified myself and asked him to send the transcript to me immediately.

The transcript was an amazing bit of intelligence, which, in one go, destroyed all the lies and the deception that the Pakistan Army had built up about the operation being organized by the jehadi militants. I rang up the secretary R&AW and explained my hunch that this conversation could be of a very senior Pakistan Army officer speaking to his chief, Pervez Musharraf, who was in China. I also stressed that his agency should, therefore, keep these telephone numbers under continued surveillance, which the R&AW did.

By the time we gathered for the Cabinet Committee on Security (CCS) meeting the next day, I was almost certain that the taped conversation was between Pakistan's Chief of General Staff (CGS), Mohammad Aziz Khan and his chief, Pervez Musharraf. This was confirmed when we replayed the audiotape. The tape revealed to the CCS and other participants in the meeting that the whole operation in Kargil was no jehadi operation but a military aggression, planned and executed by the Pakistan Army.

The R&AW intercepted another conversation two or three days later. By now the vital importance of such an intercept was well known. Instead of sharing it with the DGMI or me at the first instance, R&AW sent it to the national security advisor, Brajesh Mishra, and the prime minister. On 2 June 1999, I accompanied the prime minister and the national security advisor to Mumbai to attend a naval function to commission INS *Delhi*. On our flight back, the prime minister asked me about the latest intercept. When Brajesh Mishra realized that I had not seen it, he got this omission corrected immediately on our return.

This anecdote has been narrated to show how our intelligence system tends to work at the highest level and that too in a war situation. There is a strong tendency to hoard information so as to gain the upper hand in the turf competition. Rather than have the message expeditiously transmitted to the agencies that need to prepare their future plans, presenting it to higher-ups becomes more important. (See Appendix 2 for the record of the conversation between General Pervez Musharraf and Lieutenant General Mohammad Aziz Khan.)

5

The Fog of War

A factor that contributed the most to our surprise and to the fog of war was our inability to identify the intruders for a considerable length of time. Who were they? Were they militants or Pakistani Army regulars?

A S STATED IN CHAPTER 1, ON 10 MAY 1999, I LEFT FOR AN official visit to Poland and the Czech Republic.

A service chief's visit to a foreign country has to be planned much in advance. The Ministry of Defence (at the ministerial level), the Ministry of External Affairs and the Prime Minister's Office (PMO) approve such a visit twice; initially as an annual plan keeping in view factors such as reciprocity, good relations or a new military diplomacy initiative. After approval, information regarding incoming and outgoing visits is intimated to the concerned foreign governments through the high commission or the embassy. The second time, documents on the 'visit abroad' giving the exact itinerary, are processed through the Ministries of Defence, External Affairs and Finance, and then through the Cabinet Secretariat and finally the PMO. This second approval for me to visit Poland and the Czech Republic, on which we were dependent for some important defence equipment, was received just two to three days before the scheduled date of my departure.

The situation on the Kargil and Siachen front, as known to us till then, did not indicate any need for me to cancel my planned visit. The Director General Military Operations (DGMO), Lieutenant General Nirmal Chander Vij, had visited Leh and Kargil on 4–5 May 1999. He did not get any inkling of the Pakistani intrusion in his interaction with the commanders there. The Northern Army commander, Lieutenant General Hari Mohan Khanna, visited Headquarters 15 Corps on 8 May 1999. Except for the usual exchange of fire from small arms, mortars and artillery, there were no situation reports of any intrusion. Even the intelligence report given by Tashi Namgyal (a resident of Garkhun village near the Batalik ranges) to the local unit

(3 Punjab) and Headquarters 121 (I) Infantry Brigade indicating the presence of unidentified people in the higher reaches of the Batalik sector and the subsequent patrol clashes had not been reported to the Army Headquarters till then. In the daily report of 8 May 1999 prepared by the Military Operations Directorate, there was mention of a clash with a Pakistani patrol in the Turtuk area, after which one soldier was reported missing. On the night of 9–10 May, heavy artillery shelling was reported near Headquarters 121 (I) Infantry Brigade in Kargil. Some shells hit the Brigade Ammunition Point, which was located in a mountain re-entrant. On enquiry, the Northern Army commander informed me that this was a 'chance hit' on the Brigade Ammunition Point.

On 12 May evening, when I was in Warsaw, Brigadier Ashok Kapur, my military assistant, spoke to the deputy military assistant in New Delhi. He learnt that some militants had infiltrated into the Batalik sector and that Headquarters 3 Infantry Division was taking action to clear the area. Ashok Kapur conveyed this information to me. Early next morning, before leaving Warsaw for Cracow, I spoke to the DGMO. He informed me that: (a) as per Headquarters Northern Command's assessment (till then), about 100 to 150 jehadi militants appeared to have infiltrated into Kargil, mostly in the Batalik sector. It was 'localized infiltration'. (b) Elements of two units from 3 Infantry Division had been moved to Batalik. (c) Defence Minister George Fernandes, accompanied by the Northern Army commander and GOC 15 Corps, Lieutenant General Krishan Pal, was visiting Partapur (in the Shyok Valley, Ladakh), Leh and Kargil on that day. (d) The Vice Chief of Army Staff (VCOAS), Lieutenant General Chandra Shekhar, had apprised the Chiefs of Staff Committee (COSC). The situation, he said, was being handled appropriately at the division and corps level. At the dinner hosted by our ambassador, Nalin Surie, that evening, I asked our host if he had any information about the jehadi militants' intrusion in the Batalik sector and if there was any message for me. Nalin told me that there was no information about the infiltration in Batalik, nor was there any message for me. Also, there was no mention of infiltration or intrusion in the national media reports on the Internet.

On 14 May, I visited a cavalry formation of the Polish Army near Goleniow. The DGMO informed me in the evening that the defence minister, the Northern Army commander and GOC 15 Corps, after visiting Kargil, Leh and Partapur, had gone over to Srinagar. The defence minister had briefed the media in the evening and stated that the infiltrators would be thrown out in the next forty-eight hours.[1]

On 15 May, I left for Prague in the Czech Republic, on the second leg of the visit. In the afternoon, Ambassador Girish Dhume informed me that as per some Pakistani media reports on the Internet that day, 'Pakistani Mujahideen had captured some Indian areas near the LoC in Jammu and Kashmir'. There was no official confirmation from New Delhi, although some Indian newspapers had reported infiltration by the Mujahideen (jehadi militants) in the Kargil sector. I gave him the picture as known to me till then and also remarked that jehadi militants do not usually capture territories.

That evening, the DGMO conveyed to me that as per the latest assessment of Headquarters Northern Command, the number of infiltrators was more: in the range of 250 to 300. The units deployed in the Batalik sector were in contact with some of them. An officer patrol in the Kaksar sector was missing. A search party sent to locate the lost patrol had been involved in a clash in the same area. Headquarters 15 Corps had now warned 56 Mountain Brigade of 8 Mountain Division located at Sharifabad (near Srinagar) that it should be ready to move to Dras at short notice. One of its battalions, 8 Sikh, was moving towards Dras and would start deploying immediately. I advised as follows: (a) We should make greater use of helicopter reconnaissance. (b) If Headquarters Northern Command were to ask for more troops for the Kargil sector, that could be allowed from 8 Mountain Division. (c) The COSC should be kept informed about the developments.

On 17 May, I had a long conversation with the DGMO and the VCOAS. They reported that except for the identification of

---

[1]'Infiltration Will Be Pushed Out in 48 Hours: George', *Daily Excelsior*, 15 May 1999.

infiltration in some more areas, there was not much progress. Patrols sent by the units and the brigade to combat and oust the infiltrators had either failed or made little progress. They pointed out that the number of infiltrators could be more. GOC 15 Corps and the Army commander, Northern Command, were still very confident that they would be able to eliminate the infiltrators soon. We discussed the situation. As jehadi militants seldom capture or hold onto any territory, Pakistan Army involvement appeared to be more than usual. The overall picture was, however, hazy and unclear. I advised the VCOAS that in the COSC meeting next day, he should seek assistance from the Air Force, particularly armed/attack helicopters for further surveillance and detection of the intrusion. He should also consider warning 6 Mountain Division located at Bareilly for induction into Ladakh for any future contingency.

On 18 May, I was told that, in the COSC, the air chief had not agreed to our request for additional support other than transport helicopters. The reasons given were that attack helicopters could not operate at that altitude and that the use of air power would escalate and enlarge the dimensions of the conflict. The VCOAS had projected these aspects in the Cabinet Committee on Security (CCS) also but his viewpoints were rejected.

It must be placed on record that, throughout this period, there was no suggestion from the defence minister, or anyone else, for me to cut short my visit. My staff and I were ringing up New Delhi every day. On 17 May, I asked the DGMO and the VCOAS if I should return to New Delhi immediately. Both advised me that as the situation was well within the capability of 15 Corps and Northern Command, there was no need for me to do so. Meanwhile, I had asked the defence attaché, Colonel Balakrishna Nair, to check return journey flight alternatives. He informed us that by cancelling the last one-and-a-half days of the official programme, we would gain only seven to eight hours in returning to New Delhi via London.

On 19 May (when I was on my way to New Delhi), GOC 15 Corps, Lieutenant General Krishan Pal, addressed a press conference in Srinagar. He described the situation as 'a local counterinsurgency operation' and declared that the jehadi militants in Kargil had been backed by the Pakistani Army 'to revive the defeated proxy war and to internationalize the situation by building up war hysteria'. He stated that this was 'a local situation to be dealt with locally'. He could not confirm whether the intruding groups had regulars amongst them. Krishan Pal pointed out that it was a 'time-consuming operation' for which no specific timetable could be given. The media reports about the use of helicopters, gun ships and aircraft by India were not correct, he clarified. He was hopeful that all the groups of infiltrators would be eliminated in a few days as they were simply on a 'suicidal mission'.[2]

On balance, then, the decision to continue with my trip abroad or cancel a part of it was purely circumstantial. There had been complacency in the routine surveillance during winter months at the local level. Poor intelligence assessments kept harping on the situation as 'jehadi militants' intrusion'. All commanders in the chain of Northern Command – in fact, even the defence minister – had visited the affected area during this period. They had repeatedly conveyed confidence in being able to handle the 'local situation' successfully at their levels. Towards the end of the visit, I had to take into account various factors such as the considerations of diplomacy and protocol on a formal visit to a friendly country (our ambassador had no official intimation of the Kargil situation), the speculations or ringing of alarm bells that would be caused due to the sudden termination of my visit and the time that could be gained by rearranging the return journey.

When I returned to New Delhi on 20 May, as per the normal custom, the DGMI, Lieutenant General Ravi K. Sawhney, received me at Palam Airport. He gave me the latest information and an assessment of the current situation. When I reached home, the DGMO updated me on all actions taken till then by corps, command and Army Headquarters.

The next day, we had a long briefing-cum-discussion during the COSC meeting in the Operations Room at Army Headquarters. The VCOAS, who had visited Srinagar on 19 May, gave us his

---

[2]'300–400 Pak Infiltrators Trapped in Drass – Kargil Corps Commander Extends DM's 48-hour Deadline', *Daily Excelsior,* 19 May 1999.

impressions. He informed us that the exact number of intruders, their identity and the extent of deployment in some sectors were still not clear. Several patrols, he added, had been sent out to ascertain these details. The extent of intrusion, the positions held by the intruders and the intensity of machine-gun, mortar and artillery fire indicated that the Pakistan Army was involved in this intrusion. The induction of 56 Mountain Brigade from 8 Mountain Division into Dras was nearly complete. Some Rashtriya Rifles units were also moved to the Dras–Kargil sector for providing rear-area security. It was decided that the Army Headquarters needed to locate additional reserves for handling offensive or defensive contingencies in Ladakh. Accordingly, a brigade from 6 Mountain Division was cleared for this purpose. For security reasons, this brigade was asked to move by road on the Manali–Upshi axis. The remaining division was kept ready so that, if required, it could begin moving at short notice. Headquarters Northern Command was informed that I would be visiting Udhampur, Srinagar and Kargil on 22 May.

A factor that contributed the most to our surprise and to the fog of war was our inability to identify the intruders for a considerable length of time. Who were they? Were they militants or Pakistan Army regulars? During my telephone conversations from abroad, and during my initial briefing on returning home, I was informed that our intelligence reports, and almost all radio intercepts, indicated that the intruders were jehadi militants from Pakistan. On the basis of the few visual contacts, they were reported to be wearing black salwars and kameez. The Pakistan DGMO (Lieutenant General Tauqir Zia) in his tele-conversation with our DGMO continued to deny any knowledge of the ground situation.[3]

Although civil and military intelligence agencies kept reporting that the intruders were jehadi militants from Pakistan and perhaps a few local militants, our doubts stemmed from the fact that the jehadi militants never defend territories. They never put up a sustained fight from sangars (emplacements made with loose stones) or hold any ground for long. The intensity

---

[3]He only wanted to know our impressions and reactions.

of the mortar and artillery fire indicated that the Pakistan Army was involved and was closely supporting the intruders. Something was amiss! We, therefore, asked Headquarters Northern Command and 15 Corps to get as much enemy identifications as possible at the earliest.[4]

Later, I raised the issue of the intruders' identity in one of the CCS meetings. Heads of R&AW (Arvind Dave) and the Intelligence Bureau (S. K. Datta), and even the secretary of the National Security Council Secretariat (NSCS), Satish Chandra, felt that the composition was approximately 70 per cent jehadi militants and 30 per cent Pakistani regulars. On my insistence, the prime minister asked the NSCS to review the whole issue of jehadi militants' involvement and prepare a report for the CCS. A few days after the telephone conversations between the Pakistan Army Chief of General Staff, Lieutenant General Mohammad Aziz Khan, and General Pervez Musharraf were intercepted, Satish Chandra came up with a fresh assessment. He reported that nearly 70 per cent of the intruders appeared to be Pakistani regulars and only 30 per cent were jehadi militants. I questioned this assessment and pointed out that all the evidence available with the Army indicated that the intrusion was by the Pakistani Army. Except for the radio intercepts, which could be a well-planned deception, we had not obtained a single piece of evidence suggesting the presence of militants amongst the intruders. The prime minister did not pay much attention to my statement but the secretary, NSCS, pointing to the heads of R&AW and the Intelligence Bureau, whispered to me: 'General Malik, *inki bhi to laaj rakhni hai*' (we have to save their honour too). I consider this remark unforgettable.

This incident has been narrated to underscore our strategic and tactical intelligence failure in assessing the real intentions of the Pakistanis. Their military planning was going on alongside the negotiations for the Lahore Declaration. Pakistan used the jehadi militants' façade to carry out the Kargil intrusion with regular Army troops. Our intelligence agencies kept reporting

---

[4]When we captured Tololing on 17 June 1999, we had gathered enough evidence to show to the world that we were facing regular troops of the Pakistan Army and not militants.

the intrusion as 'jehadi militants' activities'. Having reported the existence of jehadi terrorists' camps inside Pakistan-Occupied Kashmir, and having 'assessed' their likely activities during the summer months, these agencies persisted with the jehadi militants' version. The black salwar-kameez evidence on the ground and daily radio intercepts of jehadi militants' conversations supported this intelligence picture.

I will end this chapter with another story that highlights the fog of war. On 9 June, I had had a long day in Headquarters 15 Corps in Srinagar. After a detailed operational briefing by the corps commander, we discussed deficiencies of weapons and equipment in the corps, particularly with respect to the units deployed in the Kargil sector. Things were in a rather dismal state. I had called all the general staff officers who controlled these items and others responsible for holding them. After going into details, I gave instructions to the Army and Command Headquarters' staff to release the required items from depots outside Northern Command. I also gave instructions for interformation transfers.

I had retired to my room around 11 p.m., when an agitated deputy military assistant, Colonel Vijay Chopra, came in. He exclaimed: 'Sir, the situation on the ground is worse than it was at the time of our last visit. People in 15 Corps Headquarters, it seems, are not telling you the whole truth.' I asked him why he thought so. He replied: 'Sir, on your last visit when you were listening to corps commander's briefing, I counted the number of red pins (indicating enemy presence) on the map. There were thirty-six pins. This time, the number of red pins has gone up to forty-eight.' He then asked: 'How is that possible?' He was convinced that there was some cover-up. Hence, I explained to him: 'Red pins indicated confirmed or suspected enemy locations. Last time, they were still trying to locate the enemy in our territory. If they have now got confirmation of enemy presence at more places, so much the better! It shows the fog of war has started to lift. Once we have located the enemy, it will be easier to destroy him.'

That reply, I think, helped him to sleep better that night.

6

The Reckoning

I was convinced that the Air Force must make its presence felt by using its power in Kargil and, if necessary, elsewhere. Our substantial superiority in the air and on the seas must be brought to bear on the enemy to create the necessary strategic asymmetry, not only in Kargil and Ladakh but also along the entire western border.

All three services are national security assets.... For any combat situation, we must employ all three services optimally, in an integrated manner.

A N EARLY LESSON THAT I LEARNT IN MY PROFESSIONAL CAREER was that the first situation report on, or assessment of, any event was seldom a balanced one. It was either overoptimistic or overpessimistic. Based on the inputs of such a report, every commander must make his own appraisal, preferably by visiting the ground himself.

On 21 May, we had a long briefing-cum-discussion during the Chiefs of Staff Committee (COSC) meeting in the Military Operations Room at Army Headquarters. I was informed about how our first patrol, which began its quest following the information given by a civilian, had encountered intruders in the Batalik sector. Thereafter, our patrols had encountered a large number of intruders in all battalion-defended areas of 121 (I) Infantry Brigade. The intruders' count appeared to be over a thousand now. They were well armed and supported with mortars and artillery. Having occupied the dominating heights, they were interfering with our movements not only on the national highway but also on the smaller roads and tracks going up to our posts on the LoC. None of our posts on the LoC or in the rear areas had spotted infiltration by the intruders. There had been no encounters at or near the posts. As the threat posed by the intruders started becoming increasingly evident, approximately two battalions from within 3 Infantry Division (1/11 Gorkha Rifles and 12 JAK Light Infantry) had been hastily inducted into the affected areas and placed under the command of Headquarters 70 Infantry Brigade, which was now deployed and given responsibility of safeguarding the Batalik sector.

Two battalions from the Kashmir Valley (1 Naga and 8 Sikh) had been inducted and deployed in the Dras sector. These battalions were placed under the command of Headquarters

56 Mountain Brigade, which had taken over this sector. Some Rashtriya Rifles units had also been moved to Dras and Kargil for providing rear-area security.

Although we were fairly certain that the Pakistan Army was involved in the intrusion, we could not obtain authentic evidence to indicate the extent of its involvement. The intruders wore civilian clothes of the Mujahideen but conducted themselves as well-trained Army personnel. Over the last few days, artillery shelling by the Pakistan Army had intensified. Intercepts of the Pakistan radio network and our own intelligence reports, however, continued to indicate that the intruders were Pakistani jehadi militants.

I was briefed in detail about the Cabinet Committee on Security (CCS) meeting of 18 May, wherein we had been asked to clear the intrusion and also to exercise restraint and avoid an escalation of hostilities. When the VCOAS, Lieutenant General Chandra Shekhar, sought the use of helicopters and offensive air support from the Indian Air Force, the CCS rejected his proposal. The reason can be attributed to the disagreement on the issue within the COSC. It is also possible that the need to 'exercise restraint' may have been engendered due to the ongoing Track-2 dialogue between India and Pakistan.[1]

As mentioned in Chapter 5, the VCOAS, who had visited Srinagar on 19 May, gave us his impressions. He next showed us an aerial photograph (taken on 17 May by the Aviation Research Centre, New Delhi, and delivered to the Army Headquarters on 19 May) that showed a Pakistan Army helicopter flying along our side of the LoC. This evidence also indicated the involvement of the Pakistan Army.

The exact number of intruders, their identity and deployment in some sectors were still not known. Several patrols were sent out for finding out this information. So far, they had not achieved any success. Our troops had also failed to recover any ground occupied by the intruders on our side of the LoC. Meanwhile, our casualties were now occurring on an almost daily basis.

---

[1] R.K. Mishra (India's Track-2 interlocutor with Pakistan) was in Islamabad on 17 May. The Indian military was not aware of the Track-2 dialogue process.

During briefings in Udhampur and Srinagar, I was informed about the tactical responses of the local formations in checking and clearing intrusions, and about the immediate movement of troops ordered by the Headquarters of 3 Infantry Division, 15 Corps and Northern Command to the area of operations. Both the Army commander and the corps commander gave me their assessment of the situation.

By now, it was clear that the intrusion extended from the Mashkoh sector under 121 (I) Infantry Brigade to Subsector West (SSW) under 102 Infantry Brigade. The intruders were holding several tactically important features along this front. They had been able to construct tactically located sangars (emplacements made with loose stones) and shelters, which enabled them to observe troop movements from long distances and fire at them. Except for one aerial photograph taken by the Aviation Research Centre on 17 May, it had not been possible to acquire any other aerial or satellite imagery. The intruders possessed all the weapons normally issued to infantry battalions. They could rain down intense and accurate artillery and mortar fire on troop movements on the roads and tracks. Their composition appeared to be a mix of Pakistani jehadi militants and regular soldiers. They were supported not only by long-range, heavy-calibre machine-guns and artillery but also by helicopters (which helped with their logistics). Neither the intruders nor the Pakistani troops from across the LoC had ever attempted physical assaults on our posts.

Early clearance of the Zoji La pass by the Border Roads Organization had enabled the movement of 56 Mountain Brigade and other troops from the Kashmir Valley into the Kargil sector. Headquarters 70 Infantry Brigade, which had been reinducted into the sector in October 1998 before the closure of Zoji La, had been made responsible for the Batalik sector. It had been given two additional battalions, which had finished their tenures in the Siachen sector and were awaiting deinduction from Ladakh. Meanwhile, Tactical Headquarters of 3 Infantry Division had moved from Leh to Kargil to control all operations east of Zoji La.

I got the distinct impression that the ground-level reaction up to that stage had been mostly in the form of counterterrorist operations. Also, I felt that the movement of additional units and subunits at the brigade and divisional levels had been done in haste. The hastily moved units and subunits had neither adequate combat strength nor logistic support. They were being tasked at brigade and division levels in an ad hoc manner without any detailed planning.

Due to lack of any success so far, the commanders and the staff in both headquarters appeared quite tense and dispirited. They had lost some of the enthusiasm and optimism displayed by them during my earlier visits. I chastised them a bit about the infiltration and poor surveillance in 3 Infantry Division, particularly in 121 (I) Infantry Brigade, and then exhorted them to undo what had been done by the enemy and ensure that no one gets away. We discussed operational prioritization of the sectors in which intrusion had taken place and the need for deliberate planning of operations in view of the nature of the terrain and the entrenched enemy on the mountaintops with a long field of vision and fire. I pointed out that we must establish the identity of the intruders as soon as possible and to collect detailed information about their precise locations in the area of intrusion. I emphasized that we must ascertain the intruders' identities within the next few days. If required, I added, operations should be planned for this purpose.

Meanwhile, it was necessary to ensure operational balance on the LoC and the Actual Ground Position Line (AGPL), as the enemy did not appear to have shown his full hand yet.

While in Srinagar, I learnt that due to inclement weather, it was not possible to fly to Kargil that day and that a briefing of the CCS by me had been scheduled for the morning of 24 May. There was a lot on my mind that required quiet reflection on my part as well as discussion with my colleagues. So, I returned to New Delhi that evening.

The overall situation appeared to be much worse than what had been conveyed to me and what I expected it to be. The intrusion obviously was planned and executed not by the jehadi militants but by the Pakistani Army. Pakistan had taken the initiative and surprised us. It was a war-like situation and we were reacting to it like we did in 1947–48 and 1965. The government expected us to clear the intrusion and restore the sanctity of the LoC as early as possible but there was one stipulation: *we had to achieve our objective without crossing the LoC or the border.* I had a fairly good knowledge of the terrain in these sectors. I knew that it would be extremely difficult, and time consuming, for 15 Corps to evict the enemy from this area unless we created a suitable strategic superiority, and thus asymmetry, vis-à-vis the enemy, for the troops to operate. The corps would need additional formations, apart from artillery and logistical support. For achieving operational success in the intruded sector, we had to ensure that the Pakistani Army was not able to build up on its success after the Kargil intrusion.

It was apparent that Pakistan still had some secrets up its sleeve. Its game plan and its overall political or military objectives were still not clear. We needed more information in this context. Meanwhile, the Pakistan Army had to be deterred from making adventurous moves anywhere else. In a dynamic war situation, it was essential to be prepared for all contingencies that may arise either due to enemy action or to achieve our own political and military aims under the changed circumstances. The situation demanded much greater military effort for creating a strategic asymmetry along the entire Indo–Pak front and also for achieving escalation dominance.

The Pakistan Army had been proactive. It had taken the initiative and achieved tactical surprise, leading to penetration along a limited front. We needed to react strategically – where our strength lay – and escalate the hostilities, if and when necessary.

The first thing I had to do was to explain the operational situation and its serious political and military implications to my colleagues in the COSC and get them on board to fight the war jointly. I was convinced that the Air Force must make its presence felt by using its power in Kargil and, if necessary, elsewhere. Our substantial superiority in the air and on the seas must be brought to bear on the enemy to create the necessary strategic asymmetry, not only in Kargil and Ladakh but also along the entire western border.

Admittedly, the Army, Navy and Air Force were faced with their respective problems when it came to timely mobilization for war. But these problems could be overcome, if all three services planned, coordinated and implemented a joint military strategy, and more importantly, put across our points of view to the CCS in unison. The Pakistani war machine was plagued by the same shortcomings as we were. Due to shortage of funds, virtually no modernization was taking place and a large part of the Pakistan Army was being utilized for governance and for performing internal security duties.

The CCS appeared to be exercising restraint and was reluctant to escalate the conflict. Its members had either not received full information and the correct assessment of the Pakistani Army involvement or had some other political reservations about which we (the heads of the armed forces) did not know yet. We needed permission for larger mobilization to gain a strategic advantage. The relevant questions that arose in this context were as follows: Would the CCS allow conflict escalation and the induction of the other two services in this effort? Would escalation dominance work in the nuclearized Indo–Pak environment, and where political leaders indulged in rhetorical statements frequently? How would the government handle international opinion? How long would that diplomatic effort take? Under these circumstances, what political objectives were likely to be laid down? Would the government be prepared to declare war and go the whole hog? I needed to discuss all these matters with my staff, COSC colleagues, the national security advisor, Brajesh Mishra, and also in the CCS.

Of the three services, the Army takes the maximum time to complete its mobilization and is the most visible. Unless the top political leadership could declare a war, we had to achieve such mobilization without causing alarm both in the country and in the rest of the world. In the existing circumstances, how soon could we launch an offensive, if permitted? How would the climate impact our war effort? Also, we needed to take stock of our important inventories and reassess urgently our capabilities for defensive and offensive operations.

A Joint Military Strategy

On 23 May, I gave my own assessment of the situation and presented my thought processes to the VCOAS and the operational staff in the Operations Room. I then went to meet the Navy chief, Admiral Sushil Kumar, whose office was in the same corridor. After bringing him up to date with the prevailing circumstances, I discussed the need for enlarging the scope of the fighting and for carrying out joint services planning.

My logic for such an integrated approach at the level of the COSC was simple. All three services are national security assets. A single-service approach to defence and operational planning at the level of the armed forces chiefs, though outdated, tends to continue in our country due to its peculiar higher defence control organization and due to the fact that there is no chief of defence staff or chairman, chiefs of joint staff. For any combat situation, we must employ all three services optimally, in an integrated manner. The allocation of exact missions thereafter is a matter of detailed coordination, keeping in view factors such as the characteristics and capabilities of assets available with each service, the level of joint training and the degree of interaction among the services. In our country, where the political leadership and its civil advisors have virtually no knowledge or experience of warfare, differences in the opinions of the professionals are often played up. Such a tendency makes it extremely difficult for the political leadership to overrule any interservice argument. Such differences must be resolved at the level of chiefs of staff.

Sushil Kumar readily agreed with me as far as the integrated approach and employing all our assets optimally were concerned. He felt that such a step would not only give us maximum strategic and tactical advantage but also enable us to be prepared for any conflict escalation. Both of us realized that the Air Force chief, Air Chief Marshal Anil Yashwant Tipnis, may require some more convincing as, till that stage, he had not agreed to the use of air power in the COSC. He had two reasons for his stand: attack helicopters would not be able to fly at that altitude and the use of air power would escalate and enlarge the conflict. Consequently, the CCS, in its meeting of 18 May, had not allowed the use of air power including armed helicopters. On 19 May, Anil Tipnis had addressed a long letter to me, with a copy to Sushil Kumar, stating that there was considerable misconception about the use of air power and its political and operational implications. He wanted the COSC to discuss this issue again and then have a standard operating procedure prepared for the purpose. This letter was a bit upsetting and untimely, but I did not react to it.

I invited Sushil Kumar and Anil Tipnis for a COSC meeting in my office at 4 p.m. on 23 May. As this was to be an important meeting, and could become sensitive, I decided to keep it restricted to the three of us.

In the meeting, I gave my assessment of the situation and explained that it was necessary to gain the strategic initiative in order to facilitate the operations of 15 Corps and Northern Command. I observed that we had to be prepared for war escalation, either by Pakistan or by us. In such an eventuality, all the three services would be fully sucked into the war. It would, therefore, be desirable to take certain preparatory steps immediately. I suggested that the Air Force should use air power in Kargil and Ladakh to assist the 15 Corps' operations and, hereafter, we should carry out joint planning for war. I emphasized that it would be helpful to ensure unanimity over this issue before the CCS meeting scheduled for the next day but also made it clear that if any of my colleagues was not agreeable to my suggestion, I would oppose his view in the CCS meeting.

My picture of the ground, analysis and the resultant discussion on the future course of action convinced my COSC colleagues about the validity of the suggestion. We took a unanimous decision to recommend joint strategy and joint operational planning and action, including the use of naval and air power in the CCS meeting.

Briefing in the Operations Room

My first impression of the CCS meeting in the Operations Room the next day was that an unusually large number of civilian officers from the Prime Minister's Office, the Cabinet Secretariat, the Ministry of Defence, the R&AW, Intelligence Bureau and other ministries and agencies had walked in. There was a great deal of inquisitiveness and anticipation on the part of the cabinet ministers and officials. However, many officials appeared to have turned up not for making any useful contribution but only to know 'what next'. The meeting went on for more than ninety minutes.

I briefed the CCS about various factors such as the operational situation, the terrain, the gaps in our defences, the manner in which the intruders had managed to infiltrate into our territory, the heights they had been able to occupy till now, the overall intelligence picture and the conduct and the handling of the intrusion by the Pakistan Army personnel, although they continued to deny it officially.

In my presentation, I stated that, in the Kargil sector, the Pakistan Army had intruded into the areas of Batalik, Kaksar, Dras and Mashkoh with the aim of holding ground permanently so as to interdict the strategic Srinagar–Kargil highway and the road from Kargil to Leh along the Indus River. The enemy had entrenched himself at strategic locations along the dominating heights and was supported by an array of armaments such as artillery, air defence weapons, machine-guns and other heavy-calibre weapons. The intrusion would change the alignment of the LoC as delineated in 1972 and also affect our movement along these roads. In the Turtuk sector, the Pakistan Army was attempting to outflank our defences in SSW by moving up the Mian Lungpa (a gully in the mountains across the LoC) to the Ladakh Range and then rolling down the Turtuk Lungpa. Such movement could render our defences untenable in this area and enable the Pakistanis to capture Turtuk and dominate the road along the Shyok River. There were some reports that Pakistan was planning to initiate insurgency in Turtuk.[2]

My appraisal of the situation was that, lately, since Pakistan was losing ground in Jammu and Kashmir, it had launched this operation. The political objectives were to create a situation that would enable the Pakistanis to negotiate on Jammu and Kashmir from a position of strength and to internationalize the Kashmir issue once again. Pakistan's objectives, from a military viewpoint,

---

[2]In June 1999, we recovered a large cache of arms and ammunition from Turtuk village. Twenty-four suspects were arrested and handed over to the civil police. They disclosed Pakistani plans to initiate insurgency in Turtuk, Chalungka, Thang, Tyakshi and Pharol.

appeared to be as follows: (1) to cut off the strategic Srinagar–Leh road (thereby creating a crisis situation for us); (2) to alter the status of the LoC permanently for strategic and territorial gains; (3) to divert our attention from anti-terrorist operations in the Kashmir Valley; (4) to revive insurgency in Jammu and Kashmir (if the Dras and Mashkoh sectors came into Pakistan's possession, it could drive a strategic wedge into our territory east of Zoji La and could facilitate infiltration towards Pahalgam and the Kashmir Valley); and (5) to capture Turtuk and a part of the Central Glacier in the Siachen sector.[3]

So far, I pointed out, our response had been as follows: ensuring that we did not lose any existing post to the intruders; keeping the road communications open; locating, containing, isolating and evicting intrusions; and holding 'reserves' ready for any contingency.

I then brought to the notice of the CCS the strategic discussions held in the COSC the previous day. It was necessary, I emphasized, to gain the strategic initiative in order to facilitate operations of 15 Corps and Northern Command. I also stated that we had to be prepared for war escalation, either by Pakistan or by us, and in such a situation, all the three services would have to be prepared and act cohesively.

On behalf of the COSC, I then sought permission for the use of air power and the deployment of the Navy. I had been told that, at the political level, the minister for external affairs, Jaswant Singh, had opposed the use of air power in the CCS meeting on 18 May. While seeking permission this time, I recall, looking more at him than at the prime minister or anyone else. To my surprise and great relief, there was no objection from anyone. The CCS approved our proposal readily and wanted the

---

[3]According to a Pakistani defence analyst: 'Pak military strategy for the limited offensive was that by July [1999], the Mujahideen would step up their activities in the rear areas, threatening the Indian lines of communications at pre-designated targets, which would help isolate pockets, forcing the Indian troops to react to them. This would create an opportunity for the forces at Kargil to push forward and pose an additional threat. India would, as a consequence, be forced to the negotiating table...' Shauqat Qadir, 'An Analysis of the Kargil Conflict 1999', *RUSI Journal*, April 2002.

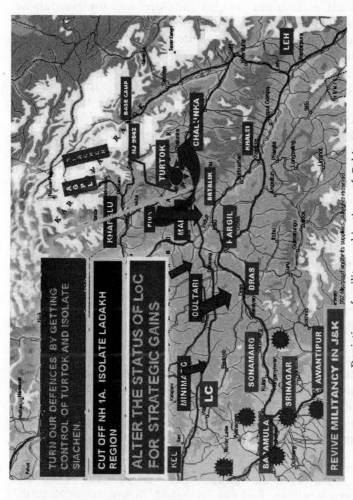

Depiction of military objectives of Pakistan.

(*Note:* The map is neither accurate nor drawn to scale; it merely depicts the geographical area.)

intrusion along the LoC to be cleared at the earliest. Jaswant Singh insisted that our forces should *not* cross the LoC or the international border. Brajesh Mishra, on behalf of the CCS, reiterated this statement as a term of reference.

Such a 'restraint' at this juncture was understandable. Pakistan's political motives were not clear and the identity of the intruders was doubtful. Due to the sustained inputs given by all intelligence agencies, and also owing to the Pakistani radio deception, no one was in a position to authenticate whether the Pakistan Army was using jehadi militants or carrying out the operation by itself. Besides, a war effort at the national level required a great deal of preparation. A considerable amount of work had to be done on the diplomatic front, particularly because only the previous year (1998) India and Pakistan had blasted their way out of nuclear ambiguity and had upset the United States of America and other powers, including the UK, China and Japan. The nuclear factor too must have been weighing on the mind of the prime minister and his CCS colleagues, though this aspect was never mentioned or discussed in the meetings.

In my summing up, I accepted that the operational situation was definitely more serious than that made out by the assessment so far. I stated that we needed to investigate the intrusion further and to learn how that had happened. But I felt that this was not the time for such an investigation; it should be done later.

By this time, I could sense that the long faces in the audience had become longer. The CCS had been conveyed an unambiguous picture of the ground realities and the implications militarily and politically. If there were doubts in anyone's mind these were clarified; if there were any expectations from Track-2 dialogues, these were dispelled.[4] I concluded my briefing by informing the CCS that the Army had codenamed the operation in the Kargil sector as Operation Vijay (victory) and that we would take all

---

[4]On 22 May 1999, the Pakistani prime minister, Nawaz Sharif, after a meeting with the Pakistani Army chief, General Pervez Musharraf, had declared that Pakistan would 'give a befitting response to India, if New Delhi launched any misadventure at the Line of Control'. 'PM, COAS Discuss Indian Build-up at LoC', *The News* (Pakistan), 23 May 1999.

necessary action and ensure that ultimately *vijay* would be ours. There were no further discussions and the meeting ended on that note.

That night, Prime Minister Vajpayee spoke to his Pakistani counterpart Nawaz Sharif. Vajpayee told him that 'we will not allow any intrusion to take place in our territory. We will clear our territory'.

Some analysts in the USA, who have written about the Kargil war after listening to the Pakistani briefings, have described the infiltration as a 'limited probe'. This viewpoint is unacceptable. A 'limited probe' would be a small-scale incursion to *learn* about occupied/unoccupied areas and to ascertain the adversary's capability to defend those areas. The probing element's ability to return to home ground, or reverse the course without conflict escalation, is one of the main features of a 'limited probe'. The risk involved is limited and controllable. On the other hand, in the Kargil area, Pakistani troops had intruded 8–10 kilometres deep into the Indian territory over a frontage of 160 kilometres. They were able to effectively interdict a vital communication link: the Srinagar–Kargil–Leh Highway, on which the entire civil population of Ladakh and the military forces deployed there were dependent for most of their sustenance. Moreover, the exit was not planned, nor was it possible, after infiltrating nearly one-and-a-half-brigade-strength force into strategically sensitive areas in depth without getting enmeshed in a serious combat. The Pakistani political and military objectives, as described earlier, were strategic in nature. Evidently, the whole process of concept, planning and preparation, on the part of the Pakistanis – including posting of additional officers to the Northern Light Infantry battalions, providing additional combat and logistical support and chalking out the radio deception plan – was worked out or confirmed at the Pakistan General Headquarters level.

The Juggernaut Gets Moving

Immediately after the CCS meeting, fresh operational instructions were issued to Headquarters Northern Command in two parts. The first part, dealing with operations on our side of the LoC, was directed to eliminate all direct or indirect interference on the Srinagar–Kargil–Leh road, stabilize the situation in all sectors and remove intrusions through *deliberate* operations. The sectors were prioritized, the immediate induction of additional troops was indicated and Northern Command was specifically advised on the security aspects of all road communications in Jammu and Kashmir and in the unoccupied areas along the LoC and the international border. This command was also advised to hand over the counterinsurgency responsibility and the grid in Jammu and Kashmir to the Rashtriya Rifles and place the central police forces, which were under the command of 15 and 16 Corps, under the director-general, Rashtriya Rifles. The aim was to free these two corps of the internal security responsibility so that they could concentrate on conventional operations on both sides of the LoC and the international border. The second part of operational instructions dealt with the punitive response, i.e., action across the LoC, should that become necessary. All other commands were also duly warned to be on the alert and be prepared for any escalation.

The next few days were spent on a series of activities. For instance: working out a detailed military strategy as well as operational planning; ordering movements of formations to the front or interim locations; finalizing the corps operational plans in each command; allocating and positioning additional resources required by them; and, of course, close monitoring of the operations in 15 Corps and Northern Command. The crux of our military strategy was to adopt an aggressive posture in the air, on the sea, and all along the LoC and the international border with Pakistan to prevent that country from focusing only on Kargil and also to maintain our own capability for undertaking offensive and defensive operations at very short notice. We decided to abide by the political terms of reference as given, but had to keep our military options open.

As per the Union War Book, the Government of India should by now have declared a 'warning period' or a 'precautionary state' for general mobilization to take place. But India and Pakistan were not fighting a regular war and the CCS was not willing to escalate hostilities. With a declared 'policy of restraint', the government could not 'declare' any such state. The Union War Book did not cater for a 'hotting up' period or low-intensity

The Pakistani prime minister, Nawaz Sharif, with his Indian counterpart, Atal Behari Vajpayee, among others, just before the Lahore talks (February 1999) (*Courtesy:* Bhawan Singh, *India Today.*)

The awesome heights of Kargil.

The snow-clad mountains of Kargil.

The barren landscape in Kargil – a treacherous battlefield.

The rugged terrain in Kargil.

Tiger Hill in all its majesty.

operations, i.e., operations short of a regular war scenario. The government, however, had no objection to the armed forces preparing for any contingency. The situation was complex since a large number of activities necessary for the preparation for hostilities hinged on other ministries of the government (such as Railways, Surface Transport, Petroleum and Natural Gas), which, in turn, get into the act only on the declaration of the 'precautionary stage' and the decentralization of financial powers in its wake. As a result, the preparation process was severely constrained. The regular CCS meetings, however, enabled us to get over most of the bureaucratic hassles.

The movement of formations and units – both types: combat as well as combat support – to and within Northern Command was given high priority. For example, 8 Mountain Division, which was a Northern Command reserve and deployed in a countermilitancy role in the Kashmir Valley and whose two brigades had already moved to Dras and Mashkoh sectors, was to disengage completely and take over operational responsibility of these two sectors by 1 June. Similarly, 39 Mountain Division was instructed to disengage from countermilitancy operations and be available to 16 Corps for any contingency, including offensive tasks. Additional Rashtriya Rifles battalions were moved to Northern Command for countermilitancy operations. Four additional Bofors (155-mm) medium artillery regiments and one 122-mm rocket battery were moved to the Kargil sector to achieve greater fire superiority. Now, 6 Mountain Division, already warned, was moved by different roads to Baltal and Kargil. Its Tactical Headquarters was moved by air to Srinagar on 26 May. The movement of additional air-defence regiments and Army helicopter flights (reconnaissance and observation) were also ordered.

'Holding' or 'pivot' formations on the international border and the LoC (10, 11, 12, 15 and 16 Corps) were given instructions to exert pressure on the Pakistani military through forward deployment, active patrolling and surveillance. Strike formations (1, 2 and 21 Corps, 6 Mountain Division, 27 Mountain Division, 39 Mountain Division, 50 Para Brigade and 108 Mountain Brigade) were ordered to deploy some elements on the international border and the LoC, which would monitor enemy activities, liaise with holding formations and facilitate offensive operations when necessary. Operational logistic requirements, i.e., ammunition, reserves of arms, equipment and vehicles of these formations, were to be moved close to the international border and the LoC. We decided to go in for a graduated and incremental build-up of strategic reserves including dual-tasked formations from the east. These moves were to be carried out without disturbing normal train or road traffic and with maximum security so as not to cause any alarm.

In the following weeks, 446 military special trains rolled towards the western (Pakistan) border to carry troops and logistical equipment. The holding formations, 6 Mountain Division (except its Tactical Headquarters) and 4 Mountain Division were moved by road from Bareilly and Allahabad (both located in Uttar Pradesh) to their assigned operational locations. Dual-task formations located in the northeast (23, 27 and 57 Mountain Divisions) were moved to their assigned corps in the west or to interim locations close to the western border. Also, 108 Mountain Brigade was moved from Port Blair in the Bay of Bengal to the west coast by sea. Several tactical headquarters and most of the paramilitary and special forces units were moved by air. More than 19,000 tons of ammunition were moved from various depots, mostly across the Zoji La pass for additional troops deployed in the Kargil–Leh sector.

The Indian Navy had issued instructions for an alert before the CCS meeting and had deployed INS *Taragiri* on a barrier patrol off the coast of Dwarka (in Gujarat). Immediately after the meeting, the Navy added two information warfare Dornier aircraft and also deployed INS *Veer* and INS *Nirghat* near Okha (also in Gujarat). Instructions were issued by the Navy and the Ministry of Shipping so that our shipping fleet would not be caught unawares at sea. Naval staff carried out an analysis of Pakistan's vulnerability as far as oil was concerned and started planning to interdict Pakistani oil tankers. The Navy chief, Admiral Sushil Kumar, also decided to supplement the Western Naval Fleet with selected units of the Eastern Naval Fleet and moved the latter from the Bay of Bengal to the Arabian Sea. This step enabled the Navy to extend the range of its deployment. The naval projection of 'reach and mobility' had an immediate impact.

Pakistan started providing escorts to its oil tankers as they moved out from the Gulf to Karachi. At one stage, Sushil Kumar turned so aggressive that I had to lightheartedly caution him not to start a full-scale conventional war before all the three services were ready!

The Indian Air Force had so far been providing Mi-17 helicopter sorties for airlifting of troops in the Kargil and Leh sectors for redeployment and for the evacuation of casualties. On 21 May, a Canberra on a reconnaissance mission, while flying along the LoC in the Batalik sector, had been hit by enemy fire. But it was able to return safely. The IAF responded very quickly after the CCS approved of the employment of air power on our side of the LoC. It deployed its forces and launched the first close-support air strikes with MiGs and armed Mi-17 helicopters on 26 May morning. This move conveyed our strategic resolve to the enemy. After 23 May, there were no professional differences whatsoever that could affect our teamwork or planning in the COSC.

Unfortunately, the very next day, we lost two MiG aircraft. One MiG-27 was lost over the Batalik sector at approximately 1100 hours due to an engine flameout. The pilot, Flight Lieutenant Nachiketa Rao, was able to bail out. He landed inside Pakistan territory and was captured by the Pakistanis.[5] His colleague, Squadron Leader Ajay Ahuja, flying a MiG-21, tried to ascertain Nachiketa's location and the wreckage of the MiG-27. In the process, his aircraft was shot down by a surface-to-air missile. He also bailed out and was captured. But his captors, instead of making him a prisoner of war, killed him. On 28 May, we were subjected to one more shock when an armed Mi-17 helicopter was shot down while attacking the Tololing feature near Dras. That incident caused widespread depression, but also led to a steely resolve amongst the armed forces to eliminate the intrusion, whatever be the cost.

The Air Force thereafter became more determined in its mission. It began innovating (and practising) ways and means to become more effective and to avoid any further loss. It

---

[5]He was handed over to the Indian high commissioner in Islamabad on 12 June.

started employing a weapons delivery system with a global positioning system (GPS). When some troops on the ground complained about poor accuracy in engaging targets, the IAF employed Mirage aircraft and used laser-guided bombs to achieve greater precision. The air chief, Anil Tipnis, and I visited and addressed our field formations together.[6]

The Kargil Synergy and War Management

After the CCS meeting on 24 May, the three chiefs were closely enmeshed in a politico-military decision-making process. In consultation with Brajesh Mishra, the national security advisor, we prepared a list of essential weapons and equipment required urgently by each service, and sent it across to the Ministry of Defence. We were assured that the material would be procured within two to three months.[7]

The CCS met on an almost daily basis till the second week of July 1999. Besides the prime minister and the other CCS members, these meetings were attended by the national security advisor, the cabinet secretary, the three service chiefs, the secretaries of the Defence, Home, Finance and External Affairs Ministries, the heads of the Intelligence Bureau and R&AW and the secretary, National Security Council Secretariat (NSCS). Sometimes, for some specific purposes, special invitees were also called in. The prime minister would be flanked by other CCS members, the national security advisor and the cabinet secretary on one side of the table. I would sit opposite him along

---

[6]Lately, a former air officer commanding-in-chief (AOC-in-C), Western Air Command, has often criticized the politico-military strategy used during the Kargil war in the media. He has also made unsavoury remarks about the Army and its senior hierarchy. During the war, I never heard *any* reservations about the war strategy from the air chief in the COSC and CCS meetings, or even informally. The AOC-in-C was an operational commander; in charge of air operations during the Kargil war. He was not part of the politico-military strategic or the decision-making set-up. I wonder if he ever conveyed his disagreements to his air chief and what answer did he get!

[7]Except for a few items, we did not get much during the course of the war.

with my services colleagues and other secretaries and executive heads of departments.

The meetings would generally begin with the heads of the intelligence agencies giving fresh information or follow-up results. The service chiefs then briefed the participants by providing the details of the previous days' operations. They also presented envisaged plans that required CCS clearance or coordination. All politico-military-diplomatic aspects were considered/discussed. The international environment was monitored continuously. The foreign secretary gave his briefing on our own diplomatic initiatives and reactions from different countries. The home secretary provided information on the domestic political and law and order situation. The defence and finance secretaries noted all envisaged procurements, movements of troops and material and other actions that had major financial implications and required procedural clearances. Complete synergy and consensus could be discerned among the various organs of the government – whether it was political control or military actions – from political direction to execution in the field and to proactive diplomacy. It was a refreshing change in the decision-making process, both at the political level as well as at the Armed Forces level: open and direct. The political leadership received the views of the service chiefs first-hand. After discussions, the concerned executive authorities, including the three chiefs, received directions from the prime minister. National Security Advisor Brajesh Mishra, who was always accessible and a very effective troubleshooter, facilitated this process creditably. All these developments led to a very integrated approach to 'war management' with the political, economic, diplomatic, media and military aspects meshed together cogently.

At the level of the armed forces, regular military briefings were carried out in the Army Headquarters' Military Operations Room almost daily. Besides the three chiefs, representatives of the Ministries of Defence, External Affairs, Home and the intelligence agencies attended these briefings. Officers from the operational directorates of all three services, who were nominated to brief the media along with the joint secretary of the Ministry of External Affairs, who dealt with public relations, would also attend sometimes. The daily briefings were followed by an 'in-house' discussion on a 'need-to-know' basis.

Army commanders and select corps commanders visited the Military Operations Directorate for planning and interaction on an 'as-required' basis. Such visits not only facilitated contingency planning, but also ensured a high degree of security. The Military Operations Directorate, as always, consisted of a team of professionally competent and dedicated officers, led by Director General, Lieutenant General Nirmal Chander Vij and Assistant Director General, Major General J.J. Singh (both became Army chiefs later). Two other important staff officers, Brigadier M.C. Bhandari and Colonel Ashok Sheoran, prepared my daily operational briefs. Due to a sudden increase in the workload and responsibility of the Military Operations Directorate, some officers from the Perspective Planning Directorate were inducted into this team. Two of them were amalgamated with the desks responsible for the Southern and Western Commands in order to relieve extra officers needed for carrying out operations in Northern Command.

During the course of the war, the three service chiefs briefed the president of India (twice), the vice-president (once), all governors and chief ministers (once) and an all-party meeting in the Parliament House (once) on the progress of operations.

The Hotline

We followed (and still continue to follow) the practice of the directors-general of Military Operations of India and Pakistan speaking to each other over the telephone hotline every Tuesday. If a particular Tuesday happened to be a public holiday on either side, they would speak to each other the next day. This arrangement had been a very useful confidence-building measure. We reviewed this arrangement in the light of the new circumstances, and decided to let it continue. The CCS was informed about our decision.

The conversations over the hotline often provided an illuminating insight into the Pakistani thought processes and perceptions. Such exchanges proved even more useful later when the Pakistan Army sought withdrawal from our territory and a fair amount of coordination had to be achieved for this purpose.

In May 1999, the Pakistan DGMO, Lieutenant General Tauqir Zia, feigned ignorance about the infiltration when our DGMO, Lieutenant General Nirmal Chander Vij, brought this fact to his notice and informed him that this act was a serious violation of the Shimla Agreement and an attempt to alter the status of the LoC. During these conversations, Tauqir Zia would gleefully often refer to Siachen, and attempt to link it with the situation in Kargil.

On Monday, 24 May, the Pakistan DGMO conveyed a message that the telephone conversation scheduled for the following Tuesday be held on Wednesday, 26 May. When this conversation was being held, he appeared a bit disturbed, particularly on account of our air power employment in the Kargil sector and heavy artillery shelling, as well as Prime Minister Vajpayee's telephone conversation with Nawaz Sharif. He complained that we were flying fighter aircraft very close to the LoC. He also wanted to know what had transpired between the two prime ministers! Our DGMO conveyed to him categorically that 'we shall do everything within our power to liquidate the intrusions'. He also observed that our Air Force was flying *within* our territory for this purpose and, therefore, we did not need inform anyone. The Pakistan DGMO then pointed out that we should not attack their regular posts or fly into their territory. Otherwise, he added, they would be forced to react. For the first time, he also spoke about 'defusing the situation'.

The Shadow Boxing

As anticipated, the clearance of our strategy by the CCS on 24 May and the employment of air power caused events to move rapidly. From 26 to 30 May, several significant developments took place.

Prime Minister Vajpayee declared that the new situation was not infiltration but a move to occupy new territory and all 'steps will be taken to clear the Kargil area'. Replying to a question, he affirmed that our troops would not cross the LoC. Later, the government spokesman said that the intrusion had been 'obviously' undertaken 'with full complicity and support of the Government of Pakistan'.

On 26 May, Defence Minister George Fernandes met and briefed opposition party leaders and the heads of the US and the UK missions in New Delhi.

On 27 May, Pakistan's Prime Minister Nawaz Sharif made the first mention of the use of nuclear capability in the Kargil war. He was quoted as saying that the people of Pakistan were 'confident for the first time in their history that in the eventuality of an armed attack, they will be able to meet it in [sic] equal terms'. Officially, Pakistan issued a warning that 'it will take necessary steps to defend itself and retaliate'.[8]

On 26–27 May, we obtained the most invaluable piece of intelligence of the war: a telephone conversation between the Pakistani Chief of General Staff, Lieutenant General Mohammad Aziz Khan and his chief, General Pervez Musharraf, who was then in Beijing (see Chapter 4 as well as Appendix 2).

On 28 May, Nawaz Sharif offered to send his foreign minister, Sartaj Aziz, to New Delhi.[9] It was obvious that Pakistan was rattled by the new developments. It was blowing hot and blowing cold simultaneously.

---

[8]'Indian Action Unwarranted, Says Pak', *The Hindu*, 27 May 1999.
[9]'Nawaz Offers to Send Sartaj Aziz to New Delhi', *The News* (Pakistan), 29 May 1999.

7

Turning the Tide

During the media briefing on 23 June 1999, a journalist asked me if we were at 'war' with Pakistan. My reply was: 'Let us not get involved in semantics. For soldiers fighting on the border, it is war.'

A FTER 24 MAY 1999, EVERYONE IN THE CABINET COMMITTEE on Security (CCS), the Chiefs of Staff Committee (COSC) and all other officials dealing directly with the CCS were 'on board' as far as the assessment of the situation in the Kargil sector and our politico-military strategy to deal with the developments were concerned. The strategy made clear to one and all was that although India was a victim of intrusion and was exercising the maximum restraint, it was determined to get the intrusion vacated. As the military was not to cross the border/LoC, there was no formal mobilization or declaration of war.[1]

As a follow-up to this politico-military strategy, the three chiefs (Indian) had to work out their military strategy and plan of action, which involved the deployment of forces in such a manner that we could cross the international border and LoC at a short notice and thus exercise pressure on Pakistan and prevent its forces from focusing only on Kargil. For the military the immediate tasks ahead were as follows:

---

[1] It needs to be restated here that even at this stage the intelligence assessment was that the intruders in the Kargil sector were mostly jehadi militants (irregulars) along with some regular Pakistani Army personnel. They were being provided intimate artillery fire and logistic support by the Pakistan Army, which was probably controlling their operations.

The military was neither aware of, nor taken into confidence regarding, the Track-2 dialogue that had been going on through the interlocutors.

- Issue instructions for the mobilization of forces and ensure preparedness on the international border/LoC with Pakistan with a view to achieving strategic asymmetry.
- Induct additional troops and resources into Jammu and Kashmir, particularly the Kargil sector, and create a superiority that would enable 15 Corps to get the intrusion vacated.
- Ensure that the additional forces to be deployed on the Pakistan border/LoC were in a state of operational readiness, which would enable them to undertake defensive or offensive operations at short notice.
- Maintain alertness on the border with China.
- Monitor the military situation closely, particularly in 15 Corps.

Even though we were to follow a policy of restraint and the military was politically mandated not to cross the border or the LoC, in a dynamic situation like war, we had to cater for all contingencies. Further escalation of the war could not be ruled out due to Pakistani action or for achievement of our objectives under the changed circumstances. My instructions, therefore, were that our forces should be deployed and maintained in such a state of readiness so that, given six days' notice, we should be in a position to launch an offensive anywhere across the international border or the LoC. This objective was to be achieved as soon as possible, with maximum security and without disturbing the normal air, rail and road traffic or other civilian activities along the border. We also decided that in view of the enemy threat on the Srinagar–Kargil–Leh road in the area east of Zoji La, we should immediately take measures to optimally utilize the alternative route to Ladakh, i.e., the Pathankot–Manali–Upshi–Leh road. Such measures would require enlarging the scope of the existing logistic infrastructure and facilities along this road.

While our operational staff was duly conveying instructions to all the command headquarters and facilitating their implementation, I decided to visit the Northern, Western and Southern Commands and all corps that were part of these commands (on their order of battle): to discuss, update and approve the operational plans of each corps. Intercommand and interservice operational activities had to be synchronized. Such a step would also give me an opportunity to share perceptions with their senior commanders and staff and visit as many field formations as possible to address Sainik Sammelans (troop gatherings) to motivate the rank and file. During June–July 1999, I travelled along the northern and western border extensively, visiting various headquarters and deployments near Jammu, besides Pathankot, Jalandhar and Bathinda (all three in Punjab), Chandimandir (in Haryana) and Bikaner, Jaisalmer and Barmer (all three in Rajasthan). Of all the formations, Northern Command and 15 Corps had to be accorded priority.

As Army chief, I was not directly involved in the day-to-day tactical operations in the Kargil sector. These operations were planned and conducted at the division level and controlled by Headquarters 15 Corps and Northern Command. However, it was essential for the Army Headquarters to monitor their development closely. As on 25 May, we had suffered twenty-nine casualties (soldiers either killed or missing) and about thirty wounded. Many intruders had been killed but we did not make any gains on the ground. We were in a state of undeclared war.[2] There was a need to remove ad hocism, infuse greater determination for implementing revised plans and raise the morale of the troops on the ground. Also, accountability had to be emphasized at the level of formation commanders.

Meanwhile, in the next few days, based on the Army Headquarters' directions, Headquarters Northern Command formulated detailed operational strategy and gave specific instructions for 15 Corps. The operational strategy involved the following tasks: containing and isolating intrusion; exterminating the threat to National Highway 1-A; safeguarding surface communications in other sectors; occupying gaps between defences with enhanced surveillance; and systematically eliminating existing intrusions in the given order of priority. Like other formations, 15 Corps was to be ready for selective offensive tasks at short notice.

---

[2]During the media briefing on 23 June 1999, a journalist asked me if we were at 'war' with Pakistan. My reply was: 'Let us not get involved in semantics. For soldiers fighting on the border, it is war.'

Headquarters Northern Command laid down some specific objectives such as Tiger Hill, Point 5100 and Tololing, and called for the interdiction and destruction of enemy administrative bases there. Next, 15 Corps was directed to occupy positions that would stop enemy movement coming up from Piun and Chuar (both in Pakistan) along mountainous routes to the area of Chorbat La on the LoC.

Headquarters 8 Mountain Division was directed to assume responsibility of the Dras–Mashkoh sectors, east of Kaobal Gali. After consulting Army Headquarters regarding the missions that could be assigned to the headquarters and brigades of 6 Mountain Division, the deployment areas for this formation were indicated by Headquarters Northern Command in its operational directions to 15 Corps.

A Visit to Srinagar, Dras and Kargil

On 30 May 1999, I visited Srinagar, Dras and Kargil, accompanied by Defence Minister George Fernandes, who wanted to see the ground realities for himself. He also wanted to address the civilian population at Kargil. This was my first visit to these locations after returning from my trip abroad and after the current fighting began. Three high-ranking officers, Lieutenant General Krishan Pal, GOC 15 Corps, Major General Mohinder Puri, GOC 8 Mountain Division, and Major General Ashok Hakku, GOC 6 Mountain Division, joined us at Srinagar on our onward journey to the war zone. En route, I told Mohinder Puri that he would take over operational responsibility for the Dras and Mashkoh sectors.[3] I advised him to carry out deliberate planning (i.e., no hurrying up and also detailed preparations) and promised to give whatever support he needed. The decision to move 8 Mountain Division had been deliberate. This division was a Northern Command reserve formation.[4] Both the brigades deployed in the Dras and Mashkoh sectors had been part of this division before their induction across Zoji La.

---

[3]GOC 15 Corps had already warned him.
[4]I had myself commanded this formation from 25 December 1989 to 20 May 1991 and we had moved from the northeast of India to Jammu and Kashmir.

At Dras and Kargil, I found the atmosphere lackadaisical, as if some routine activity was going on. At both places, bunkers had been constructed next to existing barracks, without realizing that these barracks could draw enemy artillery fire or air strikes and thus make the bunkers vulnerable and movement in the area extremely dicey. The Tactical Headquarters of 3 Mountain Division had been moved from Leh to the erstwhile Headquarters 121 (I) Infantry Brigade located in Kargil. Brigadier Surinder Singh, commander of this brigade along with his Tactical Headquarters, had moved to a new location at Kaksar. The brigade commander received us at the helipad and took us to his old office, now occupied by Major General V. Budhwar, GOC 3 Infantry Division. He was visibly unhappy on having been ousted from his permanent location. Earlier, as the commander responsible for the entire Kargil sector, he had failed miserably in ensuring the surveillance of his sector and yet had submitted certificates every month to the division that there had been no intrusion. When I asked him a few questions, he replied that he could not hear me properly due to an old ear injury.[5]

On reaching the Tactical Headquarters of 3 Infantry Division, Budhwar briefed us on the operational situation. There was little to cheer about. After the briefing, I sent the brigade commander away with the defence minister, who wanted to address the civilian population in Kargil town. In their absence, but in the presence of his corps commander, I gave a piece of my mind to Budhwar on the manner that he, his formations and his staff had conducted themselves till now and handled the situation.[6]

Diplomacy and Defence

Meanwhile, diplomatic pressure from Pakistan and the international community was building up on New Delhi to talk

---

[5]This was the day when I decided to consult others about sidestepping him.

[6]This reprimand apparently had a salutary effect, because, thereafter, there was a distinct improvement in the formation. It performed extremely well, particularly in the Batalik sector and the Subsector West (SSW).

to Islamabad. Initially, the Pakistani Prime Minister Nawaz Sharif suggested that air strikes (within our own country) be stopped as a 'precondition' for talks. When this suggestion was rejected outright by India, he offered to send Foreign Minister Sartaj Aziz to New Delhi. The Government of India accepted this offer. What greatly worried my military colleagues and myself was that any political negotiations or attempts to seek a diplomatic solution at this point of time would result in a militarily disadvantageous solution for us; that could even lead to humiliation, as had happened in 1962 (when China invaded India). So far, we had not been able to recapture any tactically significant area from the intruders in the Kargil sector.

On 5 June 1999, while returning from Headquarters Northern Command, I decided to address the entire Indian Army through a special log. The log, dictated to the DGMO (Nirmal Chander Vij) in the aircraft, read as follows:

From the COAS to all ranks(.)
Firstly (.) the enemy has violated the Line of Control in 3 Infantry Division Sector in area Batalik to Dras and made some intrusions into our territory with strategic and political aim (.) in the last few days, our troops, some of whom had to be inducted from outside this sector, have managed to stall the enemy's operations thus denying him the fulfilment of his mission (.) we have succeeded not only in containing the enemy but also in pushing him back from his original forward positions (.) hard battles are being fought all along in the Kargil sector(.)

Secondly (.) this intrusion by the enemy has thrown a big challenge before us (.) we have a very clear and precise task and that is to get our territory vacated and liquidate the intrusion (.)

Thirdly (.) while our operational plans are being put into action and preparations are afoot, the Ministry of External Affairs is having diplomatic dialogue with Pakistan (.) this process, however, should not distract us from our mission (.) our challenge clearly remains to rid our land of intruders (.) this mission has to be accomplished with all the resolve and fortitude at your command (.)

Fourthly (.) May God be with you all (.) (log ends).[7]

On 7 June 1999, the Indian prime minister in his address to the nation asserted: 'I do want to make it plain: if the stratagem now is that the intrusion should be used to alter the Line of Control through talks, the proposed talks will end before they have begun.' He added: 'Have confidence in the ability of our armed forces. The armed forces shall accomplish this task and ensure that no one dares to indulge in this kind of misadventure in future.' This spirited address was a great morale booster for the armed forces.

Sartaj Aziz arrived in New Delhi via China on 12 June. He projected a three-point formula: (a) a ceasefire; (b) a joint working group to review the LoC and its demarcation on the ground; and (c) a reciprocal visit by the Indian foreign minister the following week. This formula was emphatically rejected by New Delhi. More importantly, Jaswant Singh, India's minister for external affairs, through his gestures and his loud voice, projected by the electronic media, made it amply clear that under no circumstances would India negotiate until and unless the Pakistani intrusion was completely vacated. He affirmed that 'the aggression has to be undone, militarily or diplomatically, whichever is done first'.

To me, Jaswant Singh's was not just a political response but also one that reposed trust and confidence in the Indian military. The responsibility on us had become heavier!

Soon thereafter, the CCS decided to send copies of the tapes (on which the telephone conversation between Pakistan Chief of General Staff Lieutenant Mohammad Aziz Khan and General Pervez Musharraf had been recorded) to Pakistan's Prime Minister Nawaz Sharif through Vivek Katju, India's joint secretary in the Ministry of External Affairs.[8]

In the first week of June, Prime Minister Vajpayee once again made a public statement that India would not cross the

---

[7]Log number 198/05 June 99/MO3.
[8]R.K. Mishra (India's Track-2 interlocutor) accompanied Vivek Katju on his visit to Pakistan.

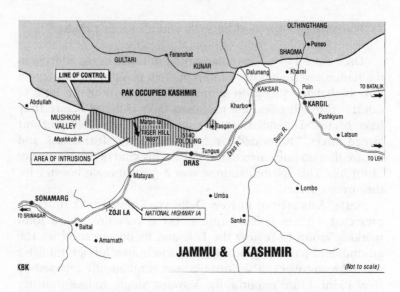

Pakistani intrusions in the Mashkoh and Dras sectors.
(*Note*: The map is neither accurate nor drawn to scale;
it merely depicts the geographical area.)

international border or the LoC. I raised the issue with him and
Brajesh Mishra, and requested that our prime minister should
not make such a statement in future. When Prime Minister
Vajpayee gave me an enquiring look, I told them that CCS
directions so stipulated, and we were following them. But suppose
we could not throw the intruders out from Kargil, I pointed out
that the military would have no alternative but to cross the
international border or the LoC. The prime minister did not
respond to my statement. But Brajesh Mishra promptly arranged
an interview with a TV channel. In the interview, he said that
'not crossing the border and the LoC holds good today. But we
do not know what may happen tomorrow.'

The middle of June was the most anxious period of the war
and possibly the closest when we came to enlarging the conflict
area. Bitter fighting was going on in all sectors but we had yet
to win any battle. On 16 June, Brajesh Mishra informed the US
national security advisor, Sandy Berger, that India would not be

able to continue with its policy of 'restraint' for long and that our military forces could not be kept on leash any longer. He added that the Government of India might have to let them cross the border any day. According to Brajesh Mishra, the US Administration took this message quite seriously.

The pressure for escalation was increasing on us. Informally, I learnt that the National Security Advisory Board, which included stalwarts like K. Subrahmanyam (a well-known defence analyst), J.N. Dixit (a former foreign secretary) and three former service chiefs, had recommended to the CCS, through Brajesh Mishra, that the Indian military should be allowed to cross the border/ LoC. Two former Army chiefs, who were not members of the National Security Advisory Board, also came out loud and clear in the media that, without crossing the LoC, it would be impractical to flush out the intruders.

In the COSC and in the Military Operations Room, we were monitoring the situation closely and keeping our escalation option open. Even though the political terms of reference were clear and justified, my colleagues in the COSC and I never considered these terms as non-reviewable or unalterable. We were prepared for all contingencies. On 18 June, I again warned all Army commanders to 'be prepared for escalation – sudden or gradual – along the LoC or the international border and be prepared to go to (declared) war at short notice'.

Our military build-up along the western border was going on smoothly. Along with the concerned Army commanders, I visited every Corps Headquarters to discuss and 'lock in' their operational plans. Gradually, military operations staff and operational logistics staff in the Army Headquarters redeployed the strike and reserve formations and issued instructions for stocking forward logistics bases in accordance with approved operational plans. Also, 108 Infantry Brigade from the Andaman and Nicobar Islands was positioned on the west coast for 'training in amphibious operations'. The juggernaut was moving steadily.

The middle of June was also the period when we felt that the Pakistani Army was showing some signs of nervousness. On 15 June, the Pakistani DGMO asked our DGMO as to why India was escalating the situation along the international border by deploying troops including armour. He then complained that the

Indian Air Force had fired rockets at the Pakistan village of Dorian in Kel (opposite our Machhal sector). After some further conversation, he raised the issue of escalation once again and said that both directors-general needed to sit down together and analyse the maps pertaining to the LoC and the international border. One could make out that, at that stage, Pakistan did not want to escalate but defuse the situation. There were repeated suggestions from the Pakistani DGMO to keep the operational activity confined to the LoC. Having started the war, he was now advising us how to conduct it!

On 20 June, Nawaz Sharif once again stated: 'Kargil is an aspect of [the] Kashmir issue.... If the Kashmir issue is not resolved once for all according to the wishes of the Kashmiri people, many more Kargil-like issues can crop up.'[9] This rhetorical threat and its implications were discussed in the CCS meeting the next day. It was obvious that we had to be prepared for an escalation. The National Security Council Secretariat (NSCS) staff was asked to prepare an intelligence assessment on Pakistan's intentions and options.

The escalation was avoided when our forces recaptured Tololing and Point 5140 in the Dras sector (details given later). Thereafter, we began achieving steady success in our operations. A few days later, Air Chief Anil Tipnis sought permission from the CCS for his fighter pilots to cross the LoC while engaging the Pakistani logistic base Munthodhalo, which was located very close to the LoC but inside our territory in the Batalik sector. The Air Force fighter pilots were facing great difficulty in going through their flying circuit within our territory to engage this important target due to its close proximity to the LoC. Tipnis's request had been approved in the COSC and we (Sushil Kumar, the Navy chief, and myself) supported him. But the CCS rejected the request. The fact that, despite this handicap, the Air Force pilots were able to engage and destroy this target is a tribute to their skills and determination.

---

[9]'Sharif Warns of More Kargil-like Situations', *The Times of India*, 21 June 1999.

The Recapture of Tololing

Let us get back to military operations on the ground.

In the Dras sector, the enemy had occupied Tololing, which is located at a distance of 5 kilometres from Dras and dominates the Srinagar–Kargil–Leh highway. This was the deepest penetration made by Pakistan in this sector. The Tololing–Point 5140 complex enabled the enemy to interdict our build-up along the highway and prevent the movement to our posts on the LoC. The capture of Tololing was essential so that we could get a foothold in the enemy's defensive layout and then proceed to clear the other intrusions.

On 22–23 May, 56 Mountain Brigade (then under 3 Infantry Division) had attempted to capture Tololing in a hurry and failed. The brigade launched another attack on the Tololing–Point 5140 complex on 13 June, this time fully prepared. After gallant hand-to-hand fighting that lasted five days, we were able to capture Tololing on 17 June and Point 5140 on 20 June.

While this battle was going on, Nirmal Chander Vij spoke to the Pakistan DGMO and told him that we now had concrete evidence of Pakistan Army units being involved. A number of identity cards had been recovered from the bodies of Pakistani soldiers. We had also recovered Survey of Pakistan maps with the LoC clearly marked on them. When the Pakistan DGMO refused to accept this reality, Vij asked him for his fax number and then faxed a copy of a map to him.

At that point of time, we needed a major success, which had eluded us till then. The public relations officer (Army) and my media advisor, Captain Manvinder Singh,[10] had often conveyed to me that the media teams wanted me to explain the military situation and answer their questions. I was hesitant to do so till we had achieved a significant success. Although I wanted more, the recapturing of Tololing was a great morale booster and I was satisfied with this accomplishment. After this event, I was ready to face media persons and was able to brief them with adequate confidence and authority on 23 June.

---

[10]From a Territorial Army battalion of the Parachute Regiment. He is now a Member of Parliament.

When I entered the hall in South Block, New Delhi, ready for the media briefing, it was overflowing with Indian and foreign journalists. Several TV channels covered the briefing live. In the preliminary remarks, two points were made. One: There was no doubt in our mind that the Pakistan Army had 'conceived, planned and executed the Kargil incursion'. It *was* the Pakistani Army that had intruded into our area. Assertions to the contrary by Pakistani Prime Minister Nawaz Sharif and others in the establishment in Islamabad were not true. Arms, equipment and documents captured from the enemy at Tololing were displayed as evidence. Two: Pakistan's alleged ambiguity about the LoC was full of 'mischief'; it was also 'wrong, dangerous and unacceptable'. We showed maps of the area delineated after the Shimla Agreement with signatures of senior military officials of both India and Pakistan to the media. As further evidence, we also displayed the Survey of Pakistan military map captured at Tololing, which had the LoC unequivocally marked on it.

While answering questions, I emphasized the following: (*a*) the terms of reference given to the armed forces not to cross the LoC were a constraint, but we were reviewing the situation all the time (if it became necessary to cross the LoC, we would take it up with the CCS); (*b*) our arms and equipment shortages notwithstanding, we would fight with whatever we had; and (*c*) there was a need for us to look beyond Kargil. The last statement had political as well as military connotations.

Meanwhile, the forward movement of Indian soldiers along the ridgelines and mountaintops of Kargil, one of the most difficult terrains in the world, became unstoppable. Pak-occupied positions fell one after another. We captured Point 5140 (Dras) on 20 June, Point 5203 (Batalik) on 21 June, Three Pimples (Dras) on 29 June, the Jubar Complex (Batalik) on 2 July, Tiger Hill (Dras) on 4 July and Point 4875 (Mashkoh) on 7 July.

The indomitable fighting spirit, the grit, the determination and the resolve of our troops during the Tololing–Point 5140 battle made everyone among the civil and military leadership in New Delhi realize that we could do it. This success also instilled in us the confidence that we could continue our offensive action within the terms laid down by the given political directive.

The terrain in the Batalik sector.

Post-Tololing Track-2 Dialogue

Some journalists and commentators have written about another attempt to resume the Track-2 political dialogue in the last week of June. At that point of time, according to these commentators, Pakistan put forward a four-point formula as follows:

- Appropriate steps to be taken by both sides to mutually respect the LoC.
- Immediate resumption of the composite dialogue initiated under the Lahore process.
- Islamabad to use its influence on the Mujahideen and request them to disengage.
- Finding an expeditious solution to the Kashmir dispute within a specified time frame.

The third and fourth points, it may be noted, give a clear impression of what Pakistan wanted to achieve (with regard to Jammu and Kashmir) from the Kargil intrusion using the Mujahideen façade. Pakistan also came up with the suggestion that if the aforementioned four points were acceptable, Nawaz Sharif could be invited to Delhi.[11] The Track-2 dialogue fell through at this stage because Prime Minister Vajpayee rejected all four points, or any ceasefire, and instead demanded that 'Pakistan must withdraw its forces from Kargil, or else New Delhi would take appropriate action.'

---

[11]Nasim Zehra, *The News* (Pakistan), 27 July 1999 and Amit Baruah, 'The Plan That Failed', *The Hindu*, 28 July 1999. See also, Robert G. Wirsing, *Kashmir in the Shadow of War: Regional Rivalries in a Nuclear Age* (M.E. Sharpe, New York, 2003, pp. 31–33). It needs to be emphasized here that these Track-2 developments were not known to the COSC.

8

'We Shall Fire the Last Shot'

Indian battalions recovered over 270 dead bodies of Pakistani soldiers after recapturing posts occupied by them. Some of the dead soldiers were found to have been half buried in shallow pits. Others had simply been covered by stones or left in the open by withdrawing Pakistanis. Indian troops gave all of them a burial befitting a soldier as per Muslim rites.

A WAR IS THE ULTIMATE TEST FOR ARMIES AND THEIR SOLDIERS. Victory in war is achieved because battles are won. At the cutting edge of every battle, besides the quality of the weapons and equipment available, are factors such as the military skill of troops, camaraderie, regimental spirit, and, above all, the will power and the resolve to win.

The Indian Army can be proud of its ancient and near-unequalled tradition of selflessness, devotion to duty, sacrifice and valour when called to battle. The Indian soldier is a remarkable human being: spiritually evolved, mentally stoic and sharp, physically hardy and skilled. Whenever well led, he has given everything he is capable of. The war in Kargil will go down in military history as a saga of unmatched bravery, grit and determination. All units responded with alacrity and with their characteristic steadfastness and perseverance.

Most of the credit for victory in Kargil, quite deservedly, goes to the bravery and dedication shown on the battlefield by soldiers and young officers. They were upfront, not hesitating to make any sacrifice to uphold the regimental and national pride and dignity. On the basis of great determination, high morale and brilliant junior leadership, our troops performed superbly. There were countless acts of gallantry, displays of steely resilience, single-minded devotion to duty and tremendous sacrifices.

In India, during a war situation, the Army chief is engaged mostly in politico-military strategy, distribution and deployment of resources and, finally, the synchronization of resources in the different theatres. He does not get involved at the tactical level unless a continuously serious situation requires his intervention. In such an eventuality, he has to go through the laid-down command-and-control channel of command, corps and divisional headquarters. In a nutshell, the Army chief monitors activities at the tactical level, assists and advises at the operational level and works at the politico-military level.

During the Kargil war, Army Headquarters was not involved in the detailed operational planning of the battles. Such planning was always left to Headquarters Northern Command and its formation commanders. There were few situations that demanded my direct intervention. Nevertheless, I visited Srinagar, Kargil and Leh almost every week. I met commanders at all levels to monitor and assess the ground situation and to ascertain their problems and requirements, without interfering in their operational planning or conduct of day-to-day activities. I would invariably address the commanders and troops to raise their morale. In one such address at Moghalpura (8 Mountain Division) on 28 June 1999, I had said, 'the enemy has started the fight, but it is we who will fire the last shot. The war will end only on our terms.'

The narrative that follows summarizes the military operations as they were conducted in different sectors. It also describes the heroic actions of some soldiers who displayed the most extraordinary valour, courage and grit to achieve what would have appeared impossible under normal circumstances. It must be remembered, however, that for every single brave deed noticed and recognized, there are many that go unnoticed in the fog of war. To those unnoticed deeds and to the gallant men who performed them, I offer my sincere apologies.

THE DRAS SECTOR

As mentioned in Chapter 7, the Tololing ridgeline, which was occupied by the regular Pakistani troops, is less than 5 kilometres from Dras town and the Srinagar–Kargil–Leh national highway. From this ridgeline, the intruders could effectively dominate the highway through observation and artillery fire; they could thus seriously impede the foot and vehicular movement from the highway to deployments on the LoC. Every summer after the Zoji La pass opens, this highway is the lifeline extensively used for carrying civil and military traffic. The highway needs to be kept open for the 'winter stocking' of essential commodities for the Ladakhis and for the military garrisons. Although small groups of Army vehicles continued to ply by night through this stretch of the road, their number was inadequate for civil and military requirements. The early clearance of Pakistani intruders from Tololing and adjacent mountaintops was, therefore, given the highest operational priority.

By the third week of May 1999, our patrols established contact with the Pakistani intruders at Tololing, Point 5140 and Point 4875, overlooking the highway and the Mashkoh Valley. On 17 May, 56 Mountain Brigade of 8 Mountain Division was inducted into Dras and given the responsibility for eviction operations in this sector. Brigade Commander A.N. Aul drew up plans to clear the Tololing complex of the enemy, while simultaneously developing operations in depth to cut off the enemy's routes of maintenance.

In the Dras sector (see p. 176 for the map), 8 Sikh and 1 Naga battalions conducted preliminary operations. While 8 Sikh succeeded in establishing the extent of intrusions in the Tiger Hill complex and occupied Pariyon ka Talab (literally meaning 'the fairy pond') with a view to cutting off the supply route to that area, 1 Naga launched a series of attacks on the Tololing–Point 5140 complex. These battalions achieved some success in ascertaining the enemy locations and strength, but at a heavy cost.

Eventually, 56 Mountain Brigade went on to recapture Tololing, Point 5140, Point 4700 and Three Pimples. Also, 192 Mountain Brigade under Brigadier M.P.S. Bajwa, which was inducted later, evicted the enemy from Tiger Hill.

Over a hundred artillery guns, mortars and rocket launchers were deployed to achieve overwhelming fire-power superiority in this sector. The valiant officers and men who participated in some of the bloodiest battles here won many awards, including three Param Vir Chakras (PVCs), India's highest gallantry award.

The Tololing and Tiger Hill battles, beamed live to millions of TV viewers by the news networks, have now become part of the national folklore. To commemorate the memory of those who gave up their lives in these battles, a memorial has now been constructed near the battle site on the highway.

The Initial Assault on Tololing

In third week of May 1999, when the information available revealed that only six to eight intruders were occupying each feature on Tololing ridgeline, 56 Mountain Brigade entrusted the task of evicting them to 18 Grenadiers. This battalion was given only four days to carry out reconnaissance, conduct acclimatization training for high-altitude conditions and prepare for the attack. The attack was launched on 22–23 May, with artillery, mortar fire and medium machine-guns (MMGs) in support. But when the troops reached close to the objective from three directions, a heavy volume of artillery fire was directed against them. The enemy also used direct firing weapons like heavy machine-guns (HMGs), MMGs and air defence (AD) guns. As a result, all companies were pinned down in the open. The brigade then realized that it was not pitted against the Mujahideen or jehadi militants, but against regular, well-trained soldiers. An MMG-mounted Cheetah helicopter tried to fire on the objective but that proved ineffective.

On 26 May, the first air strikes were launched against the intruders. While the initial impact was limited, such strikes succeeded in our troops attaining operational ascendancy and confidence, so crucial in war. Major R.S. Adhikari, a company commander, was asked to direct fire on the enemy positions from an armed Mi-17 helicopter on 26 and 27 May. But this fire had little effect.

On 27 May, 1 Naga tried to secure Point 5140 with a view to cutting off Tololing from behind. When the Nagas got close to the objective, the enemy rained heavy machine-gun and other small arms fire on them. The company commander and thirteen soldiers were wounded. Point 5140 could not be captured but the strength of the entrenched enemy there was revealed.

On 28 May at 11:30 a.m., an enemy Stinger missile shot down a Mi-17 armed helicopter, which crashed into the Tololing Nala.

The situation was dismal. Enemy fire was accurate and sustained. Only night brought some relief, but this was the time to launch one more assault. At this stage, only five batteries were available for the complete Dras sector, which was not enough to cause major destruction. All available approaches to

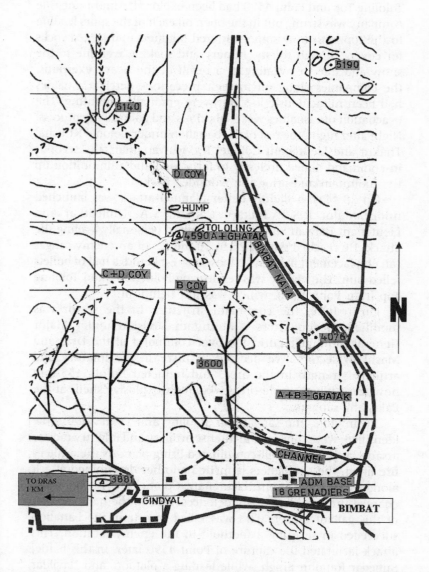

Battle of Tololing:
The role of 18 Grenadiers.
(*Scale*: One square = 1 sq. km.)

Tololing Top and Point 4590 had been explored. Almost one rifle company was strung out in the open on each of the spurs leading to the top with only some scattered boulders and jagged rocks for cover. Though thirsty, hungry and soaking wet due to the snow and due to sweating as a result of the heavy exertions, the companies clung on to their precarious perch. Casualties had been miraculously low but were gradually mounting. The evacuation of casualties was a laborious and painstaking process. Night after night, the rest of the battalion under Colonel Khushal Thakur and Lieutenant Colonel R. Vishwanathan, the second-in-command, toiled tirelessly to ferry food and ammunition up the mountain and bring the wounded back.

On 28 May, a slightly better planned attack was launched under Major R.S. Adhikari, Captain S.A. Nimbalkar and Lieutenant Balwan Singh, with Adhikari personally leading the attack. He reached within 25 to 30 metres of an enemy sangar (an emplacement made with loose stones) before a hail of bullets felled him. The enemy was reinforcing Point 4590 and Tololing Top from Point 5140, which was just behind it.

On 1 June, the command structure in the sector was modified. Headquarters 8 Mountain Division under Major General Mohinder Puri took over command of the Dras and Mashkoh sectors. We decided to increase the infantry and artillery strength in the area, and inducted Bofors 155-mm howitzers, which could fire 45-kg, high-explosive shells at the Pakistani sangars.

Meanwhile, the sangars on Tololing and Point 4590, now identified, were subjected to intense artillery and infantry mortar assault, as part of a well-coordinated firing plan. As the artillery fire lifted, the Grenadiers launched another determined attack along the southern spur. Lieutenant Colonel R. Vishwanathan charged through the enemy defences. Due to the heroic efforts of this gallant officer, who was killed in action, the battalion succeeded in securing a foothold in the enemy location. This attack facilitated the capture of Point 4590 later. In this battle, Subedar Randhir Singh, while leading a platoon, and Havildar Ram Kumar too showed exemplary fighting spirit and dedication.

All these sacrifices were not in vain. Some ground had at last been gained, although the battle for Tololing was not yet

The author encouraging the soldiers on the battlefront during one of his visits.

Some of seemingly inaccessible features in Kargil
(Subsector Haneef): *Top*: Saddle between Points 5590 and 6041
with the Karchan Glacier in the foreground.
Middle: Point 5590 and Point 5720.
Bottom: Point 5220.

Brigadier Devinder Singh (with his arm raised) and the author, among others, during the course of an operational briefing.

The author during one of his frequent visits to Kargil, to gain first-hand information and to boost the morale of the troops.

The author with commanders and staff officers of 8 Mountain Division and the GOC 15 Corps.

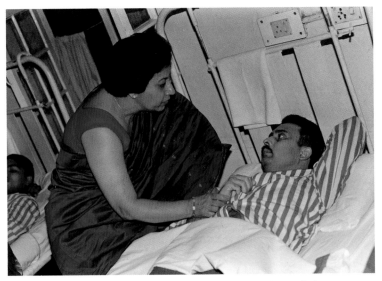

Dr Ranjana Malik, the author's wife and president of the Army Wives' Welfare Association, reassuring a wounded soldier in an Army hospital.

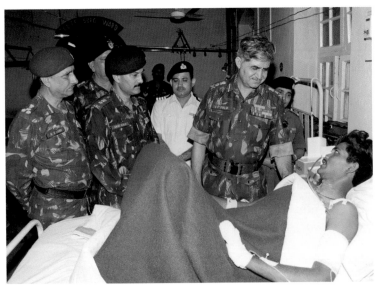

The author enquiring about the condition of an injured soldier at an Army hospital.

over. For another week, the Grenadiers resolutely hung on to their position.

Capture of Tololing: The First Victory

After going in for some more preparations, A.N. Aul, commander, 56 Mountain Brigade, nominated 2 Rajputana Rifles for carrying out further assaults to capture the Tololing ridge. While this battalion practised bunker-busting techniques and completed its acclimatization cycle for operations in high-altitude terrain, additional artillery regiments began to be deployed in the Dras sector. All of them commenced preparation and planning for the crucial assault.

The 2 Rajputana Rifles' attack commenced on 12 June. 'C' Company led by Major Vivek Gupta and 'D' Company under Major Mohit Saxena set out for the assault. The other two companies ('A' and 'B' companies) established fire bases and were nominated as reserves for the attack. 'D' Company went in first along the southwestern approach towards its objective, Point 4590. Despite facing withering fire at close range, the company succeeded in establishing a foothold. At this stage, the 'C' Company assault was launched. The latter closed in towards Tololing Top after intense hand-to-hand fighting. Vivek Gupta himself led the reserve platoon to Tololing Top. Despite suffering grievous wounds, this gallant officer continued to lead his men to evict the last of the enemy from there. At this critical hour, Captain Mridul Kumar Singh, a young artillery forward observation officer (FOO) took over the company, rallied the men and deployed them on the objective to ward off the inevitable counterattacks. The Pakistanis reacted with a vengeance. The loss of Tololing Top was a major setback for them. The counterattacks launched by them were beaten back by 'C' Company.

The commanding officer of 2 Rajputana Rifles, Lieutenant Colonel M.B. Ravindernath, then launched 'A' Company under Major P. Acharya to capture the rest of Point 4590. Despite the close proximity to our own troops at Tololing Top, effective artillery fire was brought down on this objective. Simultaneously, 'B' Company was tasked to clear the northern slopes of Tololing.

On 13 June, 2 Rajputana Rifles was finally able to recapture the Tololing feature.

In this hard-fought, crucial battle, Subedar Bhanwar Lal, Company Havildar Major Yashvir Singh, Havildar Sultan Singh Narwaria and Naik Digendra Kumar displayed inspiring bravery. A major contribution was made by Captain N. Kenguruse, who with the Commando Platoon, had been tasked to establish a block between Hump (a feature with about ten high grounds on the same ridgeline about 500–700 metres north of Point 4590) and Tololing, and prevent any enemy reinforcements from reaching Tololing. Lieutenant Colonel Ravindernath exhibited dedicated and distinguished leadership qualities.

Building on the Success

At this stage, 18 Grenadiers was ordered to maintain the momentum of attack and exploit the success to recapture Hump. Embittered by the loss of its forward-most outpost in Dras, the enemy kept pounding the Tololing ridgeline with heavy artillery fire. The Grenadiers lost twelve men in a sudden burst of concentrated artillery shelling before their H-hour (the time at which an assault begins). This was a huge setback but Khushal Thakur rallied his men and regrouped them for the attack. Now seething with anger at the loss of their comrades, the Grenadiers drove the enemy out of Hump and the adjacent Bumps.

In the different battles for Tololing, Major Amrinder Singh Kasana of 41 Field Regiment showed himself to be an indefatigable and an exemplary gunner officer. He was a battery commander with 18 Grenadiers but he volunteered to continue with 2 Rajputana Rifles during its assaults. He participated in four consecutive attacks: on Tololing, Hump, Rocky Knob and Point 5140.

After more than three weeks of bitter fighting, Tololing Top–Point 4590 were back in our hands. We had won our first victory in the Kargil conflict. Here, 18 Grenadiers had set the stage and 2 Rajputana Rifles finished the task against overwhelming odds and at a great price; 2 Rajputana Rifles captured a large quantity of the enemy's weapons and ammunition, including rocket launchers and 81-mm mortars.

The large haul of weapons, held only by regular forces, and the capture of some vital documents, shattered the myth that Pakistan had so assiduously struggled to create – that the men who had intruded across the LoC were Mujahideen or jehadi militants.

Throughout the battle of Tololing, we in Army Headquarters knew that heavy fighting was going on. It was a touch-and-go situation till Hump was secure in our hands. The last week was crucial. I had visited the area on 30 May, when it was in Pakistani hands, and again after we had captured it. As Army chief, I was anxious, but could not afford to convey my anxiety to anyone by asking far too many details; nor could I interfere with the battle that was planned and conducted at the brigade level. The list of casualties kept growing. We lost three officers, four junior commissioned officers (JCOs) and sixteen other ranks; forty-nine personnel were wounded. The enemy losses were put at twenty-seven, based on the number of bodies recovered; sixty others were assessed as 'killed and wounded'.

I could say very little till the entire Tololing feature was captured, which happened on 17 June. The events that transpired during the battle made me think of the difficult days ahead, when we had to clear the enemy from other areas. But after realizing the determination and the fighting spirit of our troops, I was convinced that we could do it.

Tololing was the first turning point in the Kargil war for us. We never looked back thereafter.

Capture of Rocky Knob

In mid-June 1999, 13 JAK Rifles and 18 Grenadiers were tasked to recapture Point 5140 (about 1500 metres north of Tololing on the same ridgeline) by 56 Mountain Brigade. The first objective, Rocky Knob (at the base of Point 5140 and about 800 metres away provided the best avenue for mounting an attack on Point 5140) was allotted to 13 JAK Rifles. The attack commenced on 15 June. Intense artillery shelling preceded the assault. As the battle raged on, the commanding officer had to be evacuated due to medical reasons. Major Y.K. Joshi, the second-in-command, was promoted to the rank of lieutenant colonel and given the reins of the battalion in the middle of the battle. The battalion also lost Major A.S. Jasrotia to the heavy shelling on its base camp.

During the course of the assault some enemy sangars proved almost invulnerable to attack by missiles and rocket launchers. These sangars were shielded from (indirect) artillery fire due to the lie of the ground. As these sangars were holding up the attack, the brigade decided to use the direct fire of 155-mm Bofors medium guns. Accordingly, a troop of guns was redeployed in a position from where the targets on Rocky Knob could be observed. The Bofors guns took a heavy toll, and the enemy then began to flee from the sangars under direct fire. Soon thereafter, 13 JAK Rifles rushed forward and captured Rocky Knob and Humps IX and X. In the skirmish, eight enemy soldiers were killed and many more injured. A large cache of arms and ammunition was recovered. Major S. Vijay Bhaskar of 'A' Company made a substantial contribution to the success of his battalion. Leading his men from the front, he displayed exceptional courage and determination.

Capture of Point 5140

On 18 June, detailed reconnaissance of the enemy's defences at Point 5140 was carried out by 13 JAK Rifles. Due to the large size of the objective, the brigade planned to capture it by resorting to a multidirectional assault: 18 Garhwal Rifles from the east, 1 Naga from the southwest and 13 JAK Rifles from the south. On 19 June, the objective and adjacent mountain features were engaged by bringing into play the entire divisional artillery and infantry mortars available in the Dras sector. A large number of guns, including some in a direct firing role, were employed. 'B' and 'D' Companies of 13 JAK Rifles climbed the southern slope leading to Point 5140 and managed to surprise the enemy. In this battle, Captain Vikram Batra showed exceptional bravery and leadership. In a daredevil assault, he killed four Pakistani soldiers in hand-to-hand combat. His success signal and call to his commanding officer 'Yeh dil maange more' ('the heart wants more', based on the wording of a popular advertisement for a soft drink) are the stuff legends are made of. Captain S. S. Jamwal led the

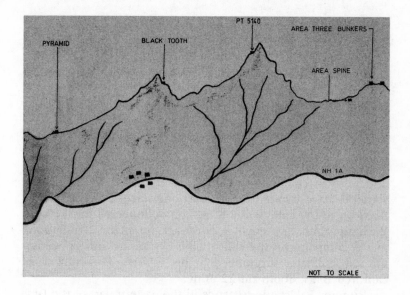

Point 5140 and the surrounding area.

final assault on Point 5140. The enemy had put in place seven sangars on Point 5140: two at the highest point and five towards the east. By the morning of 20 June, all these sangars were cleared and the Pakistanis driven out from Point 5140.

In the battle for Point 5140, the other personnel of 13 JAK Rifles who displayed remarkable courage and leadership were: Captain Sanjeev Singh, a young officer commissioned into the Army Service Corps (ASC) and serving on attachment with the battalion; Naik Dev Parkash, a section commander; and Rifleman Mehar Singh. The commanding officer, Lieutenant Colonel Y.K. Joshi, planned the battle and responded to the changing situations very competently.

Black Tooth and Area Rocky

The next coordinated attack of 56 Mountain Brigade required 1 Naga to capture Black Tooth and Area Rocky. The Nagas approached their objectives, which lay to the southwest of Point 5140, from the direction of the Tololing Nala and managed to establish a firm base on 18 June. The next night, 'A' Company was tasked to capture Area Rocky and 'B' Company Black Tooth. The steep re-entrants and the sheer cliffs along the approach permitted climbing only on all fours. After a pitched close-quarter battle that lasted over one hour, 'A' Company captured Area Rocky on 19 June. 'B' Company's progress towards Black Tooth was comparatively slower: its repeated attempts throughout the night to establish a foothold here failed. Reconnaissance during daytime revealed that the enemy at Black Tooth had set up well-coordinated defences with medium and heavy machine-guns covering all approaches. 'B' Company's standoff lasted two more nights. At one stage, a rope had to be fixed on to the cliff. Sepoy K. Ashuli volunteered for the task. With superhuman strength and courage, he led the assault group of the company up the cliff. In this action, he was grievously injured and later succumbed to his injuries. Finally, 1 Naga captured Black Tooth on 22 June.

By now, Pakistani resistance in the eastern part of the Dras sector was almost eliminated. Next, 1 Naga took over defence of the Tololing–Point 5140 complex. Eventually, its area of responsibility was extended right up to the LoC.

Assault on Point 4700

The Point 4700 ridgeline lies to the west of Point 5140. The enemy had consolidated himself in this position after being evicted from Tololing and Point 5140. Now, 18 Garhwal Rifles was ordered to capture this position.

The move towards the objective commenced on 28 June. Throughout the operation, the Garhwalis were subjected to artillery and small arms fire. Captain Sumeet Roy, with the personnel of 'D' Company, executed an outflanking move along a treacherous route and succeeded in achieving an element of surprise. This enabled the battalion to capture Point 4700 Top.[1] In this battle, Major Rajesh Sah, 'C' Company commander, Captain

---

[1]Unfortunately, on 3 July, due to enemy artillery shelling, the officer sustained injuries, to which he succumbed later.

M.V. Sooraj, Naik Kashmir Singh, Rifleman Anusuya Prasad and Rifleman Kuldeep Singh displayed conspicuous gallantry and leadership.

After capturing Point 4700 and consolidating its position for a day, 18 Garhwal Rifles went in for an attack on two nearby enemy-held features called Rocky and Sangar on 30 June. By 1930 hours, both these objectives were captured. This success enabled 56 Mountain Brigade to keep the enemy's supply route in the area under observation and subject it to effective fire and also to link up with Junction Point, the meeting point with the Three Pimples ridgeline. That would also lead to another important feature on this ridgeline, Point 5100, lying to its northwest.

Area Three Pimples

Three Pimples is a cluster of sharp, imposing mountaintops. This area is located near Point 5100 on the Marpola ridgeline, west of Tololing Nala. The Three Pimples complex consists of three main features: Knoll, Lone Hill and Three Pimples. This complex dominates the national highway, Dras village and Sando Nala. From here, the enemy could observe the movement of troops and armaments and subject them to artillery fire. Close reconnaissance by 2 Rajputana Rifles revealed that Three Pimples and Point 4700 were well held with at least six sangars in place. The task to capture Three Pimples was given to this same battalion, which had broken the stalemate at Tololing.

On 27 June, I happened to visit Headquarters 8 Mountain Division and 56 Mountain Brigade at Dras. That very evening, 2 Rajputana Rifles was preparing to attack Three Pimples. To encourage the battalion and to wish it good luck, I asked Mohinder Puri if I could be connected on telephone to Lieutenant Colonel M.B. Ravindernath, the commanding officer of 2 Rajputana Rifles. Ravindernath along with his small party was then located near the forming up place for the assault. He, I believe, was taken aback when he learnt about the telephone call from the Army chief. He spoke to me in whispers, probably due to their close proximity to the enemy. I enquired about the battalion and wished him and his men good luck in their mission. This must have been a rare occasion in military history when an Army chief spoke to a battalion commander just when the latter was close to a forming up place in a battle! The success achieved by 2 Rajputana Rifles would not have been possible but for the inspiring leadership of Ravindernath. Throughout Operation Vijay, particularly during the battles of Tololing Top and Point 4590, he went about his tasks with a missionary zeal and provided exemplary leadership to his men.

For two hours before the assault, twenty artillery fire units (about 120 guns, mortars and rocket launchers) bombarded the objectives with high-powered explosives. Most of these units were made up of the Bofors 155-mm medium guns. Some Bofors guns were employed in the direct-fire role. ('Direct firing' is when the target is seen from the gun position and engaged through a low trajectory.) 'D' Company, led by Major Mohit Saxena, and 'A' Company, led by Major P. Acharya, went in for the assault. Both companies suffered heavy casualties due to the rugged terrain near the objectives, which resulted in slow movement and prolonged exposure to the enemy's automatic weapons. The leading platoon of 'A' Company, despite the casualties, pressed ahead and established a foothold on Knoll by midnight.

The Bofors guns were put in place to fire directly on the targets on Knoll, which allowed the company to regroup. Major Acharya, the company commander, and Captain Vijayant Thapar personally led the attack. Both these gallant officers suffered severe injuries but continued to lead their men forward. They achieved success but, in the bargain, made the supreme sacrifice.[2]

Despite the loss of their officers, the remaining soldiers of 'A' Company stood fast and held on to their position. An enemy counterattack in the making was dispersed with concentrated fire from our own medium guns. Soon after this happened, 'B' Company linked up with 'A' company on Knoll. With close-range observation on Three Pimples now available, the enemy position was plastered with accurate artillery fire.

---

[2]Both these officers had written letters to their homes just before going in for the attack. These letters reflected determination, regimental spirit and extraordinary devotion to duty.

Lone Hill was an imposing feature with sheer cliff faces covered by enemy MMGs. The moonlit night made the company's task more difficult as the enemy could detect movement of the Rajputana Rifles' personnel over long distances. Mohit Saxena, who had displayed outstanding courage in the battle of Tololing, once again managed to lead his company through a treacherous route without getting noticed. He assaulted the enemy position from the south. To accomplish this feat, he had to climb a sheer rock face over 200 feet high. His daring leadership enabled his men to capture Lone Hill. Along with him, Rifleman Jai Ram Singh of the assault platoon also displayed extraordinary bravery and camaraderie with this officer. 'D' company was assisted in this battle by Captain N. Kenguruse, the Commando Platoon commander. Without any special mountaineering equipment, he scaled a sheer rock face barefooted, literally hanging on by his fingers and toes. After reaching the top, this fearless officer killed two enemy soldiers, who were manning a universal machine-gun, and later another two with his commando knife, before he was fatally wounded.

Over one hundred artillery guns made their presence felt in this battle and took a heavy toll. Leaving behind their well-entrenched positions and a huge stockpile of ammunition and rations, the enemy vacated Three Pimples on 29 June.

Tiger Hill

Tiger Hill towers majestically above all other mountaintops in its vicinity. Although located almost 10 kilometres north of the Srinagar–Kargil–Leh highway, the enemy position on this mountaintop dominated parts of this highway. After the recapture of Tololing and the adjacent features, evicting the enemy from this well-fortified position became a priority.

As the sharp triangular top of Tiger Hill was clearly visible from the highway, and appeared almost impossible to capture, the media had projected the entire episode as a national challenge.

Brigadier M.P.S. Bajwa, commander, 192 Mountain Brigade, assigned the mission of capturing Tiger Hill to 18 Grenadiers, now rested and recouped after their achievements at Tololing and Hump, and to 8 Sikh, which was already deployed at its base.

Tiger Hill.

Both these units were assisted by a crack team from the High-Altitude Warfare School, with maximum possible artillery, engineering and other combat support.

Throughout the last week of June 1999, 18 Grenadiers probed to establish the extent of the enemy's defences and to scout for suitable routes for the assault. A simultaneous multidirectional assault emerged as the best strategy. The commanding officer of 41 Field Regiment drew up an elaborate artillery fire plan. Individual guns were ranged so as to cover each objective. Bofors guns were used in a direct firing role once again, with inspiring accuracy. On the day of the assault, nearly 120 field and medium guns, 122-mm multibarrelled Grad rocket launchers and mortars rained death and destruction on the enemy at Tiger Hill. The Air Force, too, targeted Tiger Hill on 2–3 July, and hit the bull's-eye several times during its missions.

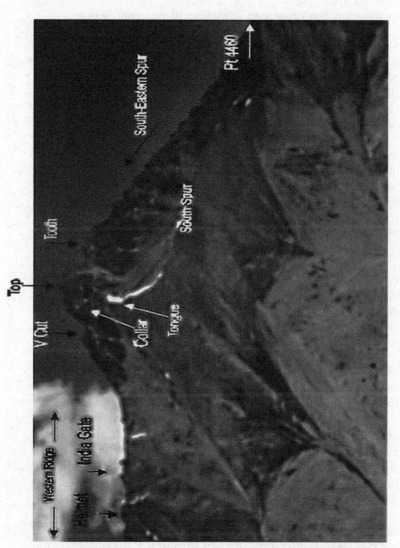

Some features related to Tiger Hill.

For the first time in India's military history, a TV channel covered the battle live: a sign of progress and transparency, not to mention the on-screen depiction of our confidence.

The Tiger Hill feature extends about 2200 metres from west to east and about 1000 metres north to south. The main extension is towards the west, on which there are two prominent protrusions. The first, approximately 500 metres west of Tiger Hill, had been named 'India Gate', and the second, 'Helmet' (located another 300 metres away). Approximately one company of 12 Northern Light Infantry (Pakistan) held the whole feature.

At 1900 hours on 3 July, 18 Grenadiers commenced its multidirectional assault under the cover of bad weather and darkness, supported by the firepower of artillery and mortars. 'A' Company captured an intermediate position called Tongue by 0130 hours on 4 July. Further advance along the southeastern spur leading to Tiger Hill Top was stalled due to accurate fire by the enemy from India Gate, Helmet and Top.

Meanwhile, Captain Sachin Nimbalkar led the 'D' Company assault from the east. His company had to negotiate a steep escarpment using mountaineering equipment, despite the darkness and the inclement weather. His approach took the enemy by surprise. After some firefighting, 'D' Company was successful in occupying the eastern portion of Area Collar, which lay within 100 metres of Tiger Hill Top.

On another front, 'C' Company and Ghatak (commando) platoon under Lieutenant Balwan Singh also surprised the enemy, this time along the difficult northeastern spur and obtained a toehold just 30 metres from the top.

At 0400 hours on 4 July, after a carefully orchestrated artillery bombardment, Sachin Nimbalkar and Balwan Singh along with their men approached Tiger Hill Top by climbing a sheer cliff and caught the enemy unawares. After a spell of hand-to-hand fighting, they succeeded in capturing the objective. Although 18 Grenadiers held the Top now, linking up with them was not easy. When the initial surprise wore off, the enemy started gearing up for launching counterattacks.

One of the most difficult tasks during the course of a battle is to maintain one's hold on the ground captured, before the next assault can be launched. Throughout the next morning artillery duels continued. Casualties mounted on both sides. The

Grenadiers hung on to their precarious perch with grit and determination. Grenadier Yogendra Singh Yadav and his team members exhibited exceptional courage during this assault.

Grenadier Yogendra Singh Yadav

Grenadier Yogendra Singh Yadav was part of the leading team of the Ghatak (Commando) Platoon tasked to capture Tiger Hill Top on the night of 3/4 July 1999. The approach to the Top, at a height of 16,500 feet, was steep, snow-bound and rocky. He volunteered to lead the assault and fix a rope for the rest of his team to follow.

The Ghataks succeeded in surprising the enemy. On seeing his team reach the Top, the enemy reacted violently and opened up intense automatic machine-gun, grenade and rocket fire killing Yogendra Singh Yadav's team commander and two colleagues. The further advance of the platoon was stalled. Realizing the gravity of the situation, Yogendra Singh Yadav crawled up to the enemy position to silence it and sustained multiple bullet injuries. Disregarding his injuries and braving the thick volley of enemy bullets, he continued towards the enemy's sangar and lobbed grenades inside, all the while firing from his rifle. He killed four Pakistani soldiers in close combat and silenced the automatic fire. In this action and while repulsing a counterattack, Grenadier Yadav was hit in his left arm and right leg. Undeterred, he crawled forward to destroy yet another sangar. Inspired by this fearless daredevilry, the rest of the Ghatak Platoon fell upon the enemy's position with vengeance and succeeded in capturing Tiger Hill Top, a high-priority objective.

For most conspicuous courage well beyond the call of duty, Grenadier Yadav was decorated with the Param Vir Chakra, the nation's highest gallantry award.

At this stage, 8 Mountain Division realized that it would not be possible to evict the enemy from Tiger Hill completely as long as his supply lines along the western spur were intact. Mohinder Puri and M.P.S. Bajwa then issued orders to 8 Sikh to attack and capture Helmet and India Gate (both located on the western spur) so that enemy reinforcements to Tiger Hill Top could be prevented. The move was also intended to cut off the enemy's supply route.

The western spur of Tiger Hill extended up to 1.5 kilometres. The approach to the spur, where 8 Sikh was deployed, lay along a steep rock face. An ad hoc column of 8 Sikh, led by Major Ravindra Singh and Lieutenant R.K. Sehrawat, comprising four JCOs and fifty-two soldiers, climbed this rock face under poor visibility conditions and was able to capture India Gate after a tough fight. In this battle, Subedar Nirmal Singh led the assault platoon. He was engaged in hand-to-hand fighting till the end and was also responsible for beating back a counterattack.

Despite heavy casualties, 8 Sikh exploited its success up to Helmet and captured this objective on 5 July.

The enemy launched two counterattacks with forty to fifty personnel, but 8 Sikh fought gallantly and was able to repulse them. Naib Subedar Karnail Singh and Rifleman Satpal Singh, who were part of a platoon deployed on the reverse slope of Helmet, showed exceptional courage. In one of these counterattacks, Captain Karnal Sher Khan of the Pakistan Army was killed. His body was subsequently handed over to the Pakistani authorities.[3] Other bodies of the Pakistani soldiers found scattered around the battleground were collected and buried appropriately.

In New Delhi, I had remained anxious all through the night of 3 July. The next morning, Krishan Pal, GOC 15 Corps, rang up at 0600 hours to inform me that 18 Grenadiers had captured Tiger Hill Top and also that heavy fighting was going on. After consulting him and Nirmal Chander Vij, we decided to await confirmation from the GOC 8 Mountain Division. At 0730 hours, Mohinder Puri confirmed to me that the enemy would not be able to dislodge 18 Grenadiers from Tiger Hill Top. I duly informed Brajesh Mishra and the prime minister, who was scheduled to address a public meeting in Haryana at 1000 hours. The defence minister was on his way to Amritsar. When he landed at the airport, I gave him this exciting news.

---

[3]Karnal Sher Khan was awarded Pakistan's highest gallantry award.

The date, 4 July 1999, was important for one more reason. Nawaz Sharif was due to meet the US president, Bill Clinton, later in the day. About ten to fifteen hours before their meeting, we made sure that the whole world came to know about the recapture of Tiger Hill, and thus the likely outcome of the war.

For some time, Pakistan even denied the existence of such a mountain feature and labelled the entire operation as a figment of our imagination; the loss of Tiger Hill was a hard physical and psychological blow. In India, a wave of jubilation and relief replaced the gloomy mood of the people.

On 8 July, after the entire Tiger Hill objective had been cleared and the situation stabilized, 18 Grenadiers hoisted the Indian tricolour on Tiger Hill Top. Throughout its tenure in the nearly two-month-long war, the battalion acquitted itself with high professionalism and honour. Displaying unshakeable determination and collective valour, all its members covered themselves with glory and notched up two of the finest victories for the Indian Army. After the war, as the battalion requested a UN mission, Army Headquarters sent it to Sierra Leone (West Africa). There too, the battalion successfully carried out a major rescue operation (Operation Khukri).

THE MASHKOH VALLEY SECTOR

The Mashkoh Valley provided a possible route of infiltration into the Kashmir Valley as well as a direct passage (i.e., without having to go through the Valley) into the Doda–Kishtwar–Bhaderwah areas of the Jammu Division. Here, 121 (I) Infantry Brigade had carried out counterinfiltration operations in the previous summer. But, in April 1999, the brigade/division had not taken up counterinfiltration positions. Such a situation enabled the Pakistanis to reach up to Point 4875, which dominated the Srinagar–Kargil–Leh national highway between Zoji La and Dras.

Operations of 79 Mountain Brigade

Of all the features in the Mashkoh Valley occupied by the Pakistanis, Point 4875 was tactically the most important. Its top

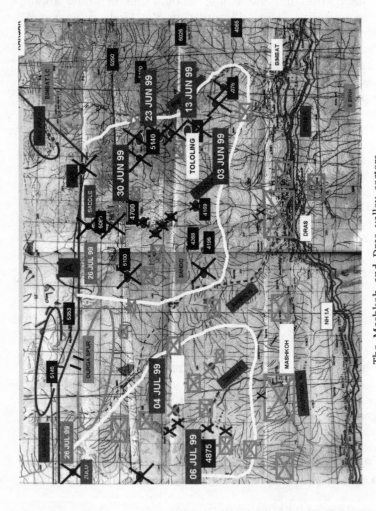

The Mashkoh and Dras valley sectors.

(*Note:* The map is neither accurate nor drawn to scale; it merely depicts the geographical area.)

and forward slopes overlooked a nearly 30-kilometre stretch of the national highway from Moghalpura to Dras. Those manning the Pakistani artillery observation post at Point 4875 could easily spot convoys moving on the road and bring down artillery fire on them. The movement of vehicles from Matayin to Dras had to be restricted to the hours of darkness. The flying of helicopters too was jeopardized. The pilots had to resort to low flying, hugging the Pandras ridgeline. Although eviction of the enemy from the rest of Mashkoh Valley was a comparatively lower-priority task, early clearance of Point 4875 became a high-priority mission.

The responsibility for operations to clear the Point 4875 complex in the Mashkoh sector was assigned to 79 Mountain Brigade, under Brigadier Ramesh Kakar. A number of preliminary operations were carried out to eliminate the enemy observation posts between the road and Point 4875. From 8 June onwards, 2 Mahar launched a series of attacks on the Daingoya Byang Thung (DBT) Ridge and captured a part of the ridgeline.

Point 4875

The capturing of this objective was assigned to 13 JAK Rifles, the battalion that had distinguished itself at Point 5140 in the Dras sector. On 1 July 1999, this battalion congregated in the Mashkoh Valley. After three days of planning and preparation, the attack was launched with the support of twenty-one fire units (126 guns, mortars and rocket launchers were employed). An ad hoc column of fighting porters from the battalion carried the ammunition and placed it in forward locations selected as a fire base.

The artillery fire plan began to be put into place at 1900 hours on 4 July. As dusk began to melt into night, the objectives were lit up by hundreds of flashes due to bombs exploding on contact with their targets. Soon, direct firing Bofors guns joined the melee. For the next two hours, the gun positions of artillery regiments in 8 Mountain Division presented a scene of frenetic activity. A major portion of such activity involved carrying heavy shells and cartridges from ammunition pits to the guns in a steady stream so that the required rate of fire could be maintained.

The assault on Flat Top, which was adjacent to Point 4875 and part of enemy defences on this objective, began with 'A' Company under Major S. Vijay Bhaskar moving along the eastern slopes of the south spur that led to Point 4875 and 'C' Company under Major Gurpreet Singh proceeding along the western slopes of the same spur. After the artillery fire lifted, MMGs from the fire base (commanded by Captain Vikram Batra) fired tracer rounds to assist the assault companies in maintaining the proper direction. By attacking from two sides, the battalion managed to divide the enemy's attention. But when the companies came close to the objective, they were pinned down by accurate small arms and MMGs fire from Point 4875. Despite several valiant attempts, the two companies could not make further progress. When daylight came, the soldiers found themselves strung out on the mountain in the open.

The forward observation officers with 'A' Company and 'C' Company, Captain B.S. Rawat and Captain Ganesh Bhatt, respectively, then pounded the objective with artillery fire for several hours. Faggot missiles were used to destroy some

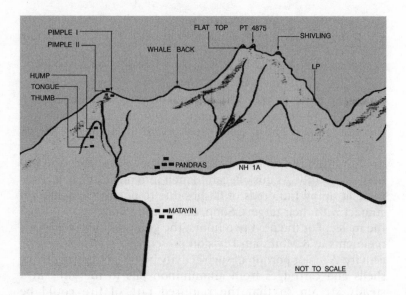

Point 4875 and surrounding features.

enemy sangars. The companies assaulted the enemy position once again and were able to capture Flat Top by the afternoon of 5 July. In close-quarter battles, Riflemen Sanjay Kumar and Shyam Singh displayed outstanding valour.

Rifleman Sanjay Kumar

Rifleman Sanjay Kumar volunteered to be the leading scout of the attacking column tasked to capture area Flat Top of Point 4875 in the Mashkoh Valley on 4 July 1999. Enemy automatic fire from one of the sangars posed stiff opposition and stalled the progress of the column. Rifleman Sanjay Kumar charged the enemy sangar with utter disregard for his personal safety. In the ensuing hand-to-hand combat, he killed three Pakistani soldiers and was himself seriously injured. However, despite his injuries, he continued to fight and charged on to the second sangar that had been interfering with the attack. The enemy fled from the scene leaving behind one machine-gun.

Although Rifleman Sanjay Kumar was bleeding profusely from his wounds, he refused to be evacuated. His actions motivated his comrades to capture area Flat Top from the enemy. For his most conspicuous gallantry against heavy odds leading to the capture of an important objective, Rifleman Sanjay Kumar was awarded the Param Vir Chakra, India's highest gallantry award.

The next day, the enemy subjected these troops to heavy artillery shelling and intermittent MMG fire. Additional reinforcements were sent under Major Vikas Vohra and Captain Vikram Batra. Heavy fighting continued near the objective. Both sides fired missiles and rifle grenades at each other. The opposing troops were so close that, besides the staccato of small arms, verbal exchanges carried on throughout the night. In this action, Captain Naveen Anaberu Nagappa of 13 JAK Rifles was seriously injured.

It became clear that the enemy location immediately to the north of Point 4875 would have to be captured. Captain Vikram Batra volunteered to undertake this task and lead his men to accomplish the mission.

Captain Vikram Batra

On 7 July 1999, Captain Vikram Batra volunteered to lead an attack to recapture the area north of Point 4875 from where the enemy was interfering in the operations of 13 JAK Rifles. The task involved an assault along a narrow ridge to clear a heavily fortified feature.

Personally leading the assault, Captain Batra engaged the enemy in a fierce hand-to-hand fight and killed five enemy soldiers at point-blank range. During the assault he sustained grievous injuries but refused to yield ground. He rallied his men, pressed home the attack and finally succeeded in achieving what had seemed to be a militarily impossible task. Inspired by this extraordinary display of fearlessness and raw courage from their leader, the troops overcame the enemy and captured his position. Earlier, on 20 June 1999, Captain Vikram Batra had displayed sterling leadership qualities, by leading from the front, to physically assault enemy positions on Point 5140 in the Dras sector. He had launched a daredevil assault and had personally killed four intruders in a hand-to-hand fight.

For his unparalleled feats of conspicuous personal gallantry, exemplary junior leadership and selfless devotion to duty, Captain Vikram Batra was posthumously awarded the Param Vir Chakra, India's highest gallantry award.

The bodies of a large number of Pakistani soldiers had been recovered during this prolonged battle. On 15–16 July, these bodies were buried with full respect and honour in the presence of the media at the Point 4875 complex. On the feature, 13 JAK Rifles remained deployed to assist 2 Naga and 17 Jat in their missions.

Pimples 1 and 2 and Twin Bumps

The task to recapture Pimples 1 and 2 and Twin Bumps were assigned to 17 Jat and 2 Naga, respectively.

On 26 May, 17 Jat battalion had been inducted into the Mashkoh Valley. This battalion captured Point 4540 three days

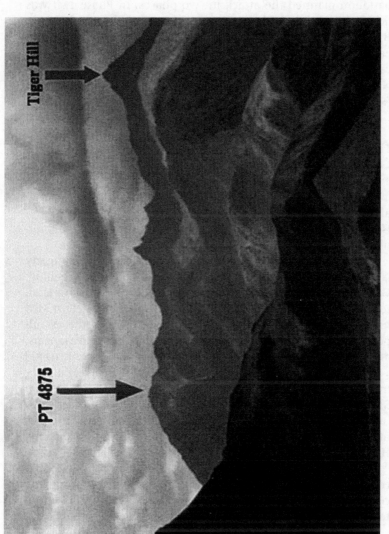

Point 4875 in relation to Tiger Hill.

later, but its attempts to capture Point 4875 had to be shelved then due to strong enemy defences. Now fully prepared, the battalion planned the attack in two phases. In Phase 1, it was decided to capture Pimple 1 from the southwest and Whale Back (a 100 metres by 50 metres feature located 300 metres east of Pimple 2) from the south. In Phase 2, the plan was to capture Pimple 2 and thereafter consolidate the success up to North Spur. The battalion was allotted twelve artillery batteries (seventy-two guns and mortars) and additional three 155-mm Bofors howitzers in a direct firing role.

Two companies launched the assault on the night of 4 July. The next day morning, 'A' Company captured Pimple 1 and 'D' Company, Whale Back. The battalion recovered twenty-eight enemy weapons, after this battle.

Phase 2 of the attack was launched twenty-four hours later, after subjecting the enemy to a heavy dose of artillery fire. Here, 'B' and 'C' Companies led the attack from the direction of Whale Back.

While moving towards the objective, the 'C' Company commander was seriously injured and had to be left behind. Captain Anuj Nayyar, the young company second-in-command, took over. The gallant officer, highly motivated and determined to achieve success for his company, decided to lead the assault personally. After he and his men had cleared three enemy sangars, an enemy rocket-propelled grenade hit him. The intrepid youngster had discharged his huge responsibility in an exemplary manner and sacrificed his life. At this critical juncture, Captain Shashi Bhushan Ghildyal, the forward observation officer, took over the company. He continued with the assault to wrest a part of the Pimple 2 objective. During the hand-to-hand fighting here, Havildar Kumar Singh displayed conspicuous gallantry.

Soon, 'B' Company was sent up as a reinforcement. Both companies then consolidated their gains under the 'B' Company commander. Pimple 2 was finally captured on 8 July, after 13 JAK Rifles cleared the nearby feature named Ledge.

Throughout this action, Colonel Umesh Singh Bawa, the commanding officer of 17 Jat, exhibited exemplary leadership and successfully repulsed two enemy counterattacks on Pimple 2.

As 2 Naga was assigned to launch an assault in Phase 2, the battalion gained a little more time to complete its preparations. Twin Bumps were comprehensively bombarded over a prolonged period by the complete artillery fire power available in the Dras and Mashkoh Valley sectors. As a result, when the assault of 2 Naga began on the night of 5 July, enemy resistance had been substantially reduced. The Nagas made steady progress in their approach towards the objective, but due to the long and arduous climb involved, their operation extended into daytime. At first light, the enemy launched a counterattack, but it was beaten back. The Nagas had to put down the last attempts at resistance by the enemy during daytime.

By now, the infantrymen had come to lean heavily on the gunners, having witnessed at close range the havoc that well-directed artillery fire could cause to enemy defences and, in turn, to the enemy morale. They had seen direct hits from medium guns destroy enemy sangars completely. The battery commanders and forward observation officers had fought shoulder to shoulder with them and suffered the same hardships and privations. Captain R.J. Prem Raj of 158 Medium Regiment (Self-Propelled) (SP) was the forward observation officer with 2 Naga during the battalion's assault on Twin Bumps on 5–6 July. During the assault, even as Prem Raj directed artillery fire on to the enemy position with devastating effect, he was hit by enemy sniper fire. Though gravely injured, he continued to direct artillery fire and very gallantly assisted in the capture of the objective.

On 6 July, Twin Bumps were captured. The enemy had now been effectively evicted from all his positions close to the highway in the Mashkoh Valley sector.

On 8 July, the commanding officer of 2 Naga, nominated Captain Deepankar Kapoor Singh Sharawat to lead a raid on an enemy mortar position west of Twin Bumps. Sharawat and his raiding party successfully infiltrated the enemy position. On reaching the mortar position, the party located the enemy sentries. Rifleman Imliakum Ao volunteered to move ahead. He did so stealthily and silenced the sentries.

Sharawat then led the assault on the mortar position, and having taken the Pakistanis by surprise, quickly overran their position. His bold and determined action led to the recovery of three 120-mm mortars, two 81-mm mortars, three G-3 assault rifles and some valuable documents.

I received the information about the exploits of 2 Naga early on the morning of 9 July. Having served in Nagaland on two occasions, and having known the (then) chief minister, S.C. Jamir, well, I rang him up on the spur of the moment and shared 2 Naga battalion's achievements of the previous night with him. He thanked me and asked if he could mention this news in the State Assembly that was in session on that day. I confirmed that he could do so and told him that I would send a letter to that effect. The chief minister made the announcement in the State Assembly amidst thunderous applause.

These three units continued to build upon their success and carried out further operations till 12 July, when the ceasefire came into force. In these operations, 79 Mountain Brigade recovered fifty-four bodies of Pakistani soldiers and large quantities of arms, ammunition and rations.

Operations of 50 (Independent) Para Brigade

We inducted 50 (I) Para Brigade into the Mashkoh Valley sector in the third week of June 1999. After acclimatization, the brigade launched operations to secure the heights east and west of Kirdi North, with a view to progressively expanding operations on the Bakarwal Ridge and other mountain features along the LoC.

On 7 July, 6 Para, assisted by troops from 1 Para (Special Forces) (SF), captured Point 4745 without much resistance from the enemy and then went on to secure the western shoulder of Kirdi North on 10 July.

Operating along the Bakarwal Ridge, 7 Para captured Point 4700 on 11 July. Five sangars with makeshift overhead protection were found at Point 4700. Some arms, ammunition and other war-like stores were recovered from there. Thereafter, due to the ceasefire, offensive operations by the para brigade were suspended. Later, when the Pakistani troops failed to withdraw completely from our side of the LoC despite the agreement to do so, offensive operations were resumed after taking permission from the prime minister. During that period, a simultaneous advance from Kirdi Nala and the ridge north of Point 4700 led to the swift occupation of important heights on the LoC by us: 7 Para occupied Point 4960 and 6 Para secured Point 4905.

Operations West of Kaobal Gali

The area to the west of the Kaobal Gali (and the Zoji La pass) was the responsibility of 28 Infantry Division. The terrain here is similar to that in the Kargil sector. Here too, there were gaps in the deployment along the LoC. It was, therefore, necessary to ensure that any Pakistani attempts to intrude into Indian territory were pre-empted. The unit deployed in this area, 8 Jat, carried out vigorous patrolling and launched operations to dominate the areas along the LoC. The unit achieved some notable successes in this extremely rugged, high-altitude terrain and occupied positions that dominated the Pakistani defences in the area.

Zulu Spur

When Pakistan failed to honour the agreement to withdraw completely to its side of the LoC after the ceasefire was announced in mid-July, operations had to be resumed to clear the remaining pockets of resistance. Zulu Spur, located in the Mashkoh sector, was one such area that had to be attacked. The main features of the Zulu Spur complex included Tri-junction, Zulu Ridge and Sando Top. This complex dominated the area across the LoC.

The attack planned by Brigadier M. P. S. Bajwa, commander, 192 Mountain Brigade, was divided into two phases. In Phase 1, 3/3 Gorkha Rifles was designated to capture Tri-junction. The operations began on 22 July, with 'C' Company under Captain Hemant Gurung, leading the assault. When he sustained serious wounds, Major S. Saini, the second-in-command, came forward to finish the job. Captain Amit Aul (son of Brigadier A.N. Aul, commander of 56 Mountain Brigade) and Riflemen Dhan Bahadur and Dinesh Gurung showed exemplary bravery in evicting the enemy and clearing the sangars.

'D' Company under Major Pallav Mishra now surged forward to assault the base of Zulu Spur. The forward observation officer,

Captain Nandan Singh Mehra of 'C' Company, who was part of the assault team on Tri-junction, volunteered to join 'D' Company to participate in his second operation in two days. He brought down effective artillery fire, which enabled the assault echelon to close in with the enemy. Despite stiff resistance, 'D' Company secured this objective on 24 July. The enemy withdrew to Zulu Top. At this stage, the engineer teams removed approximately 550 mines and a large number of improvised booby traps.

Phase 2 was to be launched by 9 Para (SF). When a firm base for this phase had been secured, 'A' Team of 9 Para (SF) under Major Sudhir Kumar, who was my ADC till seven days ago, attacked Zulu Top on 24 July. The team made slow progress as minefields had to be negotiated and ropes had to be fixed all along the route. Sudhir Kumar opened up the route to the top and reached the crest on 25 July. The battle for Zulu Top continued for some more time. Sudhir Kumar and Naik Kaushal Yadav showed exceptional gallantry in this action. Later, 9 Para (SF) team was reinforced with troops from 3/3 Gorkha Rifles and, together, they drove the enemy out of Zulu Spur.

Major Sudhir Kumar

Sudhir was thirty years old when he celebrated his last birthday in my house on 24 May 1999; the day I briefed the CCS first time on the Kargil war!

Balraj Kakkar, my ADC (Security), recommended him to me as his own relief before quitting the Army. Both belonged to the same unit, 9 Parachute Commandos. Sudhir was slightly older and senior. He had more battle experience and had been awarded the Sena Medal for gallantry twice. He had been wounded in the last action but was now physically fit. After he reported to me, I learnt that he had topped a Special Forces course in the USA. Fondly and out of respect for his competence, he was called 'colonel' during that course!

In the performance of his duties, I found Sudhir always very alert, responsible and mature. He was well read and took interest in all types of books. Off parade, he was full of life. He had a good sense of humour and enjoyed company.

During his last Lohri with us in the Army House, he sang many Hindi, Punjabi and Himachali songs.

A bachelor, he was reticent about his family initially. Gradually, we learnt about them. His father had retired from the Army as a subedar. Sudhir was very fond of his mother to whom he wanted to give every possible comfort. He had a physically handicapped younger brother, and a sister studying in college. Being the eldest, he felt responsible for the family. He was in no hurry to get married.

Gradually, like other ADCs, he became a member of our family. Being the oldest and seniormost, he felt more responsible. He would guide other ADCs in the office and at home. He spoke less to me but would chat more easily with my wife. He travelled with us very often, within India and abroad.

I recall his trip with us to Vietnam. The Vietnamese officers, friendly and hospitable, kept proposing toasts to India, Indo–Vietnam friendship, between our armies, and to our delegation. At one stage, I felt that the younger lot was getting into a competition to see each other under the table. Sudhir was enjoying all that on a separate table. He gave me a reassuring look conveying that he understood the game and would not let anything untoward happen. Next day we were taken to the famous Qu Chi tunnels, an area which had withstood every type of American aerial and ground attacks during the war. The three-storied tunnel network, now preserved as a historical and motivational monument, was a self-contained, underground, Viet Cong unit, which was never overrun. The size of the tunnels gets narrower as you go down, from one storey to the one below. I walked through the top one but on being good-humouredly challenged, Sudhir insisted on going through all three. He wanted the Vietnamese officers to know our fitness standards. During our return journey in Singapore, where I had an official engagement for a day, he purchased a laptop and a mobile phone.

When the Kargil war started, Sudhir had finished his tenure with me and asked to be sent back to his unit fighting the war. Not wanting to break the laid-down norms, or his spirit, I let him go. The Army House gave him an affectionate send-off that he richly deserved.

Within ten days of his departure, I learnt that he had led his 'A' Team to capture Zulu Top, over 5200 metres high in the Mashkoh sector, on 25 July 1999. In this action, thirteen Pakistani soldiers belonging to the 19 Frontier Force were killed. (We returned their bodies after the Pakistanis raised a white flag.) Our own casualties were five soldiers killed. As per papers received by the Board of Officers in the Army HQ subsequently, Sudhir was recommended for a Vir Chakra.

A few days later I saw Sudhir in Srinagar. His Para Commando Team had reverted to anti-terrorist operations in the Kashmir Valley. He had come specially to see me, and was wearing the Viet Cong jungle cap given to us by the Vietnamese officers during our visit to Qu Chi Tunnels. I asked him about his attack on Zulu Ridge without any acclimatization. He smiled and said: 'Sir, you know that I am a Pahari (from the mountains). I don't need acclimatization.' With a smile, I told him not to break the laid-down rules again.

Three days after my return to Delhi, during breakfast, on a sudden impulse, I rang up Lieutenant General Krishan Pal, GOC 15 Corps. I told him to be careful in employing Sudhir and his team. Sudhir was a brave and an over-enthusiastic lad who would volunteer for every challenging mission. We should not allow him to take risks day after day. My wife, who was also at the breakfast table, could not believe what I had done. I had never said such a thing earlier for anyone.

Exactly a month after Kargil war was over, my wife and I were returning from Gurgaon (near New Delhi) after visiting Major Sushil Aima's bereaved family. In the car, I received a phone call informing me that, while leading an assault on a terrorists' hideout in Haphruda forest [in Kupwara disrtict, Jammu and Kashmir], Sudhir had been fatally wounded and died before he could be evacuated to hospital.

Sudhir, who had already operated in this jungle earlier, was tasked to search and destroy a terrorists' hideout. He and his buddy Naik Kheem Singh had spotted and surprised the terrorists deep in the jungle. In the ensuing fire fight, they had killed nine terrorists. It was a daring action, led all the way from the front. Sudhir was recommended for, and received, Ashok Chakra, the highest gallantry award during peacetime.

On 29 August 1999, the nation lost a gallant and a specially gifted soldier. My loss was personal!

As in other places, large quantities of weapons, ammunition, equipment, rations and stores were recovered. The enemy had also left behind a large number of documents that revealed the planning that had gone into Operation Badr.

On 27 July, the Pakistanis asked for a flag meeting and permission to evacuate the dead bodies of their soldiers. This permission was granted by GOC, 8 Mountain Division, Mohinder Puri. In that flag meeting, the Pakistani troops agreed to implement and abide by the terms of the ceasefire in full.

THE BATALIK SECTOR

In the Batalik sector, the LoC cuts across the Indus River between Batalik and Marol and then runs roughly along the Shangruti and Chorbat La watershed on the Ladakh Range at heights that are well above 16,000 feet. Thereafter, the LoC dips a bit towards Subsector Haneef (SSH) south of the Shyok River. Troops of 5 Northern Light Infantry (Pakistan) had intruded 8–10 kilometres in the unheld area, lying to the west of Chorbat La. They had occupied four ridgelines, which jut southwards like the fingers of a hand from the knuckle along Chorbat La watershed. These ridgelines – Jubar, Kukarthang, Khalubar and Point 5203–Churubar Po – vary in height from 15,000 feet to 16,800 feet. Here, 70 Infantry Brigade under Brigadier Devinder Singh had arrived just in time to ensure that the enemy did not extend the intrusion to dominate the Leh–Batalik–Kargil road.

Preliminary Operations

Initially, in the Batalik sector, the progress of operations was extremely slow. Preparations for attacks took a long time. The firm bases established by the assaulting troops were two to three days' marching distance from our administrative base. The routes along which men and equipment had to move were visible to the enemy and could be easily interdicted.

Among the preliminary operations launched in the Batalik sector was an attack by 1 Bihar on Point 4268 on 29 May. Due to a lack of adequate intelligence about the enemy defences and also due to (initial) inadequacy of artillery, the battalion achieved only partial success. A few enemy sangars were captured in an attack led gallantly by Major M. Saravanan. In one of the sangars, a pay book of a regular Pakistani soldier was recovered. Naik Ganesh Prasad Yadav and Naik Shatrughan Singh displayed conspicuous bravery and endurance in this action. But, despite tremendous efforts, the unit could not hold on to the feature.

To start with, the main thrust of the attack in this sector was concentrated on the western flank. But many of the western approaches along the Gragra Bar Nala were under the effective

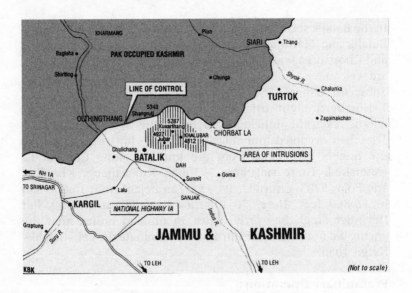

Pakistani intrusions in the Batalik sector.
(*Note*: The map is neither accurate nor drawn to scale;
it merely depicts the geographical area.)

domination of enemy's defences in the Shangruti complex (a 16,000-feet-high mountaintop on the Pakistani side of the LoC). As the offensives undertaken by us were not bearing fruit, it was felt that the main effort should be shifted from the west to the east, where Point 5203 would be able to provide the springboard for further operations along the Khalubar ridgeline and Chorbat La. After a review of the situation and after detailed discussions in the Military Operations Room towards the end of May 1999, Nirmal Chander Vij sought the views of the Army commander Northern Command and GOC 15 Corps on this issue. They both agreed and issued appropriate instructions to 3 Infantry Division and 70 Infantry Brigade.

Point 5203 and Point 4812

On 9 May 1999, 12 JAK Light Infantry was inducted into the Batalik sector. The battalion was then in the process of being deinducted from Ladakh. In fact, the advance party of this battalion had left for Delhi when it was ordered to move to Batalik.

Initially, the battalion was given the task of driving a wedge between the enemy's defences at Point 5203, the eastern extremity, and the Point 4812–Point 5287–Point 5000 complex (the Khalubar ridgeline). The battalion accomplished this task by infiltrating through the Junk Lungpa Nala. Next, 12 JAK Light Infantry, Ladakh Scouts and 10 Para (SF) succeeded in cutting off the enemy's supply route to Khalubar from the east. Major Vikas Mehta led a company attack and captured Point 5390 (16,700 feet) on 1 June. Because they could be clearly observed by the enemy during daytime, Major Mehta's troops, including the fighting porters, had to move by night in order to avoid interdiction by the enemy during their long climb through the Junk Lungpa Nala. Point 5390 provided unhindered observation and enabled the unit to bring down sustained and accurate artillery fire on the enemy positions.

On 6 June, Headquarters 70 Infantry Brigade tasked 12 JAK Light Infantry, along with a company of 5 Para, to recapture Point 5203, a formidable feature. The assault was launched from the Junk Lungpa Nala position after an extensive artillery fire plan had been drawn up. The battalion secured a foothold on the feature. The next night, this position was counterattacked, which resulted in a hand-to-hand fight. Captain Amol Kalia and his men fought bravely and beat back the counterattack. In this endeavour, a young Kashmiri soldier, Lance Naik Ghulam Mohammad Khan, used his rocket launcher effectively and made a major contribution. Unfortunately, thirteen soldiers of 12 JAK Light Infantry were killed in the counterattack that night. That was a heavy blow to the battalion.

For twelve days, troops of 12 JAK Light Infantry and 5 Para remained engaged with the enemy from the foothold secured on Point 5203. During this period, several acts of gallantry were performed. For instance: Subedar Bahadur Singh displayed exemplary determination, and fighting spirit, by climbing to the rugged top unnoticed and killing two enemy soldiers.

Although our troops demonstrated a great deal of courage and perseverance, the progress of the operation was slow. Consequently, I decided to visit a forward location, Handranbrok, on 10 June, accompanied by the corps and divisional commanders. We noticed that the brigade commander and his main headquarters were lagging far behind the forward troops due to poor communication with Headquarters 3 Infantry Division. That should not have happened in the battle. It is the responsibility of the higher formation to ensure that communication is extended to the lower formation moving ahead. My visit, and my giving of a piece of my mind to everyone, proved useful because, thereafter, both brigade and divisional commanders took to leading from the front and achieved notable successes.

To recapture Point 5203, a multidirectional attack was launched on 20 June, with two more companies of Ladakh Scouts joining the fray. While the troops of 12 JAK Light Infantry advanced from their foothold on Point 5203, Captain B.M. Cariappa of 5 Para steered his company through a circuitous route for an attack by infiltration and cleared the enemy position systematically.[4] The Ladakh Scouts' companies joined

---

[4]On 22–23 July, when the Pakistanis failed to honour their commitment to withdraw completely to their side of the LoC, Captain Cariappa led yet another assault on Area Conical on the LoC. In both actions, the officer showed commendable leadership and bravery.

the Paras quickly and this important objective was secured on 21 June. The seven Pakistani soldiers who were killed in this action were given a military burial by the troops of 12 JAK Light Infantry.

Brigadier Devinder Singh, while directing operations, was injured in a forward location at the base of Point 5203 on 22 June. Undaunted, he merely went in for some first aid and carried on with his duties till the end.

The loss of Point 5203 dealt a big blow to the enemy in the Batalik sector and proved to be a huge morale booster for 70 Infantry Brigade. An assailable flank had now been created, from which operations could be launched to evict the enemy from the Khalubar ridgeline.

The Stangba–Khalubar Ridgeline

The Padma Go–Khalubar ridgeline, located west of Point 5203, dominates Junk Lungpa in the east, Gragrio Nala in the west, the Kukarthang feature to its southwest and Muntho Dhalo, the logistic base of the enemy, in the northwest. The ridge, running north-south from the LoC, is razor-like, with vertical cliffs and rocky outcrops. The enemy positions on the ridgeline comprised: Point 5229, Padma Go, Dog Hill and Point 5000 (all on the Padma Go ridge); the Point 5287 complex; the Khalubar complex; and the Point 4812 complex (all on the Khalubar ridge). The Khalubar ridge was the hub of enemy defences in the Batalik sector.

Headquarters 70 Infantry Brigade made plans for the early capture of the long Khalubar ridgeline by launching simultaneous attacks from Junk Lungpa at several positions. In the north, Ladakh Scouts (Indus Wing) under Lieutenant Colonel Amarjit Singh Chandhoke were tasked to capture Point 5000, and also two other areas, namely, Stangba and Padma Go. In the middle of the Khalubar ridgeline, 22 Grenadiers was given the task of establishing footholds astride Point 5287, which were to be subsequently enlarged by 1/11 Gorkha Rifles. In the south, 12 JAK Light Infantry was assigned to capture Point 4812. The aim was to cut off the enemy's routes of maintenance and withdrawal as well as drive him out of his positions at Jubar, Kukarthang and Tharu subsequently.

Point 4812

In a brigade-level attack, 12 JAK Light Infantry was tasked to capture the Point 4812 complex situated at the southern extremity of the Khalubar ridgeline. In this action, Captain K.C. Nongrum demonstrated outstanding gallantry while leading his troops towards the objective and while eliminating the opposition en route. Havildar Satish Chander, a leading section commander, also made a significant contribution by clearing several enemy sangars.

Besides Captain Nongrum, seven brave soldiers were killed. For the next two days, the battalion hung on to its position but could not make further progress. After being reinforced with two reserve columns, the battalion launched a fresh assault and recaptured the objective on 3 July. The unit also captured the first Pakistani prisoner of war, Naik Inayat Ali, while he was trying to escape from Point 4812.

Khalubar

On 30 June, 22 Grenadiers launched the initial assault on Khalubar. Three expert mountaineers from a Vikas battalion (comprising troops of Tibetan origin) assisted 22 Grenadiers in their assault up the steep and rugged slope. They had to overcome stiff enemy resistance before they could secure two small footholds on the Khalubar ridgeline, south of Point 5287. The battalion could not make further headway, but Major Ajit Singh's company managed to hold on to the top against all odds. Very soon, 1/11 Gorkha Rifles, the reserve battalion, was inducted to enlarge the footholds secured by the Grenadiers and also to capture Khalubar.

The 1/11 Gorkha Rifles battalion had been in the process of moving from Ladakh to a peace station when it was inducted into the Batalik sector on 9 May to participate in the initial operations of 70 Infantry Brigade for securing the Yaldor axis that led to Ganasok, Junk Lungpa and further north to Khalubar (in the west) and Point 5203 (in the east). While waiting for these operations to get underway, the second-in-command, Lieutenant Colonel Amul Asthana, had sent a handwritten forces' inland letter direct to me, thereby violating the laid-down channel of correspondence. This letter pointed out the deficiencies in the machine-guns, mortars and communications equipment in his unit. (His unit had handed over most of the equipment in its custody to the relieving battalion in Siachen.) Apparently, the unit was in no state to fight with such major deficiencies. That letter set me thinking and I spent a whole day in Headquarters 15 Corps, making enquiries in the concerned branches. I instructed Army Headquarters to carry out rationalization of medium machine-guns, mortars and other such small arms and radio equipment on an all-India basis. We had to withdraw some material from other commands, and from some battalions of Rashtriya Rifles, which had been raised without receiving the government sanction for equipping these battalions till then. The reserve stocks of such weapons and equipment held in the ordnance depots for war had been used up to equip these Rashtriya Rifles battalions. On my orders, Headquarters 15 Corps met the requirements of 1/11 Gorkha Rifles immediately. I also made sure that no one in the chain of command took any action against Lieutenant Colonel Asthana for violating the channel of correspondence!

Towards the end of June, 1/11 Gorkha Rifles remained busy in degrading the enemy's defences at Jubar and Churubar Sispo, west of the Khalubar ridge. On 2 July, the battalion moved from Yaldor to a forward assembly area at the foot of Point 4812. The build-up for the attack was completed the next day. Meanwhile, the brigade artillery comprising field, Bofors and 130-mm high-explosive shells destroyed enemy sangars and disrupted his communication and supply lines. After climbing up a mountainside for seven hours, the Gorkhas reached their objective on the Khalubar ridge. Some of the most heroic deeds of valour were witnessed in this part of the battle.

The capture of Area Bunkers, the enemy position immediately south of Khalubar, by Lieutenant Manoj Kumar Pandey and his men facilitated the capture of Khalubar. Meanwhile, the commanding officer, Colonel Lalit Rai[5] linked up with Ajit Singh

[5]Colonel Lalit Rai had been commanding 17 Rashtriya Rifles during counterinsurgency operations in the Doda district of Jammu and Kashmir when he was flown into Batalik to take over command of 1/11 Gorkha Rifles.

of 22 Grenadiers. Lalit Rai's knee was seriously injured, but he continued to lead his men who had to fight with the enemy at close quarters for the next three days. Some others who fought gallantly included Naik Gyanendra Kumar Rai and Havildar Bhim Bahadur Dewan. The battalion eventually cleared the enemy from Khalubar on 6 July and linked up with 12 JAK Light Infantry deployed in the south.

Lieutenant Manoj Kumar Pandey

Lieutenant Manoj Kumar Pandey, a young officer of the 1/11 Gorkha Rifles, fearlessly participated in a series of boldly led attacks at Khalubar. On the night of 2–3 July 1999, as his platoon approached its final objective after an arduous climb lasting several hours, it came under heavy and intense enemy fire from the surrounding heights. Manoj's platoon was nominated to clear the interfering enemy positions. Manoj quickly moved his platoon to an advantageous position and sent one section to clear Pakistani sangars from the right, while he himself proceeded to clear four other enemy sangars, which were interfering with the attack from the left. Fearlessly charging up to the first sangar, braving a hail of bullets, he killed two enemy soldiers and went on to assault the second. He destroyed it by killing two more enemy personnel.

While clearing the third sangar, Manoj was injured on the shoulder and legs by enemy fire. Undaunted and without caring for his grievous injury, this spirited young officer personally led the assault on the fourth sangar, urging his men on. He succeeded in destroying it with a grenade but even as he hurled a grenade inside, he sustained a medium machine-gun burst on his forehead at virtually point-blank range, to which he succumbed. This singular daredevil act of the young officer provided the critical foothold to the Gorkhas that finally led to the capture of Khalubar.

Lieutenant Manoj Kumar Pandey was awarded the Param Vir Chakra for his outstanding acts of bravery.

The enemy suffered heavy casualties and left behind a huge quantity of weapons and ammunition, including US-made Stinger missiles. It was noticed that many enemy posts were without water and rations. We intercepted several radio messages from Pakistani posts complaining about lack of food and heavy Indian shelling. One Pakistani soldier was heard stating that they were 'living like dogs and there is no place to sit here'. As this area faced the south, and the sun, for a longer period, the snow here had melted much faster. With no snow near the sangars that could be melted to obtain water, the Pakistanis had to go down several kilometres to fetch this vital liquid from the streams. In that process, they suffered heavy casualties due to our small arms and artillery interdiction.

Padma Go

Stangba, Point 5000 and Dog Hill lie on the Padma Go ridge that runs north from the Khalubar–Point 5287 complex. Eventually, this feature meets the LoC. It was necessary to evict the enemy from this ridgeline so that operations to the west of the Khalubar–Point 5287 complex could be carried out unhindered. This task was allotted to the Indus and Karakoram (KK) Wings of Ladakh Scouts.

On the Padma Go ridge, 70 Infantry Brigade planned to capture Point 5000 first and then, using it as a firm base, set in motion operations up to Padma Go (about 16,500 feet). These operations were to be conducted simultaneously with the 1/11 Gorkha Rifles attack on the Khalubar ridgeline so that the enemy's attention would be divided.

One of the columns of the Ladakh Scouts launched an attack on Point 5000 on 30 June. Despite having to negotiate steep escarpments and waist-high snow at places, the column succeeded in capturing the objective. Further progress was slowed down due to the domination enjoyed by the enemy. The Padma Go objective was softened over the next few days with concentrated artillery and infantry mortar fire. In the renewed attacks on 5–6 July, Dog Hill was captured despite stiff resistance and a foothold was established on Stangba North. In this battle, Naib Subedar Tashi Chhepal displayed exemplary bravery and leadership. Thereafter, two columns under Major John Lewis and Captain N.K. Bishnoi attacked the formidable Padma Go feature. The objective was captured on 9 July. The Ladakh Scouts then went on to seize Point 5229, close to the LoC.

The loss of the Point 4812–Khalubar–Point 5287–Padma Go ridgeline broke the back of the enemy defences in the eastern part of the Batalik sector. While JAK Light Infantry troops, the Gorkhas and the Ladakh Scouts were systematically rolling up enemy's defences on the Khalubar ridgeline, other battalions of 70 Infantry Brigade were simultaneously launching assaults on enemy positions at Jubar and Tharu.

Jubar, Tharu and Kukarthang

With the recapture of the Point 4812–Khalubar–Point 5287–Padma Go ridgeline, the enemy's routes of maintenance and withdrawal were seriously threatened. Now 70 Infantry Brigade was well placed to tackle the Jubar, Tharu and Kukarthang complex from the west.

In a brigade-level operation, 1 Bihar was tasked to recapture the Jubar complex. Simultaneously, 17 Garhwal Rifles was asked to assault and recapture Area Bumps (1 and 2) and Kalapathar (one of the company objectives in the same area) and then continue north up to Point 5285 located at the junction of the Jubar and Kukarthang features.

The attacks on Jubar and Tharu were preceded by concentrated artillery fire. In an innovative action, the division employed some 122-mm Grad multibarrel rocket launchers[6] in a direct firing role to pulverize enemy defences. These launchers were deployed close to a pass on the Batalik–Kargil road where they were at the same height as the Jubar complex. With great professional pride, the gunners saw their ammunition destroy the targets. Direct hits shattered several enemy sangars.

On 29 June, 1 Bihar launched its attack. Phase 1 of the attack went off as planned and the Pakistanis were driven out from

---

[6]Grad in Russian means hail. For the enemy, it must have been a lethal hailstorm.

their sangars on the Jubar Observation Post (OP) on 30 June. A counterattack by the enemy was repulsed after inflicting heavy casualties. Jubar Top, immediately north of Jubar OP, proved to be a tough nut to crack. Heavy exchanges of fire continued between the contending troops throughout the next day and resulted in large numbers of casualties on both sides. A second attempt to capture Jubar Top on the night of 30 June with a fresh company was also unsuccessful.

The standoff lasted five days. During this period, artillery and infantry mortars continued to engage the targets. Air strikes were also planned and executed whenever the weather permitted. Fortuitously, artillery guns and infantry mortars of 1 Bihar hit the enemy's ammunition dump behind Jubar and it blew up completely. This caused panic amongst the enemy soldiers deployed on the Jubar Top and they began to thin out thereafter. In order to exploit the situation, a fresh attack was launched on the night of 6 July. Major K.P.R. Hari led the attack under the cover of heavy enemy artillery and small arms fire. He and other members of his team scaled a cliff face leading to Jubar Top from an unexpected direction. Undetected, they reached within 50 metres of the enemy's position and captured Jubar on 7 July.

The next day, the battalion cleared Point 4924 and recovered a large cache of arms and ammunition, apart from the dead bodies of a number of Pakistani soldiers, all of which had been left behind by the fleeing enemy.

In the finest tradition of the Indian Army, and as a reflection of the esprit de corps in the battalion, 1 Bihar had also recovered the dead bodies of Major M. Saravanan, Naik Ganesh Prasad Yadav and two other soldiers who had been killed on Point 4924 in an earlier attack on 29 May. It was gratifying for the battalion to finally capture a feature that had eluded its grasp earlier.[7] On 9 July, 1 Bihar added another feather to its cap by recapturing

---

[7]At this time, our national spirit and respect for the soldiers were so high that a Union minister, the late Ranganathan Kumaramangalam, personally escorted the body of martyr Major Saravanan to his hometown in Tamil Nadu, where a solemn farewell was given.

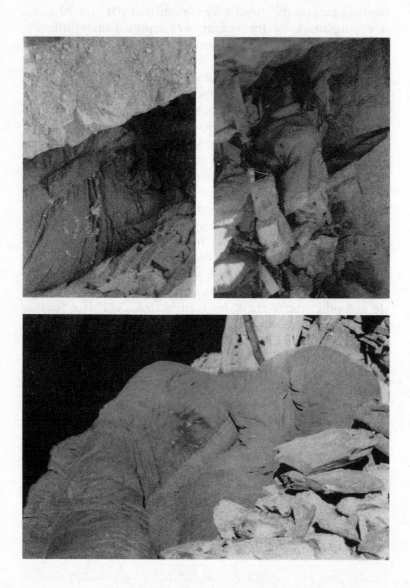

Bodies of Pakistani soldiers recovered from trenches.

the Tharu feature (Point 5103) after an arduous climb to over 15,000 feet; the battalion then linked up with 1/11 Gorkha Rifles at Kukarthang. (Tharu is a dominating feature on the Kukarthang ridgeline.) The assault was preceded by several days of pounding of the enemy positions by the divisional artillery; the enemy did not put up much resistance.

Area Bumps, Kalapathar and Point 5285

On the night of 29 June, 17 Garhwal Rifles launched simultaneous attacks on Area Bumps and Kalapathar, enemy positions on the Jubar ridge, north of Point 4926. These attacks were also intended to draw the enemy's attention away from the main thrust and pin down his reserves. It was a long climb to the objective. All companies were exposed during daytime, except one platoon of 'A' Company led by Captain Jintu Gogoi. This platoon made steady progress and, braving heavy machine-gun fire and artillery shelling, reached the objective at Kalapathar but then found itself surrounded. In the hand-to-hand combat that resulted, Jintu Gogoi led his platoon skilfully and manoeuvred it out of the enemy's reach but was himself grievously wounded.

The battalion firmed in near this location. Snowfall on 2–3 July delayed further operations. Finally, as part of simultaneous brigade attacks on several features on 6–7 July, the Garhwalis recaptured Kalapathar (on 7 July). The same night, Captain Ajay Rai led a platoon and secured a position, north of Area Bumps, near the enemy's Muntho Dhalo logistic base that had already been hit by the fighter aircraft of the Indian Air Force. The route to Point 5285, a dominating feature near the junction of Jubar and Kukarthang ridgelines, now lay open. The assault on Point 5285 was launched on 9 July. As a result of factors such as the objective's proximity to the LoC, the enemy's ability to interfere effectively with the attack from several vantage points, heavy snowfall and the hazards of rugged high-altitude terrain, the progress was slow. But the battalion fought bravely and captured the objective the very next day.

Kukarthang

The long-delayed attack on Kukarthang was launched by 1/11 Gorkha Rifles on 8 July. By now a much larger quantity of guns and ammunition had become available in the Batalik sector and a devastating punch in the form of concentrated artillery and mortar fire set the stage for the attack.

On 8 July, 'A' company captured Point 4821, and despite heavy artillery and automatic fire of the enemy, 'D' company was able to secure Ring Contour. Both these enemy positions were enroute to Kukarthang Top. By early morning of 9 July, the Kukarthang ridge, which, till recently, appeared daunting, was cleared of all enemy positions. The enemy had vacated most of them. As at other places, mopping up and consolidation operations revealed a large cache of arms, ammunition and rations. Also, many dead bodies of Pakistani soldiers were found.

Chorbat La

Chorbat La, the eastern extremity of the Kargil sector, lies on the massive watershed of the Ladakh Range between the Indus River and its northern tributary, the Shyok River. Soon after the intrusions were detected in the Batalik sector, we assessed that the enemy was likely to expand the area of operations to include the tactically important Chorbat La, which was held by a small detachment of the Border Security Force (BSF). This pass would provide an additional axis to the enemy to sustain troops that had intruded into the west Batalik area and Turtuk.

Keeping all these factors in mind, it was decided to secure Chorbat La firmly by occupying defensive positions on both flanks. Major Sonam Wangchuk's company, made up of men from the Indus and Karakoram Wings of the Ladakh Scouts, was assigned the task of reinforcing Chorbat La. While most of these men climbed the steep mountains, fourteen of them were lifted by Cheetah helicopters directly on to the ridgeline on 20 May and thus succeeded in pre-empting the enemy. Major Wangchuk's leadership and exploits in these operations have already become legendary.

The Ladakh Scouts

Till the end of Operation Vijay, the Ladakh Scouts had two wings: the Karakoram Wing (deployed on Ladakh's eastern front with China) and the Indus Wing (deployed on the southern Siachen Glacier and in SSW). The headquarters of both the wings and most of their companies were actively involved in the operations against the Pakistani intruders. Physically fit and well accustomed to the harsh terrain and climate from their childhood, Ladakh's brave men were psychologically attuned and had been battle hardened over decades of operational commitments at Siachen and the Line of Actual Control with China.

The Ladakh Scouts acquitted themselves with an inspiring tenacity of purpose and indomitable courage and played a stellar role in the Batalik sector.

In recognition of the outstanding valour of their men and their sterling performance, the Ladakh Scouts were awarded the Unit Citation and, later, in a special ceremony at Leh, I presented them with the Chief of Army Staff Banner. I also approved their request to recognize the Ladakh Scouts as a full-fledged regiment of the Indian Army and put them at par with all infantry regiments of the Indian Army.

On 30 May, Subedar Chhering Stobdan's patrol was involved in a close encounter while trying to evict enemy troops climbing up an ice wall to occupy a dominating feature. He shot down two enemy personnel, who were later identified as regular soldiers of the Pakistani Army. Havildar Tsewang Rigzin displayed conspicuous bravery when he was ordered to occupy a steep position on the ridgeline along the LoC at 15,500 feet to pre-empt enemy occupation and infiltration.

Two additional companies of the Karakoram Wing of the Ladakh Scouts were rushed to the area to occupy high mountain features such as Point 5440, Point 5498 and Point 5520. By 2 June, the Chorbat La ridgeline had been adequately secured and the Pakistani intrusion effectively contained. Subsequently, the occupation of the ridgeline enabled our artillery to interdict

Pakistani supply routes and administrative bases. This factor also ensured that the enemy could not use the supply route on the Piun–Siari axis (coming from Skardu in the Northern Areas) for its troops deployed on the LoC in this area.

In the Chorbat La area, the operations of 70 Infantry Brigade and 102 Infantry Brigade had to be synergized and coordinated in Subsector Haneef (SSH). The 155-mm Bofors howitzers as well as 130-mm medium guns of 3 Artillery Brigade were employed frequently to influence the battle in Batalik and SSH.

By 9 July, almost the whole of the Batalik sector had been cleared of the enemy. Six prisoners of war were captured. I visited Headquarters 70 Infantry Brigade once again at Ganasok. This time, I gave a well-deserved pat to Devinder Singh, along with a bottle of Scotch whisky – a small personal gesture of appreciation – to share with his colleagues. I also met and gave small gifts to some personnel of the brigade who had fought exceptionally well and promoted V. S. Bhalothia of 12 JAK Light Infantry to the rank of colonel (already chosen by the Army Selection Board), which he richly deserved.

The Last Battle in Batalik

When the Pakistanis failed to honour their commitment to withdraw from all Indian territory up to the LoC, 70 Infantry Brigade had to resume operations to capture Point 5300 and the neighbouring heights.

By 12 July, the brigade had been deployed on the dominating heights all along the Batalik sector and enjoyed an excellent field of observation, which enabled them to bring down indirect fire with near pinpoint accuracy on the enemy. And it was for the same reason that the Pakistanis did not want to vacate their positions on the last few features held by them inside Indian territory. The recapture of these positions would enable the Indian Army to occupy the LoC at a number of places and dominate the ridgelines and valleys.

In the Chorbat La area, 14 Sikh was tasked to capture Point 5310 (17,500 feet) on 22 July. The Unit Commando Team led by Lieutenant Praveen Kumar accomplished this feat. The team attacked the feature from three different directions after scaling a near-vertical cliff by fixing rope ladders. After capturing this feature they were able to inflict heavy casualties on the enemy located opposite SSH using artillery and mortar fire.

In Batalik, 1/11 Gorkha Rifles, from the Khalubar ridgeline, had already captured Point 5190 on 10 July. They were poised to attack Point 5300. But it was only on 22 July that they were given the green signal to capture this objective. Two companies of 5 Para also launched an attack simultaneously along with the Gorkhas. One of these companies secured Conical Feature near the LoC on 23 July. The second company of 5 Para encountered a deep minefield en route to its objective, Ring Contour, and suffered heavy casualties. On 24–25 July, the Pakistanis launched two counterattacks but the paratroopers fought back and repulsed both. Meanwhile, the Indus Wing of the Ladakh Scouts battled heavy odds to secure a foothold on Point 5239. By 26 July, the Gorkhas, the paratroopers, paracommandos and the Ladakhis together had recaptured the last remaining mountain features that were held by the Pakistani intruders on the Indian side of the LoC in the Batalik sector. Three Pakistani soldiers were killed and the rest ran away.

SUBSECTOR HANEEF

The Southern Glacier as well as the Subsector West (SSW) (Turtuk–Chalunka), east of Chorbat La, was as much a beehive of activity as the Kargil sector. Due to the inaccessible nature of the terrain and also due to tactical inexpediency, there were wide gaps in the deployment of troops along the LoC and the Actual Ground Position Line (AGPL) in this subsector.

After a clash between patrols in the area in May 1999, when some minor intrusions (200–500 metres) were discovered, Brigadier P. C. Katoch, commander, 102 Infantry Brigade, decided to pre-empt any further intrusions by occupying defences along all important mountain features up to Chorbat La on the Ladakh Range and the watershed. Also, the decision to occupy defences along the Turtuk Lungpa, a track and *nala* flowing from the Ladakh Range to Shyok River past Turtuk, prevented further ingress by the enemy and provided us a firm base for launching attacks to evict the intruders. Next, 9 Mahar deployed a company

west of the Turtuk Lungpa and another company at Tyakshi
Spur with positions along the Ramdan Lungpa to further
strengthen our defences in the Turtuk area. The battalion
subsequently attacked and captured Point 5220. Ladakh Scouts
occupied supporting positions in this area. Subedar Lobzang
Chhotak and Sepoy Tsering Dorje proved to be exceptionally
courageous in these operations.

At the end of May, 11 Rajputana Rifles, a battalion that was
in the process of leaving after completing its tenure at the
Central Glacier, was inducted through the Turtuk Lungpa to
occupy defences on the LoC at Point 5500 and adjacent areas.
Here, personnel from 5 Vikas assisted 11 Rajputana Rifles. On
6–7 June, an attempt was made to capture Point 5590 by a patrol
led by Captain Haneef-ud-din, an Army Service Corps officer
serving on attachment with 11 Rajputana Rifles. The patrol,
moving at a height of 18,500 feet, approached the enemy position
but came under heavy fire. Despite grave injuries, Captain
Haneef-ud-din took up position and kept on engaging the enemy
till the remaining patrol succeeded in establishing a foothold on
the mountain. He succumbed to his injuries thereafter. In
recognition of this gallant young officer's determined leadership,
the new sector occupied during Operation Vijay, south of
Subsector West (SSW), was named Subsector Haneef (SSH). In
this action, Naib Subedar Mangej Singh, who was assisting
Haneef-ud-din on this patrol, conducted himself in an exemplary
manner.

In the first week of June 1999, Headquarters 102 Mountain
Brigade received an intelligence report that the Pakistanis had
planned to initiate insurgency in Turtuk. Based on this report,
searches were carried out in Turtuk and neighbouring villages.
Large quantities of arms and ammunition were recovered during
the searches and twenty-four suspects were apprehended and
handed over to the civil police.

Point 5770

In the Southern Glacier lies the Chulung La on the Saltoro
Range, devoid of snow for about five months a year. Indian
troops occupy its eastern shoulder while the Pakistanis occupy

the western one. Pakistan had made several attempts in the past to capture the eastern shoulder as that would permit it to cut off our Gulab Complex and the SSW and allow a thrust towards Chalunka in the Shyok Valley. Towering above the western shoulder stand the twin glaciated peaks of Point 5770 on the Saltoro Range. The Pakistanis had established a post named Pimple some distance below. By occupying Point 5770, they would have been able to choke off our Bahadur Complex and facilitate the capture of Chulung La. Therefore, a decision had been taken way back in December 1997 to occupy Point 5770.

In the summer of 1998, 4 JAK Rifles, assisted by three units, namely, a High-Altitude Warfare School (HAWS) team, 5 Para and Ladakh Scouts, established posts north and south of Point 5770. But all attempts to secure the top proved unsuccessful due to permanent ice overhangs and falling icicles. The enemy later noticed these posts and periodic exchanges of fire had become a norm.

In June 1999, appreciating that the enemy would try to secure Point 5770 once again, 102 Infantry Brigade came up with a bold plan to attempt to capture it directly from the east, after a stiff 1-kilometre perpendicular climb. A task force of six personnel (two each from 27 Rajput, Ladakh Scouts and HAWS) under Major Navdeep Singh Cheema was selected and trained to lead the assault. To achieve stealth and surprise, it was decided that artillery firing would not be resorted to unless it became necessary for the safety of the task force. Due to heavy snowfall, the fixing of ropes for the assault on Point 5770 could commence only on 25 June. On 26 June, a rifle shot was heard from the direction of the summit. Undaunted, the fixing of ropes continued. On 27 June, the six-man task force commenced the ascent at 0700 hours. After seven hours of arduous climbing, they reached the top, but to their horror, found that eleven Pakistani Army personnel had already reached there from their post, Pimple. The Pakistanis were unaware of the Indian task force that had stealthily crept up from an unexpected direction. Some of them were busy constructing a sangar, two were writing letters and some resting in a makeshift fibreglass hut nearby. Major Navdeep Singh Cheema took the courageous decision to assault the Pakistanis along with his colleagues and was successful in killing all of them. Eight weapons, including a mortar, were captured. Immediately thereafter, all hell broke loose. The Pakistanis let loose intense artillery and mortar fire and missiles in the next three hours. Fortunately, the task force did not suffer any casualties. In this operation, Captain Shayamal Sinha and Havildar Joginder Singh, both from the High-Altitude Warfare School, and Rifleman Sewang Morup of the Ladakh Scouts, exhibited exceptional valour at the time of the final approach and assault. This was one of the toughest and the most audacious operations, at par with the capture of Bana Top in 1987 in the Northern Glacier.[8]

Soon after the war was over, we received a request through our defence attaché in London to return the body of a young Pakistani officer, Captain Taimur Malik, of the Special Service Group, attached to 3 Northern Light Infantry, who had been killed at Point 5770. Captain Taimur Malik's grandfather, who was living in London, had approached the Indian defence attaché and wanted his request to be conveyed to me. On receipt of this message, we got young Taimur's and other bodies exhumed from the area. They were returned to the Pakistan Army near Kargil, with proper military honours.

In the subsequent operations in Subsector Haneef, 13 Kumaon captured some of the highest features that witnessed fighting during Operation Vijay, including Point 5810, Point 5685 and the Ring Contour. Also, 11 Rajputana Rifles succeeded in capturing the daunting feature Point 5990, where Captain Haneef-ud-din had been killed earlier. These operations were conducted on some of the most formidable mountain features in the world, under the most trying climatic conditions, with fortitude and the utmost devotion to duty.

THE KAKSAR SECTOR

The terrain in the Kaksar area along the LoC is generally glaciated with heights ranging above 15,000 feet. The main ridge comprising the Point 5608–Point 5605–Point 5280 Spur

---

[8]See under 'The Revenge for Siachen', Chapter 2. Point 5770 has now been rechristened Navdeep Top.

Junction is a watershed with smaller ridges emanating on both sides of the LoC. The approach to the main ridge is confined to the glaciated valleys between smaller ridges and can be observed from the main ridge. Movement along the valleys and ridge tops is very difficult.

The details of vacation of the southwest spur of Point 5299, Bajrang post, in March 1999 by the 4 Jat battalion after obtaining permission from the brigade commander but contrary to the laid-down instructions of Headquarters 15 Corps, have already been narrated in Chapter 4.

On 14 May 1999, a five-man patrol of 4 Jat, led by Lieutenant Saurabh Kalia, had disappeared in the Kaksar sector after losing contact with the base. It was almost a month later, i.e., on 8 June, that the Pakistan Army returned their mutilated bodies to the Indian Army. From the condition of the bodies, it became evident that the Indian soldiers had been tortured and had died in captivity. When the media reported this news, the whole nation was upset. The situation was particularly traumatic for the families of personnel on this patrol. The emotions ran so high that many people from the strategic community in New Delhi wanted us to escalate the war immediately. The prime minister, then in Lucknow, rang me up to ascertain the condition of the bodies of our soldiers returned by the Pakistan Army. I requested him not to react to the media reports till an independent body had conducted a proper postmortem. We requested the International Committee of the Red Cross and also the Indian Red Cross to carry out the postmortem. Both agencies declined to do so. Ultimately, the postmortem had to be done by doctors in the Army Hospital, Delhi Cantonment.

After he saw the postmortem medical reports, the Indian external affairs minister, Jaswant Singh, briefed the media personally and made some very strong comments, which were fully justified.

Such conduct is not simply a breach of established norms, or a violation of international agreements; it is a civilizational crime against all humanity; it is a reversion to barbaric medievalism.

Jaswant Singh

I was myself very upset and angry, and told Nirmal Chander Vij to raise this issue with the Pak DGMO immediately. I asked him to convey our disgust at the Pakistanis' treatment of our prisoners of war.[9] The DGMI, Ravi K. Sawhney, was told to show the postmortem reports of these men to selected defence attachés located in New Delhi.

On 15 May, after Saurabh Kalia's patrol went missing, 4 Jat had dispatched another patrol led by Lieutenant Amit Bhardwaj (with thirty-two men) to the South West Spur of Point 5299 (Bajrang post). The Pakistani soldiers fired upon this patrol. In the encounter, one soldier was killed and ten were wounded. Amit Bhardwaj and another soldier were declared missing on 20 May. Their bodies were recovered from the site of the encounter after the ceasefire came into effect.

On 17 May, another patrol was launched by 4 Jat under Major Vikram Singh Shekhawat to extricate Amit Bhardwaj's patrol, which had come under heavy fire of the enemy. After carrying out this task, this patrol took up a position close to Point 5299. In this action, Major Shekhawat was wounded.

On 18 May, a company each of 28 Rashtriya Rifles and 8 Battalion, Border Security Force, were deployed along the smaller ridgeline emanating from Point 5299 area towards the Srinagar–Kargil road to prevent the enemy from extending his position towards the road. On 28 May, 14 JAK Rifles was placed under the command of Headquarters 121 (I) Infantry Brigade.

Further operations to evict the enemy from Kaksar were inordinately delayed because 14 JAK Rifles took a long time to settle down and locate the enemy defences in the area. The lack of progress in the Kaksar sector till 10 June was one of the reasons for sidestepping Brigadier Surinder Singh, commander, 121 (I) Infantry Brigade. Brigadier O.P. Nandrajog relieved him on 19 June. The troops nominated for evicting the intruders could be redeployed only by 25 June. The razor-sharp ridgelines in the Kaksar sector, located at an average height of 17,500 feet, also made it difficult to build up logistics for launching the offensive. A large number of fighting porters had to be

---

[9]This was done on 15 June 1999.

employed to carry ammunition; many people from nearby villages volunteered for this job.

The plan to evict the enemy envisaged recapturing Point 5605, Point 5280 and the Spur Junction on the main ridgeline. Preliminary operations were launched on 28 June, and assault teams were in place by 1 July. The full-fledged operations resumed on 5 July, but had to be called off in the second week (of July) because the ceasefire had been announced and the Pakistanis had offered to withdraw. When the ceasefire was agreed to between the DsGMO of India and Pakistan, Kaksar was the first sector to be vacated by the Pakistani Army personnel. They commenced withdrawal from the intruded area on 9 July and vacated it by 11 July. Our troops occupied positions in this area by 15 July.

After the war, one day, Sudha Narayan Murthy, wife of Narayan Murthy, then chairman of Infosys Ltd., rang me up. She asked for names and addresses of personnel who had been captured by the Pakistani Army in Kaksar and then killed after interrogation. I had these details sent to her. In a rare gesture of sympathy, she met the families of these personnel and also gave them monetary assistance from the Infosys Foundation, which is involved in citizens' welfare programmes.

End of Military Operations

When military operations in Kargil ended on 26 July 1999, the Indian Army had captured eight Pakistani Army soldiers and a large number of weapons, ammunition, equipment and documents. Some details are now given.

Weapons and Ammunition Captured in War

- 12.7-mm anti-aircraft machine-guns   04
- Universal/medium/general purpose machine-guns   40
- Heavy machine-guns with tripods   9
- Rifles (G3/AK/Chinese/M16/auto/SLR)   80
- Rocket launchers (RPG)   14

Captured identity cards of Pakistani Army personnel.

Captured pay books of Pakistani Army personnel.

PERSONAL DIARY OF LT MD MAAZ ULLAH KHAN SUMBAL OF 8 NLI

Captured diary of a Pakistani officer *(cont.)*

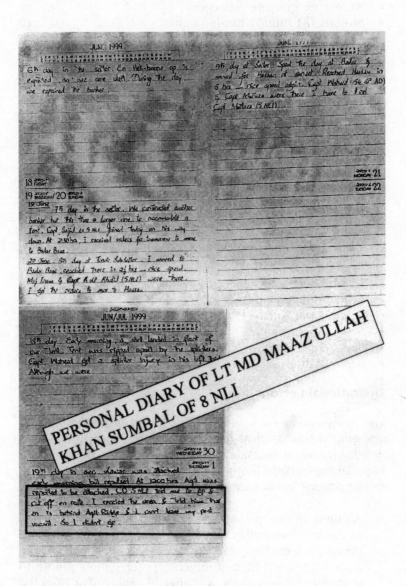

Captured diary of a Pakistani officer.

- Automatic grenade launchers   05
- Mortars (81 mm/51 mm/60 mm)   10
- 120-mm mortars   03
- Sniper rifles   06
- 23-mm gun   01
- 14.5-mm KPVT   01
- PIKA machine-gun   04
- 37-mm twin barrel air defence (AD) gun   01
- Stinger missile with launcher   02
- 105-mm howitzers   03
- Assorted ammunition   6 tons
- Mines   4432
- Grenades   952

Prisoners of War

- Naik Inayat Ali   5 Northern Light Infantry
- Sepoy Hunar Shah   -do-
- Sepoy Sher Baz Khan   -do-
- Sepoy Mohammad Ayaz   -do-
- Sepoy Fazal Aman   24 Sind
- Sepoy Abdul Hamid   33 Frontier Force (FF)
- Sepoy Salik Khan   -do-
- Sepoy Ashraf   19 Frontier Force (FF)

Operational Lessons

The Army conducted several studies to record and implement operational and tactical lessons from this operation. These detailed lessons are outside the scope of this book. However, ten important operational lessons, which I believe would be of interest to the general public, are given as follows:

1. All units and formations require a certain minimum period of reorientation when there is a change in their role and operational environment. This includes a change of role from counterterrorism/insurgency/peace-station profile to conventional operations, a change of deployment from the plains to a high-altitude area, or from defensive to offensive operations.

2. All formations/units/subunits require sufficient time for recce, planning and preparation for any offensive mission. This must never be compromised. Assaulting troops must have up-to-date information of the terrain.

3. In the high-altitude mountains, classic set-piece unidirectional attacks, even attacks from two directions, are less likely to succeed. During Operation Vijay, multidirectional attacks with lesser strength were found to be the only successful method of unbalancing the enemy and maintaining the momentum of the attack.

4. The application of combat superiority for an attack even up to the ratio of 8:1 was found to be inadequate. In a majority of cases, attacks succeeded when the ratio went as high as 9:1.

5. When troops are required to scale heights, particularly above 14,000 feet, and still be fit enough for a 'hand-to-hand' fight after reaching the top, physical fitness gains paramount importance.

6. In high-altitude warfare, more than anywhere else, a young profile of officers and men in combat units is vital.

7. There is much greater need for artillery and its ammunition, as the rate of movement in high-altitude mountains is very slow.

8. The impact of high altitude and cold on all weapons and equipment needs to be monitored and taken into account during battles.

9. Logistic bases have to be located as far forward as possible, with multiple means of transportation. For close logistic support, the Army needs its own fleet of light and medium-size helicopters. Helicopter evacuation of casualties is the most effective method at high altitudes.

10. For combat in high-altitude mountains, the Army must continuously look for lighter weapons and equipment, particularly for its infantry.

9

Combat and Logistic Support:
A Crucial Input

Conflict termination occurred on our terms. The Pakistan Army was forced to beat a hasty retreat only because our forces, including artillery, broke the enemy's will to fight.

The Gunners

IN MOUNTAIN WARFARE, THE INFANTRY SPEARHEADS THE ATTACK but the spearhead has to have a strong shaft. That is none other than the artillery.

Operation Vijay was a high-intensity operation in high-altitude mountains, with a fairly large amount of unconventional artillery support. The enhanced reach and versatility of weapons and ammunition now available could give the artillery enough opportunity to cause destruction and damage in a more effective and responsive manner than had been possible in the past. But we badly missed weapons-locating radars and other equipment for ensuring more accurate target acquisition and surveillance.

Enemy targets on both sides of the LoC were engaged. Nearly fifty fire units comprising artillery guns, howitzers, mortars and one rocket battery were employed in the area of operations for various purposes: for destroying given objectives, for supporting the infantry attacks (described earlier) and for carrying out counterbombardment. In all, these units fired nearly 250,000 rounds/rockets over a period of ninety days. The medium guns fired nearly 30 per cent of the total ammunition. Sometimes, in a space of five minutes, over 1200 rounds of high explosives were fired on objectives such as Point 4875, Tololing and Tiger Hill.

As an effective innovation in mountain warfare, field guns, the 155-mm Bofors howitzers, 130-mm medium guns and even 122-mm Grad multibarrel rocket launchers were employed in a direct firing role. In this role, targets were engaged at distances up to 17 kilometres.

Several forward observation officers and battery commanders, while moving with assault troops, were exposed to small arms fire and, in the process, got injured or killed. On some occasions when a company commander became a casualty, the forward observation officer took over command of the rifle company and led it to capture the assigned objective.

The list of the gallant individuals whose exploits ensured success is long. Major K.A.S. Kasana, 41 Field Regiment, Captain S.B. Ghildyal, 315 Field Regiment, Captain R. Jery Prem Raj (posthumous), 159 Medium Regiment, and Gunner S.G. Pillai (posthumous) of 4 Field Regiment were awarded Vir Chakras. Brigadier Lakhwinder Singh, Headquarters 8 Mountain Artillery Brigade, Colonel N.A. Subramanian, 315 Field Regiment, and Colonel Sanjay Saran, 15 Field Regiment, were awarded Yudh Seva Medals. Thirty-four gunners were awarded Sena Medals (Gallantry). Three artillery units, 141 Field Regiment, 197 Field Regiment and 108 Medium Regiment, were given the Chief of Army Staff's Unit Citation.

The Army Aviation Corps

The Army aviators performed exceedingly well. Two squadrons, which participated in the war, flew over 2500 missions and logged over 2700 flying hours. Most of the missions were flown at the upper extremity of the flight envelope (i.e., the minimum and maximum heights above sea level within which a chopper is expected to fly efficiently) of the helicopter fleet. Two hundred and forty troops and about 200 tons of material were initially lifted by helicopters to old and new posts that were to engage the enemy. Helicopters evacuated over 900 casualties from the battlefront, mostly from makeshift helipads, despite the enemy's small arms' and artillery fire. Of the total number, 785 casualties were lifted, in 734 missions, by Cheetah (Alouette) helicopters.

Major Gautam Shasikumar Khot and Major Prabhu Nath Prasad, were awarded Vir Chakras. Other awards received by the Army Aviation Corps were one Yudh Seva Medal, three Sena Medals (Gallantry) and one Sena Medal (Distinguished).

The Corps of Engineers

The sappers have always had to perform unglamorous but herculean tasks: laying/lifting mines, booby traps or other obstacles, or building roads, bridges, helipads, field defences and living accommodation. Twelve engineer regiments were deployed during the Kargil war. The Sappers constructed about 8 kilometres of Class 9 (a measure pertaining to the width and gradient of the road on which trucks can move) roads, 250 kilometres of new mule tracks and 20 kilometres of foot tracks. They improved upon 30 kilometres of mule tracks and built nearly seventy helipads. Their most challenging task was lifting mines and booby traps left behind by the withdrawing Pakistani troops, without any markings on the ground. They recovered about 5000 mines manually. That speaks volumes for their professionalism and courage.

The creation of the communication and logistic infrastructure takes several years. Such a process requires a great deal of advance planning and provisioning of resources. The requisite infrastructure was created to avoid operational constraints in future. The engineers rose to the occasion and performed very well during and after the Kargil operation. They procured and transported stores, at times by helicopter, and worked on projects at a fast pace. The speed of track construction in particular was commendable. During this operation, Captain Rupesh Pradhan was awarded the Vir Chakra. Eight sappers won Sena Medals (Gallantry).

The Corps of Signals

In modern warfare, multiplicity of media, alternative routing and state-of-the-art equipment are essential for ensuring responsive and survivable operational communications. At high altitudes and amidst mountains, the portability of equipment and the security of communications are the other key elements. The Corps of Signals had a mix of new and old equipment. But it was less than adequate. The equipment required to ensure security of communications was both poor and insufficient. It was generally not available in infantry battalions and artillery regiments. The Defence Research and Development Organization

(DRDO) and other production agencies had promised to deliver it, but had not been able to do so.

Despite these handicaps, the Corps of Signals supported the operations very effectively. In addition to providing the normal communications network, they also came up with innovative arrangements such as the Iridium satellite telephones for artillery observation posts, Inmarsat satellite terminals between headquarters and hand-held walkie-talkie sets to monitor the movement of convoys and the progress of logistic stocking. Fax facilities were made available even at the battalion headquarters level.

We realized that holding of operational reserves of signal equipment, including secrecy devices, in the theatre of war, was critical for the efficient conduct of operations. The management of the electro-magnetic spectrum by a single agency to ensure that communication and other networks functioned efficiently was also highlighted.

Logistic Support

Providing logistic support for a large force operating in a high-altitude region, which is glaciated, underdeveloped, avalanche prone, blizzard swept and extremely cold, is not easy. The Pakistan Army failed to achieve this objective, and so did we in the beginning. We were handicapped because of a very short warning period, sudden accretion of our force levels, particularly the induction of artillery and 5000 tons of ammunition, and enemy interference along the Srinagar–Kargil–Leh highway.

Moreover, the provision (and movement) of ammunition, fuel oil and lubricants, rations, engineering stores and clothing had to be suddenly expanded to a high level. The Army logistics teams worked tirelessly and innovatively to keep the momentum going during the entire course of the war.

Transportation

The Animal Transport (AT) Battalion personnel proved their golden worth during the Kargil war. Naib Risaldar Prem Singh was awarded the Sena Medal. The 874 AT Battalion became the first Army Service Corps (ASC) unit to be awarded the Chief of Army Staff's (COAS) Unit Citation. Some of the Mechanical Transport Battalion personnel such as Sepoys V. Paneer Selvem and Gopinath Maharana, both awarded the Sena Medal, were killed while performing round-the-clock duty.

On the technical side, there were many problems to be overcome. The operations were launched at a time when the stocks built up for the previous winter season were nearly consumed. Fresh stocking for the seasons ahead had not commenced. The sudden heavy induction of troops made it difficult to find road space for movement of vehicles carrying other logistical material. The onus of ensuring smooth supply fell on local depots and the composite platoons of the ASC battalions in the Kargil sector. The transport battalions completed the necessary stocking, despite heavy enemy shelling, and despite the fact that the breed of vehicles was new for the drivers; they had either limited experience or none at all in handling them. Such a state of affairs necessitated rapid acquisition of driving skills and administrative acumen, and coordination of efforts among all the battalions involved.

The Medical Corps

The Army Medical Corps personnel, right from a regimental aid post up to the advance base hospital and the military hospital, worked with customary professionalism and dedication. Of the 1361 casualties admitted to various hospitals, only fourteen succumbed to their injuries. This achievement is remarkable by any standards anywhere, particularly considering the inhospitable terrain conditions and the seriousness of the injuries in the forward areas. The regimental medical officers worked bravely under fire. Captain Somnath Basu sustained severe injuries but refused to be evacuated and continued at his post. He performed over fifteen operations every day in his field ambulance. One medical officer was awarded the Yudh Seva Medal and two others were decorated with Sena Medals (Gallantry).

The Army Ordnance Corps

The Army Ordnance Corps had the unenviable duty of fulfilling a suddenly enhanced requirement of practically all items required for war except rations and fuel. It goes to the credit of this corps that the requirement of nearly 300 guns, mortars, rocket launchers, small arms' ammunition and other related equipment was always fulfilled. Nearly a hundred special trains were run to move ammunition and other stores from various depots to the railhead at Jammu, from where they were transported to the front.

The Electrical and Mechanical Engineers

The Electrical and Mechanical Engineers have to ensure that all weapons and equipment are shipshape and in perfect working condition. These engineers are also responsible for the recovery and repairs of armaments. During the course of the Kargil war, most repairs were carried out *in situ* and, at times, under enemy shelling. Spares were lifted to the forward positions in helicopters that were being used for casualty evacuation. All helicopters with the formations were serviced, repaired and kept flying right through the war. It is worth noting that over 650 vehicles were recovered, 200 engine assemblies replaced and 5000 miscellaneous repairs carried out *in situ*. Captain M. V. Sooraj of the Electrical and Mechanical Engineers, while serving with 18 Garhwal Rifles, was awarded the Vir Chakra. Two other officers serving with infantry battalions received the Sena Medal (Gallantry).

Other Units

The Corps of Military Police, the Postal Service, the Remount and Veterinary Corps and several other smaller organizations also contributed to the logistic support.

Profiles of Collective Courage

Soon after the capture of Tololing, some commanders suggested that we should announce awards for exceptional gallantry while the war was going on, a practice followed earlier. As these awards were given for individual actions, sometimes they created discrimination and envy within units. To avoid that possibility, we decided to recognize collective actions and contributions of units. Such an award, instituted for the first time in the history of the Indian Army, was called the 'COAS' Unit Citation'.

The following units, which performed admirably, were awarded the COAS' Unit Citation in the Kargil war:

- 8 Sikh.
- 13 JAK Rifles.
- 1 Bihar.
- 17 Jat.
- Ladakh Scouts.
- 18 Garhwal Rifles.
- 1/11 Gorkha Rifles.
- 2 Naga.
- 18 Grenadiers.
- 12 JAK Light Infantry.
- 663 Recce and Observation Squadron.
- 141 Field Regiment.
- 2 Rajputana Rifles.
- 666 Recce and Observation Squadron.
- 108 Medium Regiment.
- 197 Field Regiment.

10

The Army Family Support System[1]

What was truly touching was the spirited reply that most soldiers gave when asked how they were. 'Bilkul theek hain!' (absolutely fine!) was the usual reply, and they expressed their fervent desire to get back into action. Sitting by the side of soldiers with grievous gunshot wounds, amputated limbs, multiple splinter injuries and penetrating injuries to the eyes, one admired their courage and overt bravado.

---

[1]This chapter has been contributed by Dr Ranjana Malik, my wife, who was the president, Central Army Wives' Welfare Association, from 1 October 1997 to 30 September 2000.

THE ARMY IN INDIA IS SUPPORTED BY A UNIQUE NON-OFFICIAL welfare organization. This organization is unique because it handles a very large number of soldiers' welfare activities and has the maximum insight into the Indian military sociology. Such an organization probably does not exist anywhere else in the world. It comprises, and is led by, Army wives only. Its structure and welfare activities run alongside the entire command hierarchy of the Army.

The Army Wives' Welfare Association (AWWA), with its closely interlinked centres, embodies a vast network that reaches out to the families of all Army personnel, including the families of the deceased, the wounded and the ailing. It is active in all Army stations across the country. The AWWA played a significant role in maintaining the morale of the soldiers fighting the Kargil war.

AWWA: The Human Face of the Army

An 'Army wife' in India is generally viewed with considerable admiration. The most important quality she possesses is supreme courage in the face of tremendous adversity. She is the brave woman behind the soldier. Over years of being married to a soldier, she learns to understand the daunting challenges of her husband's career. She accepts the demands of his profession stoically and stands by him through his trials and tribulations. As the 'Army wife' goes through long periods of separation, difficulties, despair and anxiety, she learns to mask her feelings while continuing to look after the home, the children and, sometimes, the elderly parents too. To the Indian soldier, it is this constant reassurance and solace from the domestic front that lend intrinsic strength to his grit and determination and spur him on to achieve legendary heroism and display indomitable valour.

The AWWA is the 'human face' of the Army. It is a voluntary – more of a self-help – organization dedicated to the welfare of the families of serving soldiers and of ex-servicemen belonging to the Army. AWWA's motto is 'Caring and Sharing'. It reaches out to all those who need help and exhibits concern towards those in distress. Having gained vast experience over the years, the 'Army wives' have managed to develop a deep commitment to the organization and they have been working with sincerity and compassion to fulfil their goals.

At the apex of the organization is the president, Central AWWA, the wife of the incumbent Chief of Army Staff. The president sets guidelines and provides the impetus at the highest level. Down the family tree come the individual presidents of the regional AWWAs at the levels of the commands, corps, division and area. At the grassroots level, humanitarian activities take place in the family welfare centres in the regiments or the units. Every unit commander's wife, with her team of ladies, maintains close and constant interaction with the families of soldiers under her jurisdiction.

At the apex level, based on past experience and current requirements, various AWWA committees have been formed with volunteers chipping in. These committees take care of a variety of people and institutions. For instance: the widows and families of the deceased soldiers; the wounded and disabled soldiers; the field area families; the Asha schools (for the specially challenged children); the children's hostels; and the centres where women are encouraged to undergo training in a vocation of their choice to make them economically self-reliant. Committees have also been set up for the designing, printing and distribution of Asha greeting cards and the AWWA journal. Some committees deal with production units called 'Parishram' (hard work).

For the AWWA, the war did not begin with Operation Vijay. For decades Army soldiers have been engaged in anti-terrorist and counterinsurgency operations in Jammu and Kashmir and in the northeastern states. The various committees of the association have been playing an active role all the time. When the actual operations began and the number of people needing help increased, the efforts were stepped up without any difficulty. Relief measures did not need to be initiated from scratch; the prime requirements were giving clear-cut directions, prioritizing relief and morale-raising measures, streamlining of diverse activities, and, above all, getting on earnestly with the tasks on hand.

During the war, thousands of messages expressing solidarity from various organizations and individuals (within the country and outside) poured in. The upsurge of feeling for the soldiers was overwhelming. These factors motivated every member of the AWWA to identify a role for herself and work with renewed vigour.

During the war, the president, Central AWWA, met Usha Narayanan, the wife of the president of India, and briefed her about the magnitude of the task at hand and the priorities. Suman Krishan Kant, the wife of the vice-president of India, who was also the president, Mahila Dakshita Samiti, asked her to address heads of a large number of women's organizations to inform them about the herculean tasks that the AWWA had to perform and how they intended to handle the challenges posed by these tasks.

The efforts of the AWWA, at this stage, were focused towards the following activities:

- Caring for the families of the soldiers killed in battle.
- Caring for the seriously wounded and disabled soldiers in various hospitals.
- Caring for the families living in cantonments when the husband has been posted in a field area.
- Reaching out to soldiers in the battlefield.
- Setting up of collection centres for relief material received and for making arrangements for dispatching it to other formations and hospitals.

The president, Central AWWA, wrote letters to a wide range of people, including the command AWWA presidents, the wives of general officers commanding of the corps and divisions, all centre commandants and colonels of the regiments, asking them to establish immediate contact with the families of the martyrs. Since the families of soldiers live in different parts of the country, it finally becomes the responsibility of the AWWA members in the area closest to the soldier's hometown to help the grieving families.

When the bodies of deceased soldiers and officers started arriving at the Palam Airport Technical Area in Delhi, and were solemnly and ceremoniously received, volunteers from the AWWA were present to lend a hand to the shattered young wives, grieving mothers and other distraught family members. The spectacle of the coffins, draped in the national flag, was always poignant: bodies of young men returning to their grieving, but proud, family members. The AWWA president made it a point to go there each time the caskets arrived. The AWWA members visited all the families, shared their sorrow and lent a shoulder for them to weep on. They made it clear that they could be contacted at all hours. It was important for the grieving families to feel that the sacrifice of their loved ones was not in vain and that the nation shall forever remain grateful to them. Such an assurance was of utmost importance and the families had to be assured repeatedly.

War leaves an indelible mark on each family. When the guns cease to boom and national sympathy ebbs, the members of the AWWA have to continue doing their work to wipe the tears of those anguished people who are fighting quietly to come to terms with their loss.

The nature of the interaction with each family and the advice and guidance to be offered have to be based on individual circumstances. The long-term requirements of the families have to be kept in mind and they have to be advised on how to invest their money wisely, for themselves, for their children's future and for acquiring a dwelling unit. In many cases, the elderly tended to squander the compensation money away in setting up commemorative parks, erecting statues and arranging feasts for the community. The young widow had, perforce, to watch helplessly. She was invariably told that all these steps were being taken to perpetuate her husband's memory.

There were a large number of job offers for the young widows from industrial houses. Also, there were vacancies for them in computer courses or in technical and semi-technical courses. It was necessary to ensure, to the extent possible, that the woman in question got a job commensurate with her status and that she could lead a life of respectability. In a society where widow ostracism and widow exploitation have to be guarded against, the community needs to be adequately sensitized.

The Central Government announced substantial compensation packages for the war widows or parents/dependents of unmarried soldiers. The state governments also pitched in to contribute fairly large sums to the affected families.

As the Kargil war was being televised by many channels and as information about the casualties was available on the Internet, the images and the statistics made a powerful impact. Contributions started pouring in from a wide variety of sources. These contributions were sent to the assigned families. As the widows received substantial assistance from the government and non-government organizations (NGOs), often the large sums of money became the source of a tussle between the young widows and their parents-in-law. As per government rules, when a soldier got married, all benefits go to the wife. Such a state of affairs tended to leave the parents, who were often financially dependent on their son, without any monetary support. Consequently, a lot of bitterness and resentment were generated. In view of this distressing experience, modifications in the rules and procedures were suggested to the Army Headquarters. These modifications have now been introduced. The most significant modification stipulates that the compensation, the ex gratia payments and the pension can be divided between the soldier's wife and his parents.

In some cases, young widows of Army officers, who were eligible and showed a keenness to join the armed forces as commissioned officers, were encouraged to go through the selection procedures. After selection through the Union Public Service Commission, five such women underwent training at the Officer's Training Academy at Chennai. One of these young widows had remarked: 'We do not want [our] husbands' pension. We would like to do something for the Army for which our husbands gave their lives.'

Taking Care of the Wounded, Grievously
Injured and Disabled Soldiers

Hundreds of critically injured soldiers poured into the field hospitals in different parts of the war zones. Such soldiers were transferred from the field hospitals to the 92 Base Hospital at Srinagar and from there to the command hospitals at Udhampur (Jammu and Kashmir), Chandimandir (Haryana) and Delhi. While most political and social leaders wanted to be seen visiting these hospitals amidst the glare of TV cameras, scores of AWWA volunteers from the Patients' Welfare Committee worked silently behind the scenes, reaching out to the wounded and sick, reassuring them and consoling them. A gentle hand on a feverish brow, a reassuring pat on the shoulder, or a clasp of a sick one's hand – all this while answering their service- or family-related questions and gently assuaging their feelings – was extremely helpful.

Often, the wounded soldiers arrived in blood-splattered clothing, straight from the grisly battlefield. Naturally, they had no personal clothing or toiletries with them. The AWWA rushed to provide them with fresh undergarments, shaving kits, soaps and shampoos, sleeping suits, airbags, slippers, Thermos flasks, writing material and pens and magazines in regional languages. AWWA 'get-well cards' with personal handwritten messages signed by the president were placed on their bedside tables. As piles of encouraging and supportive letters arrived from all over, the AWWA volunteers read them out to the individual recipients; they also replied to letters on their behalf. Some volunteers took along their cell phones every evening so that the bed-ridden patients could speak to their loved ones.

What was truly touching was the spirited reply that most soldiers gave when asked how they were. '*Bilkul theek hain!*' (absolutely fine!) was the usual reply, and they expressed their fervent desire to get back into action. Sitting by the side of soldiers with grievous gunshot wounds, amputated limbs, multiple splinter injuries and penetrating injuries to the eyes, one admired their courage and overt bravado. Yet, when nobody was around, many of these soldiers would be overcome with fear and uncertainty, wondering what would happen to them once they were out of the Army on account of the serious injuries suffered during the war. The AWWA members could understand their apprehensions. It was so very vital to reassure them repeatedly that they would get the best of medical aid, be it treatment or wheelchairs or artificial limbs. The soldiers were informed that they would be given adequate monetary compensation for their losses.

The AWWA ensured that copies of videotapes on Endolite Limbs were sent to all command hospitals so that the amputees could see for themselves the ease with which people fitted with artificial limbs could function and thus draw inspiration. A large number of private sector companies, NGOs and individuals helped by sending a variety of items such as airconditioners, refrigerators, water coolers, television sets, bedsheets and pillows.

In Delhi, the AWWA organized a piano recital by Brian Silas within the Army Hospital premises one evening, which was attended by all patients, including many on crutches and in wheelchairs. Some of them were bandaged from head to toe, but that did not deter them. All of them sat around the pianist and listened with rapt attention to the soul-stirring and haunting melodies. Finally, one patient limped up to the microphone on the stage. He sang the patriotic number, 'Aye Mere Watan Ke Logon...'[2] in a voice choked with emotion. When he raised his voice to reach the high notes, many people sitting there wept.

Field Area Families

For all the families living in cantonments, whose husbands, fathers or sons were posted in the field, the duration of the Kargil war marked a period fraught with fear, anxiety, tension and stress. Each day's news (on the television, over the radio and in the newspapers) made them aware of the fierce battles that were being fought at very high altitudes. The members of

---

[2]The original song was penned by Pradeep (in the wake of the 1962 Indo–China war) and set to tune by C. Ramchandra. This song apparently brought tears to Prime Minister Jawaharlal Nehru's eyes when he heard Lata Mangeshkar sing it on stage.

the AWWA looking after these families were particularly active. They regularly visited their colonies and met the ladies. They reassured them, by providing the necessary information about their husbands obtained from the Army Information Cell opened at Udhampur, and, most importantly, by letting them know that the AWWA members were with them all the time, praying for the welfare and well-being of their loved ones. These volunteers took special care of the children: they organized coaching classes for them, set up a mobile library and periodically took them out to exhibitions. At frequent intervals, the Central AWWA president addressed the families collectively: not only to keep up their spirits but also to protect them from falling victim to any loose talk or rumour mongering.

Contact with Fighting Soldiers

The president, Central AWWA, wrote a personal note to the commanding officer and also to the subedar major of every unit involved in Operation Vijay. She highlighted the fact that all members of the AWWA were constantly thinking of them and the soldiers of their units and praying for them. The AWWA members wished all of them great success. Every week, 5000 packets of sweets were dispatched to forward areas, courtesy Indian Air Force planes. Each packet also contained a handwritten note of good wishes from a member of the AWWA. Some individual replies received from the soldiers and young officers were overwhelming and touching. Many soldiers were not aware where these sweets had come from. So, many replies were addressed to the manager, AWWA Company. Some others reached the sweet shop that had packed these boxes. From there, the letters were redirected to the Central AWWA office in New Delhi.

While all letters expressed appreciation for the sweets, the thoughts and the sentiments expressed in them made one feel proud of the soldiers.

A young officer, Captain Arjun Sardana from the 141 Field Regiment, writing from a post in Kaksar (located at 15,000 feet) on behalf of his team-mates (three officers and fifty jawans), observed: 'You will appreciate that these little acts of kindness mean a lot to soldiers sitting at isolated posts, cut off from the rest of the world. I must mention here that more than the content, it is the expression of genuine love and concern for the soldiers that has moved us and we shall treasure these as "priceless treasures".'

Another young officer, a major from Ladakh Scouts, Samir Rawat, wrote: 'On behalf of the men with me, I would like to thank you for everything that you have been doing for us and believe me, it's a big morale booster. It heartens us to know that we have your good wishes to throw the enemy out right up to his own backyard.'

Yet another young soldier of 6 Para, Sunil Sharma, noted: 'Sitting on these heights of India, we are guarding the frontiers. The citizens of India should live without fear. If you continue to send sweets like this, we would march not only to Lahore but right up to Islamabad! Pakistan would realize once and for all what the Indian Army is.'

Ravi Kumar Sharma of 13 JAK Rifles (from Tololing) wrote on behalf of all men of D Company expressing their gratitude.

Ravinder Singh from 21 Para (Special Force) described the difficult, arduous climb, even as they were facing heavily armed enemy troops, when they lost a fellow-soldier. As they sat dejected and demoralized, these sweet packets along with food packs were delivered to them. This gesture made them realize how much their countrymen cared for them and were cheering them. He added that, with renewed vigour and determination, they mounted an attack the very next day and achieved success. They had avenged their colleague's death.

In reply to such letters, the president wrote (in Hindi) to each one of them, telling them what the AWWA stood for; she also pointed out that all its members prayed for their success.

The AWWA members met hundreds of ordinary people each day. The response of such people coming to express their solidarity with our soldiers was gratifying. A young woman donated to the AWWA the money that her parents were planning to spend on her twenty-first birthday. Children from a primary school came to hand over their pocket money. An inspector general of police, Jija Madhavan Hari Singh, held an exhibition of her paintings and donated the proceeds to the Army Central

Welfare Fund. Two greeting cards and a sum of two rupees were received from Namrata Ramakrishnan from Indore along with a letter, which read as follows: 'My children are deeply moved by what our soldiers have done for our country. They have lost their father in an accident when they were very little and I am trying my best to inculcate good values in them. I am sure you will understand that they don't know the value of money as yet and hence the small amount enclosed is from their piggy banks. I will be very grateful if these cards reach the Kargil area and the children will be thrilled if a soldier acknowledges receipt of their cards along with their small contribution.' The letter was sent to the troops through Headquarters 8 Mountain Division and their acknowledgements were sent to her.

The president appeared on various TV channels and participated in several radio programmes essentially to make the people at large aware of the humanitarian role played by the AWWA. She also brought into focus all the help that could be provided to the soldiers through this association. Through write-ups in national dailies and news magazines, the AWWA kept reminding people of the sacrifices made by the soldiers and the need to help them to the extent possible.

As the president tellingly put it: 'It takes so little to make people happy – just a touch if we know how to give it, just a word aptly spoken, just a moment to help those incoherent with pain, just a smile to let people know that they are important.'

With a tenacity of purpose and a philosophy rooted in compassion, the AWWA continues (and will continue) to support the regular Army not only in carrying out its diverse activities but also in achieving its goals.

Handing over bodies of Pakistani soldiers to the Pakistan Army.

Victory! Soldiers holding aloft the Indian tricolour atop one of the recaptured peaks.

Indian soldiers in a triumphant mood.

The author along with the Air Force chief, Air Chief Marshal Anil Tipnis, among others, in a celebratory frame of mind.

The three chiefs together: the author, Air Chief Marshal
Anil Tipnis and Admiral Sushil Kumar.

11

Partners in Victory

...we three service chiefs...were regularly invited to participate in the proceedings of the Cabinet Committee on Security. This step provided a refreshing change in the decision-making processes, both at the political level as well as at the services' level, since the political hierarchy could get to know the views of the armed forces first-hand and, simultaneously, the three chiefs could obtain clear-cut political directives directly from the prime minister.

IN SHARP CONTRAST TO THE PLANNING AND CONDUCT OF operations by the Pakistan Army, which did not consult the other two services (the Air Force and the Navy), not to mention many senior officers within its own ranks, our groundwork and the execution of Operation Vijay were done on an institutionalized basis. Barring an odd incident, there was complete synergy and unity of effort among the three services.

After I returned from abroad and reviewed the operational situation, the three service chiefs were closely involved in the activities of the Chiefs of Staff Committee (COSC). The chiefs were regularly invited to participate in the proceedings of the Cabinet Committee on Security (CCS). This step provided a refreshing change in the decision-making processes, both at the political level as well as at the services' level, since the political hierarchy could get to know the views of the armed forces first-hand and, simultaneously, the three chiefs could obtain clear-cut political directives directly from the prime minister.

Besides the aforementioned, regular briefings were carried out on a daily basis in the Military Operations Room of the Army Headquarters, which were attended by the appropriate representatives of all the three services. Similar briefings also were carried out in the Military Intelligence Directorate, again on an almost daily basis.

The Indian Air Force

The role of the Indian Air Force in the Kargil conflict – called Operation Safed Sagar – was quite different from its conventional role in a war. As the magnitude of the intrusion became clear, it became necessary to employ air power for various purposes:

to support ground operations; to carry out reconnaissance; to interdict enemy supply routes and logistic bases; to destroy enemy footholds; and, most importantly, to establish strategic and tactical superiority over the enemy. The use of air power also ensured a secure air space for the Army and Air Force helicopter operations.

Besides influencing the war at a strategic level, the Air Force carried out its operational missions as effectively as possible, given the terrain configuration and the available technical capabilities.

The Air Headquarters had ordered the Western Air Command to 'adopt precautionary measures' before 25 May 1999. The Air Force joined in the offensive actions against the Pak intruders after political clearance was given on 24 May with the proviso that the LoC should not be crossed. Once the Air Force (and the Navy) entered the fray, our firm resolve to evict the intruders became very clear to Pakistan. The rest of the world began to take notice that the intrusion was not a routine Indo–Pak border skirmish in Jammu and Kashmir.

In the initial stages, i.e., up to 25 May, the IAF provided helicopter support to airlift troops in Ladakh. Some aircraft and helicopters were deployed in Jammu and Kashmir and a slew of armed helicopters fitted with armour plating, a defensive countermeasure dispensing system and a global positioning system went in for training at the Tosha Maidan firing ranges along the Pir Panjal mountains in the Kashmir Valley. In the second and third weeks of May 1999, the request from the Army for sending in Mi-35 attack helicopters or Mi-17 armed helicopters against the intruders could not be complied with. The Mi-35 attack helicopters were not employed due to the terrain elevation. The request for Mi-17 armed helicopters was not accepted by the Air Force due to 'want of political clearance'.[1]

---

[1]The need for political clearance for the employment of Mi-17 armed helicopters against terrorists and Pakistani Army personnel within Indian territory is a debatable point. Personally, I feel that in view of operational urgencies and the need to take early decisions, such a requirement can be discussed and cleared at the highest levels in the Command or Service Headquarters. There is no need for political clearance.

(cont.)

A Canberra photoreconnaissance mission[2] was undertaken on 21 May. The aircraft was hit by a shoulder-fired surface-to-air missile in the Batalik sector but managed to return to base safely.

In order to support the Army operation on the ground, the Air Force engaged the intruders with bombs, rockets and other specialized ammunition in order to soften their locations. The Air Force also focused on the interdiction of supply lines of the intruders to choke them logistically. The hostile terrain and the targets, often dug into mountain slopes, made visual spotting and engaging of targets very difficult. Forward air controllers (Air Force officers who are trained to engage targets close by from our ground positions or from a helicopter flying near the target) were not available in sufficient numbers to guide the fighter aircraft to these targets. Besides, such aircraft had to remain far away from the target to ensure their own safety from being hit by surface-to-air missiles.

As already narrated in Chapter 6, on 27 May, we lost two MiG fighter aircraft: one due to engine flameout and the other due to its being hit by enemy surface-to-air missile when it flew very low to ascertain the location of the pilot and wreckage of the former aircraft.

On 28 May, we suffered another setback. An Mi-17 armed helicopter was lost while attacking the Tololing feature in the Dras sector, well within our territory. This helicopter, not equipped with a countermeasures dispensing system, had completed its mission and was turning back, when an enemy surface-to-air missile brought it down.

After these losses, the Air Force generally kept out of the range of Pakistani missiles, fired at them from a standoff distance,

---

In most other countries, such helicopters are a part of the Army establishment and inventory. In India, these are Army assets, flown and maintained by the Air Force. The 'armed' or 'attack' helicopters would be far more effective in ground support operations if they are made part of the Army establishment.

[2] The use of the Canberra, a 1950s' vintage, slow-speed aircraft, is a reflection on our poor capability for carrying out surveillance or photoreconnaissance missions in the mountains.

and thus attempted to neutralize the enemy's air defences. The armed helicopters were pulled out of offensive action.

Initially, apart from rocket attacks, the fighter aircraft dropped heavy bombs (250–1000 kg) in dive attacks. The pilots had to cater for variable wind speed and pressure density conditions at high altitudes while engaging targets with free fall bombs. Even a very small human error of judgement or a technical error could lead to the bomb missing the target by miles. ('Missed by a mile' is literally true in the mountains!) Later, the global positioning system for weapon delivery from high and medium altitudes was innovated. After that, the attacks were carried out from outside the enemy air defence weapons' range and from above the cloud base, if any. In this area, the Mirage 2000 proved to be the most successful fighter plane. It was able to optimally use its sophisticated navigational attack system. After 6 June, this aircraft was loaded with the laser-guided bombs (delivered through the paveway guidance system) and achieved good results.

In the last week of June, some incidents were reported by the troops on the ground wherein the heavy bombs that were dropped without any navigational aid fell far away from the targets and dangerously close to our own troops. As these incidents caused some concern at the lower level, the air chief and I decided to visit our lower formations/wings/squadrons in the Kashmir Valley and the Kargil sector and speak to the troops jointly. The visit was extremely helpful in confidence building and in motivating them to accomplish their mission.

Nearly fifty Air Force and Army radars were deployed in the control and reporting centres on the western front. A number of mobile observation flights were located along the LoC and the Indo–Pak border. Transport aircraft were utilized to induct a large number of units and formation headquarters apart from meeting logistic requirements. In all, the Air Force notched up 1050 strike and escort sorties (550 strike missions and 500 escort missions), 483 air defence sorties, 152 reconnaissance sorties and 24 miscellaneous sorties. They also flew 2185 helicopter sorties, mostly for the evacuation of casualties and other logistic purposes.

The Air Force had to face serious limitations due to the mountainous high-altitude terrain, the narrow flying corridors, the lack of effective ordnance delivery systems and the stipulation not to cross the LoC even when engaging important targets very close to it. *No targets were engaged by the Air Force across the LoC.* However, it is to the great credit and dedication of the Indian Air Force that its personnel continued to experiment and evolve new techniques throughout the operations to overcome these handicaps.

The Air Force's efforts at gathering electronic intelligence and at carrying out photoreconnaissance could not provide any worthwhile inputs. Its fighter and photoreconnaissance missions were ineffective, as these aircraft were not adequately equipped to overcome adverse weather conditions, particularly when there was a low cloud base. This was a major handicap during the war.

Air Chief Marshal A.Y. Tipnis	Air Headquarters
PVSM, AVSM, VM, ADC	New Delhi 110011
Air HQ/15042/CAS	07 July 99

My Dear Chief

1. The whole Nation has been witness to the courage, tenacity and single-minded devotion of our Army Officers and Jawans at Kargil. All personnel of the Air Force join me in applauding the indomitable spirit of our Army. We are happy that we were able to contribute to the joint effort.

2. We salute our brave comrades-in-arms of the Indian Army who have fought so valiantly and set a shining example of self-sacrifice in the cause of our Motherland.

    With warm regards,

                                      Anil Tipnis

General V.P. Malik,   Army Headquarters
PVSM, AVSM, ADC   New Delhi 110011
A/00043/1/COAS   10 July 99

Dear Tippi

1. Thank you for your DO letter No. Air HQ/15042/CAS
    dated 07 July 99 conveying compliments on the
    performance of Army in **OP VIJAY**.
2. As you are aware, these successes could not have been
    achieved but for our Air Force having jointly performed
    with equal valour and commitment in complete
    coordination. The success in the operations is therefore
    attributable to our synergized joint effort.
3. On behalf of all ranks of the Army, I reciprocate the
    appreciation and express gratitude to you and all ranks
    of the Air Force for their important part in OP VIJAY.

With warm regards,

                                                Yours sincerely,
                                                    Ved Malik

Air Chief Marshal A.Y. Tipnis, PVSM, AVSM, VM, ADC
Chief of the Air Staff,
Air Headquarters,
New Delhi 110011

The Kargil war highlighted the importance of close air support
and ground support missions in high-altitude mountainous terrain
and also underlined the fact that the Air Force needs to be
adequately equipped for such missions.

Other significant lessons learnt from Operation Safed Sagar
were as follows: the need for improved tactical and strategic
intelligence-gathering mechanism and wherewithal; better
dissemination of intelligence; and the necessity for closer, real-
time liaison between the Army and the Air Force at all levels.
The conflict also highlighted the operational urgency for handing
over armed and attack helicopter assets to the Army.

The Indian Navy

The Indian Navy gave the codename 'Operation Talwar' to its operations during the Kargil war. The Navy's contribution at the strategic level, though much less visible as compared to that of the other two services, was an important factor that helped us in winning the war.

The Naval Headquarters took notice of night landing facilities being provided at the Pasni (a town situated on the Arabian Sea coast in the Sind province of Pakistan) airfield in the third week of May 1999; the first indications of 'enhanced activities' on the maritime front. Keeping in mind the experience of the 1965 conflict, when the Pak Navy had launched a surprise attack on Dwarka (situated in coastal Gujarat),[3] instructions were issued to remain alert and to enhance security measures. On 21 May 1999, the Western Naval Command deployed INS *Taragiri* on barrier patrol off Dwarka. Two Dornier aircraft of the Information Warfare Squadron commenced electronic support measures probes just outside the Pakistani air defence identification zone. Wartime routine was introduced at all levels. At this stage, the aim was not to be surprised at sea. A specialized group of officers were tasked to address the requirements of operational analysis, assessment and planning.

After the CCS meeting on 24 May, the assistant chief of Naval Staff (Operations) and his subordinate staff began to attend daily briefings in the Military Operations Room of the Army Headquarters. In the light of the decisions taken in the CCS and COSC meetings, the Navy decided to supplement the Western Fleet with selected units from the Eastern Fleet. The loading of certain Western Fleet units commenced on 25 May, and a major combat force was deployed off the Saurashtra (in Gujarat) coast for sounding an early warning and also for deterrent purposes.

Meanwhile, Pakistan's patterns of oil imports – including the type, the extent and the origin – were analysed from the available data, essentially for planning tanker interdiction, should the situation so warrant. When this information reached the Pakistan

---

[3]The Pakistan Navy continues to celebrate the day (7 December) as 'Pakistan Navy Day'.

Navy, it went into a red-alert mode and its warships began escorting the oil tankers.

The deinduction of 108 Mountain Brigade from Andaman and Nicobar Islands was used by the Army and Naval Headquarters to project it as 'preparation and training for an amphibious operation', thus opening a new dimension to the maritime activity already in progress in the Arabian Sea near the Pakistani coastline.

The Navy also helped out the Army in many ways. For instance, it provided specialized equipment and survey parties to the Army to enable the latter to locate enemy gun positions on the international border and the LoC. The activities of the Navy's newly inducted Information Warfare Dornier Squadron from Naliya (Gujarat) was extended for executing surveillance and electronic intelligence tasks along the western land border to locate enemy air defence radars. The success of this mission resulted in an institutionalized framework for conducting joint operations.

Priority Message
FROM NAVAL HEADQUARTERS

TO: ARMY HEADQUARTERS &
AIR HEADQUARTERS

PERSONAL FOR: COAS & CAS

1. WITH ADMIRATION AND PRIDE ALL RANKS OF THE INDIAN NAVY SALUTE OUR INDIAN ARMY AND AIR FORCE FOR THEIR STUNNING FEATS AT KARGIL UNDER DAUNTING CONDITIONS. AND NOW THE CAPPING SUCCESS AT TIGER HILL SAYS IT ALL.

2. AS WE GUARD THE SEAWARD FLANK THE INDIAN NAVY FEELS INSPIRED AND MOTIVATED BY THE INTREPID ACTION OF OUR COMRADES IN THE ARMY AND AIR FORCE.

GOOD HUNTING. GOD BLESS.

SUSHIL KUMAR
ADMIRAL
05 JULY 99

General V.P. Malik   ARMY HEADQUARTERS
PVSM, AVSM, ADC   NEW DELHi 110011
A/00043/1/COAS   10 July 99

Dear Sushil,
1. Thank you for your warm appreciation of the performance of our officers and jawans at Kargil. Your message gives us the encouragement to carry on our endeavour until each and every intruder is evicted.
2. Your 'warning' to Pak Navy has been an extremely useful contribution. The enemy is now fully aware that he faces the synergized effort of the Indian Armed Forces.
   With warm regards,

Ved Malik

Admiral Sushil Kumar, PVSM, UYSM, AVSM, NM, ADC
Chief of the Naval Staff
Naval Headquarters
New Delhi 10011

12

The Pakistani Withdrawal

...a war is fought to achieve a given political aim. It that aim has been achieved, it makes little sense to continue with the war.

Who Was Putting Pressure on Whom?

WHILE OUR MILITARY OPERATIONS WERE GATHERING momentum and achieving success in recapturing important positions occupied by the enemy every few days, we learnt from the Cabinet Committee on Security (CCS) meetings that the US Administration was now in close touch with the Governments of Pakistan and India. In this context, US President Bill Clinton spoke to Prime Ministers Atal Behari Vajpayee and Nawaz Sharif on several occasions, particularly after mid-June 1999.

On 24–25 June 1999, General Anthony Zinni, commander-in-chief of the US Central Command, who was considered a close friend of Pervez Musharraf, visited Islamabad on instructions from the White House. He met Pakistani political and military leaders and conveyed a rather blunt message: 'If you don't pull back, you're going to bring war and nuclear annihilation down on your country. That's going to be very bad news for everybody.' Zinni, in his book, has added: 'Nobody actually quarreled with this rationale. The problem with the Pakistani leadership was the apparent national loss of face. Backing down and pulling back to the Line of Control looked like political suicide. We needed to come up with a face-saving way of [sic] this mess. What we (the USA) were able to offer was, a meeting with President Clinton, which would end the isolation that had long been the state of affairs between our two countries, but would announce the meeting only after a withdrawal of forces. That got Musharraf's attention: and he encouraged Prime Minister Sharif to hear me out.'[1] (These

---

[1]Tom Clancy and Anthony Zinni, *Battle Ready* (Berkley Books, New York, 2004, pp. 346–48.)

extracts are from General Zinni's book. During the course of the war, we did not have any intelligence inputs on his meetings in Islamabad.)

After the futile visit to India by Pakistan's Foreign Minister Sartaj Aziz, the Pakistani authorities were now looking for a honourable way to end the battle. According to Nawaz Sharif, he 'seriously wanted the war to come to an end'. Sharif has also stated that Pervez Musharraf asked him: 'Why don't you meet Clinton? Why don't you ask him to bring about a settlement?'[2]

Bruce Reidel, special assistant to President Clinton and senior director for Northeast Asia and South Asia affairs, has written that in the last days of June 1999, Prime Minister Nawaz Sharif began to send out requests to see President Clinton directly to plead his case. On 2 July 1999, Sharif spoke to President Clinton and appealed for American intervention immediately to stop the fighting and to resolve the Kashmir issue. The next day, Nawaz Sharif became more desperate and told President Clinton that he was ready to come immediately to Washington. For his part, President Clinton emphasized that he 'had to come to the United States knowing two things: first, he had to agree to withdraw his troops back across the Line of Control; and second, I [President Clinton] would not agree to intervene in the Kashmir dispute, especially under circumstances that appeared to reward Pakistan's wrongful incursion.'[3] In the face of such a stand taken by the US president, Nawaz Sharif told him that he wanted desperately to find a solution that would allow Pakistan to withdraw with some cover. Sharif informed Clinton that he would be in Washington on 4 July 1999.

Pervez Musharraf was a party to the decisions taken at the meeting of the Pakistan Defence Committee of the Cabinet on the eve of Nawaz Sharif's departure for Washington. Musharraf saw him off at the airport on 3 July.[4]

---

[2]'Nawaz Sharif Speaks Out', interview with Raj Chengappa, *India Today*, 26 July 2004.

[3]See Bill Clinton, *My Life* (Alfred A. Knopf, New York, 2004, p. 865).

[4]According to the Pakistani journalist Ayaz Amir, Nawaz Sharif went to the USA 'to pull the Army's chestnuts out of the fire'. 'Retrieving the Lost Years', *Dawn* (Pakistan), 5 December 2003.

There should be no doubt in anybody's mind that surprised by the intensity of our attacks and after seeing the writing on the wall as far as military operations were concerned, Pakistan was now seeking a face-saving device. Moreover, it was internationally isolated. During this period, President Clinton spoke to Prime Minister Vajpayee and tried to persuade him to visit Washington at the same time as Nawaz Sharif. Vajpayee categorically refused to do so.

The 'desperate' meeting that the Pakistani prime minister sought was fixed for 4 July 1999, despite that day being a holiday (it was the American Independence Day). As mentioned earlier, twenty hours before Nawaz Sharif could meet President Clinton, we had recaptured Tiger Hill. For all practical purposes, this development meant that the tide had turned inexorably in our favour.

Talks were held between President Clinton and Prime Minister Nawaz Sharif at Blair House, Washington D.C., and their outcome was in the form of a joint statement. The relevant excerpts are as follows:

- President Clinton and Prime Minister Nawaz Sharif share the view that the current fighting in the Kargil region of Kashmir is dangerous and contains the seeds of a wider conflict.
- They also agree that it was vital for peace in South Asia that the Line of Control in Kashmir be respected by both parties, in accordance with their 1972 Shimla Agreement.
- It was agreed between the President and the Prime Minister that concrete steps will be taken for the restoration of the Line of Control in accordance with the Shimla Agreement.
- The President urged immediate cessation of the hostilities once these steps are taken. The Prime Minister and the President agreed that the bilateral dialogue begun in Lahore in February [1999] provides the best forum for resolving all issues dividing India and Pakistan, including Kashmir.
- The President said he would take personal interest in encouraging expeditious resumption and intensification of those bilateral efforts once the sanctity of the Line of Control has been fully restored.

- The President reaffirmed his intent to pay an early visit to South Asia.

In his monograph,[5] Bruce Riedel has highlighted three aspects of the Clinton–Sharif meeting: (a) The US insistence that Pakistan must withdraw its troops to its side of the LoC; (b) why was [the] Pakistan Army making preparations to develop strategic weapons for possible use and thus 'messing with nuclear war'; and (c) Nawaz Sharif's repeated pleading for direct US intervention in the Jammu and Kashmir dispute. (This is further evidence of why he had agreed to the military launching operations in Kargil.)

Again, according to Bruce Reidel, on 3 July, as the US officials prepared to play host to Nawaz Sharif, they received 'disturbing evidence that Pakistanis were preparing their nuclear arsenal for possible deployment'.[6]

The next day, the meeting started with Nawaz Sharif asking for the United States' direct intervention in the Jammu and Kashmir dispute and fixing a timetable for that purpose. He showed Clinton a non-paper (i.e., a draft) wherein 'the two Prime Ministers (Vajpayee and Sharif) would agree to restore the sanctity of the LoC and resume the Lahore process. Nawaz Sharif said that at first India had agreed to this non-paper but then changed its mind.'[7]

President Clinton insisted on the restoration of the sanctity of the LoC. He also insisted that the Pakistani forces withdraw to the LoC and that Pakistan should follow the Lahore Declaration. When Nawaz Sharif attempted to get round the suggestion on the withdrawal of Pakistani forces to the LoC, the US president confronted him with the latest information given to him by his staff. Clinton asked Sharif if he knew that the Pakistani Army

---

[5]Bruce Reidel, 'American Diplomacy and the Kargil Summit at Blair House', Policy Paper Series 2002, Center for Advanced Study of India, University of Pennsylvania.

[6]Ibid.

[7]Nawaz Sharif was most probably referring to the Pakistani four-point formula, which had been rejected by Vajpayee in June 1999, after we captured Tololing. See Chapter 7.

was preparing its nuclear arsenal for possible use and a nuclear war between India and Pakistan appeared imminent. Nawaz Sharif, as per Bruce Reidel, denied that he had ordered their missile force or nuclear weapons to be readied. He then agreed to sign the joint statement. President Clinton next called Prime Minister Vajpayee to preview the joint statement before he and Nawaz Sharif signed it.[8] Clinton's impression after the meeting was that 'Sharif had come in order to use pressure from the United States to provide himself cover for ordering his military to diffuse the conflict'.[9]

During the meeting, President Clinton also warned Nawaz Sharif that unless he did more to help the United States in apprehending or killing Al Qaeda leaders, he would have to announce that Pakistan was in effect supporting terrorism in Afghanistan. Nawaz Sharif then agreed to the United States' proposal to train sixty Pakistani commandos, who would go into Afghanistan and get hold of Osama bin Laden; something that Pakistan was not agreeing to earlier.[10]

How Serious Was the Nuclear Threat?

There is no doubt that the Pakistani political leaders, including Nawaz Sharif himself and the foreign secretary, Shamshad Ahmad, had been making provocative public statements about using nuclear weapons. We in India never took them seriously. India's national security advisor, Brajesh Mishra, had conveyed our contempt for such rhetoric through an interview given by him to the media. Other than one or two intelligence reports indicating that Pakistan Army personnel were noticed cleaning up artillery deployment areas and missile launch sites at the Tilla Ranges, we had no specific reports that the Pakistan Army was readying its nuclear arsenal. Moreover, till then, Pakistan had not created any nuclear command and control structure for utilizing strategic weapons and for decision-making in this sphere. At least, we had no such information. However, in view of the

---

[8]Bruce Reidel, op. cit.
[9]Bill Clinton, op. cit.
[10]Ibid.

intelligence reports about the Tilla Ranges being readied for possible launching of missiles and repeated statements being made by their political leaders and non-military senior officials, we considered it prudent to take some protective measures. Accordingly, some of our missile assets were dispersed and relocated.

On 5 July, Brajesh Mishra informed the CCS about the possible test firing of another Agni 2 missile by India. This decision had probably been taken jointly among the national security advisor, the scientific advisor to the defence minister and the head of Defence Research and Development Organization (DRDO) and the prime minister. We were being informed about the tentative date. I reminded the prime minister that missile testing at this time did not gel with the government policy of 'strategic restraint', particularly when the armed forces had been pointedly directed not to escalate the conflict situation. After some discussion had taken place, the proposal to carry out the test was dropped. (I am usually in favour of such tests but am against the use of 'missile rattling' for scoring political points.)

Developments on the Ground

Events over the next few days moved rapidly. On 6 July 1999, when the Directors General Military Operations (DsGMO) of India and Pakistan held their scheduled telephonic conversation, our DGMO, Lieutenant General Nirmal Chander Vij, conveyed to his counterpart that we were now in possession of several Pakistan Army official documents and personal letters belonging to their officers, all of which revealed Pakistani duplicity. He also told him that there were so many dead bodies of Pakistani soldiers on the Indian side that it had become difficult to identify them individually. He then gave him the names of various units that had been detected so far. The Pakistani DGMO appeared quite rattled. He ended the conversation abruptly, saying that he had nothing to discuss.

I visited Kargil and other forward areas to assess the operational situation. We were now in full control. The tide was running in our favour and was in full flow. On my return to New Delhi, during the course of a telephone interview to Shekhar Gupta, editor-in-chief, *The Indian Express*, I affirmed that we had made substantial and decisive gains. I also informed him that the results were now coming in fast, the mood everywhere was upbeat and the morale was high. By this time, 90 per cent of the intrusion in the Batalik and Dras sectors had been cleared. After recapturing Tiger Hill and Point 4875, 79 Mountain Brigade and 50 Para Brigade were poised to undertake major operations to clear the rest of the Mashkoh Valley sector and sever the supply route of the intruders originating from a place called Gultari.

On 8 July, Prime Minister Vajpayee called me to his residence. Only he and Brajesh Mishra were present in the room where we met. The prime minister informed me that Pakistan had agreed to withdraw its forces to the LoC. He wanted to know my reaction. My immediate reaction was that the Indian Army would not accept such a withdrawal. The armed forces had suffered many casualties. My question was: Now that events were swinging in our favour, why should we let the enemy escape? In any case, I told the prime minister and Brajesh Mishra that I needed to consult my colleagues in the Chiefs of Staff Committee (COSC) and also formation commanders on this issue.[11]

A few hours later, there was another call asking me to come over to the prime minister's residence. This time he asked me how much more time would we take to clear the rest of the Pakistani intrusion. I replied that it might take two to three weeks; hopefully two weeks to finish the work. But I needed to keep one week as reserve. He then mentioned that we had already suffered heavy casualties, and asked whether we would suffer any more. I responded by pointing out that we were fighting a war initiated by someone else and that our effort always was and would be to minimize the casualties. I, however, observed that some more casualties could not be ruled out during these operations. Before I left the prime minister's residence this time, he also told me that, as per the constitutional requirement, the country had to go through the elections for the Parliament

---

[11]Apparently, either the two prime ministers, or their interlocutors, had already discussed the Pakistan Army withdrawal issue before I was called to give the military reaction.

within a specified period. He stated that time was running out and this requirement had to be fulfilled very soon.

Meanwhile, my colleagues in the COSC, the Vice Chief of Army Staff (VCOAS) and the DGMO had been requested to attend an urgently convened meeting at my house. We discussed the various crucial issues in detail (during the meeting, the DGMO kept speaking to the Northern Army commander on the phone). Several questions were raised: Should we accept the withdrawal of the Pakistani forces? If we did so, what would be the political and military implications? What should be the methodology adopted to ensure such a withdrawal? How would the Pakistani forces conduct themselves during this exercise? What contingencies could we face during this period and how should we prepare ourselves to meet them?

There was a perceptible shift in the political situation now. We could carry on with the eviction operations, but there was little chance of our being permitted to cross the LoC. There could be political and military implications in carrying on with the operations even up to the LoC. We could lose international and domestic support that we had been able to muster so far. One has to bear in mind that a war is fought to achieve a given political aim. If that aim has been achieved, it makes little sense to continue with the war. However, we did have serious doubts whether the Pakistani forces would actually withdraw. They simply could not be trusted. Our main apprehension was that Pakistani troops could occupy some important features close to the LoC, where logistic support would be easier to obtain, and indulge in extensive mine laying on their withdrawal routes.

After lengthy discussions among and within the services, we agreed that we could accept a phased withdrawal of the Pakistani forces from sectors to be *prioritized by us*. This was because we felt that the Pakistan Army and its leadership could not be wholly trusted; their sincerity needed to be tested. In the first phase, we decided that a ceasefire along the entire front should not be agreed to; it should be restricted to the sector in which the withdrawal was to be carried out. We also emphasized that a time frame for withdrawal should be laid down so that the Pakistani forces would not be able to lay mines or booby traps during withdrawal.

Keeping all these points in mind, I once again went to the prime minister's residence at night and conveyed our recommendations as well as reservations. The prime minister accepted these views. He instructed that all our recommendations and reservations should be built into the proposed withdrawal plans for the Pakistani forces and conveyed to the Pakistani DGMO.

In all these conversations with the prime minister, there was never any hint of political pressure. They were simply consultations between the highest political authority and the chairman, COSC, as it should always be.

The Pakistani Withdrawal

The next day (9 July) evening, the Pakistani DGMO called our DGMO, Nirmal Chander Vij, for holding an unscheduled conversation. Apparently, the Pakistani DGMO had received instructions from his prime minister and the Pakistan Army chief for the withdrawal of forces. Consequently, he wanted to work out the details. He set the ball rolling by stating that as the political top brass on both sides had shown the good sense to de-escalate the conflict, his leaders had persuaded the Mujahideen to honour their commitment. Vij asked him how had they suddenly managed to gain so much control over the Mujahideen who had been operating in Jammu and Kashmir for so many years. Vij gave his counterpart the identities of two Pakistani Army officers who had been killed in the Dras sector and told him to give up this Mujahideen façade, which, he pointed out, could no longer convince anyone.

The two of them then worked out the nitty-gritty of the withdrawal plan for the Pakistani troops, starting with the Kaksar sector on 11–12 July 1999. The Pakistani DGMO suggested a general ceasefire during the withdrawal of Pakistani troops, which was rejected by Vij. Finally, they agreed that the ceasefire would be applicable only to the Kaksar sector and that the details for withdrawal from the remaining sectors would be formulated later.

The CCS was kept informed about this telephone conversation and the new developments.

On 10 July, in the CCS meeting, we were informed that Pakistan was agreeable to holding a one-on-one meeting of the DsGMO to work out details for the withdrawal of Pakistani forces from the rest of the Kargil sector. I welcomed the idea but declined to send our DGMO to Pakistan for such a meeting. It was agreed later that the meeting would be held on our soil, in the Border Security Force (BSF) premises at Attari near Amritsar. I briefed the DGMO at the Army Headquarters and took him along to the next CCS meeting (11 July forenoon) for a political briefing before he left to meet his Pakistani counterpart at 1330 hours at Attari.

The DsGMO reviewed the progress of the Pakistani withdrawal from the Kaksar sector and then agreed to follow a procedure on the following lines:

- In the affected sectors of withdrawal, Pakistani troops must go well across the LoC.
- The schedule will be: Mashkoh – 12–15 July, Dras – 14–15 July, Batalik (up to Turtuk) – 15–16 July.
- After the stipulated time, our (Indian) troops would move from south to north and anyone left on our side will be cleared out, the way we deem suitable.
- No new post shall be established within 1000 metres of the LoC on either side in the gaps between the Indian and Pakistani posts that were held before and during the war.

The Pakistani DGMO was specifically told to avoid taking recourse to misinterpreting the alignment of the LoC, as such a step would not be accepted.

The Indian DGMO made it clear that there was no ambiguity with respect to the delineated LoC. He also highlighted the fact that we were dealing with the regular Pakistani Army and not Mujahideen. He asserted that any attempt to retain or set up a new post on the LoC to gain tactical advantage shall be attacked and cleared by us and also that Pakistan would be solely responsible for creating such a situation.

The Pakistani DGMO raised the question of missing personnel and dead bodies. He was informed that the dead bodies of their soldiers had been buried locally with full military honours and religious rites and that, wherever possible, their photographs had been taken. The Indian DGMO stated that, if desired by the Pakistanis, we could send these photographs and also papers and other items found on the bodies to them. The details of the prisoners of war in our custody at that time were conveyed to the Pakistani DGMO, who, in turn, confirmed that there were no Indian prisoners in his custody.

Next, the Pakistani DGMO assured our DGMO that his side would not make any attempt to leave behind any mines and booby traps. He specifically requested that we should keep in check our 'very aggressive media' and those official spokespersons making belligerent statements.

At the end of the discussion, our DGMO displayed the marked Pakistani maps and several original identification documents of Pakistani soldiers. The Pakistani DGMO cursed the '*ahmak*' (fool) who had marked interformation boundaries on his map. A folder containing the incriminating material was given to his staff officer.

During the meeting, Pakistani DGMO wanted both armies to consider de-escalation in other areas as well. What was the purpose of deployment during the monsoons, he queried.[12]

On the ground, the withdrawal of Pakistani troops from different sectors commenced smoothly. The DsGMO spoke to each other frequently, sometimes more than once a day. The Pakistani DGMO sought an extra day for pulling out from the Mashkoh sector. This request was granted. At the end of the accepted time frame, we found that, while withdrawing, the Pakistanis had laid mines and booby traps indiscriminately, particularly in the Mashkoh sector. Also, despite the 1000-metre distance agreement, they remained deployed in several pockets. Some of these pockets were vacated after we reported them to the Pakistani DGMO. But three pockets close to the LoC *on our side* – Zulu Spur in the Mashkoh sector, Ring Contour in the Dras sector and Area Saddle in the Batalik sector – remained occupied by the Pakistanis. The details of these three intrusions

---

[12]According to Lieutenant General Vij, throughout the meeting, the Pakistani DGMO appeared tense and not his normal self.

were faxed to the Pakistani DGMO, but to no avail. One possible reason could be that they were still hoping to link these intrusions to the Siachen sector.

At the request of the Pakistani DGMO, we arranged to return the dead bodies of two Pakistani Army officers, including Captain Karnal Sher Khan, who was subsequently awarded the Nishan-e-Haidar, the highest gallantry award in Pakistan.[13]

The Announcement of Elections

While these activities were going on during the agreed ceasefire period and there was a lull in the fighting, India's chief election commissioner (CEC), M.S. Gill, promulgated orders on 11 July 1999 for holding the next parliamentary elections. That announcement changed the mood of the CCS members all of a sudden. From then onwards, I found them and the secretaries of various ministries spending more time discussing election scenarios and arrangements rather than the war situation. For the armed forces, the war was not yet over because the intrusions had not been fully vacated. Our troops were still engaged with Pakistani troops at several places. In the vacated areas, they were busy locating and lifting mines and booby traps put in place by the enemy. I strongly felt that the military implications of the announcement of the election schedule for the war situation should have been considered and the COSC consulted. I mentioned this aspect to the prime minister, who pointed out that the CEC was an autonomous authority. There was nothing that we could do now except to log a lesson for the future. I, therefore, conveyed my views to M.S. Gill over the phone the very next day.

Meanwhile, the withdrawal of the Pakistani troops, which was extended by one day after 16 July, came under dispute. The Pakistanis claimed that they had pulled out completely and had gone over to their side of the LoC. However, according to the information available to us, they were still occupying three features on our side, close to the LoC. Despite a discussion over

---

[13]Company Havildar Major (CHM) Lalak Jan Dohet also received the Nishan-e-Haidar for gallantry in the Kargil operations.

the hotline between the DsGMO of India and Pakistan, the stalemate over this issue continued.

On 21 July, I briefed the prime minister on the latest operational situation. I said that it would not be possible for the armed forces to conclude Operation Vijay successfully till the three Pakistani pockets on our side of the LoC were cleared. I pointed out that we needed his approval to use force for evicting the Pakistanis. He gave the go-ahead signal. All the three pockets were cleared by 25 July. (Details of these operations have already been given in earlier chapters.)

The next day, the Indian DGMO, Nirmal Chander Vij, along with his colleagues from the Navy and the Air Force, held a press conference and announced that all intrusions of Pakistani troops had been cleared. '...With this, the mission assigned to the Armed Forces by the Government has been accomplished', he declared.

The prime minister and his CCS colleagues visited the Military Operations Room on 27 July, to meet senior officers of the three services, and to compliment the armed forces on the successful mission accomplishment.

On 30 July 1999, I sent my own message of appreciation to all ranks of the Army and also pointed to the challenges ahead:

I convey my deep appreciation, felicitations and sense of fortitude to all ranks for the successfully concluded Operation Vijay. This operation will go down in the annals of Indian history as one fought through grit and determination by our Jawans (soldiers) and an example of outstanding performance on the part of the junior leadership. Planning and execution at all levels were of a high order.

I would also like to put on record the Army's appreciation of the role of the Air Force and silent support of the Navy.

Along with a grateful Nation, I salute our brave Officers, Junior Commissioned Officers and Jawans who made the supreme sacrifice to uphold the integrity of the country. To take care of those who laid down their lives, and others who have been disabled, the Government has announced a number of schemes. We resolve to take care of all the affected families.

There has been an upsurge in public sentiment and support to the Army's performance in this conflict. The entire Nation rose as one to applaud our people. The extensive media coverage highlighted the difficult nature of the operations. The public responded overwhelmingly by contributions to the Defence Funds. Funeral ceremonies of our martyrs were spontaneously attended in large numbers, expressing sympathy and solidarity with their families. Thousands of letters and messages of support and concern have been received by me and in the names of the Jawans from every part of the country. There is now a new image of trust and dependability of the Army in the minds of our countrymen in the 'Year of the Jawan'.

The Kargil conflict is over, but we continue to remain in the grip of the ongoing proxy war in J&K. In spite of all adversities and repeated engagement in various operations, the Army has always risen to the call of our Nation with a singular aim of victory in mind. We still have many challenges ahead. Suitable measures are being instituted to upgrade our capability in consonance with the tasks that lie ahead. Assimilation of modern technology and enhancing the combat potential shall remain our uppermost concern. Welfare and morale of all ranks shall be addressed suitably to ensure that both the fighting spirit and capability remain supreme.

May God be with you! Jai Hind!

13

Crying Nuclear Wolf

. . . the political leadership in a democratic country tends to be more responsible, cautious and restrained on the possible use of nuclear weapons. In a crisis situation, such leadership exercises greater control over these weapons. On the other hand, the military leadership tends to take chances and risks. A communication gap between the two forms of leadership — or any person/s not being part of the decision-making loop — can create serious problems.

A T THE LAHORE SUMMIT IN FEBRUARY 1999, PRIME MINISTERS
Atal Behari Vajpayee and Nawaz Sharif had recognized that
the nuclear capabilities acquired by both India and Pakistan had
added 'to their responsibility for avoiding a conflict between the
two countries'. They had reiterated their determination 'to
implementing of Shimla Agreement in letter and spirit' and
agreed 'to intensify their efforts to resolve all issues, including
the issue of Jammu and Kashmir'.

The memorandum of understanding (MoU) signed by the
foreign secretaries of India and Pakistan on the occasion called
for the two nations 'to engage in bilateral consultations on
security concepts and nuclear doctrines with a view to developing
measures for confidence building in the nuclear and conventional
fields aimed at avoidance of conflict'. The MoU listed seven
other significant clauses on nuclear and conventional CBMs,
consultations and communication between the two sides, as
given in Appendix 1.

In Pakistan, however, even when there is a civilian
government, the security policy, the nuclear weapons
infrastructure and its command and control are supervised by
the Army. As stated in Chapter 2, the Pakistani Army perceived
that several political and military advantages would accrue to
the country as a result of the Kargil operation (known as
Operation Badr). Besides altering the status of the LoC and
effectively interdicting the strategic Srinagar–Kargil–Leh
highway, this operation was expected to revive militancy in
Jammu and Kashmir and highlight this dispute internationally.
Operation Badr was expected to greatly increase military and
economic costs for India without endangering Pakistan's security.
Apparently, the Pakistani military high command saw no

contradictions among the Lahore Declaration, the MoU and the launching of Operation Badr.

Nuclear weapons too played an important role in shaping Pakistan's military strategy for the Kargil episode. There was a strong belief that Pakistan's demonstrated nuclear weapons capability in May 1998 was sufficient to prevent the escalation of the situation in Kargil to a full-scale conventional war level. The military high command headed by Pervez Musharraf was confident about Pakistan's 'nuclear shield'. The Pakistani military believed then, as it still does, that it could safely conduct a low-intensity conflict or a limited war in Jammu and Kashmir and that its nuclear capability would prevent a conventional Indian attack. During the conflict, a senior Pakistani Army officer was quoted as stating: 'The Indians cannot afford to extend the war to other areas in Kashmir, leave aside launching an attack across the international boundary because of the risk of conflagration.'[1] Having persuaded Nawaz Sharif of the merits of intervention across the LoC, the military high command had launched the military campaign in the Kargil sector under the Mujahideen façade. The operation was progressing smoothly as per plan till India, after 24 May 1999, decided to raise the ante and create strategic asymmetry by committing all three services for waging land, air and sea battles.

When the Indian Air Force fighters took to the skies on our own side of the LoC, when our Western and (part of) Eastern Naval Fleets were mobilized in the Arabian Sea and our Army formations started deploying along the entire western border, both the political leadership and the military leadership in Pakistan were surprised. Such a response was not expected and not catered for by them.

On 26 May, the Pakistani DGMO queried our decision to employ the Air Force. He then stated that we should not attack their regular posts or fly into their territory. For the first time, he spoke about 'defusing the situation'.

The next day, Nawaz Sharif made the first mention of nuclear capability with reference to the Kargil war. He said that the people

---

[1] Quoted by Zahid Hussain in 'On the Brink', *Newsline* (Pakistan), June 1999.

of Pakistan were 'confident for the first time in their history that in the eventuality of an armed attack, they will be able to meet it in [*sic*] equal terms'. Officially, Pakistan issued a warning that 'it will take necessary steps to defend itself and retaliate'.

On 28 May, Nawaz Sharif offered to send his foreign minister Sartaj Aziz to New Delhi.

On 31 May, for the second time, Pakistan raised the nuclear alarm. Pakistan's foreign secretary, Shamshad Ahmad, who had himself signed the MoU on strategic weapons along with the Lahore Declaration, explicitly warned: 'We will not hesitate to use any weapon in our arsenal to defend our territorial integrity.'[2] The leader of the House in the Senate, Raja Zafarul Haq, declared that Pakistan would use nuclear weapons if imperative for its security, and added: 'The purpose of developing weapons becomes meaningless, if they are not used when they are needed.'[3]

It needs to be remembered that, at that time (May 1999), about one year after Pokhran II and the Chagai nuclear weapons tests, neither India nor Pakistan had put in place a properly worked out and approved nuclear doctrine or command and control structure for their strategic forces. Although these statements did not make much military sense, as intended, they were promptly highlighted by the foreign media and raised hackles in political circles around the world.

National Security Advisor Brajesh Mishra termed Shamshad Ahmad's statement 'utterly irresponsible' in a TV interview. On 2 June, *The Times of India* titled its editorial 'Crying Nuclear Wolf', evidently inspired by the aforementioned statement. This statement was thereafter denied by Pakistan.

Deeply concerned about the escalation of war between two geographically contiguous nuclear-capable states, the international community began to take greater interest in the Kargil conflict after 26 May.[4] 'There is always the possibility of events spinning out of control. Clearly, the ingredients are there

---

[2]'Pakistan May Use Any Weapons', *The News* (Pakistan), 31 May 1999.
[3]'N Weapons Can Be Used for National Security: Zafar', *The News* (Pakistan), 31 May 1999.
[4]When the Indian Air Force joined the war.

for miscalculation,' said Karl Inderfurth, the US undersecretary for South Asia.[5]

In mid-June 1999, when fighting on the Tololing feature was still going on, Brajesh Mishra told his US counterpart, Sandy Berger, that India could no longer keep its armed forces on leash and that an escalation of the conflict could not be ruled out. Prime Minister Vajpayee too threatened to carry the fighting beyond the LoC, if Pakistan did not withdraw its forces from Jammu and Kashmir.

When the Pakistan Army's role was exposed and the details of the Pakistani intrusion were highlighted, the international community started demanding the immediate withdrawal of that country's troops from Kargil, accusing Islamabad of sending them across the LoC. The US Congress adopted a resolution recommending the suspension of loans from international financial institutions to Pakistan until it withdrew its troops to its side of the LoC. The G-8 and the European Union called for the intruders to pull out forthwith and for Pakistan to respect the sanctity of the LoC.

(The political and military circumstances leading to the Bill Clinton–Nawaz Sharif meeting on 4 July, which culminated in the signing of a joint statement in Washington D.C., have been described in Chapter 12.)

After agreeing to withdraw the Pakistani forces, Nawaz Sharif claimed that a fourth Indo–Pak war had been averted. He also observed that 'it becomes difficult to find a winner after a war between two atomic powers'.[6] Later, Pakistan's minister of state for foreign affairs, Mohammad Siddique Kanju, declared that the Clinton–Sharif meeting 'had averted a wider conflict in a nuclear environment'.[7]

Nawaz Sharif's stand created considerable confusion in Pakistan. In the beginning, the fighting in Kargil had been depicted

---

[5]Karl Inderfurth, 'Risks High in Kashmir Clash, Even Huge, US Experts Warn', *The New York Times*, 30 May 1999.

[6]'Withdrawal Aimed at Diplomatic Solution, PM', *Dawn* (Pakistan), 13 July 1999.

[7]'Wider Conflict Averted, Kanju Tells National Assembly', *Dawn* (Pakistan), 7 August 1999.

by Pakistan's officially controlled electronic media as a major victory of the Mujahideen and a military setback for India. But soon the bubble burst. The unilateral withdrawal of forces from across the LoC lifted the Mujahideen veil, or whatever was left of it, from the face of the Pakistan Army. Pakistan's public learnt about Indian forces recapturing many posts and also about the involvement of the Pakistan Army in the Kargil operations. Such a withdrawal also belied official claims that Pakistan was invulnerable as a result of its nuclear deterrence capability.

These developments led to a serious debate not only on the efficacy of Pakistan's nuclear strategy and the effectiveness of its nuclear deterrence but also on the other aspects of the Kargil war. Given all this confusion and turmoil, the Pakistani political leadership attempted to shift the responsibility for the crisis on to the military high command by stating that the prime minister had not been fully briefed about the Kargil operation. The Army chief Pervez Musharraf promptly denied this allegation. The failure of the Kargil operation, and then the attempt to blame the Army leadership for such a state of affairs, resulted in extremely strained relations between Nawaz Sharif and the Army leadership, culminating in the military coup in Pakistan on 12 October 1999.

Currently, under the Musharraf regime, domestic compulsions continue to dictate the internal response to the Pakistan Army's Kargil initiative. Pakistan's military still depicts the Kargil operation as a military success and holds the political leadership responsible for capitulating to external pressure and opting for a unilateral withdrawal. It continues to claim that the Kargil episode (as well as the Indo–Pak military standoff in 2001–02) demonstrates the effectiveness of their nuclear deterrence in that it prevented a conventional military attack by India. But there are a couple of unanswered questions in this claim. If it was a military operation and a success, does it imply that the official Pakistan Army doctrine approves Mujahideen operations or the Mujahideen façade for its conventional operations? Is this doctrinal change due to the current nuclear status on the subcontinent and due to India's conventional superiority? If the answers are in the positive, we can expect such operations again.

A few days after Bruce Reidel's monograph ('American Diplomacy and the Kargil Summit at Blair House', Policy Paper Series 2002, Center for Advanced Study of India, University of Pennsylvania; see Chapter 12) was published, Celia Dugger of the *New York Times* asked for my comments on it. I observed that during the Kargil war in June–July 1999, other than one or two intelligence reports indicating that the Pakistan Army personnel had been noticed cleaning up artillery deployment areas and missile launch sites at the Tilla Ranges, we had no reports that Pakistan was readying its nuclear arsenal. Jingoistic rhetoric apart, there was no credible evidence or threat that nuclear weapons would be used during the conflict.

'Isn't it possible that the US Administration had more information about this than Indian intelligence agencies?' she next asked. My answer was that President Clinton was speaking to Prime Minister Vajpayee every few days. Also, the US national security advisor, Sandy Berger, was regularly in touch with Brajesh Mishra. Were the nuclear threat real, my firm opinion was that he would have conveyed such vital information to Prime Minister Vajpayee, who, in turn, would have told us (the three service chiefs).

Given such a background, the questions that come to mind are: Did the threat of a nuclear exchange extend beyond mere rhetoric? Was the nuclear-related intelligence input to the US president exaggerated? Was the US president using this information to arm-twist the Pakistani prime minister and thus exploiting the well-known communication and decision-making gap between the political leadership and the Army?

My impression is that the Pakistani nuclear rhetoric, combined with reports on the deployment of the Indian Army on the western border and Pakistani Army preparations in the Tilla Ranges, caused the nuclear hype and hoopla in the Western media. The coverage of the nuclear danger factor was speculative and exaggerated. The 'doomsday forecasting' suited the non-proliferation policy of the West, and, after 4 July 1999, helped in claiming much greater success for President Clinton's personal intervention in the crisis than it deserved. Under these circumstances, the Western media cannot be faulted.

Because of the Pakistani high-decibel nuclear rhetoric during the war, Western media journalists and researchers have often asked me hypothetical questions. Would Pakistan have resorted to nuclear weapons if the Indian armed forces had crossed the border or the LoC? If they had done so, what was likely to be India's response? My answer to these questions has been that Pakistan and India have consciously avoided causing much collateral damage to population and industrial centres in the wars fought in 1947–48, 1965 and 1971. I also pointed out that since the 1990s, India and Pakistan had been used to 'existential deterrence' (this term implies that although not tested and officially declared, nuclear weapons deter aggression by virtue of the simple fact that they exist). The Kargil crisis, I clarified, was pitched at a higher rung because both nations had by then demonstrated their nuclear capabilities overtly. Finally, I stated that since India had conducted the various operations during the war in a responsible manner and had exercised a good deal of restraint, where was the chance for Pakistan to think in nuclear terms? Brigadier Shauqat Qadir[8] has put forward a Pakistani view and stated that, during the Kargil conflict, even a conventional war was never a possibility, let alone a nuclear war.

Many Indian strategists believe that so long as a US naval fleet is present in the Arabian Sea, or its troops are located in Pakistan or Afghanistan, Washington would not allow Pakistan to use its nuclear weapons.[9] There are others who feel that the USA does not have much influence on Pakistan when it comes to the latter's vital national security decisions. They cite the examples of the USA failing to (a) stop Pakistan from going nuclear in May 1998, (b) prevent a military coup in Pakistan in October 1999 despite issuing stern warnings in September that year and (c) make Pakistan pursue/arrest Osama bin Laden before or after 11 September 2001.[10] While the US officials themselves deny having much influence over Pakistan, the fact

---

[8]Shauqat Qadir, 'An Analysis of the Kargil Conflict 1999', *RUSI Journal*, April 2002, p. 26.

[9]K. Subrahmanyam, 'Indo–Pak Nuclear Conflict Unlikely', *The Times of India*, 2 January 2002.

[10]Suba Chandran, 'Limited War with Pakistan: Will It Secure India's Interests?' Arms Control, Disarmament, and International Security (ACDIS) Occasional Paper, University of Illinois, August 2004.

remains that they have been, and shall remain, very sensitive to any nuclear threat emanating from Pakistan, or by any other country to Pakistan.

I must emphasize that the risk of a nuclear war cannot be taken lightly by anyone. So what danger do we face today? The danger, I believe, lies much less in the existence of nuclear weapons on the subcontinent – many nations have much larger stockpiles of such weapons – but more in their *intended* use, not to mention factors such as chances of irresponsible proliferation, falling into the hands of irrational characters like Osama bin Laden and the possibilities of accidents.

In India, nuclear weapons are meant only for defence; we have a declared policy of '*no first use*'. Such weapons serve more as political instruments rather than as military tools; they are 'antidotes to blackmail' and are 'likely to be conducive to – rather than subversive of – strategic stability in South Asia'.[11] India has made its nuclear policy and doctrine transparent and these subjects have often been publicly debated. Ever since the initial irresponsible statements made by some political leaders soon after the Pokhran II tests (conducted in May 1998), indulging in nuclear rhetoric has been discouraged at political and official levels. During the Kargil war, India's response on the nuclear issue was measured, low key and dismissive of reckless statements and threats by some jingoistic elements. Thereafter too, despite frequent provocative media questioning, the Government of India has shown responsible restraint. The political decision makers all over the world tend to be cautious about exercising military options when there is even a remote possibility that doing so could prove potentially dangerous.

In Pakistan, the situation is noticeably different. It is the Army that controls the nuclear infrastructure and policy. The nuclear weapons programme is the preserve of a close circle of policy makers confined to the military establishment and chosen partners from the bureaucracy and the scientific community, in whose perception, their nuclear weapons counter

---

[11]Ashley Tellis, 'India's Emerging Nuclear Doctrine: Exemplifying the Lessons of the Nuclear Revolution', *NBAR Analysis*, The National Bureau of Asian Research, Seattle, May 2001.

India's nuclear capability as well as conventional superiority. The political leadership, which tends to be more responsible and cautious (as the Blair House incident has shown; see Chapter 12), is normally not kept in the decision-making loop. Till date, Pakistan has not announced its nuclear doctrine and has rejected a 'no-first-use' policy. The nuclear policy and doctrine have been kept deliberately ambiguous. Lieutenant General Khalid Kidwai, the head of the Strategic Planning Division, which services Pakistani's National Command Authority, once admitted that the president, who was also the Pakistani Army chief, took 99 per cent of the decisions as far as nuclear issues are concerned. Kidwai also spelt out the bottom lines (or thresholds) for the use of nuclear weapons to a research group from Italy. Although he stressed that the nuclear capability was defensive in nature, the thresholds articulated happened to be vague and flexible.[12]

In my opinion, it is very unlikely that the Pakistani Army, which controls the nuclear weapons today, and cannot by any stretch of imagination be considered 'irrational', will resort to nuclear weapons unless Pakistan's vital interests are threatened and its very existence is at stake. Even under such circumstances, the Pakistani top brass would have to very seriously consider India's nuclear response. The political decision makers in India may appear tentative, or lacking a proactive approach, but they have never hesitated to respond courageously to serious national security challenges as per nationally accepted policies. To that extent, nuclear weapons do provide some strategic stability, and the danger need not be blown out of proportion.[13] It is factors such as Pakistan's ambiguity in the nuclear weapons sphere, its proactive use of the 'nuclear shield' to support jehadi terrorism, nuclear proliferation and the possibility of nuclear weapons coming into the possession of irrational elements that tend to make such weapons dangerous.

---

[12]'Nuclear Safety, Nuclear Stability and Nuclear Strategy in Pakistan', a concise report of a visit by Landau Network – Centro Volta, Villa Olmo, Via Cantoni 1, 22100 Como (Italy) (http://www.mi.infn.it/-landnet).

[13]Rajesh Rajagopalan, *Second Strike – Arguments about Nuclear War in South Asia* (Penguin Viking, New Delhi, 2005).

The strident rhetoric that hits the headlines, whenever there is military or diplomatic tension between India and Pakistan, gives the impression that nuclear capability is also used to send signals; it is sometimes wielded as an instrument of coercive diplomacy. Nuclear signalling on the subcontinent, however, remains murky and is an imperfectly understood practice. Pakistan has been indulging in such signalling much more than India, probably to make its deterrence policies appear more credible. Leaders in both countries have to realize that these signals could be misread or misinterpreted. Nuclear signalling during a major crisis gets clouded because the messages are interpreted differently by domestic, crossborder and international audiences at the same time. In a critical situation, greater clarity can be achieved with more discipline and caution and also with fewer spokespersons interacting with the media on such issues.

The crux of the matter is: For how long can Pakistan use the 'signalling ploy' to stir up international concerns over a nuclear war resulting due to the Kashmir dispute? Currently, Pakistan is facing an international backlash due to factors such as its perceived role in fomenting and sustaining terrorism, the nature of its military command and control and irresponsible proliferation of nuclear technology, thanks to the efforts of its scientist Abdul Qadeer Khan.

An important lesson learnt from the Kargil war is that the political leadership in a democratic country tends to be more responsible, cautious and restrained on the possible use of nuclear weapons. In a crisis situation, such leadership exercises greater control over such weapons. On the other hand, the military leadership tends to take chances and risks. A communication gap between the two forms of leadership – or any person/s not being part of the decision-making loop – can create serious problems.

14

'We Shall Fight with Whatever We Have!'

The persistent problems with regard to the modernization of the armed forces…are generally the inadequacy of funds for capital purchases, the inability to develop and produce the required weapon systems and equipment indigenously in time and the extremely tedious procurement and decision-making procedures. Currently, we can also add political witch hunting and the scare of getting involved in scams to the aforementioned problems.

EVERY SERVICE CHIEF TRIES HIS BEST TO MODERNIZE THE FORCE during his tenure. For me too, modernization was a key result area when I took over as Army chief in October 1997. The persistent problems with regard to modernization of the armed forces, which have not been resolved till date, are generally the inadequacy of funds for capital purchases, the inability to develop and produce the required weapon systems and equipment indigenously in time and the extremely tedious procurement and decision-making procedures. Currently, we can also add political witch hunting and the scare of getting involved in scams to the aforementioned problems.

In the 1990s, due to a serious shortage of foreign exchange and owing to a very tight fiscal situation, the annual allocation for defence kept decreasing: from 3.59 per cent of the GDP in 1987–88 to 2.31 per cent in 1996–97. The Eighth Defence Plan, prepared during 1991–92, remained an exercise on paper only as the Cabinet Committee on Security (CCS) did not approve it. The Army was consequently forced to evolve the 'bottom-line' concept – holding less than 70–80 per cent of authorized weapons, ammunition and equipment in units and as war reserves in Army depots. The annual budget available for capital purchases (modernization) was extremely low. During these years, on account of raising new combat and Rashtriya Rifles units, low-intensity operational commitments and annual maintenance and training requirements, the war wastage reserves kept depleting faster than they could be replenished.

In 1997–98, the Army budget was Rs 16,384 crore. After accounting for maintenance, works (i.e., construction of accommodation, storage and connected facilities) and contractual liabilities, only Rs 230 crore or 1.4 per cent was available for funding modernization schemes. All the years of neglect had had a serious negative impact on making up deficiencies and led to setbacks for the modernization of the armed forces.

While addressing the prime minister and his CCS colleagues who had participated in the Combined Commanders' Conference (held on 20 October 1997 in New Delhi), I had stated that as far as the condition of the Indian Army was concerned, 'the spirit is strong but the body is weak'. I had pointed out that the continuous depletion of the defence allocation had resulted in huge deficiencies of arms, ammunition and equipment in the Army. In addition to these deficiencies, more and more weapons and equipment were going 'off road' due to the non-availability of spares.

The Army generally follows the principle that critical weapons and equipment should be available over three generations covering a span of twenty-five to thirty years so as to ensure a balance between our fiscal demands and operational readiness. Generation 1 corresponds to equipment that can be categorized as 'obsolescent' (twenty to thirty years' vintage). Generation 2 encompasses equipment that has 'matured' (ten to twenty years' vintage). Generation 3 refers to 'affordable state-of-the-art' equipment (up to ten years' vintage). When these three categories are nearly equally balanced, such a state represents a cost-effective equilibrium between modernization and operational effectiveness.

In 1998, most of our infantry equipment was of 1960–70 vintage. Moreover, such equipment was in short supply due to the raising of the Rashtriya Rifles (consisting of thirty battalions) without the requisite armaments and other material being sanctioned for these battalions. The Rashtriya Rifles battalions, deployed for counterterrorism operations in Jammu and Kashmir and elsewhere, had to be issued weapons and equipment from Army reserves. The state and availability of the weapons and equipment in other combat units and combat support units were no better. Except for a small number of tanks, infantry combat vehicles, Bofors and air defence guns of Generation 2 vintage, all other weapons and equipment were really old.

We gave a presentation highlighting the Army's state of preparedness, budgetary requirements and procurement procedural difficulties to various officials including the finance secretary, the defence secretary and the expenditure secretary. After providing all the relevant details, I ended by stating: 'Keeping in view our shortages and deficiencies, we do not get adequate budgetary allocation. But even when we do get something, our procurement procedures are such that we can seldom spend the given amount.'[1]

When I got the next opportunity to address the prime minister and his CCS colleagues in October 1998, I stated:

The Army has been making a case for a higher fiscal allocation to support its modernization programmes for many years. But for one reason or the other, there has only been a linear yearly increase to take care of inflation. In fact, in some years, there has been a negative growth; even inflation was not addressed. Faced with growing hollowness, we contrived a concept of "bottom-line" requirements but we are now over Rs 14,800 crore in deficit for equipment. With increasing deficiencies of arms, ammunition and equipment, the Army's modernization programmes are in a state of terminal illness.... On assuming my assignment as COAS [Chief of Army Staff], and having taken stock of our modernization programmes, the state, as I saw it then, compelled me to order a suppression of 50,000 personnel. That would help generate an additional Rs 870 crore in the Ninth Plan, starting with around Rs 100 crore in the current financial year. We followed this up by a cut in the non-fighting force, saving and redeploying nearly 20,000 personnel. I am constantly reviewing ways and means to derive greater value for money, both in terms of fiscal discipline and inventory controls. These measures shall

---

[1]Besides lack of funds, our procedures are unresponsive, cost escalatory, frustrating and demoralizing. Vendors create and exploit the 'scam phobia'. We do believe in self-reliance but the problem is that even in critical areas, the development and production agencies make promises, and then fail to keep them for years on end. I have no doubt that by streamlining procedures, we can get 20 to 30 per cent additional value from our allocation.

continue unabated. But there is a finite limit to what we can do. Unless additional funds are earmarked, future planning is not possible and the erosion in our combat edge will soon become uncorrectable.

In my presentation, I recommended:

- Consideration of higher allocation to the capital account to hold the creeping hollowness in the equipment profile of the Army.
- Additional allocation for Rashtriya Rifles and Special Forces.
- Consideration of a "defence reserve fund" to offset the "rush of March" syndrome (a hasty effort to spend the budget before the end of every financial year on 31 March).
- Decentralized and faster clearance for priority procurement items that were listed in the Ninth Plan, already approved by the CCS.

These were all issues that I kept pursuing vigorously throughout my tenure, sometimes at the cost of personal relationships. Besides the correspondence at the staff level, I kept writing to the defence minister regularly, before and after the Kargil war. In one of my letters (March 1999), I noted: 'The Army is finding that major acquisitions get stymied for various reasons and a feeling of cynicism is creeping in. By and large, the prevailing situation is that nothing much can be done about the existing hollowness in the Army. By denying essential equipment, the armed forces would gradually lose their combat edge which would show adversely in a future conflict...'

When the Kargil war began, it was not the vintage but the *deficiencies* of weapons, equipment, ammunition and spares that worried us more. Even infantry weapons such as medium machine-guns, rocket launchers and mortars, apart from signal equipment, bulletproof jackets and snow clothing for high-altitude warfare, were in short supply. I spent one whole day in Srinagar during the war in order to ascertain the state of the essential stores (stores controlled by the General Staff) in 15 Corps and Northern Command. At the end of the day, we ordered the transfer of some medium machine-guns, mortars and radio equipment from the Rashtriya Rifles to the units of 3 Infantry Division and 8 Mountain Division. There were hardly any force multipliers. Most of the small arms were without passive night sights (i.e., night viewing devices that enable observation without lighting up the object) and thus were disadvantageous for the assaulting troops. There were no laser range finders (i.e., range-measuring equipment that works with the help of a laser beam) for the MMGs or the mortars. The signal communication equipment at the unit level was outdated, in short supply and with insufficient gadgetry to ensure secrecy. What we missed most were the weapon-locating radars, which would have enabled us to engage Pakistani artillery and mortars more effectively. After long negotiations with a manufacturer, some of these radars were about to be purchased in 1997. At the last moment, the Defence Research and Development Organization (DRDO) caused this deal to be scuttled with a promise that it would develop and produce these radars in the next two years; a promise that was never fulfilled.[2]

We had to cater for a full-scale war on the rest of the western front. Despite facing acute shortages of weapons and ammunition, we took the risk of allotting extra Bofors regiments and artillery ammunition to Northern Command. This command too was beset with a major problem: it had limited special winter clothing and equipment. Consequently, all ordnance depots were ordered to issue whatever they could to meet the immediate requirement. The staff members worked round the clock to prioritize demands from each theatre of war and then they had to locate and dispatch the material to the designated destinations.

---

[2]These radars were later purchased from the same manufacturer in 2003, after the US Administration agreed to lift sanctions on selected defence purchases.

Prime Minister Atal Behari Vajpayee visited wounded soldiers in many hospitals. During one such visit I was with him when he asked a seriously wounded Garhwali soldier: 'How are you feeling? What can I do for you?'

The soldier forgot his pain. He replied: 'Sir, I will be alright in a few days and then would like to go back to my unit to fight. But I have a request. Please get us lighter weapons and equipment, which we can carry on these mountains more easily.'

The Kargil war brought to the fore yet another shortcoming: it highlighted the gross inadequacies in the nation's surveillance capability. We had sought satellite imagery from two friendly countries, but received a most unsatisfactory response. At one point of time, the DRDO made an effort, quite inexplicably, to *control* the downloading of satellite pictures. Aerial imagery, except for inputs from the Aviation Research Centre, was non-existent. Moreover, the system of interpretation and delivery was slow. On a couple of occasions, I carried air photos personally from the Operations Room in Delhi to Headquarters 8 Mountain Division in Dras.

Besides weapons and equipment, the ammunition reserves for many important weapons were low. The transport fleet in most units was much below their entitlement with most of the vehicles being very old. We had to deal with shortages of fuel containers and some varieties of oils, lubricants and greases too. Fortunately, some of these shortages were made up quickly. The CCS was persuaded to lift the decades-old ban on the erstwhile Bofors Company to enable us to purchase the urgently needed spares for the guns and other weapons purchased from it earlier.

Lifting the Ban on Spares for Bofor Guns and Other Weapons

No single issue has stymied the modernization of the Indian Army as much as the Bofors artillery gun, which paradoxically was the most useful weapon during the Kargil war.

By the end of May 1999, we had about 100 Bofors (155-mm) guns deployed in the Kargil sector. It was a risk because the situation was uncertain and could spill over to other parts of the LoC and international border. Besides, we had no spares of the guns due to the ban imposed on the manufacturers, and our inability to import them from other vendors or to manufacture them within India. Our efforts with the Ministry of Defence to get the ban lifted (agreed to by the minister at one stage) or to find an alternative source for 155-mm guns had failed during the last two years. The situation now was difficult because not only did we lack guns, but also the spares for those in action. When these guns started getting out of action due to wartime use, I raised the issue of the guns, spares and the ban with the defence minister and the CCS. Usually, whenever the CCS discusses issues of defence procurements, the chiefs of staff are not invited. I do not know how, why and when was this practice started. But the situation now was different. I was present and able to argue the case effectively as I had full information and also knew the military implications. After detailed consideration over ten days, the CCS agreed to lift the ban on the manufacturer. The cabinet secretary interpreted this for the spares of 155-mm guns only. I questioned his interpretation and said that the ban was on the company and not on the weapons it had sold. We had also purchased a number of other weapons and equipment from this company. Why should there be a need to go back to the CCS for other weapons and equipment or spares after this lifting? Fortunately, good sense prevailed!

The efforts put in and the struggles undergone by the three services to make up deficiencies and go in for modernization were hardly secrets. On 23 June 1999, when I was briefing the media, a journalist asked me as to how the Army was going to fight in the face of severe shortages. My spontaneous reply was: *'We shall fight with whatever we have.'* Someone from the Ministry of Defence brought this remark to the prime minister's attention. He told me politely that I need not have used such language. I explained that, firstly, my reply was to a direct question posed by a journalist. Secondly, I pointed out that any attempt by me to cover up would have conveyed an impression to the Army rank and file that the chief was indulging in double talk. If that happened, they would lose confidence in me. Consequently, it was essential for me to speak the truth.

When all the deficiencies and shortages were pointed out by the service chiefs to the prime minister and Brajesh Mishra, they decided to act. The Government of India agreed to procure some essential items urgently. Accordingly, prioritized lists were prepared, discussed and finalized by officials in the Ministry of Defence and the Prime Minister's Office. The items on these lists were to be procured within a given time frame. Some of these items were acquired during, and some were delivered after, the war. The ordnance factories rose to the occasion in an attempt to make up our ammunition deficiencies as quickly as possible. They were only partially successful despite their commendable response. But we faced considerable problems in obtaining items that were not available within the country and had to be imported at short notice. Most of these items fetched up much later. A major lesson learnt from this whole episode was that in every situation of 'urgent purchase' of defence items, every vendor, no matter from which country, would exploit the situation.

With regard to defence procurements in our country, the focus is now more on scams than on planning for security needs. The rather unfortunate aspect is that the short spurt in procurement of essential defence items during the Kargil war has turned into yet another 'scam' controversy and led to unwanted politicization of the entire issue.

In one of the defence minister's morning meetings during the war, a senior civil servant, who had never earlier worked in the Ministry of Defence, said to me: 'General Malik, you keep complaining about shortage of weapons. I have been to the Ordnance Depot, Jabalpur [in Madhya Pradesh]. There are thousands of rifles in good state lying in that depot.'

I was aghast at his lack of awareness. And then, rather impatiently, I told him: 'The Army does not go into combat with rifles alone. Our projected list of essential items does not include rifles.'

Without getting involved in, or passing judgement on, these controversies, I would like to emphasize that the prime objective of procuring all the aforementioned items was to bring the forces to a certain level of readiness so that they would be able to deal with the envisaged threat more effectively. How could these purchases become 'unnecessary' or 'fruitless' as soon as the Kargil war was over, as some auditors have asked? Did the intelligence agencies, the government, or anyone else, give an assurance to the armed forces that there was no threat on our borders for sometime after Operation Vijay (completed on 26 July 1999) and, therefore, we could take our own time in procuring these items? What about the deterrent factor? In fact, in October 1999, after the military coup in Pakistan and after a review of the prevailing security situation, the chiefs of staff had to remind the defence minister again to expedite the acquisition of the already projected requirement of essential weapons and equipment.

In June 2000, I wrote to the defence minister:

> I wish to bring to your notice that in the recent past no progress seems to have been made. Against availability of Rs 2777 crore for new contracts under the capital modernization budget during the current financial year, only Rs 13.70 crore, which is a mere 0.5 per cent of the available funds have been utilized so far though three months have elapsed…. It appears to me that the handful of officials in the Ordnance Wing of the Ministry of Defence who deal with most procurement cases of the Army have been busy providing case files for investigation to the Central Vigilance Commission (CVC) and Comptroller and Auditor General (CAG). That notwithstanding, we do, now, need to pay greater attention to procurement cases so that the large funds now made available to the Army due to your personal intervention are fully and fruitfully utilized.

On 10 September 2000, only twenty days before my retirement, I wrote to him once again and suggested that, as a one-time exception, an empowered committee be formed under the defence minister for ensuring essential acquisitions. This committee's recommendations could go to the CCS direct, so long as the expenditure involved was within the allotted budget of the concerned service.

But by then, despite adequate allocations, we had fallen into the habit of surrendering funds from our capital budget!

The Impact of Poor Defence Planning

A vital fact that defence planners have to constantly remember is that defence capabilities are not purchasable 'off the shelf'. The process of translating 'money' into 'capability' is time consuming. The weapons and equipment have to be manufactured or purchased, according to strict specifications, and then absorbed into the respective units. Next, tactics and procedures have to be reviewed and revised. After that, the personnel have to be trained and maintenance proficiencies built up. All these activities, obviously, cannot be performed in a jiffy! The cost and time to build up combat capabilities get multiplied – in fact, grow exponentially – with every year of neglect. (The illustration given here is self-explanatory.)

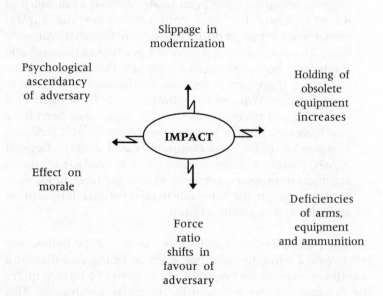

Ever since the Bofors controversy started making news (in the late 1980s), defence-related debates in Parliament focus mostly on purchases; these debates are invariably acrimonious. The opposition blames the government for the lack of defence preparedness but simultaneously kicks up a ruckus over every defence purchase. Meanwhile, the civil and military officials responsible for procurements are becoming more and more apprehensive of taking decisions. To soldiers, the proceedings give an impression that political rivalries and vendettas get higher priority than national security. The media, the CAG, the Public Accounts Committee (PAC) and the CVC, all keep harping on scams, procedural lapses and delays in the field of defence purchases. And yet, hardly anyone is punished and the dismal state of affairs continues.

There is no point in talking about a revolution in military affairs, information systems and netcentric warfare if the Indian armed forces cannot induct relevant weapons and equipment in time. We need a greater sense of responsibility and accountability on this score. No one is affected more than the soldiers who have always to be prepared for all kinds of contingencies. We must remember that the military is an organismic being; it is not a switch-on-switch-off robot.

(We shall revert to this subject and the post-Kargil procurement reforms in Chapter 19.)

The armed forces are not like a limited liability company to be reconstructed from time to time as the money fluctuates. It is not an inanimate thing like a house to be pulled down, enlarged, or structurally altered at the caprice of the tenant or owner. It is a living thing. If it is bullied, it sulks; if it is unhappy it pines; if it is harried it gets feverish; if it is sufficiently disturbed it will whither and dwindle and almost die, and when it comes to this last serious condition, it is only revived by lots of time and lots of money.

Sir Winston Churchill

15

The China Factor

In recent years, the Indian policy has been to accord high priority to maintain peace and tranquillity on the borders in accordance with bilateral agreements. At the same time, India must take prudent precautions. The Indian strategic policy towards China has, therefore, to be guided by the principle of 'cooperate but ensure security'.

IN RECENT YEARS, CHINA HAS BEEN STATING THAT IT IS pursuing an 'independent foreign policy' and that its relations with Pakistan would not be at the cost of its relations with India. During the Kargil conflict, at the political level, China did indeed articulate the above view and did maintain a neutral posture. However, at the ground level, the People's Liberation Army (PLA) had enhanced its level of activity along the Line of Actual Control (LAC) in Ladakh and opposite Arunachal Pradesh.

Ever since the Sumdorong Chu (Wangdung) incident in the disputed area in Kameng district of Arunachal Pradesh in 1986, and particularly after India's nuclear tests in May 1998, there had been an increase in the PLA patrolling along the LAC, ostensibly for 'better border management'. Such an increase could be partly attributed to the stated Chinese policy 'to improve infrastructure in the border region'. However, (*a*) the attempt to construct a road in the disputed area known as Trig Heights in June 1999 and thus alter the status quo in Ladakh, (*b*) a provocative deployment in Chantze (in the West Kameng district of Arunachal Pradesh) in July 1999 and (*c*) reports of induction of additional troops opposite Arunachal Pradesh, revealed an attempt to assert their claim over the disputed areas. This enhancement in PLA activities along the LAC coincided with the start of the conflict in Kargil. At the military level, the Chinese move indicated a demonstrative support to Pakistan, or an attempt to take advantage of our Army's involvement on the western borders.

Major Chinese patrolling activities that took place during the period were in the following places:

- *Demchok:* A strong Chinese patrol comprising approximately seventy PLA personnel was observed opposite Demchok in eastern Ladakh on 6 June 1999. Some members of the patrol party came up to Old Demchok, whereas some others moved further south along the LAC. The patrol spent approximately one hour in the area. The activity was carried out just when India had begun its operations in Kargil.

- *Trig Heights:* This is a bilaterally accepted area in Ladakh where India and China have differing perceptions of the LAC. Both countries had agreed that these differences would be resolved through negotiations and not by the use of military force. However, in the last week of June 1999, the Chinese commenced the construction of a natural surface track in the Trig Heights area. This step was assessed as an attempt to assert their claim over a disputed area.

- *Pangong Tso (a lake in Ladakh):* The Chinese constructed a track from Spanggur (Ladakh) up to the southern bank of this lake and were able to achieve the coordination of both boat and foot patrols in the area. The road construction was undertaken on a war footing with approximately 150–200 personnel employed every day.

- *Chantze:* In the first week of July 1999, the Chinese deployed troops in temporary posts in Chantze, resulting in a military standoff. It was assessed that the Chinese had inducted over one company in the area opposite Chantze, with the rest of the battalion waiting in the wings. The standoff continued till the Chinese agreed to dismantle the additional temporary posts created and withdraw the troops. By end September, both sides reverted to their old positions.

We also received intelligence reports that the PLA's director in the Department of Armament (handling the conventional weapons and equipment of the Chinese Army) visited Islamabad during the conflict to help the Pakistan Army overcome its critical deficiencies in conventional armament, ammunition and equipment. These developments and also the fact that both General Pervez Musharraf and Nawaz Sharif had visited Beijing *after* the commencement of the Kargil war did cause some concern. The 'all-weather' strategic relations between Pakistan and China are well known.

Militarily, despite the relative lack of road transport, we took care to remain well equipped and alert in West Kameng to prevent Chinese ingress/hostile action. In the Trig Heights area, our logistic vulnerability due to very scanty lines of communications did not give us a particularly comfortable military posture. That aspect notwithstanding, we increased our vigilance and patrolling to match the PLA activities, taking care to ensure that the operational situation in this area was not permitted to escalate.

China's Strategic Outlook

India shares a long boundary (about 4050 kilometres) with China, which is fast emerging as a global power, economically as well as militarily. While analysing the strategic implications of China's moves for India, one must take into account various factors such as (a) the unresolved boundary issue between the two countries, (b) China's aggressive and assertive policies as the Middle Kingdom and even after attaining independence in 1949, (c) Chinese strategic influence including regular sale of military equipment to countries that are part of India's immediate neighbourhood (Nepal, Myanmar, Bangladesh, Sri Lanka and Pakistan), (d) close strategic relations between Pakistan and China and (e) the historical fact that rapid changes in the international power equilibrium seldom take place without concomitant conflict and turbulence.

Strategic Relations between Pakistan and China

After the 1962 Sino–India border war, Pakistan, in a clever diplomatic move, had settled its boundary issue with China after ceding to it a portion of Jammu and Kashmir territory (Shaksgam valley bordering China) under its control. That move established a long-term strategic relationship between the two nations. Although China did not go in for any large-scale military manoeuvres on the Sino–Indian border during Indo–Pak wars of 1965 or 1971, it has provided Pakistan with military, technological and diplomatic support for several decades. The Pakistani military strategic community believes this relation to be a common 'Islamic–Confucian' cultural value partnership and considers it to be more valuable and durable than the Pakistan–USA strategic partnership. The Chinese refer to it as the 'lip-and-teeth' relationship. The Sino–Pakistan strategic relationship is a result of realistic compulsions and common strategic requirements.

China's Military Outlook

Over the past fifty years, China's military strategic thinking and doctrine have changed from Mao Ze Dong's 'people's war', to Deng Xiaoping's 'people's war under modern conditions' in the middle 1980s and then to Jiang Zemin's 'fighting local (or "limited") wars under high-technology conditions' in the late 1990s. Currently, Beijing's focus is on netcentric warfare using advanced systems capabilities. China's defence expenditure in 2004 was about $25 billion. It is concentrating on establishing missile forces, putting in place rapid deployment forces, creating amphibious warfare capability, improving joint services operational and logistics capabilities and developing information warfare systems.

During its period of further economic development and modernization of its armed forces, China is more likely to take recourse to diplomatic measures rather than get enmeshed in a major military confrontation. Despite underlying differences between China and the USA with respect to strategic, economic, human rights and environmental issues, both nations continue to engage each other constructively.

In the next five to ten years, China's strategic focus will be on the Asia Pacific region, particularly on the reunification of Taiwan with the motherland, and on new threats such as jehadi terrorism. China would also ensure the security of its energy sources, including sea routes and overland pipelines. Its strategic engagement and close defence ties with India's neighbours are likely to continue. Some such neighbours may even provide access to their ports and other logistic facilities to China.

China is augmenting its Rapid Reaction Force divisions in each regional army, which will speed up its intervention capability at any crisis location. Despite considerable naval modernization in the recent past, China still does not have the 'blue-water' capability to intervene or pose a threat in the Indian Ocean, west of the Malacca straits. Another significant point is that, recently, there have been substantial accretions in the PLA Air Force and also its strategic forces have undergone a great deal of modernization.

Through population management and rapid improvement of infrastructure, such as the laying of the oil pipeline, the building of the Gormo–Lhasa railway line and the upgradation of the Chengdu–Lhasa road as well as the airfields in Tibet, Beijing has been able to integrate Tibet with mainland China. This would increase China's capability to induct, deploy and sustain large forces in Tibet at short notice. In this respect, India's progress in the areas south of the Himalayan watershed has been negligible.

'Cooperate but Ensure Security'

For India, keeping in view its socio-economic and strategic priorities, an environment of peace is a precondition for pursuing human development at an ever-increasing pace. There has been a substantial improvement in the Sino–Indian economic relationship besides the expansion of the strategic dialogue between the two nations. The talks on the Sino–Indian border dispute have been upgraded to the political level. India's interest requires a cooperative relationship with China, without overlooking our past experience and Sino–Pakistan strategic relations. For their long-term development needs, both India and China need a good peripheral environment. In recent years, the Indian policy has been to accord high priority to maintain peace and tranquillity on the borders in accordance with bilateral agreements. At the same time, India must take prudent precautions. The Indian strategic policy towards China has, therefore, to be guided by the principle of 'cooperate but ensure security'.

Regions close to China, such as Kargil, the Siachen Glacier and the area to the west of the Karakoram Pass, are geographically and strategically interlinked. At the ground level, there is a need to adopt an adequately strong, integrated defensive posture with necessary logistic support. As a lesson from the Kargil operations and in pursuance of the abovementioned goal, we decided to raise Headquarters 14 Corps soon after the war. Whatever be the contours of our foreign and security policies, we need a credible dissuasive posture in Ladakh till the LoC and the Siachen dispute with Pakistan, and the boundary question with China, are fully resolved.

16

'Leave Us Alone: We Are Apolitical'

The Indian Army, Navy and Air Force have inherited a legacy of maintaining a totally apolitical stance. They have steadfastly preserved that legacy through the years. Unlike many of our neighbouring countries, the Indian armed forces have stuck to the concept of loyalty to the constitutionally elected government and thus enabled the nation to develop its unique democratic political ambience. Their oath is to the Constitution of India.

> People, if united in will and firm in convictions, are capable of successful military endeavours.
>
> Chanakya

AMONGST THE DEVELOPING COUNTRIES, INDIA STANDS OUT AS an exemplar of democratic values, where the armed forces are not involved in the affairs of state. The Indian Army, Navy and Air Force have inherited a legacy of maintaining a totally apolitical stance. They have steadfastly preserved that legacy through the years. Unlike many of our neighbouring countries, the Indian armed forces have stuck to the concept of loyalty to the constitutionally elected government and thus enabled the nation to develop its unique democratic political ambience. Their oath is to the Constitution of India. The ideologies and policies of different political parties, whether in power or in the opposition, do not concern them. They have always supported a democratic process that guarantees free and fair elections. In disturbed states, whenever required, they have ensured a peaceful atmosphere for the conduct of polls, without interfering in the electoral process. Needless to say, such an apolitical nature is a matter of great pride for the nation in general and for members of the armed forces in particular.

There are several reasons why the Indian military has remained apolitical over the years. The credit goes not only to the military and its traditions, but also to the political leadership, our egalitarian society and other well-established democratic institutions. Another important reason has been that, in the past, the political leaders or their party members did not make any attempt to politicize the armed forces. While some central and state services in India are gradually getting more and more politically influenced, the armed forces are among the last bastions to have escaped this trend. It is best that such a state of affairs continue. I am, therefore, writing this chapter out of my concern that the democratic values and systems, which have kept the armed forces apolitical, do not get eroded. If we wish to see the men and women in uniform remain apolitical, the nation will need to be vigilant and help them to maintain such a tradition. Without political consensus on serious defence issues affecting the country, there is a danger of the armed forces being politicized.

We fought the Kargil war at a time when our political system had been (and still is) going through the adjustments and compromises required by political coalitions, which are often more convenient than principled. Despite the good wishes sent through millions of letters from all over the country to soldiers, and despite the emotional bonding with the nation that touched all of us, we were affected by political crossfire of a kind that had never been experienced in the past. On several occasions, the political parties that formed the government as well as the opposition managed to drag the armed forces into needless and unsavoury controversies that could adversely affect military systems and their efficiency, and also harm their apolitical image and stature. The political exploitation of the Kargil war for electoral gains worried the military leadership as it could undermine the neutral character of the armed forces and, in the process, affect its professionalism.

The war was imposed on the nation when there was an interim Central Government constituted by the National Democratic Alliance. General elections for the Parliament were due in a few months. At the beginning of the war, political parties, like the rest of the nation, were unclear about the nature and size of the Pakistani infiltration, not to mention its purpose and rationale. When the fog of war enveloped the environment, and also when this fog started lifting, there was a justifiable concern in different quarters about the security situation in Kargil. Political parties in the opposition found an opportunity to hold the government responsible for political, intelligence and surveillance 'negligence'. This step, again, was justified, as a part of healthy national democratic process. Soon after that, some instances occurred wherein the Army was unnecessarily involved in the political crossfire.

In an attempt to clarify matters, the government organized a series of briefings and discussions in which the leaders of the political parties, governors and chief ministers of the states and Members of Parliament were scheduled to participate. The service chiefs, or their staff, were asked to brief the participants. After the briefings, before any political discussions began, the latter were requested to leave. During one such briefing, the ruling National Democratic Alliance pushed the armed forces into the morass of polemics.

On one occasion, the armed forces team, comprising the Director General Military Operations (DGMO) and his counterparts from the other two services, was summoned to the Parliament House at very short notice to brief the Members of Parliament belonging only to the National Democratic Alliance. When the opposition parties and the media learnt about this briefing, they created a furore, which was fully justified.

I was out of Delhi when this incident took place. As the name of the Air Force representative was also Malik, but with the initials S.K., some people thought that the Army chief was present at the briefing and blamed me for the entire episode.[1]

On my return to Delhi I investigated the matter, and learnt that the defence minister's personal secretary had conveyed 'ministerial instructions' to the DGMO for addressing this briefing. He had specified the time and the location of the briefing, but had not disclosed the names of the Members of Parliament (or any other details) who were scheduled to attend. When the team reached the specified room in the Parliament House, three members of the Cabinet Committee on Securiy (CCS), including the defence minister, received the officers. As the team members entered the room, they found that it was full of Members of Parliament from the National Democratic Alliance who had put

---

[1]Amongst others, Kuldip Nayar (a veteran journalist) wrote about this matter in his column in *The Indian Express*. When I gave him the correct information and explained the episode in detail, he immediately wrote a letter of apology, which was also published by the same newspaper.

their party flags on display. I wish they had just walked out of the room; unfortunately, they did not. Consequently, the attitude of the armed forces' team was viewed as politically partisan.

In the third week of June 1999, when we decided to post out Brigadier Surinder Singh, commander 121 (I) Infantry Brigade, for 'ineffective command and control', political parties from the opposition supported him openly, something that had never happened during the course of any war before. When hostilities are on, commanders and staff officers who cannot deliver are often removed from their assignment. There are numerous such instances in our military history, especially during the 1962, 1965 and 1971 wars. In this particular instance, it was the Army leadership and not the government that was involved in the decision to transfer the officer. The situation became murkier when some opposition party leaders decided to defend him in the Court of Inquiry instituted by the Army and later attempted to use the classified correspondence contained in his complaint (to the Chief of the Army Staff) to score political points through the media. There was no substance in Brigadier Surinder Singh's complaint. He began to hawk his theory about the failure of superiors to heed his 'warnings' only *after* he had been removed from the command of 121 (I) Infantry Brigade. In his complaint, he had written about a briefing when I (as COAS) visited his brigade for a few hours in August 1998, well before General Pervez Musharraf took over command of the Pakistan Army and planned Operation Badr.[2] His so-called 'warnings' were never followed up by him with his chain of command, a factor that is crucial in making operational decisions in the Army. He had been giving 'no-intrusion-in-my-sector' certificates to Headquarters 3 Infantry Division even when the infiltration was going on. After the infiltration came to light, his reactions and his orders vis-à-vis command and control were considered suspect. Consequently, wartime action was taken against him. Even though the complaint by him was written with dubious intent, it was processed as per Defence Services

---

[2]Except for this complaint, Brigadier Surinder Singh had never addressed any other letter on operational matters to the COAS.

Regulations and Army Rules. The whole issue could have been investigated subsequently, as indeed it was. But some parties chose to exploit the episode for political reasons and thus encouraged him in his activities, even though such a move involved the Army directly and tended to adversely affect the image of its leadership and the morale of the troops. No one seemed to spare a thought for the Army personnel who were fighting a war, or for the grieving kith and kin of those killed.

As the final outcome of the conflict started becoming clearer and the elections drew closer, Kargil became a political football. Everything to do with the Kargil conflict became an issue for election campaigns. There was an attempt either to put the armed forces on a pedestal or to pull them down from it.

I have already described (in Chapter 12) how the mood and the attitude of the CCS and participating officials changed as soon as the dates for the election were announced. We had a hard time in keeping the political parties at bay: those blatantly cashing in on the Kargil victory and those attempting to neutralize this effect by castigating the ruling alliance. Many political leaders, with photojournalists in tow, motivated more by political factors than by a genuine concern for the wounded soldiers, made a beeline to the military hospitals to be photographed by their bedside while handing over gifts to them. Some organizations with well-recognized political agenda distributed copies of the Bhagvad Gita and Ramcharitmanas[3] to the injured soldiers undergoing treatment in the Military Hospital, Delhi Cantonment. Others wanted to distribute refrigerators and gift items, but only in the full glare of the media. When the Ministry of Defence PRO tried to stop political visitors from taking media persons into the hospitals, both groups got visibly upset. The military leadership was again accused of being politically partisan.[4]

◆

---

[3]Hindu religious books.

[4]Surprisingly, the president of India, who is also the commander-in-chief of its armed forces and who had been briefed on the conflict twice by the three service chiefs personally, did not visit any hospital despite subtle suggestions made by me through his military secretary. I have often wondered what could be the reason for that.

On 23 August 1999, a large band of Vishwa Hindu Parishad (VHP) representatives descended upon South Block. They were carrying 20,000 *rakhis*,[5] apart from party and religious symbols, for the troops defending the Kargil border. They had brought along half-a-dozen photographers and insisted on meeting the Army chief (me). When they were refused permission, they forced their way into the Media Cell offices and handed over the *rakhis* to the staff, making sure that the TV cameras caught all the action. From the next day onwards, entry into the Army Headquarters part of the South Block was further restricted. The Army PRO soon sent out a notice to the effect that it was logistically not possible for the *rakhis* to be sent to the soldiers on the front. The failure of the mass media to ask these groups why they were indulging in such politically motivated gestures spread the wholly erroneous and indeed mischievous impression that the forces were partial to such groups.

One party went to the extent of putting up posters of the three service chiefs at a political rally in Haryana!

I brought all these happenings to Prime Minister Vajpayee's notice. He graciously acknowledged the wrong doings of the party workers belonging to the different constituents of the National Democratic Alliance and other supporting organizations. But his advice to me was: 'Do not be extrasensitive!'

In one of the near-election generous moods, the chief minister of a northern state, which is considered one of the poorest despite its rich mineral resources, wanted to give one lakh rupees to every soldier from that state who had served in the Kargil war zone. This amount was to be in addition to a large sum that had been announced for soldiers from that state who had been killed in the war. As the chief minister's gesture would have adversely affected the morale of soldiers from other states, we politely declined the offer.

No war in the past had been fought on the eve of general elections. None of them had influenced the domestic electoral

---

[5]In Hindu society, Rakshabandhan is a festival that is celebrated every year. On this occasion, a sister ties a *rakhi* (a thread with decorations attached) on her brother's wrist, and he promises to protect her from all evils.

dynamics in the way the Kargil crisis did. The inability of the political establishment to reach a national consensus at the time of war tended to affect the chain of military command and the morale of the troops. The armed forces were anguished because they were getting sucked into electoral politics as a result of the blatant attempts to politicize the war for immediate electoral advantage. At one stage, in desperation, I had to send across a strong message through the media: 'Leave us alone: we are apolitical.'[6]

I spoke about this predicament to a retired senior, who was a friend. I asked him as to how could we get our message across to the opposition parties. He advised me to meet Dr Manmohan Singh, then the leader of the opposition in the Rajya Sabha. My senior arranged a meeting with him in August 1999, and also accompanied me. Dr Manmohan Singh was extremely courteous. He appreciated the adverse consequences of the armed forces getting caught in political crossfire. He felt that the prime minister ought to call an all-party meeting on this important matter and advised me to speak to him. I did so. But like so many other issues in the government that are discussed and action promised, this matter, too, remained unattended to.

The Kargil war had no doubt thrown up many important policy challenges. These included the need for procurement and qualitative upgradation of equipment, understanding the spectrum of conflict from low-intensity operations to a full-scale war, the relationship between nuclear and conventional deterrence, a massive restructuring of the national intelligence apparatus, reworking of the higher defence organization and the promotion of greater coordination between the civilian and military establishments. But all these crucial issues were never debated in the post-Kargil war election campaign or in the Parliament by the political parties.

For sometime after the war, very few leaders from the opposition were seen at the military investiture ceremonies held

---

[6]'Leave Us Alone: Gen. Malik to Parties'. *The Indian Express*, 23 August 1999.

in the Rashtrapati Bhavan (President's House). Such a state of affairs was noticeable and many senior serving and retired officers wondered why things should be so. The ground reality is that a soldier fights for the nation, regardless of which party or group of parties is in power.

While the conflict was on, there was close coordination between the armed forces and the government, especially the Ministries of Defence, External Affairs and Home Affairs besides the Prime Minister's Office. Such cooperation indeed proved to be a war-winning factor. The services chiefs took an active part in the meetings of the CCS, which met on an almost daily basis. Informed and enlightened cooperation among the political leadership, the civil services and the armed forces, backed by public support, constituted a unique example of a successful security and strategic exercise. This sort of synchronization among diverse entities, involving consultation, decision making and resultant action, had not taken place for quite a long time; in fact, almost since the 1971 war. Soon after the Kargil war, two more serious security-related incidents came to the fore: the shooting down of Pakistan maritime reconnaissance aircraft in August 1999 and the hijacking of Indian Airlines flight IC 814 to Kandahar in Afghanistan towards the end of December 1999. (I shall not dwell on these topics, which are beyond the scope of this book.)

Upon my urging, Prime Minister Vajpayee agreed to resume the practice of monthly informal interaction with the three service chiefs over tea. This practice was started by Mrs Indira Gandhi but had been stopped by the prime ministers who followed her. During these meetings, we shared views on important strategic and security matters. These meetings helped in developing better understanding at the politico-military level and could be extremely useful during a crisis situation or when tough security-related decisions had to be taken. Yet, certain sections misconstrued this entirely laudable development as proof of the Army's 'politicization'. The Ministry of Defence and the Cabinet Secretariat also expressed strong resentment to such meetings. This practice was again stopped soon after my retirement.

It is unfortunate that attempts to make political capital out of sensitive strategic and organizational issues pertaining to the armed forces did not stop even after the Kargil war or the elections. The politicization of the Kargil war has become so sharp that the sensitivities involved in such a crucial event are seldom considered. Political rivalries have also been a major cause of delays in making essential defence purchases, thereby affecting the operational capabilities of the armed forces adversely. Even in 'aid-to-civil-authorities' operations such as the maintenance of law and order and providing disaster relief, the Army has not been spared; it has often been enmeshed in political controversies.[7]

Tall Journalism

In August 2000, an opposition party leader held a press conference and, without ascertaining facts from the Army, claimed that Pakistan was continuing to occupy six peaks on our side of the LoC in Kargil. The Army was once again brought into this political crossfire. It was alleged that the Army had not disclosed the true facts. There were several critical reports in the media the next day. Despite denials by Army Headquarters, and even by the Pakistani military spokesman, the controversy continued. A rather vicious report was published in the *Statesman*, New Delhi, in the first week of September 1999. When factual details were conveyed to the then editor-in-chief, C.R. Irani (who passed away on 23 July 2005), a journalist known for his courage and convictions, he promptly wrote an editorial entitled 'Sorry Chief! We Apologize for the Publication Yesterday'. In this column, he not only apologized but also condemned political leaders tending to denigrate the Army by making unverified statements.

In mid-2004, an attempt was made by some mediapersons to blame the National Democratic Alliance Government for the delay in the use of air power during the Kargil war. This 'blame

---

[7]'Army Caught in Crossfire', *The Times of India*, New Delhi, 23 November 1999.

game' soon snowballed into a major controversy, leading to acrimonious political rivalry. Such a controversy could easily affect the joint working between the Army and the Air Force. (In Chapter 7, I have explained the exact circumstances under which the decision to call in the Air Force was taken.) It goes to the credit of the defence minister in the new United Progressive Alliance Government (which came to power in May 2004) that, after taking into account the details of decisions taken in the thick of the Kargil war, he unequivocally set to rest all unwanted speculation, rising above narrow political interests. However, the controversy over the Comptroller and Auditor General's report on the arms and equipment purchases done during and soon after the war is still very much alive.

Even the Kargil victory day (26 July) continues to be politicized. Initially, the National Democratic Alliance Government encouraged celebrations on that day. The prime minister (Atal Behari Vajpayee), the defence minister (George Fernandes), other cabinet ministers and some political leaders participated in the functions with great fervour. But after election fever subsided (elections to the Parliament and state assemblies), the government and the National Democratic Alliance parties set the trend of going in for 'quiet functions'.[8] The United Progressive Alliance partners, in any case, have seldom spoken of the Kargil victory or encouraged celebrating the day.

Often, the excuse trotted out for holding quiet celebrations or for not celebrating at all is that the 'peace process with Pakistan' would be jeopardized.[9] This stand is surprising, particularly when our senior political leaders seldom hesitate to

---

[8]Ironically, the BJP and its allies (that form the NDA), in the opposition in July 2005, planned to observe a week-long 'Vijay Utsav' (victory celebration). 'Eye on Pak Talks, Kargil Celebration to Be Low Key,' *The Indian Express*, 22 July 2005.

[9]The same excuse was given in December 1996 also when the armed forces planned to hold silver jubilee celebrations to mark their victory in the 1971 Indo–Pak war. The cabinet secretary summoned a meeting of the secretaries to discuss the issue. The three service chiefs/their representatives had to argue the case forcefully before the president, the prime minister and other political leaders gave their consent to participate in the events.

meet and greet other world leaders and join victory celebrations commemorating the Second World War in different countries. It must be remembered that the strategic environment of a nation keeps shifting but its history cannot be altered. Neglect of the military history of the nation reflects a weak strategic culture and a lack of military confidence. One is tempted to remind our leaders and civil officials of what Earnest Renan (a well-known historian) once wrote: 'What constitutes a nation is not speaking the same tongue or belonging to the same ethnic group but having accomplished great things in common in the past and the wish to accomplish them in future.'

In any nation, accountability is a prerequisite for good governance. However, institutional or individual accountability on sensitive issues concerning national defence policies and the armed forces needs to be sought within the framework of civilian and military establishments of the country, but outside the ambit of political jingoism.

For maintaining national defence and for keeping the men and women in uniform apolitical, it is essential that we improve public awareness about defence matters and about the armed forces. In this context, it would be relevant to introspect how much our political leaders and the public at large know. Barring small urban segments of Indian society, the rest of the country has little knowledge of the armed forces: their systems, procedures, traditions and methods of functioning. Also, a general lack of awareness persists about the issues and concerns that affect the functioning of the armed forces.

During the course of any war, or soon after that, the armed forces are glorified, greatly respected and even treated with awe. In our country, very soon after the war, they feel forgotten and neglected by the political leadership and the society. This does not happen in other developed countries and their societies. The point that needs to be driven home is that the armed forces represent the most significant and ultimate instrumentality for sustaining the Indian polity and are a manifestation of the *collective* political will of the Indian state. This situation, unfortunately, is worsening progressively as the ruling elites in the country – consisting of politicians, bureaucrats and industrialists – have for the past few years virtually stopped sending their kith and kin to join the armed forces. The result has been an ever-increasing distance between our civil society, including the aforementioned three categories, and the armed forces. Most of the retired officers from the armed forces, having remained apolitical all their lives, are loath to join active politics. For the same reason, political parties seldom sponsor them for membership of the Rajya Sabha.

I would like to emphasize that awareness about the armed forces and defence matters amongst our political leaders and bureaucrats is not only desirable, but it is also an imperative so as to ensure national security and to strengthen the armed forces in all dimensions: from the psychological level right up to their operational capacities. Conversely, the armed forces should not exist in a state of insulation or isolation from the people as well as from those responsible for the country's governance.

Political 'interference' in the promotion system of the armed forces with a view to favouring 'known' officers, particularly in the senior ranks, must not be attempted at all. There is nothing more demoralizing, and nothing more erosive of the system in place in the armed forces, than to see an undeserving senior officer being promoted on the basis of 'political contacts'.

Another tendency noticed amongst some overenthusiastic secretarial staff in the Ministry of Defence is to bypass the laid-down chain of command and telephonically convey the minister's 'desire' to a lower command or staff functionary. One such instance took place in June 2000 in connection with the 'Sindhu Darshan' festival in Ladakh. I cautioned the Army and corps commanders to discourage such communications on politically sensitive issues. While the chief and his principal staff officers would know how to handle 'desires' or 'requests' from the political leaders, officers in the field have no such experience. They would take these 'desires' or 'requests' as 'directions' from the higher command.

The crucial question at this stage is: What steps can be considered immediately to improve the awareness level of our political leaders and bureaucrats given the prevailing circumstances?

First and foremost, all Members of Parliament should be made to go through 'a capsule awareness programme' on national security and on the role of the armed forces during their first session itself. The Parliamentary Committee on Defence and the Standing Committee of the Parliament on Defence Matters should be regularly briefed by the armed forces' representatives on topics such as the evolving security environment, India's defence requirements and military sociology. Members of these committees must make field trips occasionally to familiarize themselves with the ground realities. Whenever possible, they should spend a few days with the units and formations of the armed forces. The president of India, as the commander-in-chief of the armed forces, the prime minister, the defence minister and ministers of state for defence, should also visit different field areas periodically to identify themselves with the troops, get to know their working conditions and help in boosting their morale.

There is a need to reserve a couple of seats in the Rajya Sabha for retired military officers. Given the importance of national security, the specialized role that our armed forces have to play and the amount of money that is spent annually to maintain them and their capabilities, the party/parties in power at the Centre could also consider inducting at least one 'professional' (not necessarily a retired military officer) as a minister of state in the Ministry of Defence. We need to induct more students from schools and colleges into the National Cadet Corps, and then, motivate them to join the armed forces.

There is also a need to increase the interaction between the armed forces and universities and academic institutions in the country. Such interaction would be helpful in improving public awareness and understanding of national security issues as also in the training and career planning of armed forces' personnel. Many universities have already started national security-related programmes. But unlike the academic institutions in other democratic countries, there is limited interaction between our universities and the military establishment in India.

Our defence establishment, our political class and our media, all have to realize their responsibility to generate public awareness about the functioning of the armed forces.

Lastly, the repeated or prolonged utilization of the armed forces to deal with internal security situations and law-and-order problems should be minimized. Such a step too will protect the armed forces from getting 'politicized'.

17

The Information Battle

Media moulds national and international opinion. It can be a potent force multiplier, or a force degrader. Even in circumstances of proxy war, the battle for the hearts and minds is of paramount importance. There is no point in winning the battle of bullets if you lose the war as a result of alienating the masses.

> It is better to attack the enemy's mind than to attack his fortified cities.
>
> Sun Tzu

> An archer letting off an arrow may or may not kill a single man, but a wise man using his intellect can kill even reaching into [the] very womb.
>
> Chanakya

THE KARGIL WAR WAS INDIA'S FIRST 'TELEVISION WAR'. KARGIL entered homes throughout the nation, both as a battleground and as a symbol. Why and how was that objective achieved? What are the lessons for the future? These are some of the important questions that this chapter seeks to answer.

But first, a little background information needs to be provided.

The relationship between war and the projection of war (including propaganda) is as old as warfare itself. No wonder, epics such as the Ramayana and the Mahabharata are studded with war accounts. This relationship, like warfare itself, is constantly changing. As a result of phenomenal technological developments in recent times, the conduct of warfare and its impact as a result of the media blitzkrieg have played a vital role in influencing events, both on the battlefield and outside it.

Information warfare – as a psychological pressure tactic – is not new at all. Kautilya (another name of Chanakya) and Sun Tzu advocated such warfare centuries ago with a view to defeating the enemy even before a battle actually began. The information blitzkrieg started to assume crucial importance in modern warfare ever since the first Gulf War in January 1991, which elevated the importance of on-the-spot information to a level where it is now being accepted as a tool, or even a new medium, for conducting wars. What is new is the seamless and integrated approach to the dissemination of both information and disinformation, sometimes with lethal effect. In this age of information overload, the deluge of news befuddles and bewilders both the leaders and public more than ever before. The basic challenge today is how to manage real-time information. The 2003 war in Iraq took the information assault to a new dimension through 750 embedded journalists, multiple TV channels, print media and websites working round the clock. Apart from soldiers, this war also witnessed a large number of journalist casualties.

What is the strategic justification for the information war? According to the Prussian military historian Carl von Clausewitz, a trinity made up of the government, the armed forces and the people wages war. A close interplay among them is essential to ensure victory. The government establishes the political purpose or aim, the military provides the instrument for achieving the political end and the people provide the will. All three components are indispensable.

Wars involve the entire people and not just the armed forces. The civil–military interface represents an important dimension of war and has to be suitably addressed. The people at large have to be mobilized so that they contribute to the war effort. It is through the media that people at home, and abroad, are kept fully abreast of developments so that they are not misled by rumours, propaganda and disinformation spread by the enemy. During a war, the backing of the public becomes essential for building national morale, winning popular support and understanding, for influencing international opinion and for shaping diplomatic reactions. Consequently, the information onslaught has come to be recognized as the 'fourth front' of war.

Media moulds national and international opinion. It can be a potent force multiplier, or a force degrader. Even in circumstances of proxy war, the battle for the hearts and minds is of paramount importance. There is no point in winning the battle of bullets if you lose the war as a result of alienating the masses.

The United States' Joint Chiefs of Staff define information war as follows: 'Action taken to achieve information superiority in support of national military strategy by affecting the adversary's information and information systems while leveraging and protecting own information and information systems.' Simply put, it means any action taken to deny, exploit, corrupt or destroy the enemy's information and its functions, while protecting oneself from the adversary's actions and exploitation of one's own military information functions.

The information war covers several aspects, including 'public affairs'. The 'public affairs' component comprises the use of the media to keep the masses informed and to build up public support. These objectives are supposedly achieved through overt and covert dissemination of well-conceived and effectively devised messages through the media and at the same time remaining alert to offset any hostile counterattacks in this field. The foregoing discussion should give the reader an idea of how the military in democratic countries has to cope with the emerging realities of information warfare.

The United States faced a credibility gap during the Vietnam war (in the late 1960s and early 1970s), which they attributed to the conflicting versions emerging from the unrestricted reports of journalists covering the day-to-day battles from the jungle and the official military briefings in Saigon. Over the years, the powers that be in Washington D.C. had evidently learnt some lessons. In the 1991 Gulf war, the US Administration was able to convince the mediapersons to adhere to certain guidelines. Journalists were asked to accompany military units in special 'pools'. These 'pools' represented newspapers, wire services, television and radio and news magazines. 'Pool' stories were submitted for 'security review' and cleared by defence spokesmen. All information provided outside the censored 'pool reports' came from detailed, professional official military briefings or as answers to questions raised by journalists during such briefings. All these factors were expected to make the news reports credible.

It would be interesting to ascertain how information technology has worked wonders for the media and how it has affected war coverage. Factors such as multiplicity of sources, speed, instant reach, transparency and excessive inputs have been dominant. Most of these factors have been positive. But there are some negative aspects also that require to be satisfactorily dealt with. For instance, IT can beam instant multidimensional pictures of an ongoing battle to the audiences worldwide, neither fitting the images into an overall context, nor providing any analysis or assessment in most cases. Instead of giving a clearer picture of the events taking place in the battle zones, these new tools often manage to obfuscate the facts and confuse the target audience. Earlier, transmission delays and production problems allowed adequate time for editing and putting things in perspective. Today, news is invariably unfiltered – and rapid.

I learnt my first major lesson in information warfare during Operation Blue Star when the Government of India, for reasons not known to me then, imposed strict censorship on the media. (Operation Blue Star, carried out in June 1984, entailed sending in the Army to flush out Sikh militants holed up in the Golden Temple at Amritsar, the holiest shrine of the Sikhs. Many people considered this move an act of sacrilege.) Such 'gagging' of the media gave rise to a spate of potentially dangerous rumours and to a disinformation campaign about the damage caused to the structures within the Golden Temple complex. All sorts of canards were doing the rounds regarding the situation in the towns and villages of Punjab in the aftermath of Operation Blue Star. Such a state of affairs had an immediate adverse impact on the morale of troops, especially the Sikhs. Also, the people of Punjab and the neighbouring states were quite agitated. I was then commanding a brigade near Jammu. It required all the tact and support of the saner elements in the brigade to handle the situation. Four years later, under conditions that were not as difficult or complex, and when we had learnt new lessons, Operation Black Thunder (1988) conducted by the National Security Guards was a neat, well-planned job; it was a great success.

During operations carried out by the Indian Peace-Keeping Force in Sri Lanka in 1987 (Operation Pawan), those responsible for the information war did a reasonably good job. Despite their efforts, they somehow failed to get the requisite moral support

at the national level for such operations. This failure led to a
serious setback: people began raising the issue as to why the
Indian armed forces were sent to the island-nation in the first
place. A former national security advisor, the late J.N. Dixit,
who was India's high commissioner in Sri Lanka during that
period, admitted to this shortcoming:

> The political leadership as well as the civil establishment did
> not educate the public opinion about the macro-level strategic
> motivations of the Indian mediation in the Sri Lanka crisis.
> People were not informed about the complex and
> contradictory undercurrents affecting not only the relations
> between the Tamils and the Sinhalese but [also] amongst the
> Sri Lankan Tamils themselves. Nor was the public kept
> informed in precise terms about the Indo–Sri Lanka
> Agreement and the induction of the Indian Peace-Keeping
> Force being two separate exercises even though they had
> some linkages…. The result was the absence of unified
> public support for the Indian initiative in Sri Lanka and
> ambiguity and confusion about the purpose of military
> involvement even among officers of our armed forces.[1]

As I have mentioned at the beginning of this chapter, the
Kargil war (Operation Vijay) was India's first television war.
During Operation Vijay, both the military and the media were
(as they still are) on the learning curve as far as new concepts
and methodologies were concerned. We won the information
battle primarily due to factors such as full accessibility to the
media, transparency (to the extent possible), adoption of a holistic
approach towards the entire situation and, above all, the credible
daily media briefings that were conducted jointly by the officers
from the operational directorates of the Services Headquarters
and from the Ministry of External Affairs. The Army operational
staff also held briefings at Northern Command and 15 Corps
levels. These briefings not only helped the armed forces to

---

[1] Field Marshal K.M. Cariappa Memorial Lecture, New Delhi, 26 October
1997.

project the Kargil war in its correct perspective but also brought the whole nation together and raised patriotic feelings amongst the masses. Raminder Jassal, joint secretary (external publicity, XP) of the Ministry of External Affairs, Colonel Bikram Singh of the Army and Group Captain Devendranath Ganesh of the Air Force became household names. Whenever important information had to be conveyed, External Affairs Minister Jaswant Singh, Director General Military Operations (DGMO) Nirmal Chander Vij, assistant director general Military Operations, J.J. Singh, and the assistant chief of Air Staff (Operations), S.P. Tyagi, also briefed the media.[2] I myself held a session with the media on 23 June 1999 and interacted with senior journalists and editors from time to time. Many of the Indian TV channels covered the 23 June event live.

It must, however, be acknowledged that such coordination and synchronization could not have been achieved without the unstinted support of the mediapersons and our excellent rapport with them. Senior editors and other top-level journalists were always accessible (and responsive), and were willing to carry war-related news items at short notice in the print or electronic media. They were ready to give their expert advice whenever needed.

During the initial stages of the conflict, primarily due to large-scale movements of troops and security reasons, journalists were not permitted beyond the Zoji La pass. However, we soon realized that due to the civil population living in the war zone, it was impossible to stop mediapersons from entering that zone and to file stories, without the benefit of any briefings, as they perceived the ground reality. Most of the public relations officers, including some from the Army, had very little knowledge or experience of combat situations. They were unable to respond adequately, or in time, to the queries raised by the domestic and foreign mediapersons. Also, as they belonged to the Ministry of Defence ranks, they tended to be bureaucratic in their approach and, most of the time, wanted clearance from the ministry higher-ups before they would convey any information to the media or answer any queries. In addition to their services, we

---

[2]All three officers became chiefs later in their service career.

also roped in the Army Liaison Cell, which was quickly restructured, and ad hoc media centres were set up at Udhampur, Srinagar and Kargil. A multipronged strategy was evolved. The Army Headquarters set up an interactive website. While the Military Operations Directorate handled the briefings, the Intelligence Directorate worked on the psychological aspects related to war. The electronic, print and cyber media were orchestrated to meet their demands as well as our own. The Army Liaison Cell, for the duration of the war, was placed under Major General Arjun Ray, who was summoned from the Army Training Command, Shimla. He had earlier served as brigadier, General Staff, in Headquarters 15 Corps. He had an academic background and had gained adequate experience in handling the media. He attended most of the operational conferences and thus knew the macro-level situations well.

A director from the Military Operations Directorate, Colonel Bikram Singh (mentioned earlier), was assigned the responsibility for holding daily media briefings. Captain Manvendra Singh, a Territorial Army officer and a professional journalist (who later became a Member of Parliament) and systems officers from the Army Chief's Secretariat also handled many of the functions in the Army Liaison Cell to make its impact more effective.

Lieutenant General M. L. Chhibber, who had been the director of Military Operations and the Northern Army commander, also helped us in preparing some briefs for the media.

After consulting some established and respected media persons, we tried to implement the 'pool' methodology used during the Gulf war, which entailed daily briefings in Delhi, taking mediapersons to the war zone and the operational staff providing a rundown of the main events. But unlike during the Gulf war, the media reports were not subjected to censorship. Unfortunately, without a proper infrastructure (which has still not been put in place!), the ad hoc liaison system in the field suffered from certain limitations. For instance, it could not cope with the operational commitments as well as the wartime demands of the media. The Indian media, not used to being 'conducted', resented this procedure and almost boycotted the exercise. Hence, the 'conducted site tours' were discontinued after some time. After that, the mediapersons got near total freedom to move around on their own except in those areas where their lives were considered to be in danger.

Our information policy was based on the following directives:

- Expose Pakistani lies about the Pakistan Army not being involved in the operations and about the LoC in the Kargil sector not being clearly delineated. Counter any other Pakistani disinformation campaign.
- Put across the national policy of restraint, emphasize the probity of, and the justification for, our military action and support the military strategy for war.
- Make people aware of the traditional strength and the organizational capabilities of the Army. Also, highlight gallantry displayed by the troops, their high morale, the esprit de corps in and among the various units, the competent leadership and, above all, the determination to win the war.
- Convey the news from the war zone as soon as possible without compromising on security.
- *Do not deviate from the truth.* Give out only facts and establish trustworthiness. Views and analyses to be given by senior officers only.

As the war progressed, it became easy to expose Islamabad's lies and disinformation about the non-involvement of the Pakistan Army. Besides the taped telephone conversation between Pakistan's Army chief, General Pervez Musharraf, and his chief of General Staff (see Appendix 2), we made use of hundreds of Pakistani Army official documents, identity cards, demi-official letters, personal diaries, letters and photographs that were captured after every battle starting with Tololing. Some of these items were shown on the TV channels that were viewed in Pakistan also so that all doubts could be dispelled among the public there about who had initiated the war and what was happening now. Pakistan Army equipment captured during different battles was exhibited on TV from time to time.

Mediapersons were taken to places where our soldiers buried Pakistani soldiers killed in the war with due solemnity and after performing the requisite ceremonies.

The Military Operations Directorate showed the *original copies* of the maps of the Kargil sector that had been delineated after the Shimla Agreement and which carried signatures of senior Indian and Pakistani officers. Captured Survey of Pakistan maps that had the LoC marked clearly on them were also displayed.

In addition to the daily media briefings, the Army Liaison Cell organized several discussions involving senior strategic analysts including retired officers of the armed forces who wrote for the print media or participated in TV talk shows. This move helped in explaining, in broad terms, the national policy and the military strategy without going into operational details. In the field, after every battle, or after every few days, mediapersons were briefed at the corps, division and brigade level.

While carrying out counterterrorist operations, we had obtained permission from the Government of India to hand over the bodies of soldiers killed in action to their kith and kin in villages and towns anywhere in India and to give them a ceremonial cremation or burial. Despite suffering much heavier casualties during the Kargil war, this practice was continued during the war. When the media covered these events and the images began to be projected extensively, a retired senior Army officer, who was a well-wisher, advised me to discontinue the practice immediately as it could affect the national morale adversely. However, we stuck to our decision. Those visuals shown over TV channels were undoubtedly poignant. But instead of having a negative impact, they helped to bring the whole nation together and resulted in a palpable surge of patriotism. The respect and honour given by the public to the Kargil martyrs also proved helpful, to some extent, in consoling their near and dear ones. All other soldiers sincerely felt that the nation cared for them and their families. These images also helped in firming up the resolve of the armed forces personnel who were fighting the war. The power of public opinion in India could not be discounted. The pictures showing the caskets of the Kargil martyrs reaching almost all parts of India, and representing the true spirit of India's cultural and religious pluralism, surcharged the people's emotions beyond expectations. This was indeed India's first information war in which the power of the audio-visual and print media in shaping national and international opinion was demonstrated in full measure.[3]

The military and the media did not indulge in any deliberate misinformation tactics. Together, they succeeded in achieving their objectives: they effectively exposed the Pakistani lies and put paid to the disinformation campaign. The almost instantaneous war reporting, depending on the experience and the analytical capability of the journalists, was fairly objective and was extremely helpful in obtaining overwhelming public support for the war effort.

But it was not smooth going all the way! Some civilians in the corridors of power in the Ministry of Defence did not appreciate the military approach and its initiatives with regard to the information war. The public relations establishment, manned mostly by the officials from the Information and Broadcasting Ministry, felt left out. They thought that they had 'lost control'. In August 1999, when a Pakistani maritime reconnaissance aircraft flying inside our territory was shot down by an Indian Air Force fighter plane, the Ministry of Defence public relations officer reverted to briefing the media himself, without informing or consulting operational staff of the services. He made a hash of that briefing, which was televised all over the world. The next day, at my insistence and with the help of the external affairs minister, we reimplemented the Kargil war procedure that entailed joint media briefing by the Ministry of External Affairs' officials and by service officers from the Operational Directorate.

This episode, including the role of the Army Liaison Cell, became a cause of strained relations between the Ministry of Defence and the Army Headquarters. In fact, after the war, senior military participants were not even invited to one of the interministerial post-war meetings to analyse the matters relating to dealing with the media during wartime. We learnt later that the defence minister did not take too kindly to senior military officers interacting with the media. I, however, felt that we needed to change our norms and attitudes with the times. This

---

[3] *Kargil 1999: Pakistan's Fourth War for Kashmir* [The Institute for Defence Studies and Analyses (IDSA), New Delhi, p. 191].

remained a sore point between us till the end of my tenure.

During the war, we also had to face some unexpected problems due to professional competition amongst mediapersons. Some of these dicey situations occurred not due to any malintention but because our public relations officers and formation staff at lower levels were unaware of media sensitivities. When we wanted to expose deliberate Pakistani disinformation on the 'vagueness' of the LoC, the Army Liaison Cell staff recommended that a private TV channel, with our assistance and after our approval, would prepare and telecast a short documentary on the subject. The approval, however, was exploited to record video broadcasts from an Army helicopter. The competitors immediately began complaining about this development and also about the 'preferential treatment' given to the journalists of this particular TV channel. Late one night, the minister for information and broadcasting, Pramod Mahajan, brought to my notice the fact that a large number of mediapersons were up in arms over this issue. I explained to him our objective in getting the documentary made and informed him that I was not aware of the so-called 'preferential treatment' but would definitely look into the matter. The next morning, I had the situation corrected by banning any more recording of video broadcasts from Army helicopters.

The Kargil crisis took place under a caretaker government (in the aftermath of the fall of the Vajpayee Government), when the country was poised for another general election. As explained earlier, the political polarization and prevailing circumstances managed to politicize the war and drag the armed forces into the political crossfire. Regrettably, as admitted by some strategic experts and mediapersons, 'some of the media's war coverage tended to become both the vehicle and victim of such politicization'.[4]

---

[4]*From Surprise to Reckoning: The Kargil Review Committee Report* (Sage Publications, New Delhi, 2000, p. 23). Also see, 'Politics and Media Together Can Be a Dangerous Cocktail for the Armed Forces Which Could Adversely Affect Its Apolitical Nature', *Hindustan Times*, New Delhi, 25 October 1999.

Some incidents of unverified or deliberate reporting – in which events were somewhat distorted – by the media also came to light. Consequently, the Army Liaison Cell sent off complaints to the Press Council of India. In one case, a news magazine published certain stories based on interviews given by Brigadier Surinder Singh (who had his own axe to grind) and also printed some fabricated or doctored letters. All this was done without giving a chance to the Army public relations officer or the Army Liaison Cell to clarify the situation. When the editor of this news magazine was invited to a meeting by the Army authorities, he backed out, giving some excuse. The articles were so malicious and slanderous in nature that the Army Headquarters felt compelled to issue a press release (see Appendix 4) on the subject.[5] Later, the Press Council of India upheld the validity of the Army's complaint and issued a warning to the news magazine.[6]

The decisions to ban cable operators from showing Pakistan TV and to stop the Videsh Sanchar Nigam Limited (VSNL) from accessing *Dawn*'s (a Pakistani newspaper) website were, in my view, not well considered. These decisions, however, had nothing to do with the military; they were purely political.

After the war, as expected, both the Army and the media went in for self-introspection. Such introspection proved to be interesting and instructive and, sometimes amusing, too.

Most experienced journalists felt that although there were some shortcomings, but overall, it was a job well done. Many Pakistanis who met me after the war also expressed the view that our media reports had revealed the truth to them. They were very impressed with the interaction among the military, the civilians and the media. They felt that the truth revealed to them through our media reports had affected the morale of their soldiers and citizens.

---

[5]A political leader carried a copy of this issue throughout his election campaign. He would display it to the gullible vote bank that could not read or write a word of English.

[6]Press Council of India, Press Release no. PR/60/2000-PCI, dated 19 September 2000.

Analysis by the Army indicated that there was very little time during the conflict to train public relations and other staff officers on how to interact with the media or to educate mediapersons on military, strategic and operational matters. Most of the appointed public relations officers had no combat experience and, therefore, could not respond readily or confidently to strategy- and operation-related questions. Consequently, we felt that there was an urgent requirement to improve their education as far as dealing with the media was concerned and to enhance their linkages to those departments of the Army handling operations, intelligence, personnel and equipment. We also felt that the media-related infrastructure at the corps and division levels needed to be upgraded for coping with wartime contingencies.

Most scribes who visited the war front lacked adequate knowledge of military organizations, basic battle zone tactics and arms and equipment. Most of them preferred road-head reporting rather than more realistic combat reporting, which would have entailed climbing mountains and being exposed to harsh weather conditions. The electronic media teams, due to the heavy gear they had to carry, could not go beyond the road level to cover high-altitude operations. As the infrastructure or equipment for media transmission did not exist in Kargil or even at Leh, reports had to be couriered across the Zoji La pass to Srinagar and then on to Delhi. Doordarshan, the official government TV channel with the largest infrastructure and network and maximum viewership in the country, failed to capitalize on its strengths. Although Doordarshan was already interacting with the military through the Ministry of Home Affairs, it was rather slow in covering the events. A pity indeed!

After the war, I invited Barkha Dutt (a well-known TV journalist known for her courageous reporting), who had covered the war commendably, to my office. I complimented her for her professionalism. Lightheartedly, I also mentioned about her letting out classified information in her professional enthusiasm by pointing out that during her coverage, she had given away a hint that our next objective would be Tiger Hill. She had obviously surmised that from the ongoing 'softening up' of this objective by the artillery bombardment and the Indian Air Force.

During our conversation, I found that she had something else on her mind, which was troubling her. She asked me if her speaking on the Iridium satellite phone could have given away the location of our guns or troops and thus helped the enemy to engage them with artillery. When I told her that we too were using such telephones and that the Pakistan Army did not have such monitoring equipment, she appeared quite relieved.

During the course of self-introspection, some analysts and journalists questioned the role of the media during its coverage of the war. They felt that the media had gone overboard. They also felt that the impact of television had been underestimated, and the reporting and analysis were disproportionate; there was more reporting and less analysis. Some commentators went to the extent of claiming that the mass media had been 'militarized'! Others stated that the media had 'glamourized' and 'trivialized' the war. One school of thought held that the media had 'humanized' the war. All these shades of opinion, I believe, reflect the sense of morality and the social norms prevalent in various parts of the nation. They have very little to do with the military. The military will always follow the generally accepted ethical and moral norms of the nation.

The lessons learnt during the Kargil episode from the 'information battle' and the concomitant shortcomings in the various establishments were taken note of. Several recommendations were put forward for rectifying the situation. Regrettably, hardly any of them have been implemented.

It must be realized that in the earlier days, when the media networks could not reach all the regions, the government and the military could hope to control the flow of information. Nowadays, they mostly respond. That was what happened in the last Iraq war in 2003 too. That was the first fully IT-enabled war. Instant firepower was matched by instant communications and instant interpretation. In contrast to earlier wars, when military censors controlled the coverage by war correspondents, reporters in Iraq war were embedded with the American and British forces. Other journalists roamed the countryside, reporting independently, out of reach of any public relations control or censorship regulation. According to one source: 'Their unfiltered stories were dramatic in their immediacy, but, as the broader picture became clear, the initial conclusions often proved to be overblown or plain misleading. The new form of war reporting catches events at their source, when they are still history's raw material. The earlier robust reporting has given way to what is now termed as *brittle reporting*. The result can be wide, unpredictable swings in public sentiment, compounding the government's challenge of building support for the war.'[7]

Thanks to the widespread advances in technology, information in the present day and age cannot be suppressed, and attempts to do so reflect badly on any government or organization involved. In India, we have yet to fully develop the information battle concepts and procedures. Only when that is done can we make proper use of them. While doing so, it would not be feasible to follow the American techniques. We need to develop our own, taking into account the capabilities, characteristics and sensitivities of our people. If the media is to serve as a force multiplier, we need to remember that it also has a democratic responsibility to maintain vigilance and to guard against manipulation. We have to take into account a range of issues such as the domestic political rivalries, commercial interests, media competition, the impact of globalization and the ethical and moral factors as far as the media is concerned. 'Appointed' or 'sponsored' media does not carry much credibility. 'Embedded' journalism is, therefore, unlikely to succeed in India.

The communications functions in the armed forces, which deal with the public and the media, need to be reorganized and made more professional as soon as possible. The forces must train their commanders and staff so that they can effectively discharge these functions. Also, they must enrol skilled communicators through the Territorial Army, or from amongst

---

[7]David Newkirk and Stuart Crainer, 'Management Lessons from Modern Wars', *Strategy and Business*, New York, Fall 2003.

talented officers who volunteer from the combat forces. They are the individuals, who, in the future, would hold the power to wield crucial offensive and defensive strategic weapons for converting information into understanding. It is encouraging to see that our journalists have been getting worthwhile opportunities lately to report on conflicts from other hot spots of the world and are thus gaining experience in this field. Although the training of civil and military officers in the area of mass media has been going on for some time, there is considerable scope for attitudinal changes in the government officials that could lead to further improvements. The government and the media would need to keep the following points in mind:

- The awareness level vis-à-vis national security, the military and modern warfare in India is very low as compared to the Western countries.
- Most of our security and media rules and regulations are antiquated. Till they are officially changed, media inputs will remain restricted and inadequate.
- Factors such as transparency and improved information flows can help boost morale, ensure understanding and fix accountability. These factors can prevent misreporting and help in presenting facts as they are.
- TV coverage is event oriented and fast paced. Such coverage leaves hardly any time for providing background information and going in for content analysis. It is the print media that can take up the latter aspects in a detailed and credible manner.

In the light of our experiences in the Kargil war and given tremendous technological developments in mass communications, we need to review urgently the information policies and public relations system in the Ministry of Defence.

18

The Kargil Impact

. . . the dissonance between Nawaz Sharif and Pervez Musharraf culminated in the 12 October 1999 military coup in Pakistan. When I was asked in a Cabinet Committee on Security (CCS) meeting if I was surprised by this development, my reply was: 'Yes! Yes, because it took so long to happen.'

> No one starts a war – or rather no one in his senses ought to do so – without first being clear in his mind what he intends to achieve by that war, and how he intends to conduct it.
>
> Carl von Clausewitz

OVER THE PAST FIFTY YEARS, CONVENTIONAL WARFARE HAS moved down the scale as far as factors such as intensity and inclusiveness are concerned. Potential nuclear warfare has given way to restricted nuclear deterrence; total war has yielded to limited, irregular and unconventional war. Low-intensity conflicts and limited wars are being waged more frequently nowadays. The use of military power for coercive diplomacy has increased but it has seldom culminated in a war. In most cases, either the aggressor or the victim has compromised to avoid the possibility of a war breaking out. The empirical evidence points towards a significantly lowered probability of a regular, high-intensity war.

Nowadays, a war may no longer be taken to the logical conclusion of notching up politico-military victories, as was the case in the past. Even the USA, the sole global superpower, and its multinational allies were not able to achieve a definitive victory in the Gulf war of 1990–91 or in the ensuing wars in Afghanistan and Iraq. Currently, it appears that wars are being conducted with the objective of achieving political success rather than military victories.

No war is winnable, not even a limited war, without a strong and invulnerable in-built politico-military framework within a nation. A nation that can clearly define achievable political goals would always have an inherent advantage.[1]

In the Kargil war, the Pakistan Army had taken the initiative and surprised us. We were reacting to a situation, like we had done in 1947–48, 1962 and 1965, when attacked by the enemy. The political objectives, not put down in black and white but discussed several times during the conflict, were to 'get the Kargil intrusion vacated and restore the sanctity of the LoC'. We went into the Kargil war on the basis of a policy of 'restraint'. An unambiguous political term of reference was that the LoC should not be crossed. I believe there were four main reasons for such restraint.

Firstly, we had to go to war so soon after the Lahore talks between the two prime ministers that our political establishment was taken aback. No one could believe that all the goodwill and bonhomie generated through Track-1 and Track-2 dialogues had collapsed and so abruptly. There were no intelligence indicators like extra tension between opposing forces deployed on the border, termination of leave of military personnel or recall of those already on leave, unusual military movements, combat and logistic build-up and preparation of defences on the border. Although the intelligence agencies did indicate that jehadi militants would continue their attempts at infiltration across the LoC and that there would be an increase in violent activities, there was not the faintest hint that the Pakistan Army was planning or preparing to send in regular troops on a large scale into the Kargil sector. Due to these inadequacies and also due to the Pakistani Army personnel masquerading as Mujahideen, the fog of war remained thick till the end of May 1999. All these factors made the political leaders react tentatively at first and adopt a cautious approach. It was only later that they decided to escalate the situation.

Secondly, it was essential to ensure diplomatically that international opinion was sufficiently in our favour. A favourable international opinion in a war is a major force multiplier. We

---

[1]From the author's papers and presentations on 'limited wars'.

had to convince the world that India was a victim of Pakistani aggression, which had violated the Shimla Agreement and the sanctity of the LoC as laid down therein. At the international level, diplomats needed concrete proof of Pakistan's military aggression: we had to furnish irrefutable evidence to show that the infiltrators were not Mujahideen militants but regulars belonging to the Pakistan Army. Simultaneously, as a nation that had blasted its way out of nuclear ambiguity recently and caused a major setback to the Non-Proliferation Treaty, there was the need to show 'greater responsibility and restraint'. That was the main reason why we had signed the memorandum of understanding along with the Lahore Declaration.

Thirdly, the nuclear factor did play on the minds of the decision makers, although this factor posed little problems for a limited war. However, political and military planning and preparation for conflict escalation had to be carried out carefully. Escalation control was essential. It is a well-known fact that during the 'hotting up' period, the civilian political leadership in all nuclear equipped countries tends to tighten its control over the military, particularly on its nuclear and missiles assets. There is nothing wrong with that. This is where a responsible, strategic decision-making difference comes to the fore between a democratically elected government and a military or a semi-military regime.

Fourthly, if the conflict had escalated, the possibility of major powers intervening to prevent a nuclear confrontation would be there. They would have sought an early termination of the war. This *could* have left a part of Pakistan-occupied territory in Kargil in its hands, which would have been a major setback for us politically and militarily. Moreover, Pakistan and countries friendly to it would have played up the issue of Jammu and Kashmir in international fora.

For the military, the grand strategy of exercising 'restraint' was no doubt a handicap. But such a strategy was politically justified, at least to start with. The Chiefs of Staff Committee (COSC) accepted it, but did not consider it as non-reviewable or unalterable. I stated this viewpoint clearly during the media briefing on 23 June 1999. The prime minister and the national security advisor were also advised that our political leadership should not give an impression that not crossing the LoC or the international border had an all-time sanctity. In a dynamic war situation, one has to cater for all contingencies. New situations can be caused either due to enemy action or due to some other unforeseen developments. In all contingency planning, the final goal is always to achieve the given political objective. *Kargil was a limited conventional war under the nuclear shadow where space below the threshold was available, but it had to be exploited carefully.* The political embargo on crossing the line of control or the border notwithstanding, the COSC and the operational directorates of the armed forces had done their planning and preparations for escalation (crossing the border or the LoC), if that became necessary, and was authorized by the Cabinet Committee on Security (CCS).

After recapturing Tololing and Point 5140, we gained confidence to continue our offensive actions in the area of conflict successfully by adhering to the given political directive. Some retired officers and military analysts have opined that the Indian Army would have suffered lesser casualties had it opened another front and crossed the border.[2] This opinion is questionable, not only because of the given political aim and terms of reference, but also because of the new combat environment. Modern, long-range, accurate and more lethal weapon systems, deployed three-dimensionally, would increase casualties in a larger combat environment substantially. In any battle, the number of casualties on account of splinters, shell injuries and blasts is much higher than gunshot wounds caused by small arms and other direct firing weapons. In the Kargil war, fought amidst high-altitude mountains, our casualties in the actual combat were 473 personnel killed (including five from the Air Force) and 1060 wounded.[3] More than 50 per cent of

---

[2]Jasjit Singh, 'Should India Cross the Line of Control?', *The Times of India*, 20 June 1999, and Generals V. N. Sharma and Shankar Roychowdhury, former chiefs of Army Staff, 'India May Have to Cross LoC: Experts', *Hindustan Times*, 21 June 1999.

[3]Pakistan till date has not made its casualty figures transparent. According to our intelligence estimates, their Army suffered over 737 casualties, primarily due to our artillery fire. Nawaz Sharif and many others from Pakistan have given different casualty figures. In his message to the

(cont.)

the wounded personnel after treatment *within the war* zone returned to their units. Also, 53.20 per cent of the casualties suffered splinter and shell injuries, 21.07 per cent were victims of gunshot wounds and the remaining 26.73 per cent were afflicted by burns, fractures, frostbite and so on. If we had enlarged the conflict, we could have possibly captured some Pakistani territory, but the casualties on account of being subjected to fire from artillery and other weapons would have been much more.[4]

It is now clear that Pakistan, alongside the February 1999 Lahore Declaration, had consciously planned to violate the LoC by military intrusion, authorized by the combined political and military leadership. When, we in India, were trying to see through the fog of war in May 1999, Pervez Musharraf admitted that his troops had captured 500 sq. km of Indian territory across the LoC in the Kargil sector.[5] However, the Pakistan Army bigwigs, masters in operating behind smoke screens, kept insisting that the Mujahideen, and *not* the regular troops, were involved. They also insisted that the LoC in this area was not delineated and was vague, and Pakistan Army patrols, if any, were in 'no man's land'.

However, when irrefutable evidence was made available, it became clear within Pakistan, and to the world outside, that the realities were quite the opposite. We published the maps of the area with Lieutenant General Abdul Hameed Khan's (Pakistan Army) signatures on the maps accurately delineating the LoC. These maps were a consequence of the Shimla Agreement of July 1972 and were exchanged between India and Pakistan. We

---

fifteen-party Alliance for Restoration of Democracy, on 14 August 2004, he mentioned a high figure. 'Over 4000 Pakistanis Killed in Kargil War: Sharif', Press Trust of India report in *The Tribune*, 17 August 2004.

[4]The number of our casualties in some previous wars is as follows: Indo–Pak war 1947–48: killed (K) 1104; wounded (W) 3154. Indo–China war 1962: K 3250, W 548. Indo–Pak war 1965: K 3264, W 8623; Indo–Pak war 1971: K 3843, W 9851.

[5]'General Musharraf Confirms Pak Army Captured Land in Kargil', Rediff on the Net, 9 September 1999.

put on public display the Survey of Pakistan maps recovered from sangars occupied by Pakistani Army personnel inside our territory with the delineated LoC clearly shown. We also provided evidence such as captured Pakistani weapons, equipment, official letters, parade states and posting orders issued by the Pakistan Army or its formations and units to prove that it was not the Mujahideen or jehadis but the Pakistani Army regulars who were operating within our territory. The Northern Light Infantry battalions along with other Army elements that had crossed the LoC had suffered heavy casualties. The Indian soldiers buried more than 270 Pakistani soldiers who had lost their lives in the war as per Muslim customs and rites. Pakistan's perfidy had been exposed to the whole world. Its irresponsible behaviour and lack of trustworthiness as an overt nuclear power stood manifestly exposed to the international community. This arena was certainly Pakistan's Waterloo from a military-diplomatic viewpoint, perhaps the second major national setback after its military defeat at the hands of India in 1971.

As the truth filtered out, all those responsible for the catastrophe began to be vehemently condemned within Pakistan. A trenchant volley of criticism as well as expressions of agony came from senior retired military officers, top-notch journalists and political leaders. Examples of these anguished outpourings are as follows:[6]

> We should admit that Kargil has been a complete disaster and failure.... Kargil is a fiasco that has brought us humiliation and isolated us in the world while eroding our credibility. (Lieutenant General Kamal Matinuddin, former director general, Institute for Strategic Studies, Islamabad, *The News*, 25 July 1999.)
>
> There is no justification for this operation having taken place at all. Pakistan has continued to make similar mistakes (since 1947) and has not learnt any lesson from the blunders that its ruling cliques have been committing. (Air Marshal Nur Khan, former chief of Air Staff, *The News*, 25 July 1999.)

---

[6]From *Kargil 1999: Pakistan's Fourth War for Kashmir* [The Institute for Defence Study and Analyses (IDSA), New Delhi, pp. 249–50].

The ill-planned adventure in Kargil comes to an ignominious end.... The Kargil affair has exposed systemic flaws in a decision-making process that is impulsive, chaotic, erratic and overly secretive...playing holy warriors this week and men of peace the next betrays an infirmity and insincerity of purpose that leaves the country leaderless and directionless. (Maleeha Lodhi, later Pakistan's ambassador to the US and the UK, 'Anatomy of a Debacle', *The Newsline*, July 1999.)

Kargil was no trophy for Pakistan. Was it then a trauma? A harsh word to use. Someone at a recent seminar called it a catastrophe, another faux pas, yet another a debacle. And so on. What mattered was the absence of a single word in support. (Brigadier A.R. Siddiqi, *The Nation*, 4 August 1999.)

The manner we lurched into it [Kargil], unthinkingly and on the basis of a set of false assumptions, reflected the intellectual bankruptcy which holds sway in our corridors of power. (Ayaz Amir, a respected Pakistani journalist, *The Dawn*, 6 August 1999.)

[The] Kargil operation was put on the drawing board by competent military minds many years ago. "Kargil" was presented [as] a "doable" option when the time was ripe, partly as military revenge for the loss of Siachen and partly as a political device to spur the Kashmiri Mujahideen towards greater sacrifice and heroism. (Editorial, *The Friday Times*, 30 July–5 August 1999.)

Having sleepwalked into a new disaster at Kargil, we halt at the edge of a precipice. We might have won a battle but we lost the war.... Confrontation with India over the past 50 years has apparently failed. Do we have the strength to recognize other options? (M.P. Bhandara, a senior parliamentarian from Rawalpindi, *The Dawn*, 21 July 1999.)

Kargil was the biggest blunder committed in the history of Pakistan...the whole operation has cost Pakistan heavily. It has given the people of Pakistan a sense of humiliation and disgrace because they were forced to withdraw in the face of international isolation and it has led to a deep sense of betrayal on the part of the Indians who believe that the Pakistani regime was duplicitous when undertaking peace efforts in the region. (Benazir Bhutto, former prime minister of Pakistan, 'Kargil Biggest Blunder in Pak History: Benazir', *The News*, 22 July 1999.)

The Kargil episode is a very sad and tragic part of our history. The more you go into it, the more traumatic it is. (Chaudhary Nisar Ali Khan, a former minister, 'Why Can't Generals Be Tried for Treason?' An interview with Chaudhary Nisar Ali Khan, *The Indian Express*, 24 November 2003.)

Diplomatically, Pakistan's Kargil venture isolated it completely, with its credibility in international fora touching an all-time low. At the same time, India enhanced its status internationally. The global response to India's politico-military handling of the conflict reflected a major change in the world's perspective vis-à-vis India, which began to be viewed as a responsible and restrained regional power. The international community took an unprecedented position: there was an aggressor (Pakistan), a victim (India), and the victim was acting within its rights by giving the aggressor a fitting reply.

As usual, the initial reaction of Washington was to equate India and Pakistan by urging 'mutual restraint'. But by the middle of June 1999, when the USA's surveillance satellites and intelligence sources had confirmed the involvement of the Pakistan Army and accepted the credibility of our statements, there was a discernible change in the attitude of the superpower. The ground realities and the Indian position were understood and appreciated better also because of the ongoing Jaswant Singh–Strobe Talbott dialogue over strategic issues. After sometime, the US Administration began to turn the full diplomatic heat on Pakistan. The US understood that the conflict would terminate only when the Pakistan Army withdrew from the Indian territory either forcibly or voluntarily and, ultimately, India would prevail.[7] For once the US took a position that was unequivocally in favour of India. Even Henry Kissinger (a former US secretary of state), known for his pro-Pakistan tilt during the 1971 war, declared that the US viewed the LoC as sacrosanct.

---

[7]N.C. Menon, 'Misbegotten Misadventure', *Hindustan Times*, 14 June 1999.

General Anthony Zinni, commander of the United States' Central Command, was sent to Pakistan to 'advise' Islamabad to act in a responsible manner or face the consequences. Most American newspapers chastised Pakistan for causing the imbroglio and lauded India's policy of restraint and the role played by the armed forces.

By the first week of July 1999, the writing was on the wall as far as the military operations were concerned. Tiger Hill was captured on 4 July 1999, about twenty hours before Nawaz Sharif got an audience with the president of the USA. The joint Clinton–Sharif statement from Blair House on the same date re-established the political sanctity of the LoC in Jammu and Kashmir. Also, it provided a diplomatic fig leaf for the Pakistan Army's inevitable withdrawal from Indian territory. But that was not to happen before the US president had chastised the Pakistani prime minister,[8] and extracted promises from him for taking covert action against Osama bin Laden and Al Qaeda in Afghanistan.

The Pakistani domestic reactions to the Washington joint statement were bitter and the vitriol was directed towards those who initiated the war:

Sharif's Washington trip was nothing more than a shameful surrender. (*The Newsline*, July 1999.)

That the Kargil adventure was ill conceived, if not downright foolish, was becoming clear, albeit slowly, even to the congenitally blind and benighted. That consequently Pakistan swallowing its pride and not a few of its brave and gallant words would sooner or later have to mount a retreat was also becoming clear. But that the climb-down when it came would be so headlong and ill-judged, and that in the process it would leave in tatters the last shreds of national pride, should take even prophets of doom by surprise. (Ayaz Amir, *The Dawn*, 9 July 1999.)

---

[8]Bruce Reidel, 'American Diplomacy and the 1999 Kargil Summit at Blair House', Policy Paper Series, Center for the Advanced Study of India, University of Pennsylvania, May 2002.

Pakistan's bargaining position has been weakened after the Kargil fiasco. Inconsistent, even contradictory, statements issued by the government, first disclaiming any link with the Mujahideen operations in Kargil and then accepting responsibility for their withdrawal have seriously damaged Pakistan's credibility internationally. (Afzal Mahmood, *The Dawn*, 18 July 1999.)

[The] Kargil venture was launched without adequate forethought. (M.B. Naqvi, *The Dawn*, 19 July 1999.)

The tailpiece of the Kargil fiasco is difficult to match in the annals of diplomatic humiliation. (M.P. Bhandara, *The Dawn*, 21 July 1999.)

The Kargil–Washington debacle has laid bare the dangers inherent in the secretive and non-consultative decision-making mode that has been the hallmark of the PML (Pakistan Muslim League) government. (Editorial, *The Dawn*, 24 July 1999.)

Not for the first time have we snatched defeat from the jaws of victory (at Kargil). (Ikram Sehgal, *The Nation*, 24 July 1999.)

Washington's tilt towards India, post-Kargil, was a turning point in Indo–US relations. Here, I would also like to acknowledge the role that the Indian diaspora played, particularly in the USA. The Indians living abroad not only supported welfare measures for those Army personnel killed and wounded in war through large donations but also, for the first time perhaps, organized themselves into strong lobbying groups to support India's diplomacy.[9] India's politico-military strategy during the Kargil war provided ample opportunities to New Delhi and Washington to strengthen relations, reflecting a positive trend that continues even today.

Other Western countries followed the same trend. The G-8 countries condemned the Pakistan Army infiltration. They warned that they would not remain mere spectators and demanded full respect for the LoC. The Indian politico-military predicament was clearly understood at the highest levels of

---

[9]This factor became evident when I visited the USA in November 1999.

most governments prior to the crucial G-8 Summit (scheduled for July 1999 in Cologne, Germany). From the diplomatic perspective, this summit marked an important milestone in endorsing our policy on Kargil. Our military successes, without doubt, played a crucial role in this context.

The British minister of state for South Asia, Geoffrey Hoon, waxed eloquent: 'The Government of India deserves to be congratulated for the restraint and maturity with which it handled the crisis.'[10] France deferred the delivery of forty Mirage fighter-bombers to Pakistan.

In the Western media, the burial of the bodies of Pakistani soldiers killed in action, as per solemn Islamic customs and rituals, by the Indian Army (after Pakistan refused to accept them) came out as a stirring tribute not only to India's secularism but also to the exemplary conduct of its soldiers.

Perhaps the most unexpected negative response for Pakistan came from its close strategic partner, China. No doubt, the People's Liberation Army (PLA) patrols made their presence felt in some areas along the Sino–Indian border, but their numbers were far too meagre to be of any military consequence. Diplomatically, there was a radical departure from Beijing's pro-Pakistan stance during previous Indo–Pak wars. With the nuclearization of the subcontinent and the likelihood of American intercession in the event of war escalation, the Chinese were probably concerned about the fallout. One prominent Chinese newspaper warned: 'India and Pakistan should consider that intensifying the conflict runs the risk of involving Western intervention.'[11] As the war progressed and Indian military success became evident, there were subtle shifts in the Chinese stand. China chose to spurn Pakistan's overtures on Kargil and preferred to go along with the overwhelming world opinion that saw India as a victim of aggression. Pakistan was advised by Beijing to withdraw its forces, abide by the LoC and revert to the Lahore Declaration. Ever since Kargil, China's neutral stance on Jammu and Kashmir and its positive tenor on many global and regional

---

[10]Saeed Naqvi, 'The Triumph of Restraint', *The Indian Express*, 16 July 1999.
[11]*China Daily*, 26 June 1999.

strategic issues have continued to make a mark on Sino–Indian relations.

The Kargil war also served to focus international attention on the Taliban and the role of the Pakistani establishment in sustaining these fundamentalist and terrorist elements. That was long before the 9/11 attacks.

It must, however, be noted that the international community only wanted India and Pakistan to come to a settlement. The intention mostly was to ensure that India should continue its policy of restraint and not escalate the situation into a full-scale conventional war.

Even before the war was over, in fact, even before Nawaz Sharif's visit to the USA on 4 July 1999, one could feel the dissonance between him and Pervez Musharraf through the conversations that took place between directors general of military operations over hotlines and through intelligence reports. Around mid-July 1999, it became clear that after the Kargil war, the Pakistani prime minister and his Army chief would never be able to trust each other. Such a discordant situation, given the Pakistan polity, was a serious aberration. It created an internal crisis due to the disequilibrium generated among the three major centres of the Pakistani establishment: the elected government, the Army and the religious groups waiting in the wings.

Nevertheless, the Pakistani prime minister continued to support his Army chief publicly. For example, Nawaz Sharif accompanied Pervez Musharraf to the Northern Areas, which had paid the maximum price for the Pakistan Army's misadventure. Most of the casualties suffered by the Northern Light Infantry were from this area. As the Pakistan Army did not accept its role in the planning and execution of the intrusion and the ensuing conflict, the families of Northern Light Infantry soldiers and others in the region were up in arms due to their personal grief, made even more intense by the fact that they could not see the bodies of their kith and kin. These people had to be pacified by none other than the prime minister. The questionable rationale of the Kargil initiative and its aftermath caused considerable doubts in, and led to demoralization among, the rank and file of the Pakistan Army. Pervez Musharraf had to travel extensively to speak to them and restore their confidence.

The crucial question is: Why did Nawaz Sharif continue to support Pervez Musharraf if he had lost confidence in him? There could be several reasons: the existing power imbalance between the political authority and the Army in Pakistan; difficulty in taking action so soon after Nawaz Sharif had created conditions for the previous Army chief to resign; or the necessity to maintain the Pakistani Army's morale. But, most probably, it was on account of Nawaz Sharif's personal role in initiating the Kargil conflict. Eventually, as we all know, the dissonance between Nawaz Sharif and Pervez Musharraf culminated in the 12 October 1999 military coup in Pakistan. When I was asked in a CCS meeting if I was surprised by this development, my reply was: 'Yes! Yes, because it took so long to happen.'

There is no doubt that Nawaz Sharif precipitated the coup by dismissing the Army chief in such a bizarre fashion: when Pervez Musharraf was returning home by air after attending the Sri Lankan Army's golden jubilee celebrations. The seeds of distrust had, however, been sown earlier during the Kargil war. It was this fiasco that intensified the tussle between the political authority and the military leadership in Pakistan. The Pakistani Army, in all probability, had prepared itself for such a contingency. On the ground, Lieutenant General Mohammad Aziz Khan, the Pakistan chief of General Staff, and Lieutenant General Mehmood Ahmad, the GOC 10 Corps, initiated the coup. Both of them had played a major role in the planning and execution of the Kargil intrusion and were Musharraf loyalists.

Ever since Pakistan's (and India's) independence in August 1947, the Pakistani Army has ruled that country for nearly thirty years. Due to the military's dominant role in Pakistan's polity, tension has always existed between the elected civilian leaders and the Army top brass. The Kargil war, initiated by the Pakistani Army under Pervez Musharraf, provided yet another 'valid' reason to terminate the fledgling democracy in Pakistan in October 1999.

More than six eventful years have passed since that coup placed Pervez Musharraf in the most important hot seat in Pakistan. During this period, Pakistan, under his leadership, has had to cope with several geostrategic events. Musharraf's deft handling of politics and policies at home, including some timely U-turns on vital geopolitical and social issues, has enabled Pakistan to shake off the Kargil trauma, not only domestically but also internationally. Despite Indo–Pak relations oscillating between peace and war, as exemplified by events such as the Vajpayee–Musharraf Agra summit (July 2001), the military standoff (2001–02) and the Islamabad Declaration (January 2004), Musharraf has successfully managed to resume a 'peace dialogue' with India. Although his reassurance in Islamabad that 'he will not permit any territory under Pakistan's control to be used to support terrorism in any manner'[12] remains unimplemented,[13] the Pakistani and Indian guns along the LoC are, thankfully, quiet. Meanwhile, some deliberate attempts have been made by the Pakistani Army to rewrite Kargil history and to sweep that dirt under the carpet.[14] Will such attempts make the people forget about the Pakistan Army's role in Kargil? I doubt it very much. My hunch is that the ghost of Kargil would revisit Pakistan whenever Pervez Musharraf vacates the hot seat, for whatever reason.

In India, the immediate impact of the Kargil war was reflected in the expression of overwhelming public opinion. The country rose as a nation putting aside all its internal differences, be they religious, ethnic, language based, caste engendered or any other. Such a groundswell reflected 'unity in adversity', a sure sign of mature nationhood despite the fractured politics of the day. A strong feeling of patriotism not only pervaded all parts of the country but also gripped Indians all over the world. India's self-imposed restraint and the measured response in the form of determinedly beating back the aggression won it universal acclaim.

But such a state of affairs did not last long. On account of the forthcoming general elections, the Kargil conflict got

---

[12]'Pakistan–India Joint Statement', *The Dawn*, 6 January 2004.

[13]Most people in India consider it a breach of trust.

[14]Operation Badr (Pakistan's Kargil venture) is being distorted as a 'pre-emptive defence'.

immediately politicized. The ruling alliance parties wanted to piggyback on the victory achieved by the armed forces and the opposition tried to pick holes in their conduct to deny them that advantage. An intense debate began raging on the different facets of the conflict. Questions were raised on intelligence failure, as to whether or not the intrusion could have been detected earlier and as to the manner in which the infiltrators were confronted. On 24 July 1999, the CCS decided to constitute an experts' committee, with the following terms of reference:

> To review the events leading up to the Pakistani aggression in the Kargil District of Ladakh in Jammu and Kashmir and to recommend such measures as...considered necessary to safeguard national security against such armed intrusions.

The committee (named the Kargil Review Committee) comprised the doyen of strategic thinkers (also a respected columnist) in India, K. Subrahmanyam (chairman), former vice chief of the Army, Lieutenant General (retd) K.K. Hazari, well-known journalist B.G. Verghese, with Satish Chandra of the Indian Foreign Service (IFS) as the member secretary.[15] This committee, which was given total access to Army personnel and documents, submitted its report[16] to the CCS in December 1999. The report was made public barring some paragraphs and annexures. It had its share of criticism too, more due to political polarization than for any other reason. Despite the recommendation of this committee, the report was not debated in Parliament. We, in the armed forces, derived the satisfaction of being totally transparent to the committee, which helped its members collect evidence in an unbiased manner and give their opinions.

On the strategic front, the Kargil war drove home the point that although the nuclear weapons tests had made an all-out conventional war between India and Pakistan less likely, Kargil-

---

[15]This was in addition to an Army in-house enquiry ordered under Lieutenant General A.R.K. Reddy.

[16]*From Surprise to Reckoning: The Kargil Review Committee Report* (Sage Publications, New Delhi, 2000).

type military confrontations between the two nations could not be ruled out. As long as there were territory-related and other disputes, the adversary could indulge in an irregular war, a proxy war (that could lead to a conventional war), a border war or a limited war.

The Kargil war also re-emphasized that loss of territory, however remote or small, is just not acceptable to the public at large or to the political authority in India. Every Indian feels that every inch of territory has to be defended. The strategic impact of such a notion at the national level is that the armed forces take a lesser risk in trading space (losing some here but trying to capture more where there is strategic advantage!) for major offensive manoeuvres elsewhere. This is a peculiar strategic problem, and a handicap, faced by the Indian military, which intensifies in a *limited war* scenario. *Not* trading space also implies that greater attention has to be paid to surveillance and close defence of the borders or lines of controls.

We realized that the command and control of 15 Corps (Srinagar), which was looking after nearly 1490 km of the lines of control with Pakistan and China and was also handling counterterrorist operations in the Kashmir Valley and adjoining areas, were overextended. On account of prolonged proxy war in the Kashmir Valley, the corps commander in Srinagar tended to pay greater attention to the area west of the Zoji La pass. Moreover, military reserves in Ladakh were inadequate.[17] Such strategic shortcomings called for measures such as raising a separate corps headquarters, reinducting a division in place of 28 Infantry Division (which was raised primarily for the Kargil–Siachen sectors but had moved to the Kashmir Valley in 1991) and improving surveillance and the overall combat capability in Ladakh. We, therefore, raised Headquarters 14 Corps soon after the Kargil war and retained 8 Mountain Division in Ladakh. With the deployment of additional forces, with the provision of more effective command and control, and with improved

---

[17]This factor was already on our mind when we had ordered the return of Headquarters 70 Infantry Brigade from the Kashmir Valley to Ladakh in October 1998.

surveillance capability, most of the strategic and tactical shortcomings encountered during the Kargil war were overcome.

After the Kargil war, many defence analysts felt that an activist policy had now become a political imperative for India. Factors such as the absence of a proactive politico-military strategy in India in the past and New Delhi's decision not to cross the border and the LoC despite deliberate Pakistani aggression, would confirm the impression that India is a 'status-quo' nation. In other words, India does not react quickly and does not get provoked easily. Such an impression may encourage the Pakistani military to continue with its adventurous forays into Indian territory under the nuclear umbrella.

There was already a belief in Islamabad, especially among the military leaders, that India's reactive strategic mentality provided them an opportunity to push for political and military advantages in Indo–Pak disputes before the situation could escalate into a war. The Pakistan military appeared to have convinced itself that India would not resort to a full-scale war, apprehensive that it may escalate to the nuclear level.[18] Such conviction on the part of the Pakistan Army had seriously eroded India's conventional military deterrence. At another level, after the Kargil war, we had now to seriously cater for conventional and subconventional conflicts proceeding at multiple levels below an all-out, intense, conventional war threshold. These factors made the Indian Army work on a limited war doctrine, as applicable to the Indo–Pak security environment.[19]

Meanwhile, the Kargil Review Committee report brought out many serious deficiencies in India's security management system, particularly in the areas of intelligence, border patrolling and defence management. The report pointed out that despite far-reaching developments affecting India's national security in the past few decades, the country's higher and defence-related

---

[18]Such an impression may have been further strengthened during the Indo–Pak military standoff in 2001–02.

[19]'Limited War', valedictory remarks by the author in the conference organized by the IDSA, New Delhi. January 2000.

decision-making system had not changed.[20] It urged a thorough and expeditious review of the national security system by an independent body of credible experts. (A summary of this committee's recommendations is given in Appendix 3.)

The prime minister set up a Group of Ministers (ministers of Home, Defence, External Affairs and Finance) to review the national security system in its entirety and formulate specific proposals for implementation.[21] This was a historic opportunity to update the higher defence control organization and the decision-making systems.

After deliberations with members of four task forces (on intelligence apparatus, internal security, border management and management of defence, respectively), the Group of Ministers observed:

> There is a marked difference in the perception and crisis of confidence among civil and military officials in the Ministry of Defence and Services HQs regarding their respective roles and functions. There is also lack of synchronization among and between the three departments in the Ministry of Defence including the relevant elements of Defence Finance. The concept of "attached offices" as applied to Services HQs; problems of inter-se relativities; multiple, duplicated and complex procedures governing the exercise of administrative and financial powers, and the concept of "advice" to the Minister; all these had contributed to these problems. The COSC had serious weaknesses in its ability to provide single point military advice to the Government, and to resolve substantive interservice doctrinal, planning, policy and operational issues. This institution needed to be restructured to discharge its responsibilities efficiently, including the facilitation of jointness [sic] and synergy.[22]

---

[20]This was something that the Indian military had been pointing out for sometime. I had taken up this issue forcefully myself after taking over as chairman, Chiefs of Staff Committee, in January 1999.

[21]'Reforming the National Security System: Recommendations of the Group of Ministers', February 2001.

[22]Ibid.

Some other important comments of the Group of Ministers were as follows:

- There was a lack of interintelligence agencies' coordination, preparation and distribution of assessments about the adversaries with each other and the users.
- The defence planning process was handicapped by the absence of a national security doctrine and commitment of funds beyond a financial year. It suffered due to a lack of a holistic approach, interservice prioritization in annual, mid-term and long-term planning, and requisite flexibility. The planning was competitive and uneconomical. There were major differences in the doctrines and policies of the three services.
- The system governing defence acquisitions suffered from a lack of integrated planning, weaknesses in linkages between plans and budgets, endless "make-or-buy" discussions, cumbersome administrative, technical and financial evaluation procedures and the absence of a dedicated, professionally equipped common procurement structure within the Ministry of Defence.
- There was a disconnect between technological planning and development in the equipment development and in the interface between the R&D, production agencies and users, particularly in the critical linkage between services plans and the Defence Research and Development Organization (DRDO) budget.
- Finding, identifying, educating, motivating and retaining quality manpower for the armed forces had become difficult. A service career needed to be made attractive.
- There was no synergy between academic research and the government's security policy requirements. Whereas academic research was being carried out more or less in a policy vacuum, official agencies undertook their policy-making tasks without the information available with the academic community.

Decisions and Implementation

The aforementioned Group of Ministers, and later the CCS, approved several reforms/recommendations. The important recommendations that affected the politico-military establishment and the decision-making processes along with some comments on their implementation are now highlighted.

Service Headquarters' premises, which were being merely considered attached offices, were to be made a part of the 'Integrated Defence Headquarters'. This proposed new name for the Ministry of Defence was announced. However, a mere change of name has little meaning unless the working procedures and processing of issues on the file are changed. The change must be in spirit, which does not appear to have happened. For example, the Service Headquarters and the Ministry of Defence continue to maintain separate, double filing systems (maintenance of separate files on the same subject in the Ministry of Defence and Service Headquarters) on most issues, resulting in lack of transparency and confidence. The feedback so far has shown that there has been no change in the procedures or in the attitude of the officers posted in the two institutions.

The financial limit of the Services Headquarters has been increased up to Rs 50 crore (and up to Rs 100 crore in consultation with a financial advisor). The decentralization of financial decisions up to the brigadier (or equivalent) level has been promulgated. This step has improved decision-making processes for incurring 'revenue expenditure'[23] in the three services. 'Capital expenditure',[24] however, remains mostly outside the purview of the Service Headquarters.

---

[23]The 'revenue expenditure' includes expenditure on pay and allowances, transportation, purchase of ordnance stores (including supplies by ordnance factories), rations, petrol, oil, lubricants, spares, maintenance of buildings, water and electricity charges, rents and other miscellaneous expenditure for annual maintenance of each service.

[24]'Capital expenditure' includes expenditure on land, construction works, plants, machineries, equipment, tanks, new artillery guns, naval vessels, aircraft, aeroengines, dockyards and other durable assets.

A post known as 'chief of defence staff' (CDS) was to be created. The functions of its occupant were slated as follows: (a) To provide single point military advice; (b) to hold administrative control over, and manage, strategic forces; (c) to ensure intraservice and interservice prioritization of ten- and fifteen-year 'perspective plans' and also the five-year defence plans; and (d) to bring about improvement in the 'jointness' among the various units of the armed forces. Further, he was expected to work for the improvement in the uniformity of training in the three services and also reduce 'overlap' and 'replication' in them.

Unfortunately, most of the decisions pertaining to the setting up of the post of the chief of defence staff are still in limbo.

A Defence Intelligence Agency has been established as part of the integrated staff to coordinate the functioning of the different intelligence directorates in the Service Headquarters and to meet long-term strategic requirements. It is also responsible for interpreting satellite and other imagery as well as scientific data. This agency also manages the defence and military attachés posted abroad. There have been some teething problems with regard to the sharing of responsibilities and some avoidable duplication of functions among the Defence Intelligence Agency and the intelligence directorates of the different services.

A Defence Minister's Council on Production has been set up to lay down the broad objectives with respect to long-term policies and planning on production, simplification of procedures and so on with relation to equipment. The council is also required to take 'make' or 'buy' decisions on procurement of major weapon systems and platforms.

A Defence Procurement Board has been set up under the defence secretary to undertake the entire gamut of procurement functions and to bring about a higher degree of professionalism and cost effectiveness in the process. This board will deal with major acquisitions/procurement cases that require approval of the CCS. Other procurements can be undertaken at lower levels within the Procurement Directorate of the Ministry of Defence (headed by a special secretary), or in Service Headquarters (if within financial powers) with the approval of financial advisors.

In 2004–05, the Parliamentary Standing Committee on Defence, in its interim report, observed that out of seventy-five cases approved by the board in the last three years, contracts had been signed in only fifty-one cases, including forty-eight cases under the fast track procedure (much maligned after the Kargil war procurements). About one-third of such cases are still pending. This committee opined that the Defence Procurement Board had 'miserably failed' to speed up the process and seemed to have merely added one more tier to the already existing ones in the clearance of proposals, thereby causing further delays. This committee also expressed deep anguish at the abrupt policy reversal of a non-lapsable Defence Modernization Fund (with a Rs 25,000-crore corpus), which had been instituted by the previous government in February 2004 after years of persuasion. The Standing Committee recommended the setting up of another study group 'to examine the entire gamut of defence procurement procedures and structures and suggest appropriate modifications'.[25]

Actually, even after the suggestions of the Group of Ministers' report had been implemented, there has been little change in our attitude and procedures for defence modernization. Efforts towards modernization of the armed forces are not bearing fruit, primarily because of the absence of holistic and long-term defence planning. Because of the long-term financial and political commitments required in defence planning, which are not forthcoming, it continues to suffer from political and bureaucratic myopia.

India needs a holistic review of the defence planning system, not only of the procurement procedures but also of indigenous development and production facilities and their functioning. Some of our organizations have become technological ghettoes that have little to show for themselves other than slogans for self-reliance and showing off successful trials every few days. There is a need to review the work of the DRDO, ordnance

---

[25]'Demands for Grants (2004–05)'. First Report, August 2004. Standing Committee on Defence, Fourteenth Lok Sabha. Also see V.P. Malik, 'Forging the Shield: Have We Learnt Any Lessons from the Past?' *The Tribune*, 5 February 2005.

factories and defence public sector units (PSUs) and enforce institutional reforms to bring them up to the technological levels of the twenty-first century.[26]

Most military and civilian defence experts, who have been part of the government in the past, are now becoming conscious of our shortcomings in defence planning. These systemic flaws in building defence capabilities can be set right, if we can work on the following lines:

- We should prepare a long-term guidance plan with regard to national security objectives, particularly keeping the foreign factor in mind.
- Considering the time span taken to develop and produce new weapons and equipment, which is about twenty-five years, we should follow a three-tier perspective defence planning based on a fifteen-year vision plan, a ten-year indicative plan and a five-year definitive plan.
- We should make a firm commitment for financial resources or for a defence budget allocation for the definitive plan, and, if possible, for the indicative plan as well.
- Based on the security threats and challenges, we should develop integrated procurement and modernization defence plans for the definitive plan and indicative plan periods (five and ten years, respectively). Such plans should be approved by the CCS. After that, they should not be altered without the specific permission given by a designated committee comprising the defence minister and senior civilian and military leaders.
- The general staff qualitative requirements, once laid down, should not be altered unless there has been an abnormal delay in the development and production of the weapon or the equipment system.
- The "make-or-buy" decisions taken by the Defence Minister's Council on Production should include factors such as technology transfers, collaboration with foreign vendors, delivery schedules and import arrangements. There should be greater accountability for the development and manufacture of "make" items.

---

[26]From an editorial in *The Indian Express*, 13 August 2005.

- The Defence Procurement Board and its staff should have trained, experienced and committed officials on a long-tenure basis, i.e., five to seven years.
- Ordnance factories and defence PSUs should be modernized as soon as possible. If necessary, units that are old or producing non-essential, low-tech items should be disinvested. Money so earned should be utilized to technologically upgrade other factories or defence PSUs.
- Defence PSUs should be given freedom to form consortia and to go in for crossinvestment in foreign countries to obtain cutting-edge technologies. They should be encouraged to become global players in designing, production and integration of large weapon systems and platforms.
- The present system of quality assurance is unpopular with the vendors as well as the end users. This system should be reviewed.
- Currently, we are actively seeking cooperation with the USA for joint development and research, technology transfers and co-production in the field of defence. Such collaborations between the government/public sector establishments of India and private companies of the USA are unlikely to progress at the desired pace or levels. The defence sector private companies of the USA are likely to work better with Indian private sector companies. The private sector in India should be encouraged to invest and establish manufacturing units by itself, or with foreign collaboration, for defence items. Adequate incentives should be provided in terms of orders for capacity building.
- The policy on export of weapons and equipment should be made more flexible and viable for the defence industry in India.

As far as the post of the chief of defence staff was concerned, the earlier mentioned Parliamentary Standing Committee noted that the 'coordination and synergy amongst the armed forces, service headquarters and the Ministry of defence is [sic] extremely vital for expeditious decision making and also for higher defence management. The Chiefs of Staff Committee has not been able to perform their role and function [sic] in bringing together and promoting coordination amongst the services'. The committee asked the Ministry of Defence to urgently take a stand on the recommendations of the Group of Ministers so as to ensure that the post of chief of defence staff came into being immediately.[27]

Some Strategic Thoughts for the Future

Three important lessons learnt from the Kargil operations are:

- The deployment of troops for counterterrorist operations not only causes battle fatigue but also leads to a change in their orientation. Consequently, their reorientation, when necessary, and re-equipping them for conventional operations take quite some time.
- Most of our reserves in Jammu and Kashmir and the northeast were committed to counter terrorist operations. Hence, there was an operational imbalance at the start of operations in the area east of the Zoji La pass. About three weeks were needed to regain an operationally viable posture. We learnt that this mistake should not be repeated.
- Overall, the very idea of a credible conventional deterrence stood eroded. That made Pakistan audacious, and the powers that be badly miscalculated.

Pakistan appears to have convinced itself that India would not resort to war for fear of escalation and also because Islamabad possessed nuclear deterrence. As India, unlike in the 1965 war, did not cross the LoC or the international border during the Kargil war, such an impression got reinforced. The mindset was further strengthened after the Indo–Pak military standoff in 2001–02. Many Pakistani military officers and analysts in their think tanks continue to articulate that in both these cases, their nuclear deterrence had worked effectively.[28] Pakistan's political and military leaders frequently talk about their nuclear deterrence and low thresholds. In such a situation, the

---

[27]Ibid.
[28]General Musharraf has made that claim repeatedly after the aforementioned military standoff.

continuation of proxy war in Jammu and Kashmir or Kargil-type misadventures across the LoC cannot be ruled out.[29] Such irrationality combined with unpredictability on the part of the Pakistani leadership, and our inflexibility in always standing firm on high moral ground, make these challenges greater for our policy makers and for the military.

How do we face such challenges in future?

The Kargil war and events thereafter have highlighted some new trends, which have had a marked influence on the conduct of warfare and the structure of the armed forces. Some of these trends are being driven by technology; others by strategic considerations and concepts. The objectives are varied: to avoid escalation of violence; to minimize collateral damage; or to achieve success with minimum losses. Nonetheless, they have made a significant impact on strategies and tactics.

First: The separation among the tactical, operational and strategic levels of warfare is getting blurred. While there was always some degree of overlap among these levels, due to the increasingly pervasive influence of information technology on warfare, this overlap is increasing. Even a small military action along the LoC, or a terrorist act in the hinterland of the types that we have seen in the recent past, tends to become issues for consideration and decision making at the strategic level. It is a situation wherein a junior military officer is expected to understand political considerations and a political leader is expected to know the tactical and operational factors. Fast flow of information, quick assessments and transparency at these three levels are essential. Communication gaps can be fatal. To a considerable extent, all these aspects became evident during the Kargil war.

Second: We need more effective integrated command, control, communications and intelligence systems apart from faster decision making at tactical, operational as well as strategic levels of command.

Third: There is an urgent need for greater politico-military synergy. At the military level, the actual fighting during a war

---

[29]Such a threat was articulated by Nawaz Sharif soon after the Kargil war, and later even by Pervez Musharraf.

has to be conducted in a more integrated manner; hence, the need for more integrated capabilities and 'jointness' to obtain optimum results.

As already mentioned, with nuclear weapons here to stay, the probability of an all-out, high-intensity regular war will remain fairly low. Even if a conventional war does break out, it is likely to be limited in time, scope and space: some people call that a subconventional war or a limited conventional war. Such a war would have to be conducted within the framework of carefully calibrated political goals and military moves that permit adequate control over escalation and disengagement. Such precautions, however, do not rule out altogether a larger scale conventional war with nuclear or non-nuclear weapons.

Is there some space between a proxy war and a high-intensity conventional war? The answer has been given by Pakistan in Kargil and by our reaction to that country's stratagems. How small or big is this space? The answer to this question, I believe, will always be a matter of circumstance, conjecture and debate. This space becomes more exploitable if one is reacting to a Kargil-type intrusion or a proxy-war situation. To understand the factors that will impact this space, one has to consider the following factors: Who will take the initiative? What would be the international perception? Will the adversary chance nuclear retaliation even when his survival is nowhere at stake? How limited will the political and military objectives be? How big and effective will the conventional forces on both sides be? How low is the adversary's nuclear threshold? If it is very low, then why keep large conventional forces? Will the adversary heed or not heed the deterrent response of nuclear retaliation?

Almost all these factors have a bearing on escalation control. In addition, there is also the factor of 'escalation dominance'. That too has a bearing on escalation control. There is yet another factor that is peculiar but applicable to the subcontinent. Even during conflicts and wars, communications between India and Pakistan have seldom broken down completely. For instance, during the Kargil war, both at the political and military levels, the hotlines continued to work. In South Asia, we tend to fight and talk at the same time!

A limited war was, and still is, a strategic possibility so long as the proxy war continues on the subcontinent. As Ashley Tellis (a noted strategic analyst) put it in an *India Today* Conclave:

> I believe that limited war should be viewed not as a product of the proclivities of the state, but rather as a predicament resulting from a specific set of structural circumstances.[30]

A limited war does not mean limited capabilities; it refers to the optimum use of the capabilities at one's command.

I am not one of those who believes that war makes the state and the states exist only to make wars. No one in his or her right senses wants to have a war on his or her hands, least of all democracies like India and people like me who have studied, participated in and conducted wars. But the armed forces have to be prepared for all possible conflict contingencies so long as wars remain an instrument of state policy.

---

[30]'If India Seeks to Become a Great Power, It Also Has to Become a Net Provider of Regional Security.' Talk by Ashley Tellis, senior associate, Carnegie Endowment for International Peace, *India Today* Conclave, 12–13 March 2005, New Delhi.

19

India and Pakistan: Beyond Kargil

...inviting General Pervez Musharraf to Agra...so soon after the Kargil war was not the right thing to do. As usual, the military was not consulted. Many senior officers from the armed forces, and almost all those who had lost their kith and kin in the Kargil war, were surprised and upset. At the politico-military level, the result was that all the military and diplomatic gains, and sacrifices, that we had made during the Kargil war, particularly against the Pakistan Army and its leadership, were immediately forgotten.

THE BIGGEST CASUALTY OF THE KARGIL WAR, APART FROM THE lives lost on both sides of the LoC, was in the form of trust and confidence between India and Pakistan.

The Agra Summit: July 2001

After two years of 'Kargil break', the two nations decided to travel the high road to peace through the Agra Summit. Atal Behari Vajpayee's political initiative to hold talks at a summit with the new Pakistani military ruler in July 2001 surprised many in India and abroad.[1] Pervez Musharraf, who only a few days before the summit anointed himself as the president of Pakistan, carried a heavy baggage as the 'saboteur of the Lahore Summit', the 'author of Kargil war' and someone who had derailed democracy in Pakistan. Till then, he had not inspired much confidence in the people inside or outside Pakistan. Musharraf himself acknowledged that reality.[2]

India's motivations were driven by sentiment, and were of long-term consequence. Musharraf's compulsions were immediate: both at the personal and national levels. At the national level, these compulsions arose from factors such as Pakistan's low political credibility, the growing loss of international

---

[1]Brajesh Mishra, then the national security advisor, has distanced himself from this move, stating: 'The decision was taken at the political level. I was not consulted...but I would have had reservations about it.' 'Too Early to Think of Kashmir Solution: Brajesh Mishra', Indo-Asian News Service (IANS), 15 April 2005.

[2]Pervez Musharraf's televised interaction with the Indian media over breakfast in Agra on 16 July 2001.

confidence in that country, the negative impact of continuing sanctions on its economy and the politico-socio-economic crisis that affected the people. All these factors were, in one way or the other, connected to the Kargil war.

On 14 July 2001, the Agra Summit started on a cordial note with the Government of India unilaterally announcing several 'people-to-people' confidence-building measures. At the banquet hosted by the president of India, K.R. Narayanan, the same day, Pervez Musharraf said:

> I am deeply committed to finding a path towards normal relations between our countries. I would like communications to be open, trade to flourish, mindsets to change and stereotypes to disappear. The children of Pakistan and India must not be made to live under the constant shadow of conflict. They must also not be made to live in deprivation and crippling poverty. The energies of our people must be diverted to the immense and challenging task of social and economic uplift, of banishing misery and ushering in an era of progress and prosperity.

But soon thereafter, Pervez Musharraf's obsession with Kashmir took over and the road to peace became bumpy. Before the summit, I had stated:

> Musharraf is coming to the Agra Summit "with an open mind" but with Jammu and Kashmir as the "core issue" of the agenda. We have to remember that in Pakistan, Jammu and Kashmir is more a military agenda than a political agenda.... India will be speaking to a military person who heads "the keepers" of Pakistan's policies on Indo–Pak relations, particularly on Jammu and Kashmir and nuclear weapons. This is an advantage as well as a disadvantage. He does not have to take orders from anyone today and can afford to become pragmatic and flexible when confronted with India's long-standing position and arguments. But would his own mindset and his military colleagues, the Corps Commanders, and the Jehadi groups allow him that flexibility

on the Jammu and Kashmir issue? The General has made himself a prisoner of his own rhetoric on Jammu and Kashmir and Indo–Pak relationship. He once stated in Karachi that Indo–Pak relations would not improve even after the Kashmir problem is over.[3]

I had also stated:

The stakes in the Summit were very high, agenda fairly limited, and expectations low.... If Musharraf follows his predecessor military presidents, we could expect him to be courteous, apparently honest and sincere and, like all of them, good in the art of political and military deception. However, Pakistan's political and military history tells us that its military presidents tend to be strategically shortsighted. They were no Kemal Ataturks!'[4]

But even I did not expect the midnight storming out (and the subsequent flight to Islamabad) by the grim-faced general, expressing hurt and disappointment. The summit ended on a jarring note, with both sides unable to agree even to an acceptable joint statement.[5]

According to Jaswant Singh (who was then holding two portfolios as defence minister and foreign minister), the talks failed because there were conceptual differences: Pakistan's 'unifocal' approach on Kashmir vis-à-vis India's insistence on maintaining its territorial integrity and secular identity. He, however, reiterated the resolve of the Indian Government to continue with the dialogue at summit and official levels.[6]

The priorities at Agra should have been to create a measure of trust and to strengthen military and non-military confidence-

[3]'The General in His Labyrinth', *The Week*, 15 July 2001.
[4]Ibid. See also *Dainik Bhaskar*, 12 July 2001.
[5]According to Brajesh Mishra, the Agra Summit 'failed very badly'. 'Too Early to Think of Kashmir Solution: Brajesh Mishra', Indo-Asian News Service (IANS), 15 April 2005.
[6]Post-Agra Summit briefing of the media by the foreign ministers of India and Pakistan on 17 July 2001.

building measures. But the Pakistani leader was interested *only* in Kashmir. As a political leader, he conveyed the impression of being proactive, assertive and clever, someone who loved to play to the gallery. He did not observe diplomatic proprieties and tread on the toes of his hosts by meeting members of the All-Party Hurriyat Conference (APHC), an alliance of many parties in Kashmir favouring separatism, in New Delhi privately.

The important question that needs to be asked is: how do you negotiate when you have not built up mutual trust? Also, summit-level parleys cannot be conducted through the media, definitely not in the Indian subcontinent. When it comes to Indo–Pak relations, the people of both countries are far too sensitive and their emotions get charged up very easily. More than five decades of confrontation has made both Indians and Pakistanis suspicious, jingoistic and impatient. The overenthusiastic media coverage of the 'low-expectation' Agra Summit managed to raise public hopes to an unrealistically high level. Before the year was over, these hopes were shattered once again as a result of the gun battle outside the Indian Parliament (described later in this chapter).

In my opinion, inviting General Pervez Musharraf to Agra, falling backward to appease him and concede every demand of his so soon after the Kargil war, was not the right thing to do. As usual, the military was not consulted. Many senior officers from the armed forces, and almost all those who had lost their kith and kin in the Kargil war, were surprised and upset. At the politico-military level, the result was that all the military and diplomatic gains, and sacrifices, that we had made during the Kargil war, particularly against the Pakistan Army and its leadership, were immediately forgotten.

General Musharraf came to India, not as a culpable Pakistan military leader, but as a great hero and statesman. He continued to assert that terrorism in Jammu and Kashmir was the consequence of 'a freedom struggle' and Pakistan had nothing to do with it. He appeared confident that he would be able to make India sign a treaty on his terms. It was a typical Pakistan Army bluff-and-bluster attitude, about which our political leaders have so little knowledge and, therefore, are so naïve. He wanted to achieve politically what he had attempted militarily but failed.

Fortunately, due to last-minute political intervention, Indian leadership saw the light.

9/11 and Pakistan

Strategically, 2001 was a difficult year for Pakistan, not so much on account of politico-socio-economic problems, which made the Western media consider it a likely failed state, but because 9/11 reinforced this perception. The country had to bear the brunt of international censure for becoming the epicentre of global terrorism. Faced with a US ultimatum to mend its ways, Pakistan, under Musharraf, made a dramatic U-turn in its Afghanistan policy: it abandoned the Taliban and joined the coalition against terrorism. This step marked a major break from its past, and the beginning of a fresh chapter in relations between Islamabad and Washington. For Pakistan, the South Asian identity became more important than West Asian dependency. However, military and jehadi interests were not completely given up. The Pakistanis sought to obfuscate matters by attempting to differentiate between terrorists (in the West) and those who became freedom fighters (in the East).[7] Pakistan tried to justify that war against the former could continue without abandoning the latter under the new label.

The Terrorists' Assault on the Indian Parliament

On 13 December 2001, five Pakistani terrorists struck at the heart of Indian nationhood and democracy: the Parliament House in New Delhi. In the ensuing gun battle, all the five terrorists, seven Delhi policemen and one Parliament House employee were killed. This assault came after a similar but more violent one on the Jammu and Kashmir State Legislature on 1 October. The Indian nation was angered. The people wanted an immediate response. Soon after the terrorist attack, Prime Minister Vajpayee declared: 'The attack was not on Parliament but on the entire nation. We have been fighting

---

[7]Even when there is no difference in their civilian targets!

terrorism for the last two decades and the do-or-die battle is in the final stages. We accept the challenge and we will blunt every attack.' The prime minister's statement not only expressed a sense of frustration but also sent out a clear signal that India's patience was fast running out and that the threshold for Pakistan-sponsored jehadi terrorism had been crossed. In response, on 15 December, India ordered the immediate mobilization of its armed forces under the codename Operation Parakaram (meaning valour). There was no 'W' (warning) phase. The Union War Book, which lays down actions to be taken by various ministries and departments of the government when a war is considered imminent, had not been invoked. Yet, Operation Parakaram led to the largest deployment of the forces on the borders since the 1971 Indo–Pak war: larger in scale than the one carried out during the Kargil war.

The mobilization and deployment, a huge and expensive exercise by any standards, were completed in twenty days. The entire exercise was carried out efficiently, though not rapidly enough to achieve any strategic or tactical surprise. In a media conference held on 11 January 2002, General S. Padmanabhan, my successor, stated that 'mobilization was complete and the armed forces were waiting for the political nod'.

During the course of the next ten months that the military standoff lasted, at least on two occasions, India went to the brink of war. Such a war would have been a legitimate response, as self-defence, under Article 51 of the UN Charter. Had the war taken place, it would have put an end to Pakistani misperceptions of India's strategic restraint during the Kargil war, and shattered New Delhi's record of respecting the sanctity of the LoC.

But India did not go to war either in January, or even in May, 2002 when the terrorists struck again in the family quarters of an Army camp at Kaluchak (in Jammu and Kashmir). As the events subsequent to mobilization unfolded, the nod to the military to initiate the war was never given. The troops remained in a state of border deployment and alert, for offensive and defensive actions, till a review of the politico-military situation was done on 16 October 2002. After consulting the National Security Advisory Board, the Cabinet Committee on Security (CCS) ordered withdrawal of the forces from the border to their 'strategic relocation'.[8]

There was considerable speculation over the question as to why the terrorists attacked Parliament. Was it because the Agra Summit had failed? Was it because India had failed to adequately respond to an earlier attack on the Jammu and Kashmir State Legislative Assembly in October 2001? Had the Agra Summit succeeded or had India responded firmly to the October attack, would the 13 December attack on the Indian Parliament have taken place?

The general impression was that both the Pakistan Government and the jehadi organizations (Lashkar-e-Taiba and Jaish-e-Mohammad), often controlled by Pakistan's Inter-Services Intelligence (ISI) while carrying out their activities in India, had a convergence of interests. The jehadi organizations wanted to achieve pan-Islamic objectives. And the Pakistan Government was looking for ways to intensify 'militant' pressure on India without its state security apparatus getting overtly involved. The aim was to ensure that India would once again engage Pakistan politically over Kashmir.

The India–Pakistan military standoff (2001–02) was an outcome of the continued Pakistani strategy of employing terrorism as an instrument of state foreign policy. The employment of this strategy against India has been known to, and acknowledged by, many retired military officers of Pakistan. In a recent article in an Indian news magazine, Lieutenant General Talat Masood has been quoted as saying: 'His [Pervez Musharraf's] advisors keep saying Pakistan has a diplomatic imperative for supporting the militant campaign in Kashmir. Without militant struggle there would be no pressure on India over Kashmir, and the Pakistan Government will have little sway at the negotiating table. Under such circumstances, the General [Pervez Musharraf] has little choice but to keep up the guerilla war with the help of ISI-backed militants.' [9]

---

[8]The author was a member of the National Security Advisory Board and participated in the discussions on 16 October 2002.
[9]'Footprints of Guilt', *Outlook*, 8 August 2005.

The military standoff served as yet another reminder of the possibility of a proxy war escalating into a conventional war.

India adopted a two-pronged strategy for applying pressure on Pakistan during the standoff: the deployment of armed forces and a 'threat of waging a war' to back the diplomatic initiatives. The second part comprised a possible escalation to the level of conventional war. This threat was to be the instrument of last resort after all other options had been exhausted.

While mobilization and deployment were in progress, India took several measures on the diplomatic and economic fronts. On 19 December 2001, New Delhi asked Islamabad to do the following: (a) take action against the Lashkar-e-Taiba and Jaish-e-Mohammad outfits responsible for the terrorists' attacks; (b) take their leadership into custody; and (c) to freeze their financial assets and stop their access to such assets. Some of these 'actions' were taken by Pakistan, but for 'demonstration' purposes only. On 28 December, India demanded that Pakistan hand over twenty hard-core terrorists responsible for various heinous acts on Indian soil since the mid-1980s. The political focus, thereafter, shifted to this list of terrorists. These rather belated and vocal demands made the diplomatic pressure and coercive diplomacy lose their sting, and even the rationale for a war appeared unconvincing. All these developments confused most people. In the current nuclear symmetrical strategic environment, why would two nations want to go to war over twenty criminals who had at some point of time been used to carry out terrorist activities?

With the passage of time, the credibility of our diplomatic coercion was further eroded due to various extraneous factors. Elections were underway for state assemblies in Uttar Pradesh and Punjab and large-scale riots erupted in Gujarat following the burning of a train compartment at Godhra on 27 February 2002. (I shall not go into the details, which are beyond the scope of this book.) Such developments put India in an unprecedented situation wherein troops deployed on the border – nearly a division – had to be recalled to assist the civil authorities in Gujarat to maintain law and order. A few days later, there was yet another demand for Army assistance in the communally sensitive town of Ayodhya in Uttar Pradesh.

Another factor inhibiting our going to war during the stand-off was the deployment of US troops in Pakistan for Operation Enduring Freedom (war against terror in Afghanistan). The USA had also issued an advisory to foreign navies to 'lay off' Karachi harbour, which was being utilized for inducting US troops and for providing material support.

Three important lessons to be learnt from the abovementioned events and prolonged mobilization deployment are:

- Do not confuse the aims of a war or coercive diplomacy. A war is far too serious a business to be trivialized for the sake of twenty criminals.
- No country can afford to take on external forces when its armed forces have to simultaneously deal with internal crises such as riots or terrorism. Such a country will be strategically vulnerable.
- Using the armed forces for long-drawn-out coercive diplomacy is risky. Such a move tends to erode defence credibility and capability, and is unlikely to be appreciated by the international community.

Were the Indian political objectives of this ten-month-long military standoff achieved? On 20 November 2002, Defence Minister George Fernandes, while replying to questions in Parliament, asserted that the intended objectives of the forward mobilization of the military had been achieved with 'great distinction'. According to him, the mobilization exerted immense pressure on Pakistan and forced Pervez Musharraf to denounce support to jehadi militants through his 12 January and 27 May 2002 public speeches. Also, Pakistan was forced to ban a few terrorist organizations (Lashkar-e-Taiba and Jaish-e-Mohammad), close down some terrorist camps in Pakistan-Occupied Kashmir and arrest a few terrorist leaders.

Ironically, on the very day George Fernandes spoke in the Indian Parliament, Pervez Musharraf in an address to his nation stated that his 'Government had upheld the honour and dignity of Pakistan by not succumbing to Indian pressure and Pakistan had succeeded in highlighting the Kashmir cause to the international community'.

The Islamabad SAARC Summit and
the Indo–Pak Declaration

The Pakistani jehadi terrorists' assault on the Indian Parliament on 13 December 2001 and Operation Parakaram caused yet another break in the Indo–Pak dialogue. Meanwhile, in September–October 2002, India conducted another successful, internationally transparent election in Jammu and Kashmir, which resulted in a peaceful transition of power to the newly elected state government.

The threads of the Indo–Pak dialogue were eventually picked up in 2003 as a result of secret diplomatic contacts between India's National Security Advisor Brajesh Mishra and his Pakistani counterpart Lieutenant General Tariq Aziz. It took them three meetings and seven months to hammer out the differences on how to proceed to reinitiate the composite dialogue. The first important breakthrough came with the announcement of ceasefire on the LoC on 25 November 2003. The crucial last round of talks, just before the Islamabad SAARC Summit (4–6 January 2004), culminated in the Indo–Pak Islamabad announcement of 6 January 2004.

The Indo–Pak Islamabad Announcement

The President of Pakistan and the Prime Minister of India met during the South Asian Association for Regional Cooperation (SAARC) summit in Islamabad.

The Indian Prime Minister while expressing satisfaction over the successful conclusion of the SAARC summit appreciated the excellent arrangements made by the host country.

Both leaders welcomed the recent steps towards normalization of relations between the two countries and expressed the hope that the positive trends set by the confidence-building measures would be consolidated.

Prime Minister Vajpayee said that in order to take forward and sustain the dialogue process, violence, hostility and terrorism must be prevented. President Musharraf reassured

Prime Minister Vajpayee that he would not permit any territory under Pakistan's control to be used to support terrorism in any manner. President Musharraf emphasized that a sustained and productive dialogue addressing all issues would lead to positive results.

To carry the process of normalization forward the President of Pakistan and the Prime Minister of India agreed to commence the process of the composite dialogue in February 2004.

The two leaders are confident that the resumption of the composite dialogue will lead to peaceful settlement of all bilateral issues including Jammu and Kashmir, to the satisfaction of both sides.

The two leaders agreed that constructive dialogue would promote progress towards the common objective of peace, security and economic development for our peoples and for future generations.

How did all this come about? According to Brajesh Mishra: 'It was a question of assessing what were his [Pervez Musharraf's] compulsions. He desperately needed a joint statement. He was extremely keen to have a joint statement with Prime Minister Vajpayee, which he could not get in Agra.'[10]

Continuity in Change

The United Progressive Alliance (UPA) Government that came to power after the April–May 2004 general elections in India not only strengthened the ongoing dialogue but also increased its pace. Soon after he was sworn in, India's new prime minister, Dr Manmohan Singh, emphasized the normalization of relations with Pakistan as a key priority for his coalition government. After meeting Pervez Musharraf in New York on 24 September 2004, the Indian prime minister 'agreed that confidence-building

---

[10]'Too Early to Think of Kashmir Solution: Brajesh Mishra', Indo-Asian News Service (IANS), 15 April 2005.

measures of all categories under discussions between the two governments should be implemented keeping in mind practical possibilities'.

The 'Cricket Year'

By all counts, 2004 was a 'cricket year' as far as the Indo–Pakistan bilateral relations were concerned. Cricket became the engine of peace. The Indo–Pak cricket series was able to upgrade itself into a trans-border carnival, establish people-to-people contact and became the most effective form of diplomacy. The spirit of the game and the resulting bonhomie generated a strong desire amongst people on both sides not only to watch matches but also to cross over, share each other's hospitality and discover their roots in ancestral villages. Pent-up emotions burst forth as the floodgates opened. Outside the government establishments, most people forgot the bitterness and anguish caused by partition and the four wars. Despite Pervez Musharraf's 'Kashmir or nothing' parroting, which often became jarring, a great deal of optimism pervaded the atmosphere.[11] The optimism was further enhanced when the Srinagar–Muzaffarabad road (which had been closed for more than five decades) was opened for the divided Kashmiri families. The size and frequency of official and institutional delegations – from legislatives bodies, judiciary, media, cinema, trade, commerce and industry – shot up suddenly. Such sentiments, despite continuing terrorist violence in Jammu and Kashmir, enabled to keep the second round of the composite dialogue on track. There was, and continues to be, cautious optimism.

Why 'cautious optimism' when the peace process has become a people-driven initiative and there is consensus amongst all political parties in India and Pakistan? It must be remembered that the crucial factor in the whole process is the Pakistan Army. Has there been a 'change of heart' in this institution?

---

[11]Mufti Mohammad Sayeed, then the chief minister of Jammu and Kashmir, called it the 'peace tsunami' with its epicentre in Kashmir. Speech at a seminar in Jammu University on 10 March 2005.

In a recent article, Dr Ayesha Siddiqa (a well-known Pakistani defence analyst), after noting that no substantive movement had taken place in resolving Indo–Pak disputes so far, has observed:

Pakistan's own inability to take any step towards resolving the easier disputes relates to structural issues pertaining to the (Pakistan) army and the politics of the process. A closer look at the army shows an absence of sensitivity towards New Delhi. The general perception is that the peace initiative is a tactical retreat that was imperative after 9/11. Moreover, considering Pakistan's need to build economically, peace would provide the necessary respite. The process is good for PR and provides the necessary breathing space.[12]

She goes on to add:

To be fair to Musharraf, it is not possible for him to convince his generals and other senior officers of changing the old mindset regarding India. New Delhi still remains the top enemy that will have to be fought or vanquished.

Although one has often spoken of the professionalism of Pakistan's armed forces, the fact is that some policies do tend to put pressure on the socio-politics [sic] of the organization such as the long and continued association with militant organizations. Reports indicate that the connection has not been severed completely resulting in growing dissension inside the intelligence agencies and the larger organization. The division among the various ideological groups within the larger institution of the armed forces makes the peace initiative a risky project. So, while Musharraf could say a lot of positive things, he would find it difficult to put his money where his mouth is.[13]

---

[12]Dr Ayesha Siddiqa, 'The Myth of Irreversible Peace', *The Friday Times* (Lahore), 8–14 July 2005.
[13]Ibid.

There are many people on both sides of the border who would like to see such progress in Indo–Pak relations that would make the peace process really 'irreversible'. At present, it is not. It is particularly vulnerable to the acts of jehadi terrorism. The Pakistan Army's (primarily ISI) nexus with radical Islamist and Jammu and Kashmir militants has the potential to bring India and Pakistan to the brink of war yet again. The improved atmospherics have, however, created a conducive environment, which at a future date could enable discussion on various complex issues with greater confidence. Meanwhile, the dialogue on topics such as Siachen, the Wullar Barrage and Tulbul navigation projects (both in Jammu and Kashmir), Sir Creek (in the Rann of Kutch, Gujarat), terrorism, drug trafficking, economic and commercial cooperation and promotion of friendly exchanges in various fields would enter the third round between January and July 2006.

20

Pakistan: Blowing Hot, Blowing Cold

The crucial factor to be borne in mind is that so long as the motivation for terrorism is there and the terrorist infrastructure exists in Pakistan, it can increase or decrease the level of militancy...in Kashmir.

FROM ALL ACCOUNTS, IT IS EVIDENT THAT INDIA IS ON THE CUSP of becoming a major economic and military power. India is likely to attain this status in the coming two decades, despite the tremendous internal challenges and oppressive external constraints. India's gross national product is likely to overtake that of European economies. The country will become an economic magnet in the region and its growth will have an impact not only on South Asia but also on north-central Asia, Iran and other countries of the Middle East and Southeast Asia.[1] According to Professor Amitabh Mattoo, vice chancellor of Jammu University and a well-known analyst in the field of international and strategic affairs, 'India by 2020 will be in a position to make a major impact on international relations unless we shoot ourselves in the foot in the quick march to that magical date'.[2]

Professor Mattoo has highlighted the following five elements that could be taken into account while formulating the new Indian policy towards Pakistan:

- Despite the strong belief that long-term peace and stability in South Asia will not be possible until the armed forces continue to dominate the Pakistan state, a comprehensive dialogue with the powers that be is essential to reduce tensions and assuage international opinion.

[1]'Mapping Global Futures 2020', US National Intelligence Council Report, and Goldman Sachs' Global Economic Paper No. 9.
[2]Professor Amitabh Mattoo, 'Emerging India and the World'. Talk delivered at the Jammu Club on 7 March 2005.

- Despite the pathological hostility of Pervez Musharraf and his fellow-soldiers towards India, they *may* have to give up support for jehadi forces and, in fact, fight against them.
- The civil society in Pakistan must be kept engaged and people-to-people contact strengthened.
- Ways and means to get rid of minor bilateral irritants affecting the Indo–Pak relationship should be put in place.
- The resolution of the Kashmir issue would be possible only when all hostility ends. Then, South Asia can achieve economic integration and the confidence-building measures, which, in turn, would allow for greater exchange of ideas, goods and services apart from more interaction between people.[3]

India's policy towards Pakistan in the days to come is indeed important and clarity should be its hallmark. The abovementioned elements are perhaps the clearest articulation of this policy. Let us examine (or analyse) these elements in the light of foreseeable political, social and economic prospects in Pakistan that have a bearing on Indo–Pak relations. We must coldly assess as to what is happening in Pakistan, what are the compulsions of the people there and how far they can go with the 'peace dialogue'.

Politics and Civil–Military Relations

At the political level, many in Pakistan believe that their country 'will not be able to remedy its multifaceted failures in governance, economic management and foreign strategic policy unless its leaders restore civilian democratic rule, governed by a constitutional framework with appropriate checks and balances.'[4] It is generally accepted that the restoration of democracy in Pakistan would, at least to some extent, help set right the military perception of a state of permanent, inevitable conflict with India. Historically, civilian regimes in Pakistan have been less obsessed with the Indian threat and even with Kashmir. It may

---

[3]Ibid.
[4]Aquil Shah, 'Democracy on Hold in Pakistan', *Journal of Democracy*, **13**, No. 1, January 2002, pp. 74–75.

be recalled that, in 1997, Nawaz Sharif came to power in Pakistan without making India or Kashmir a major electoral issue. On the other hand, the Pakistan Army's view of India as a permanent threat justifies its own claim to relevance and primacy in Pakistani politics. Over the years, this so-called primacy has branched out to include social and economic vested interests also. Such a state of affairs has thus resulted in the growth of the normative legal and institutional foundations necessary to sustain a democratic regime being curtailed. What then are the prospects of a changeover from a 'sham democratic' to a 'true democratic' polity in Pakistan?

After the stage-managed elections in October 2002, the Pakistani president, General Pervez Musharraf, had to carry a part of the political class with him. This compulsion has, by no means, reduced the overwhelming power that the Army exercises in Pakistan politics. In fact, the Army has managed to further consolidate its political position by establishing the National Security Council in April 2004. Currently, the two political coalitions, ruling as well as the opposition, do not have any credible leader and are in a state of disarray. The military establishment's overt efforts for a national reconciliation have produced no results. There are growing internal contradictions within the Muttahida Majlis-e-Amal (MMA), Jamaat-e-Islami and Jamiat-e-Ulema Islam (JUI) and the Pakistan Muslim League (Quaid-e-Azam) [PML (Q)], which, in any case, cannot survive without military support. Ethnic and sectarian cleavages have substantially widened. The internal politics in Pakistan thus remains muddy, but opportunistic!

Pervez Musharraf till now has backtracked from the promise that he would shed his uniform. He has done little to develop institutions that could promote a democratic temper or provide an opportunity to the moderate political forces to prosper. The military continues to be the master of state politics. It is in a position to crack down fully on the sources of terrorism and religious extremism. Whether or not it chooses to do so is an entirely different matter.

The Army possesses extraordinary strength, which lies at the core of the Pakistani nation-state. Democracy, as we in India understand it, remains a distant dream in Pakistan. The well-known South Asia analyst, Teresita C. Schaffer, has made a telling observation: 'the role of military is a major obstacle impeding Pakistan's political viability.'[5]

In this context, the noted strategist Ashley Tellis has observed: 'The resuscitation of democracy in Pakistan offers no guarantee that it will successfully break out from its current morass. The absence of democracy, however, will almost most certainly ensure the perpetuation of dangerous structural trends that will lead inevitably to state breakdown.'[6]

Most other analysts also agree that the US support to the Pakistan military regime, with no accountability for political and social reforms, encourages and perpetuates the military rule in Pakistan.

A clear political field notwithstanding, after more than six years of rule, Pervez Musharraf is under pressure, politically and institutionally, to deliver.

Economics and Related Factors

Pakistan's gross domestic product (GDP) stands at about $75 billion in absolute terms and $295 billion in terms of purchasing power parity. Income per capita is low by any standards. One-third of the population lives below the poverty line and another 21 per cent subsists just above it. Massive urban unemployment and rural underemployment are noticeable. The literacy rate is about 35–40 per cent; Pakistan allocates less than 2 per cent of its GDP for education. The low literacy rate and inadequate investment in education have gradually led to a decline in Pakistan's technology base, which, in turn, has hampered the country's economic modernization. Moreover, the public health service and other social services are deteriorating.

Currently, Pakistan spends about 4 per cent of its GDP on defence; India outspends Pakistan nearly three to one.

---

[5]Teresita C. Schaffer, 'US Influence in Pakistan: Can Partners Have Divergent Priorities?' *The Washington Quarterly*, **26**, Winter 2002–03, p. 177.

[6]Ashley Tellis, 'US Strategy: Assisting Pakistan's Transformation', *The Washington Quarterly*, Winter 2004–05, p. 104.

Consequently, India is continuously able to improve its military capabilities, while allocating only 2.5 per cent of its GDP to defence.

In recent years, the Government of Pakistan has succeeded in correcting its macro-economic performance, resulting in positive developments such as rising growth rates, a reduced fiscal deficit, lower inflation and higher tax revenues. These developments have come about primarily due to the discipline imposed by the international financial institutions, some structural reforms and economic assistance provided by the USA (on account of allowing Pakistan's military bases to be used for carrying out attacks on the Taliban during Operation Enduring Freedom). The long-term economic prospects would, however, depend on the completion of structural reforms and the setting up of new institutional arrangements. The future of these arrangements would, in turn, depend upon their perceived legitimacy and the compulsions of the prevalent politics. In order to sustain the economic success, the government would also need to contain defence expenditure, increase investments in agriculture and industry to raise the employment level, alleviate poverty and utilize the human capital judiciously.[7]

The Social Environment

Pakistan was born an Islamic state, on the basis of the two-nation theory. Its religious and ideological characterization cannot possibly change. On the other hand, if any national crisis were to arise, or the country's population were to fall victim to ethnic and linguistic differences, we should expect Islam to be used as the bonding factor to achieve unity. In Pakistan politics, Islam will continue to remain a significant factor.

Unfortunately, Pakistan has also become a major melting pot of diverse shades of jehadi Islamic groups and ideas, largely because of its policies towards India and Afghanistan. Ever since General Zia-ul Haq's regime (in power in the late 1970s and most of the 1980s), the military has effectively empowered jehadi Islamic elements at the social and cultural level. This alliance

[7]Ibid.

proved to be a useful instrument in marginalizing the moderate opposition inside the country and in advancing Islamabad's regional ambitions. The experience of the Soviet Union in Afghanistan in the 1980s appears to have convinced the Pakistan military that low-intensity conflict could drive India out of Kashmir or, at the very least, make New Delhi grant significant concessions. However, the use of these groups to fuel jehad has seriously eroded the social fabric. The jehadi Islamists' worldview is incompatible with the vision of a modern Pakistan. According to a respected scholar: 'Its violent vigilantism has already become a threat to the civil society and has promoted sectarian terrorism.'[8]

Currently, the strength of the jehadis lies in their ability to muster human and financial resources. Religious institutions in South Asia are never short of these two resources. The centres run by jehadis operate charities and publish newspapers and magazines. Also, they are able to put their followers on the streets on a massive scale. In the absence of democratic decision-making processes, the jehadis can easily dominate the political discourse. Years of close contact with fundamentalists and being bombarded regularly with religious rhetoric have influenced the middle ranking and younger generation of the military officers. The ISI has a slew of officials who have assimilated Islamist beliefs, which came in handy while supporting the cause of jehad in Afghanistan and Kashmir.[9]

Strategic Issues

It is a well-known fact that in the spheres of foreign policy and security affairs, an army-run government tends to give greater weightage to military strategic issues than to grand strategic issues. The Pakistani writer on strategic issues, Dr Ayesha Siddiqa, has commented: 'The most noticeable feature of the design of Pakistan's security perception is its simplistic linearity that identifies security and national interest mainly as response to an

---

[8]Husain Haqqani, 'The Role of Islam in Pakistan's Future', *The Washington Quarterly*, Winter 2004–05, p. 88.
[9]Ibid.

external threat...Pakistan has never ventured to extend its security vision beyond India.'[10]

Post-9/11 strategic cooperation with the USA, particularly in the case of Operation Enduring Freedom, has benefited Pakistan in terms of financial resources; becoming a 'major non-NATO ally' has also helped. But such alliances also tend to place strategic constraints and influence, at times negatively, domestic and international policies of a nation.[11]

The military domination of politics will also remain a major diplomatic disadvantage for Pakistan.

From the foregoing discussion, one is inclined to draw the following conclusions:

- No serious and organized popular challenge to state authorities exists in Pakistan.
- Pakistan is far from developing a sustainable democratic system and a stable form of government due to persisting polarization (*a*) between the military and the political class, (*b*) among the three major ethnic and provincial groups and (*c*) between the jehadis and the secularists.
- The jehadis in Pakistan cannot be wished away; only the Pakistan Army is capable of containing them.
- Pakistan's economy is improving. Despite that, the economic and military capability gap between India and Pakistan would continue to grow wider.
- Despite promises and official statements, Pervez Musharraf's regime has not yet eschewed supporting terrorism as an instrument of state policy.
- The strategic outlook of the military regime in Pakistan is unlikely to change and may be expected to remain narrow and shortsighted.

---

[10]*South Asian Journal*, **3**, Lahore, Free Media Foundation, 2003.

[11]A recent example is the firing of Hellfire missiles by a US Predator (unmanned aircraft) on Damadola village of the Bajaur Agency tribal area close to the Pakistan–Afghanistan border on 13 January 2006, in which eighteen civilians, including suspected Al Qaeda operatives, were killed. The incident led to political agitations all over Pakistan and fresh tension between Islamabad and Washington.

I believe that long-term Indo–Pak rapprochement, and the benefits to both countries that would follow, would depend primarily on economic interdependence and sustained cooperative security. Such a formula has seldom failed in conflict resolution. Even when occasional differences do crop up, economic interdependence of the people astride the borders, and between countries, have enabled nations to maintain status quo. The current emphasis on 'globalization' makes it easier to follow this path.

In the near future, apart from issues of economic interdependence, there are four major security issues that would have a significant impact on the current the Indo–Pak peace dialogue: crossborder terrorism, the Siachen Glacier, Jammu and Kashmir and nuclear confidence-building measures.

Crossborder Terrorism and Jehad

For Pakistan, supporting jehadi terrorism is a strategy aimed at achieving two objectives: to keep the conflict alive in Kashmir so as to force India to negotiate to Pakistan's advantage and to make India bleed, especially in Kashmir. The Pakistan military even now believes that the jehadis and militants in Kashmir constitute its trump card, without which India would not negotiate or make concessions. Islamabad also believes that this crossborder terrorism can be calibrated, kept high or low, depending upon political exigencies. In Pakistan's perception, the higher the threat and the intensity of jehad and terrorism in Kashmir, the higher the chance of India coming to the negotiating table and suing for talks. Consequently, Pakistan is unlikely to stop supporting jehadi elements altogether, so long as the Army remains dominant in that country's politics.

The extremist groups in Pakistan are broadly divided into two groups: those that belong to and support the Al Qaeda and international jehad and those that are fighting in Kashmir. The former come mostly from the North West Frontier Province (NWFP), Balochistan and Karachi, while the latter belong to Punjab and Pakistan-Occupied Kashmir (POK). The intense international pressure and Pervez Musharraf's efforts to check terrorism-related activities in religious seminaries and their training camps have been primarily focused on the former group. So far, Pakistan has not taken serious measures to stop the activities of the latter group. Although banned, they continue to remain active under different names. They are able to gather funds, recruit new people, run radio networks and maintain small-size camps in Pakistan and POK.

The crucial factor to be borne in mind is that so long as the motivation for terrorism is there and the terrorist infrastructure exists in Pakistan, it can increase or decrease the level of militancy in Kashmir. If India were willing to engage Pakistan politically, militancy would decline. If India goes slow in the process, there could be a sudden spurt in militancy.

So far, General Musharraf has been unable to change the Indo-phobic mindset of the Pakistan military, which traditionally looks at threat and competition from India as a justification for its own relevance and primacy. He cannot afford to upset this establishment and, therefore, cannot or does not wish to eschew support to Kashmiri terrorism. But he also wants to please the Pakistani liberal elite to be able to get its support and to maintain his own liberal image.

Pakistan has yet to realize that a large democratic nation, self-respecting and sufficiently powerful – as India is – cannot afford to compromise on national interests even if a pistol is held to its head during negotiations. Strategically, it would be disastrous for India to be seen as buckling down over Jammu and Kashmir or any other dispute due to terrorists' threats.

The Siachen Glacier

Most people in India and Pakistan believe that demilitarization of Siachen is feasible. It could be the first political achievement in the dialogue to take the peace process forward. But that should not mean going back to the pre-1984 days when, without any delineation on the maps, it was possible for either side to lay claim or encroach into each other's territory. There is still immense mistrust between the two countries. Besides, in any international agreement, there is always a clause that prevents the dispute reoccurring in future. Delineation of the Actual Ground Position Line (AGPL) on the map or aerial photography, therefore, is essential so that future verification is possible if ever any party violates the agreement. Once this is agreed to, demilitarization can be undertaken over a period of two to three summers, subsector by subsector.

The Pakistan Army demands the pre-1984 situation on the ground, which is not acceptable to India.

Jammu and Kashmir

On Jammu and Kashmir, lately, there appears to have been a subtle change in Pakistan's strategy. The change has taken place primarily on what could be the future political status of Kashmir. Pervez Musharraf, a prisoner of his own rhetoric, is under pressure to show quick results on this issue. He has already dumped the traditional Pakistani emphasis on the UNSC resolutions, much to the annoyance of the hardliners.

Recently, Pervez Musharraf and some other Pakistan leaders have expressed a desire for 'limited accommodation' in terms of regions within Jammu and Kashmir. This is Pakistan's version of the 'LoC Plus' formula, a modification of the old 'Chenab Plan'.[12] In January 2006, he came up with yet another proposal: demilitarization of Srinagar, Kupwara and Baramulla (all in the Indian part of Jammu and Kashmir) and 'self-rule' in the state. Both proposals made by Musharraf were summarily shot down by the Government of India.

Under Pervez Musharraf (and the military), Pakistan is likely to keep Kashmir as the 'core' issue, which will be used as a benchmark for discussions on all major economic issues.

Nuclear Confidence-building Measures

This is one area where there is a convergence of 'concern' in both countries; also both countries face direct and indirect

---

[12]'The LoC Plus' formula implies Pakistan keeping POK territory plus acquiring additional territory on the Indian side of the LoC. The 'Chenab Plan' hawked by some Pakistani diplomats implies partitioning Jammu and Kashmir along the Chenab River as that offers a 'natural barrier'. The latter would enable Pakistan to acquire a larger chunk of territory on the Indian side of the LoC. Pakistan thus assumes that POK is Pakistani territory, not under dispute, and thus ignores Indian claims over POK and the Northern Areas.

international pressure on this count. India and Pakistan have already informed locations of important nuclear assets to each other. Pakistan would be agreeable to the setting up of nuclear risk reduction centres, and perhaps to a moratorium on nuclear testing. The provisions in this context could include safety measures and warning in the event, or likelihood, of accidents, and deployment that would reduce risks due to technical factors and misperceptions. However, a no-first-use doctrine, a regional fissile materials freeze and further development of ballistic missiles would be kept outside the purview of the aforementioned provisions.

Epilogue

There is no alternative to a gradual, incremental peace process through political, economic and military confidence-building measures. Dramatic gestures or a few summit meetings between top leaders cannot lead to lasting peace.

EVER SINCE JANUARY 2004, WHEN THE DIALOGUE RESUMED, there has been a tangible change in Indo–Pak relations. Knowing fully well that people in India and Pakistan will not support a conflict unless the other side initiates it, New Delhi and Islamabad have stopped brandishing the sword. Rhetoric has given place to reason. There are lesser allegations and accusations against each other and more debates and discussions on good neighbourly relations.

The optimists feel that despite the slow pace, the dialogue is serving a useful purpose. For the first time, there is a sincere attempt to open up people-to-people contacts and to create a mechanism for friendly negotiations. In Pakistan, like in India, there is a fair amount of national consensus on continuing with the present policy of groping for genuine peace to replace the ostensible peace. Other positive factors are:

- The frequency and the intensity of the dialogue have helped leaders on both sides to understand each other better and tacitly recognize the constraints they have to work within.
- Most people on both sides want to live in peace and are gradually becoming articulate through the media. There is a political consensus in both countries to continue the dialogue.
- Globalization and the primacy of socio-economic factors for both governments are having a positive effect.

The real problem for India in Jammu and Kashmir is providing good administration and winning the hearts of the Kashmiri people; for Pakistan, it is the military mindset of the ruling regime. India can afford to be patient. Our primary efforts should remain focused on pursuing the economic agenda (through trade and commerce) with Pakistan and on keeping our house (including Jammu and Kashmir) in order. If we can do so, political bullying over Kashmir or the menace of the terrorists' guns from across the border would become meaningless. We have the resilience, apart from the hard and soft power[1] to respond to friendly and cooperative gestures from Pakistan constructively, or to ignore the Pakistanis, if that becomes necessary. Meanwhile, India's different policy strands on Jammu and Kashmir and on Pakistan should be interwoven carefully.

Pakistan has yet to appreciate the fact that the Kargil war was the third to be initiated by that country over Jammu and Kashmir. This tally does not include the ongoing skirmishes in Siachen and the more-than-fifteen-year-old Pakistan-sponsored proxy war in the state. The strategic conditions prevailing are a lot more stringent. The Jammu and Kashmir imbroglio cannot be resolved by military means or by militancy. Any attempt to resolve a complex political problem in a hurry, without carrying

---

[1]'Hard power' includes military, economic and technological resources and other such capabilities of a nation. 'Soft power' implies its social, cultural, secular and philosophical strength.

the people of the two nations, could lead to violence on both sides of the border or the LoC.

After the devastation caused by the earthquake in Jammu and Kashmir in October 2005, which affected Pakistan-Occupied Kashmir more than the Indian part, the Government of India took some unprecedented steps to open up the LoC at a number of places to facilitate earthquake relief and to allow people of both parts of Kashmir to meet. But soon thereafter, as if on a cue, there was sudden spurt in terrorist violence by Pakistan-based terrorist groups in Jammu and Kashmir, New Delhi and Bangalore.

India's central premise is that the peace process with Pakistan should take place in a violence-free environment. If such a premise turns out to be unsustainable, the government would lose popular support for talks with Pakistan. People in India would get the impression that Pakistan is leveraging terrorist violence to extract political concessions from New Delhi. The government would thus undermine its ability and credibility to negotiate with Pakistan.

Unless Pakistan ensures the implementation of its commitments on terrorism made by General Pervez Musharraf in January and May 2002 during the Indo–Pak military stand-off, and again in the January 2004 Islamabad Declaration, in letter and spirit, there is little chance of establishing durable friendly relations between India and Pakistan.

There is no alternative to a gradual, incremental peace process through political, economic and military confidence-building measures. Dramatic gestures or a few summit meetings between top leaders cannot lead to lasting peace. Peace, as someone put it, can only be achieved through pieces. India and Pakistan have a long way to go before they can create a win-win situation for themselves. The best hope, meanwhile, is that both countries could agree to create a climate of trust and confidence: to live and let live.

In the foreseeable future, even if India and Pakistan do not go to war, which I sincerely hope they do not, people on both sides of the border can at best hope for some kind of 'no-war-no-peace situation', or, in Ashley Tellis' memorable phrase, 'ugly stability'.[2] The armed forces in India can hope for the best contingency, but they must remain prepared for the worst contingency.

---

[2]Ashley Tellis, 'Stability in South Asia', documented briefing, RAND Corporation, Santa Monica, USA, 1997, p. 51.

Text of Documents Signed at Lahore

LAHORE, 21 FEBRUARY 1999: THE FOLLOWING IS THE TEXT OF the documents signed at the conclusion of the Indian Prime Minister's visit to Lahore on Sunday [21 February].

The Lahore Declaration

The Prime Ministers of the Republic of India and the Islamic Republic of Pakistan:

Sharing a vision of peace and stability between their countries, and the progress and prosperity for their people;

Convinced that durable peace and development of harmonious relations and friendly cooperation will serve the vital interests of the peoples of the two countries, enabling them to devote their energies for a better future;

Recognizing that the nuclear dimension of the security environment of the two countries adds to their responsibility for avoidance of conflict between the two countries;

Committed to the principles and purposes of the Charter of the United Nations and the universally accepted principles of peaceful co-existence;

Reiterating the determination of both countries to implementing the Simla Agreement in letter and sprit;

Committed to objectives of universal nuclear disarmament and non-proliferation;

Convinced of the importance of mutually agreed

confidence-building measures for improving the security environment;

Recalling their agreement of 23 September 1998, that an environment of peace and security is in the supreme national interest of both sides and that the resolution of all outstanding issues, including Jammu and Kashmir is essential for this purpose;

Have agreed that their respective governments:

- Shall intensify their efforts to resolve all issues, including the issues of Jammu and Kashmir.
- Shall refrain from intervention and interference in each other's internal affairs.
- Shall intensify their composite and integrated dialogue process for an early and positive outcome of the agreed bilateral agenda.
- Shall take immediate steps for reducing the risk of accidental or unauthorized use of nuclear weapons and discuss concepts and doctrines with a view to elaborating measures for confidence building in the nuclear and conventional fields, aimed at prevention of conflict.
- Reaffirm their commitment to the goals and objectives of SAARC and to concert their efforts towards the realization of the SAARC vision for the year 2000 and beyond with a view to promoting the welfare of the peoples of South Asia and to improve their quality of life through accelerated economic growth, social progress and cultural development.
- Reaffirm their condemnation of terrorism in all its forms and manifestations and their determination to combat this menace.
- Shall promote and protect all human rights and fundamental freedoms.

Atal Behari Vajpayee   **Muhammad Nawaz Sharif**
Prime Minister of   Prime Minister of
the Republic of India   the Islamic Republic of Pakistan

Joint Statement

1. In response to an invitation by the Prime Minister of Pakistan, Mr Muhammad Nawaz Sharif, the Prime Minister of India, Shri Atal Behari Vajpayee visited Pakistan [on] 20–21 February 1999, on the inaugural run of the Delhi–Lahore bus service.

2. The Prime Minister of Pakistan received the Indian Prime Minister at the Wagah border on 20 February 1999. A banquet in honour of the Indian Prime Minister and his delegation was hosted by the Prime Minister of Pakistan at Lahore Fort, on the same evening. Prime Minister Atal Behari Vajpayee visited Minar-i-Pakistan, Mausoleum of Allama Iqbal, Gurudwara Dera Sahib and Samadhi of Maharaja Ranjeet Singh. On 21 February, a civic reception was held in honour of the visiting Prime Minister at the Governor's House.

3. The two leaders held discussions on the entire range of bilateral relations, regional cooperation within SAARC, and issues of international concern. They decided that:

    (a) The two Foreign Ministers will meet periodically to discuss all issues of mutual concern, including nuclear related issues.

    (b) The two sides shall undertake consultations on WTO-related issues with a view to coordinating their respective positions.

    (c) The two sides shall determine areas of cooperation in Information Technology, in particular for tackling of the problems of Y2K.

    (d) The two sides will hold consultations with a view to further liberalizing the visa and travel regime.

    (e) The two sides shall appoint a two-member committee at ministerial level to examine humanitarian issues relating to civilian detainees and missing POWs.

4. They expressed satisfaction on the commencement of a bus service between Lahore and New Delhi, the release of fishermen and civilian detainees and the renewal of contacts in the field of sports.

5. Pursuant to the directive given by the two Prime Ministers, the Foreign Secretaries of Pakistan and India signed a Memorandum of Understanding on 21 February 1999, identifying measures aimed at promoting an environment of peace and security between the two countries.

6. The two Prime Ministers signed the Lahore Declaration embodying their shared vision of peace and stability between their countries and of progress and prosperity for their peoples.

7. Prime Minister Atal Behari Vajpayee extended an invitation to Prime Minister Muhammad Nawaz Sharif to visit India on mutually convenient dates.

8. Prime Minister Atal Behari Vajpayee thanked Prime Minister Muhammad Nawaz Sharif for the warm welcome and gracious hospitality extended to him and members of his delegation and for the excellent arrangements made for his visit.

The Memorandum of Understanding

The foreign secretaries of India and Pakistan:

Reaffirming the continued commitment of their respective governments to the principles and purposes of the UN Charter;

Reiterating the determination of both countries to implementing the Simla Agreement in letter and spirit;

Guided by the agreement between their Prime Ministers of 23 September 1998 that an environment of peace and security is in the supreme national interest of both sides and that resolution of all outstanding issues, including Jammu and Kashmir, is essential for this purpose;

Pursuant to the directive given by their respective Prime Ministers in Lahore, to adopt measures for promoting a stable environment and peace and security between the two countries;

Have, on this day, agreed to the following:

1. The two sides shall engage in bilateral consultations on security concepts, and nuclear doctrines, with a view to

developing measures for confidence building in the nuclear and conventional fields, aimed at avoidance of conflict.

2. The two sides undertake to provide each other with advance notification in respect of ballistic missile flight tests and shall conclude a bilateral agreement in this regard.

3. The two sides are fully committed to undertaking national measures to reducing the risks of accidental or unauthorized use of nuclear weapons under their respective control. The two sides further undertake to notify each other immediately in the event of any accidental, unauthorized or unexplained incident that could create the risk of a fallout with adverse consequences for both sides, or an outbreak of a nuclear war between the two countries, as well as to adopt measures aimed at diminishing the possibility of such actions, or such incidents being misinterpreted by the other. The two sides shall identify/establish the appropriate communication mechanism for this purpose.

4. The two sides shall continue to abide by their respective unilateral moratorium on conducting further nuclear test explosions unless either side, in exercise of its national sovereignty, decides that extraordinary events have jeopardized its supreme interests.

5. The two sides shall conclude an agreement on prevention of incidents at sea in order to ensure safety of navigation by naval vessels and aircraft belonging to the two sides.

6. The two sides shall periodically review the implementation of existing confidence-building measures (CBMs) and, where necessary, set up appropriate consultative mechanisms to monitor and ensure effective implementation of the CBMs.

7. The two sides shall undertake a review of the existing communication links (e.g., between the respective Directors General of Military Operations) with a view to upgrading and improving these links, and to provide for fail-safe and secure communications.

8. The two sides shall engage in bilateral consultations on security, disarmament and non-proliferation issues within the context of negotiations on these issues in multilateral fora.

Where required, the technical details of the above measures will be worked out by experts of the two sides in meetings to be held on mutually agreed dates, before mid-1999, with a view to reaching bilateral agreements.

K. Raghunath
Foreign Secretary
of the Republic of India

Shamshad Ahmad
Foreign Secretary
of the Islamic Republic
of Pakistan

Records of Telephone Conversations

The First Conversation*

Pakistan end (P): Lieutenant General Mohammad Aziz Khan, Chief of General Staff.
China end (C): General Pervez Musharraf, Chief of Army Staff.

C: I am sorry the line is busy now.
P: Can I hold?.... Salam-ale-qum, Sir.
C: Wale-qum-Salam.
P: Sir, There is a call from Pakistan for General Pervez Musharraf.
C: Yes Sir.
P: General Aziz Khan will speak.
C: Yes.
P: Sir Colonel Hassan.
C: Yes, Hassan.
P: Sir, how are you?
C: Grace of God.
P: Sir, please speak, hello?

*The first conversation was between Lieutenant General Mohammad Aziz Khan (in Pakistan) and General Pervez Musharraf (visiting China) on 26 May 1999. Much of the conversation took place in Urdu; given here is the English translation.

C: Thank you.

P: Sir, Salam-ale-qum.

C: Yes Aziz, how are you?

P: Very fine, Sir. How is the visit going?

C: Yes, very well. OK. And, what else is the news on that side?

P: Ham-dul-ullah. There is no change on the ground situation. They have started rocketing and strafing. That has been upgraded a little. It had happened yesterday also and today. Today high-altitude bombing has been done.

C: On their side, in those positions?

P: In those positions, but in today's bombing about three bombs landed in our side of Line of Control. No damage, Sir.

C: Is it quite a lot?

P: Sir, about twelve–thirteen bombs were dropped, from which three fell on our side, which does not appear to be a result of inaccuracy. In my interpretation, it is a sort of giving of a message [sic] that if need be we can do it on the other side as well. It is quite a distance apart. Where the bombs have been dropped, they have tried to drop from a good position where they are in difficulty, from behind the LoC but they have fallen on our side of the LoC. So I have spoken to the Foreign Secretary and I have told him that he should make the appropriate noises about this in the press.

C: They (Indians) should also be told.

P: That we have told. Foreign Secretary will also say and Rashid [the press officer of the Pakistan Army] will also say. He will not, generally speaking, make any such mistake about those other bombs falling on the other side. Our stand should be that all these bombs are falling on our side. We will not come into that situation. The guidelines that they have given, we have stressed that we should say that this build-up and employment of air strike which has been done under the garb of...us [TRANSCRIPT NOT AUDIBLE HERE] actually they are targeting our position on the LoC and our logistic build-up, these possibly they are taking under the garb having intention for operation of the craft [TRANSCRIPT NOT CLEAR HERE] Line of Control, and this needs to be taken note of and we would retaliate in kind...if that happened. So, the entire build-up we want to give this colour.

C: Absolutely OK. Yes, this is better. After that, has there been any talk with them (Pakistani officials)? And meetings, etc.?

P: Yesterday, again, in the evening.

C: Who all were there?

P: Actually, we insisted that a meeting should be held, because otherwise that friend of ours, the incumbent of my old chair, we thought lest he gives some interpretation of his own, we should do something ourselves by going there.

C: Was he little disturbed? I heard that there was some trouble in Sialkot [a town in Pakistan's Punjab state].

P: Yes. There was one in Daska [another town in Pakistan's Punjab state]. On this issue there was trouble. Yes, he was little disturbed about that but I told him that such small things keep happening...[TRANSCRIPT NOT CLEAR] and we can reply to such things in a better way.

C: Absolutely.

P: There is no such thing to worry.

C: So that briefing to Mian Saheb [Nawaz Sharif] that we did, was the forum the same as where we had done previously? There, at Jamshed's place?

P: No, In Mian Saheb's office.

C: Oh I see. There. What was he saying?

P: From here we had gone – Choudhary Zafar Saheb [Lieutenant General Saeed-uz Zaman Zafar, GOC 11 Corps], Mehmood [Ahmad, GOC 10 Corps, Rawalpindi], myself and Tauqir [Zia, Pakistan's DGMO]. Because before going, Tauqir had spoken with his counterpart. We carried that tape with us.

C: So, what was he [Indian Army DGMO] saying?

P: That is very interesting. When you come, I will play it for you. Its focus was that these infiltrators who are sitting here, they have your help and artillery support, without which they could not have come to J&K. This is not a very friendly act and it is against the spirit of the Lahore Declaration. Then Tauqir told him that if your boys tried to physically attack the Line of Control and go beyond it...and that the bombs were planted on the Turtok [Turtuk] bridge and the dead body received in the process was returned with military honours and I said, I thought that there was good enough indication you would not enter into this type of misadventure, and all build-up that you are doing – one or more brigade strength and fifty to sixty aircraft are being collected – these are excuses for undertaking some operations at various places. So I had put him on the defensive. Then he said the same old story. He would put three points again and again that they (militants) should not be supported, and without your support they could not be there, they have sophisticated weapons and we will flush them out, we will not let them stay there. But this is not a friendly act.

C: So, did they talk of coming out and meeting somewhere?

P: No, no, they did not.

C: Was there some other talk of putting pressure on us?

P: No. He only said that they [the jehadi militants] will be given suitable reception. This term he used. He said, they will be flushed out, and every time Tauqir said that please tell us some detail[s], detail[s] about how many have gone into your area, what is happening there? Then I will ask the concerned people and then we will get back to you. So whenever he asked these details, he would say, we will talk about this when we meet, then I will give details. This means they are possibly looking forward to next round of talks, in which the two sides could meet. This could be the next round of talks between the two PMs, which they are expecting.... Sir, very good thing, no problem...

C: So, many times we had discussed, taken your [TRANSCRIPT NOT CLEAR HERE] blessings and yesterday also I told him that the door of discussion, dialogue must be kept open and rest, no change in ground situation.

P: So no one was in a particularly disturbed frame of mind.

C: Even your seat man [probably, Lieutenant General Ziauddin, DG ISI].

P: Yes, he was disturbed. Also Malik Saheb was disturbed, as they had been even earlier. Those two's views was that the status quo and the present position of [TRANSCRIPT NOT CLEAR]...no change should be recommended in that. But he was also saying that any escalation after that should be regulated as there may be the danger of war. On this logic, we gave the suggestion that there was no such fear as the scruff (*tooti*) of their (militants) neck is in our hands, whenever you want, we could regulate it. Choudhary Zafar Saheb coped very well. He gave a very good presentation of our viewpoint. He said we had briefed the PM earlier and given an assessment. After this, we played the tape of Tauqir. Then he said that what we are seeing, that was our assessment, and those very stages of the military situation were being seen, which it would not be a problem for us to handle. Rest it was for your guidance how to deal with the political and diplomatic aspects. We told him there is no reason [for] alarm and panic. Then he said that when I came to know seven days back, when corps commanders were told. The entire reason for the success of this operation was this total secrecy. Our experience was that our earlier efforts failed because of lack of secrecy. So the top priority is to accord confidentiality, to ensure our success. We should respect this and the advantage we have from this would give us a handle.

C: Anything else? Is Mian Saheb OK?

P: OK. He was confident just like that but for the other two. Shamshad [Ahmad, Pakistan's foreign secretary] as usual was supportive. Today, for the last two hours the BBC has been continuously reporting on the air strikes by India. Keep using this – let them keep dropping bombs. As far as internationalization is concerned, this is the fastest this has happened. You may have seen in the Press about UN Secretary-General Kofi Annan's appeal that both countries should sit and talk.

C: This is very good.

P: Yes, this is very good.

C: OK. Bye.

The Second Conversation*

Pakistan end (P): Lieutenant General Mohammad Aziz Khan, Chief of General Staff.

---

*The second conversation was between Lieutenant General Mohammad Aziz Khan and General Pervez Musharraf on 29 May 1999.

China end (C): General Pervez Musharraf, Chief of Army Staff.

P: This is Pakistan. Give me room no. 83315 (same room number). Hello.

C: Hello Aziz.

P: The situation on ground is OK, no change [TRANSCRIPT NOT CLEAR]. One of their Mi-17 armed helicopters was brought down. Further...the position is that as it had approached our position [Pakistani], it was brought down. Rest is OK. Nothing else except, there is a development. Have you listened to yesterday's news regarding Mian Saheb's speaking to his [Indian] counterpart? He [Nawaz Sharif] told him [Vajpayee] that the escalation has been done by your people [Indians]. He [Nawaz Sharif] specially wanted to speak to me thereafter. He told Indian PM that they should have waited instead of upping the ante by using Air Force and all other means. He [Nawaz] told him [Indian PM] that he suggested Sartaj Aziz [Pakistan's foreign minister] could go to New Delhi to explore the possibility of defusing the tension.

C: OK.

P: Which [referring to Sartaj Aziz's visit to India] is likely to take place, most probably tomorrow.

C: OK.

P: Our other friend [most probably, the USA] might have also put pressure on [Nawaz Sharif]. For that, today they will have a discussion at Foreign Office about 9.30 and Zafar Saheb [Lieutenant General Saeed-uz Zaman Zafar, GOC 11 Corps and acting chief] is supposed to attend.

C: OK.

P: Aziz Saheb [Sartaj Aziz] has discussed with me and my recommendation is that dialogue option is always open. But in their first meeting, they must give no understanding or no commitment on ground situation.

C: Very correct. You or Mehmood [Ahmad, GOC, 10 Corps] may have to go with Zafar. Because, they don't know about the ground situation.

P: This week, we are getting together at 8 o' clock because the meeting will be at 9.30, so Zafar Saheb will deliberate it [sic].

We want to suggest to Zafar that they have to maintain that they will not be talking about ground situation. Subsequently, DsGMO can discuss with each other and work out the modus operandi.

C: Idea on LoC.

P: Yes. The hint is that the LoC has many areas where the interpretation of either side is not what the other side believes. So comprehensive deliberation is required. That can be worked out by DsGMO. If they are assured that we are here from [sic] a long period. We have been sitting here for long. Like in the beginning, the matter is the same – no post was attacked and no post was captured. The situation is that we are along our defensive Line of Control. If it is not in his [Sartaj Aziz's] knowledge then discuss it altogether. Emphasize that for years, we are here only. Yes, this point should be raised. We are sitting on the same LoC since a long period.

C: Yes! This point should be raised. We are sitting on the same LoC since a long period.

P: This is their weakness. They [India] have not agreed on the demarcation under UN's verification, whereas we [Pakistan] have agreed. We want to exploit it.

C: This is in the Simla Agreement that we cannot go for UN intervention.

P: Our neighbour does not accept their presence or UNMOGIP [UN Military Observer Group in India and Pakistan] arrangement for survey of the area. So, we can start from the top, from 9842 [NJ 9842]. On this line, we can give them logic. In short, the recommendation for Sartaj Aziz Saheb is that he should make no commitment in the first meeting on military situation. And he should not even accept ceasefire, because if there is ceasefire, then vehicles will be moving [on the Dras–Kargil highway]. In this regard, they have to use their own argument [to remove] whatever [jehadi militants] is interfering with you [India]. That we don't know. But there is no justification about tension on the LoC. No justification.

We want to give them this type of brief so that he does not get into any specifics.

C: Alright.

P: In this connection, we want your approval. And what is your programme?

C: I will come tomorrow. We are just leaving within an hour. We are going to Shenzhen [China, near Hong Kong]. From there, by evening, we will be in Hong Kong. There will be a flight tomorrow from Hong Kong. So, we will be in Lahore in the evening, via Bangkok flight.

P: Sunday evening [30 May 1999], you will be at Lahore. We will also indicate that if there is more critical situation, it [Sartaj Aziz's visit] should be deferred for another day or two. We can discuss on Monday [31 May 1999] and then proceed.

C: Has this Mi-17 not fallen in our area?

P: No Sir. This has fallen in their area. We have not claimed it. We have got it claimed through the Mujahideen.

C: Well done.

P: But it was quite a sight...crashing straight before our eyes...

C: Very good. Now are they facing any greater difficulty in flying them? Are they scared or not? This also you should note. Are they flying any *less* closer to our positions?

P: Yes. There is a lot of pressure on them. They were talking about greater air defence than they had anticipated. They can't afford to lose any more aircraft. There has been less intensity of air flying after that.

C: Very good. First class. Is there any build-up on the ground?

P: Just like that. But the movement is pretty sluggish and slow. One or two are coming near. No. 6 [India's 6 Mountain Division]. Till now only one call sign [TRANSCRIPT NOT CLEAR], this has not reached the valley so far. Now the air people and the ground people will stay back and then the situation will be OK.

C: See you in the evening.

A Summary of the Kargil Review Committee's Recommendations

1. A thorough review of the national security system in its entirety should be undertaken by an independent body of credible experts, whether a national commission or one or more task forces or otherwise as expedient.
2. Having a National Security Advisor who also happens to be Principal Secretary to PM can only be an interim arrangement. There must be a full-time NSA and a second line of personnel should be inducted into the system urgently and groomed for higher responsibilities.
3. There must be periodic intelligence briefings of [the] Cabinet Committee on Security with all supporting staff in attendance.
4. Every effort must be made to ensure that a satellite imagery capability of world standard is developed indigenously and put in place in the shortest possible time.
5. Acquisition of high-altitude Unmanned Aerial Vehicles (UAVs) should be undertaken and institutionalized arrangements made to ensure that imagery generated by them is disseminated to concerned intelligence agencies as quickly as possible.
6. Communication interception equipment needs to be modernized and direction-finding equipment augmented.
7. The establishment of a single organization like the National Security Agency of the USA, grouping together all communication and electronic intelligence efforts, needs to be examined.

8. Adequate attention has not been paid to develop encryption and decryption skills.

9. The issue of setting up an integrated Defence Intelligence Agency needs to be examined.

10. There is no institutionalized mechanism for coordination or objective-oriented interaction between intelligence agencies and consumers at different levels. Similarly, there is no mechanism for tasking the agencies, monitoring their performance and reviewing their records to evaluate their quality. Nor is there any oversight of the overall functioning of the agencies. Accordingly, a thorough examination of the working of the intelligence system with a view to removing these deficiencies is called for.

11. Though the efficacy of the Joint Intelligence Committee has increased since it became part of the National Security Council Secretariat, its role and place in the national intelligence framework should be evaluated in the context of the overall reform of the system.

12. The development of country/region specialization along with associate language skills should not be further delayed. It is necessary to establish think tanks, [to] encourage country specialization and to organize regular exchange of personnel between them and the intelligence community.

13. In order to have a young and fit Army, colour service [service before a soldier is required to retire or to go as a reservist] should be reduced from seventeen years to between seven to ten years. Released officers and men should then be diverted to paramilitary formations. Subsequently, older cadres might be further streamed into regular police forces.

14. Improved border management necessitates a detailed study in order to evolve appropriate force structures and procedures to deal with the inflow of narcotics, illegal migrants, terrorists and arms.

15. Many experts have suggested the need to enhance India's defence outlay as budgetary constraints have affected modernization and created operational voids. Government must determine the level of defence spending in consultation with the concerned Departments and Defence Services.

16. Armed forces headquarters are outside the apex governmental structure. This had led to many negative results and it is felt that the Services headquarters should be located within the Government. The entire gamut of national security management and apex decision making and the structure and interface between the Ministry of Defence and Armed Forces' headquarters should be comprehensively studied and reorganized.

17. Beginning with Indira Gandhi, successive Indian Prime Ministers have consistently supported an Indian nuclear weapons programme but enveloped it in the utmost secrecy not taking into confidence their own party colleagues, the Armed Forces and senior civil servants. [Records in government files] establish that the Indian nuclear weapons programme had a much wider consensus than is generally believed. Accordingly, the publication of a white paper on the Indian nuclear weapons programme is highly desirable.

18. On many vital issues, sufficient public information is not available in a single comprehensive official publication. The Government must review its information policy and develop structures and processes to keep the public informed of vital national issues.

19. One of the major factors influencing Pakistan's aggressive behaviour in 1947, 1965, 1971 and 1999 has been a deliberately cultivated perception of an ineffectual Indian Army and a weak and vacillating Indian Government. Though Pakistan was discomfited in all the four military adventures it undertook, it has attempted to portray each as a narrowly missed victory. It is, therefore, necessary to publish authentic accounts of the 1965 and 1971 wars to establish the facts. It is also recommended that an authoritative account of the Kargil conflict be published at an early date.

20. A true partnership must be established between the Services and the DRDO [Defence Research and Development Organization] to ensure that the latter gets full backing and funding from the Services and the former get the indented equipment they require without delay.

21. Establishment of a civil–military liaison mechanism at various levels from Command Headquarters to operative formations

at the ground level is essential to smoothen the relationship during times of stress and to prevent friction and alienation of the local population.

22. A rehabilitation programme for soldiers who were wounded in the Kargil war and [for] others must be put in place.

23. The dedication and valour of Ladakh Scouts and J&K Light Infantry merit recognition through raising of additional units of these regiments locally.

24. The country must not fall into the trap of Siachenization of the Kargil heights and similar unheld gaps. The proper response would be a declaratory policy that deliberate infringement of the sanctity of the LOC and crossborder terrorism will meet with retaliation in a manner, time and place of India's choosing.

25. Credible measures must be undertaken in J&K to win back alienated sections of the population and attend to genuine discontent. .

26. Neither the Northern Army Command nor HQ 15 Corps nor the lower field formations had media cells, which could cater to the requirement of the press corps. It must also be recognized that the media has to be serviced at many levels – national, local and international.

27. The US Armed Forces usually operate dedicated radio and TV channels to entertain and inform their armed forces when deployed overseas. The Government should seriously consider similar dedicated facilities for the Indian Armed Forces. If such facilities had been available at the time of Kargil, some of the misleading reports and rumours that gained currency could have been effectively countered.

28. The committee was informed that Prasar Bharati [India's public sector broadcasting organization] in J&K lacks Balti and other linguistic skills to reach the people across the LOC. Unless such software and programming aspects are taken care of, mere hardware expansion may not be cost effective.

Press Note from Army Headquarters

1. We have been constrained to issue the statement only because some people with vested interests have picked on a disgruntled Brigadier who was removed from command of a Brigade for operational reasons to another appointment, after due thought and recommendations of the chain of command – a type of action that often becomes necessary in a war. Accordingly, insinuations and fabrications have been published quoting some Army documents completely out of context and some that do not even exist. It is therefore essential that the true facts must be stated.

2. It is reiterated that the only letter received by the COAS, through his Military Assistant, from Brig. Surinder Singh, ex Cdr 121 (I) Infantry Brigade, is No. 29734/SS/Confd dated 28 Jun 99 repeat 28 Jun 99, after his removal from command of 121(I) Inf Bde. This is a confidential letter wherein Brig. Surinder Singh has represented against his removal from command of 121(I) Inf Bde. In this letter he has attached several annexures of his correspondence with his Div HQs. This letter with all its annexures has already been handed over to the [K.] Subrahmanyam Committee. We believe its existence is also known to several mediamen for some time past.

3. Meanwhile, some spokesmen and a (very) few journalists have given numbers with dates of several letters supposedly written by Brig. Surinder Singh to the Chief of the Army Staff on dates between Aug 98 and Dec 98. The existence/

receipt of these letters have [*sic*] been consistently denied by Army HQ/Ministry of Defence. The 'facts' regarding some of the letters/extracts published in a magazine and a newspaper are attached with this statement. Is it just to quote and misquote the words of a disgruntled Brigadier to vilify the entire hierarchy of the Army, when inquiries into the matter are still underway? Would it have been too much for us, uniformed men who swear by the honour of the profession of arms, to expect these publications to at least approach us for our version of these purported documents? We believe it is an elementary principle of journalism. Or is an exception to be made now in the case of the Army? If so, why?

4. It is nobody's case that the principle of accountability does not apply to the Armed Forces. It is precisely for this reason that the Subrahmanyam Committee has been set up to review the events leading up to the Pakistani aggression in Kargil, and recommend such measures as are considered necessary to safeguard national security against such intrusions. To this end, the Committee is empowered to summon and investigate all witnesses and documents from the Army pertaining to this issue. We also have our own system of introspection and correction so that lessons that need to be learnt – even from a victory – must be learnt. We are serious about these things as they involve lives of our men and the security of our nation. It is not in the nature of the Army to cover facts or draw wrong lessons.

5. The entire world acknowledges the apolitical and secular nature of our Armed Forces. We perform our task with equal commitment under different Governments, unmindful of the politics of the day. If we were now to be dragged into electoral politics in so vicious a manner, it will be a sad day for the country.

6. For its effective functioning, the Army relies heavily on its ethos, tradition, discipline and its chain of command. The Kargil war may have partly ended, but insecurity on the LoC, borders and within the country continues. We appeal to all countrymen, including media leaders, please do not destroy the fabric of the organization, which has always stood by the nation.

Postscript

AFTER THE RELEASE OF THE ENGLISH VERSION OF THIS BOOK in April 2006, there have been two significant developments connected with facts about the Kargil war, which require to be commented upon.

In the book, I have mentioned about systemic failures and about the assessments that were received from the Research and Analysis Wing (R & AW), Intelligence Bureau (IB) and Joint Intelligence Committee (JIC) at the politico-military levels of the government during the period 1998–99. I have summed that up by stating: 'The failure to anticipate and identify military action of this nature on our borders by Pakistan Army reflected a major deficiency in our system of collecting, reporting, collating and assessing intelligence.' This remark has been questioned by a couple of former officers from the national intelligence agencies in the media.

Having read their statements, I feel that their reaction is more in anger and in turf defence than on the basis of any logic! First: They have not contradicted any intelligence assessments cited by me of the period one year before the war, i.e., 1998–99. We must appreciate that at the level of the Cabinet Committee on Security (CCS) and the Chiefs of Staff Committee (COSC), strategic decisions are taken on the basis of assessments and not individual reports. Second: One of them has referred to the IB director's note of June 1998. (I have written about this note in Chapter 4.) There was no mention of the Pakistan Army's preparations for a military attack by infiltration in this note. Third: This note was written on 2 or 3 June 1998. General Pervez Musharraf planned and initiated the war *after* he took over command of the Pakistan Army in October 1998. How could a military action be perceived six months before it was decided and initiated by Pakistan? Fourth: In a briefing to an American delegation in January 2003, Major General (now Lieutenant General) Nadeem Ahmed, then Pakistan's Force Commander Northern Areas (FCNA), categorically denied the presence of any Mujahideen or militants (see footnote 12, Chapter 4).

I have not tried to cover the surveillance lapses on the ground; the details have already been given earlier in the book. The point I would like to emphasize relates to intelligence assessments. If the intelligence agencies had made correct assessments, and were so convinced, then Prime Minister Atal Behari Vajpayee should have been stopped from going to Lahore in February 1999. The heads of R & AW, IB and JIC were meeting him and the NSA, Brajesh Mishra, much more frequently than I did.

One crucial question in this context is: Were there any tactical and strategic consequences of wrong intelligence assessments and our inability to differentiate between militants' and Pakistani military intrusion in the early stages of the war? Yes! At the battalion and brigade levels, you shoot at anyone crossing the LoC. But at the strategic level, such assessments *did* make a difference in our reactions to the situation. They also taught us a major lesson vis-à-vis the Kargil war.

Crossborder infiltration by militants had been (then) going on for about ten years. The initial reactions to the intrusion at the corps and command levels were prompt but weak, uncertain and yet, surprisingly, overconfident. This can be made out from the then defence minister's and 15 Corps commander's statements to the media from Srinagar in the third week of May 1999. Had there been a timely and correct assessment of Pakistan's *military* intrusion into the Indian territory, then the politico-military reactions would have been very different. In such an eventuality:

- Prime Minister Vajpayee should not have visited Lahore in February 1999.
- The Pakistani intrusion would have been immediately declared a military aggression, with all its domestic and international implications.
- I would not have gone on the official visit to Poland and the Czech Republic in May 1999.
- The air chief and the CCS would have had no hesitation in employing air power against the Pakistani military intrusion on 18 May 1999.
- The CCS could not have insisted on the Indian armed forces not crossing the LoC/border.

Some people have suggested that in view of Vajpayee's Lahore visit, the heads of intelligence agencies may have been told to play down Pakistan's terrorist-related activities till the actual intrusion. I have neither any knowledge of any such instructions nor do I believe that to be plausible. That would make the issue far too serious, implying deliberate suppression or obfuscation of facts at the cost of national security.

In the Line of Fire

On 25 September 2006 General Pervez Musharraf released his book *In the Line of Fire: A Memoir*[1] in New York. The book, in the form of a personal narration, carries his version of the war in the chapter 'The Kargil Conflict'.

General Musharraf starts the chapter as follows: '1999 may have been the most momentous year of my life, assassination attempts notwithstanding. The events of that year, and the fall of 1998, dramatically catapulted me from soldiering to leading the destiny of the nation.... It is time to lay bare what has been shrouded in mystery.' He then reveals the mystery. Seven years after the event, when endless analyses have been recorded and several dozen books written on the subject, the General states

---

[1]General Pervez Musharraf, *In the Line of Fire: A Memoir* (Simon & Schuster, New York, 2006).

that the Kargil war was a great victory for the Pakistan Army and that was undertaken because the Indian side was preparing an offensive operation. According to him: 'Indian plan of an offensive was pre-empted.... The initiative was wrested from them...finding a solution to Kashmir is owed to the Kargil conflict.'

What an imaginative version! The General is a master of fabrication! He either has very great confidence in his persuasive powers or harbours utter contempt for the people of Pakistan and the USA, who are the primary audience of this book.

General Musharraf claims that after taking over as the Pakistani Army chief (on 9 October 1998), he learnt that India had reported five 'make belief [sic] attacks' in October–early November, and that the Indians were on the verge of attacking the Shaqma sector (opposite Dras–Kargil) in summer 1999 because (a) India had been 'creeping forward' across the LoC ever since the Shimla Agreement, (b) India had not moved two reserve brigades out of Kargil–Ladakh during winter 1998–99, (c) India had procured large quantities of high-altitude equipment and special weapons and (d) George Fernandes (the defence minister) was visiting Siachen and Kargil frequently. Based on this logic, in mid-January 1999, the General approved a 'defensive maneuver' by Pakistan's 10 Corps/FCNA for 'plugging the gaps'.

He states further: 'The troops were given special instructions not to cross the watershed along the LoC.' Subsequently, he boasts that by 15 May 1999, the 'freedom fighters occupied over 800 sq. km of Indian-occupied territory...I was kept informed of all movements of freedom fighters from March 1999 onwards.... Our maneuver was conducted flawlessly, a tactical marvel of military professionalism.'

Let me present the ground realities:

- Other than Indians pre-empting the Pakistani operation in the Siachen sector (Operation Abdeel) in April 1984 and then ensuring this sector's security by preventing repeated attempts to dislodge us from there, only the Pakistanis had done the 'creeping forward' in Dalunang (Kargil sector) in the 1980s.

- In October–December 1998, apart from two or three patrol skirmishes between Indian and Pakistani troops along the AGPL, there were no 'real' or 'make-believe' attacks across the LoC or AGPL.
- Since 1991, due to continuing militancy in the Kashmir Valley and later as a result of signing of the Peace and Tranquillity Accord with China in 1993, India had carried out a gradual reduction of troops from the area east of Zoji La pass. After March 1997, only three brigades (102, 114 and 121) were left in this area; thus there were no reserve brigades. In October 1998, after an improvement in the operational situation in the Kashmir Valley, Headquarters 70 Infantry Brigade, with one battalion, was moved back to Ladakh. The brigade had to leave behind two battalions, as the reorganization of sectors in the Kashmir Valley could not be completed before the winter closure of the Zoji La pass.
- As subsequent events in the Kargil war revealed, the Indian Army did not have sufficient high-altitude clothing and equipment in this sector. No new weapons other than Indian National Small Arms System (INSAS) rifles had been inducted in the field formations.
- Defence Minister George Fernandes visited Ladakh and the Siachen Glacier frequently, partly to raise the morale of the troops and partly for gaining political points.

The fact is that there was not much jehadi activity north of Zoji La pass, and never in the Siachen Glacier area. In coming up with this imaginative, India-phobic rationale, General Musharraf conveniently ignores all political, military, strategic or logistical indicators; in this area or outside that could justify his assessment and decision to launch Operation Badr.

In his book, General Musharraf writes: 'Considered purely on military terms, the Kargil operations were a landmark in the history of the Pakistan Army. As few as five units, in support of the freedom fighter groups, were able to compel the Indians to employ more than four divisions, with bulk of its artillery coming from strike formations meant for operations in the southern plans. The Indians were also forced to mobilize their entire national resources, including their air force.'

I would like to point out that India had only 3 Infantry Division east of the Zoji La pass before the war. Also, 8 Mountain Division was inducted in end May 1999. Only these two divisions fought the war in Kargil. Yes! We had additional forces poised at different locations elsewhere for crossing the LoC or the international border – some at very short notice – should the need arise.

On the use of air power the General notes: 'The Indian Air Force was brought into action. Helicopter sorties were flown to ascertain the ingress made by the freedom fighters. However, the actions of the Indian Air Force were not confined to the freedom fighters' locations, they also started crossing over and bombarding Pakistan Army positions. This resulted in the shooting down of one their helicopters and two jet fighters over Pakistan territory.' Factually, despite severe operational and technical constraints, India's CCS rejected the COSC's request to allow the IAF to cross the LoC for engaging targets like Muntho Dhalo, that were very close to it on our side. One can also ask, since when is Tololing, where the IAF helicopter was shot down, in Pakistani territory?

As already brought out in the earlier chapters, throughout the Kargil war, the Directors-General of Military Operations (DsGMO) of India and Pakistan were in regular telephone communication with each other. The Pakistan Army top brass, masters in operating behind smoke screens, kept insisting till the end of the war that their regular troops were not involved in the Kargil war. They also insisted that the LoC was vague, and Pakistan Army patrols, if any, were in 'no man's land'.

If Pakistan's action was a pre-emptive action against a planned Indian offensive, then why did the Pakistan Army maintain the myth of Mujahideen till the time of their withdrawal? Where was the difficulty in the Pakistan Army owning up to the presence of its Northern Light Infantrymen across the LoC? Was there a need for Pakistan Foreign Minister Sartaj Aziz to be humiliated over the issue of the 'vague LoC' when Indians threw clearly demarcated maps signed by General Abdul Hamid of Pakistan and General P.S. Bhagat in 1972 at him during his visit to India during the course of war?

General Musharraf's narration conveys the impression that he was unaware of preparations for the February 1999 Lahore talks between the prime ministers of India and Pakistan. He paints a poor picture of his own country's intelligence and the other country's naivety. He remains silent on the telephone conversations between him and his Chief of General Staff of 29 and 30 May 1999 (see Appendix 2), and the meeting of the DsGMO, and on abandoning hundreds of dead bodies of Northern Light Infantry soldiers within the Indian territory. He does not mention the poor logistical planning for Pakistani troops; some of them, when captured, had been without rations and water for days. He also does not refer to his own inability to see through the strategic implications of this commando-like operation.

K. Subrahmanyam, who was chairman of the Kargil Review Committee set up by the Government of India, commenting on General Musharraf's Kargil war version, asks: 'If India was preparing for an offensive action and this move was undertaken as a countermeasure, why was this charge not made earlier when the then Pakistani foreign minister, Sartaj Aziz, visited India in June 1999? Why did it not feature in the conversations of the director generals of military operations? Why did not Prime Minister Nawaz Sharif raise the issue in his conversations with Atal Behari Vajpayee? The General claims it was a great victory for his army. Why then it is that the officers and men of the Pakistan army who fought valiantly and got killed did not get the decent burial that was their due? Why were their bodies abandoned on Indian Territory? There is no precedent in the history of warfare of a victorious army behaving this way. Why did Pakistan not own up to this victory? Why it was not advertised to the great pride of the Pakistani people till this book was published?'[2]

In attempting to pass the buck of the Kargil fiasco entirely to his political boss, General Musharraf claims that Nawaz Sharif was briefed by the Pakistan Army right through January to July 1999. However, on dealing with Sharif, whom he later ousted in a coup in October 1999, he portrays himself as an unbelievably weak and timid Pakistan Army chief: 'Prime Minister asked me

---

[2]K. Subrahmanyam, 'Heights of Deception', *The Indian Express*, 27 September 2006.

several times whether we should accept a ceasefire and withdraw. My answer every time was restricted to the optimistic military situation, leaving the political decision to him. He wanted to fire the gun from my shoulder, but it was not my place to offer it.' And then adds: 'As the Chief of the Army Staff I found myself in a very difficult position. I wanted to explain the military situation, to demonstrate how successful it had been, and point out the political mishandling, which had caused so much despair. But that would have been disloyal, and very unsettling for the political leadership.' He expresses 'consternation' on Sharif flying to the USA on 3 July 1999 and observes '...the military situation was favorable: the political decision has to be his (Sharif's). He went off, and decided on a ceasefire. It remains a mystery to me why he was in such a hurry'.

General Musharraf is economical with the truth when he claims that he told Nawaz Sharif, on 3 July 1999 before the latter left for Washington D.C., that the military situation was favourable to Pakistan. After the Indian soldiers had captured Tololing on 17 June, their forward movement along the ridgelines and mountaintops became unstoppable. Pakistan-occupied positions fell one after another. Indian troops captured Point 5140 (Dras) on 20 June, Point 5203 (Batalik) on 21 June, Three Pimples (Dras) on 29 June, the Jubar Complex (Batalik) on 2 July, Tiger Hill (Dras) on 4 July and Point 4875 (Mashkoh) on 7 July. No one, not even the Americans, are prepared to endorse the General's assessment of the military situation.

Besides, General Musharraf has chosen to ignore all the evidence to the contrary. General Anthony Zinni, who visited Islamabad on 24–25 June 1999, has written in his book *Battle Ready*[3] (co-authored with Tom Clancy): 'The problem with the Pakistani leadership was the apparent national loss of face.... What we (the USA) were able to offer was a meeting with President Clinton, which would end the isolation that had long been the state of affairs between our two countries, but would announce the meeting only after a withdrawal of forces. That got Musharraf's attention: and he encouraged Prime Minister

---

[3]Tom Clancy and Anthony Zinni, *Battle Ready* (Berkley Books, New York, 2004).

Sharif to hear me out.' The General's book does not take into account Nawaz Sharif's statement that Musharraf asked him: 'Why don't you meet Clinton? Why don't you ask him to bring about a settlement?'[4]

On the likely nuclearization of the Kargil conflict, Musharraf declares: 'I can say with authority that in 1999, our nuclear capability was not yet operational. Merely exploding a bomb does not mean that you are operationally capable of employing nuclear force in the field and delivering a bomb across the border over a selected target. Any talk of preparing for nuclear strikes is preposterous.'[5] While I am inclined to agree with this argument, everyone knows that it was the Pakistani nuclear rhetoric that created panic everywhere.

General Musharraf claims Kargil as a great diplomatic success since it internationalized Kashmir. On the other hand, it was the first time that neither China nor the United States was prepared to back Pakistan on its misadventure. Also, Kargil marked a turning point in Indo–US relations. President Bill Clinton's firm stand that Nawaz Sharif need not come to Washington unless he was prepared to withdraw his forces impressed India.

General Musharraf's factually incorrect and unconvincing narrative of the Kargil war is an attempt to whitewash a dark chapter of the Pakistan Army under his leadership: he took a military initiative that went horribly wrong – militarily, diplomatically and politically. Besides loss of face on the battlefield, his foolhardy venture isolated Pakistan, with its credibility touching an all-time low. Politically, it became yet another humiliation. When the truth about the Kargil intrusion filtered out in Pakistan, those responsible for the catastrophe were vehemently condemned. A trenchant volley of criticism (marked by agony) came from senior retired military officers like Air Marshal (retired) Nur Khan, Lieutenant General (retired) Kamal

---

[4]'Nawaz Sharif Speaks Out', interview with Raj Chengappa, *India Today*, 26 July 2004.

[5]According to Bruce Riedel's account, the Pakistani Army was attempting to escalate the conflict while being pushed back, by attempting to deploy presumably nuclear missiles, as the Americans assessed.

Matinuddin, Brigadier (retired) A. R. Siddiqi, from top-notch journalists like Najam Sethi, Maleeha Lodhi and Ayaz Amir and from political leaders such as Nawaz Sharif, Benazir Bhutto and M.P. Bhandara. All these views are well recorded in the Pakistani media. At one place, Musharraf states: 'On our side, I am ashamed to say, our political leadership insinuated that the achievements of our troops amounted to a "debacle". The Pakistan Army was called a "Rogue Army" by some.' This, in fact, was the language used in the Pakistani media.

According to Subrahmanyam, 'General Musharraf is trying to salvage his position after having survived the aftermath of the Kargil debacle for seven years. His version of events is not likely to impress political leaders, analysts or military establishments around the globe. On the issue of Kargil, the audience he is aiming at is Pakistani servicemen and common people. Presumably he relies on public memory being proverbially short.' He adds, 'India has to deal with General Musharraf as a ruler of neighbouring Pakistan. There is no alternative to that. In doing that we have to bear in mind the mindset of the leader we are dealing with. In this case, he seems to be a person who is not highly concerned about his own credibility.'[6]

In Pakistan, reacting to General Musharraf's claims, Chaudhary Nisar Ali Khan, the acting parliamentary leader of the Pakistan Muslim League (Nawaz) [PML (N)] has said: 'General Musharraf had made false claims about the Kargil operation only to gain publicity.' Khan has claimed that 'at a meeting held in the Governor's House in Lahore during Kargil operation, General Musharraf had told the Cabinet Committee on Defence that the Army was in great trouble at Kargil. The then Air Chief and the Naval Chief had expressed reservations over the Kargil situation and complained that they had not been taken into confidence before launching of the operation.' Former Senator Farhatullah Babar has pointed out that that the book is a one-sided version of critical events, namely, nuclear proliferation, war on terror, the Kargil conflict and the 12 October 1999 military takeover.[7]

---

[6]K. Subrahmanyam, 'Heights of Deception', *The Indian Express*, 27 September 2006.

[7]'Opposition Accuses Musharraf of Disclosing State Secrets', *The Tribune*, 28 September 2006.

A few days before the release of General Musharraf's book, an editorial in a Lahore publication made some scathing remarks: 'On each count, General Musharraf seems opposed to the will of the people. He doesn't want the exiled leaders to return and participate in the next elections, he refuses to extricate himself from the clutches of the unpopular mullahs and embrace the popular political parties, he insists on strong presidential powers in a weak parliamentary system, he will not allow an independent election commission and caretaker government to conduct the elections, and he seems bent on retaining his uniform and also being president. Under the circumstances, talk of restoring the writ of the state is nonsense. Is that the beginning of the end of the story?'[8] General Musharraf's self-proclaimed infallibility and imaginative achievements for the Pakistan Army, as highlighted in his book, are likely to leave him further exposed to such beliefs.

In an article published in the Pakistani newspaper *The News* on 4 October 2006, Lieutenant General Ali Kuli Khan, who was in line to become the Pakistani Army chief but retired quietly after General Musharraf superseded him, has described the book's 'numerous lies, half truths and misleading statements'. On the Kargil war chapter, the Lieutenant General observes: 'It is fairly obvious that the Kargil operations were not conceived in totality, with the result that apart from bringing ignominy to Pakistan, it also caused unnecessary misery to a lot of innocent people. I regret to say that the conception and planning at the highest level had been poor; in fact so poor that the only word which can adequately describe it is unprofessional.'

In his book, General Musharraf comes across as vain and self-centred, and is extremely frugal with the truth. His bluff and bluster, his Kashmir obsession and his anti-Indian mindset ('Not even my dead body would be landed in India') are quite vivid. All these characteristics will only increase the trust deficit, already at a premium, between India and Pakistan. The book is likely to adversely affect his credibility. It will disappoint people in India and Pakistan who, as a result of several post-Kargil

---

[8]Najam Sethi ,'State of the Nation', *The Friday Times*, 15 September 2006.

war confidence-building measures, ceasefire on the LoC and people-to-people contacts, have been hoping for durable peace on the subcontinent.

Acknowledgements

THIS BOOK IS A RESULT NOT ONLY OF THE WAR THAT THE INDIAN armed forces fought to evict Pakistani intrusion in the Kargil sector in the last year of the twentieth century but also of my forty-five-year-long association with them, i.e., with the Indian Army in particular.

A career in the armed forces implies drawing inspiration from its history, traditions, professionalism and ethical codes. The Indian soldier has always had a reputation for courage, sense of duty and honour. Other hallmarks of Indian soldiers have been discipline, loyalty and integrity. I was fortunate to imbibe all these traits and benefit immensely from them for a comparatively longer period than most. The Army career also gave me the opportunity to acquire professional knowledge and skills and hone them to perfection. I gained a lot from several excellent instructional establishments, as a student and sometimes as a teacher.

I am thus indebted to a very large number of fellow-soldiers of the Indian armed forces, who directly or indirectly influenced me from my military cadet days to the period when I became the chief of one of the largest and one of the most renowned armies of the world.

As I grew in my professional career and got the opportunity to interact with people from other services and professions at different levels, there was a great deal that I learnt from them.

It is not possible to name each of them individually but I do acknowledge my debt to all of them collectively.

My colleagues in the armed forces as well as in the central and state civil services and all others who played an active role in the Kargil war deserve special thanks. They made my task easier during the war and also when I started to write about the war.

I am also grateful to a large number of journalists, academics, senior military officers and political leaders from Pakistan whom I met after retirement. They were always respectfully friendly and candid while discussing the Kargil war and other related events.

A sizeable flock of friends and relatives persuaded me to write this book, helped me with its framework, dissected my observations and analysis, and spurred me on whenever I felt exhausted. From that long list, I would like to name a few.

Let me start with Professor Amitabh Mattoo, vice chancellor, Jammu University and a former colleague on the National Security Advisory Board, who read the first draft of the manuscript and offered his suggestions. Next, Brigadier Gurmeet Kanwal of the Observer Research Foundation, New Delhi, and Professor Rajesh Rajagopalan of the Jawaharlal Nehru University, New Delhi, who read the second draft of the manuscript and came up with more suggestions.

I would also like to express my gratitude to the following individuals from the armed forces: Major General Sheru Thapliyal, ex GOC, 3 Infantry Division; Major General V.K. Ahluwalia, GOC, 8 Mountain Division (Kargil); Brigadier Khushal Thakur, who commanded 18 Grenadiers in the Kargil war and is now commander, 56 Mountain Brigade (Dras); Major General P.C. Katoch, who commanded 102 Mountain Brigade (Siachen) during the Kargil war; and Brigadier Devinder Singh, who commanded 70 Infantry Brigade (Batalik) during the same war.

Captain Amarinder Singh, the chief minister of Punjab and the author of *A Ridge Too Far*; Air Commodore Jasjit Singh, former director, Institute of Defence Studies and Analysis, New Delhi; and Professor Sumit Ganguly, Tagore Chair, director, India Studies Program, Indiana University, USA, deserve special thanks.

I am also indebted to Lieutenant Colonel Jack Gill (the US Army), US National Defence University, Washington D.C.; Professor Stephen P. Cohen, Brookings Institute, Washington D.C.; Dr Ashley Tellis, Carnegie Endowment for International Peace, Washington D.C.; and Dr Peter R. Lavoy, director, Center for Contemporary Conflict, Naval Postgraduate School, Monterey (California).

I am deeply obliged to my publishers, particularly, Ashok Chopra, P.M. Sukumar and K.J. Ravinder, for their editorial inputs and other help.

Colonel H.K. Suchdeva, my uncle, who has been a great influence on me throughout my life, was very persuasive in making me write this book.

Finally, I would like to record my appreciation for the untiring efforts of Dr Ranjana Malik, my wife, who, despite having to endure my long hours on the computer, read the manuscript and put forward her comments and views. She has also contributed a chapter to this book. She has been my emotional and intellectual anchor not only in this endeavour but also at every stage of my life.

Index